The Narrative Art
of Charles Dickens

a

b

Two passages from the MS. of *Bleak House* (reproduced by kind permission of the Director and Secretary of the Victoria and Albert Museum) showing Dickens consciously using (*a*) the simple effect (*b*) the complex effect. See pp. 103–5, 175–6

The Narrative Art
of Charles Dickens

The Rhetoric of
Sympathy and Irony in his Novels

———

HARVEY PETER SUCKSMITH

OXFORD
AT THE CLARENDON PRESS
1970

Oxford University Press, Ely House, London W. 1

GLASGOW NEW YORK TORONTO MELBOURNE WELLINGTON
CAPE TOWN SALISBURY IBADAN NAIROBI DAR ES SALAAM LUSAKA ADDIS ABABA
BOMBAY CALCUTTA MADRAS KARACHI LAHORE DACCA
KUALA LUMPUR SINGAPORE HONG KONG TOKYO

PRINTED IN GREAT BRITAIN
AT THE UNIVERSITY PRESS, OXFORD
BY VIVIAN RIDLER
PRINTER TO THE UNIVERSITY

IN MEMORIAM

HARVEY SUCKSMITH

PREFACE

In the following study, I have examined Dickens's novels as conscious and rhetorical art and tried to arrive at his theory and practice of fiction through a comprehensive study of the available evidence, the various influences on his work, the books in his library, his letters, prefaces, and notes, above all his revisions in the manuscripts, corrected proofs, and various editions of his novels, and of course through a critical analysis of the novels. Most of the material I have used is new. Wherever I have used material already examined by scholars and critics, I hope I have done so in a way which throws fresh light on it.

The system I have used to indicate deletions, insertions, and second thoughts in the manuscripts and corrected proofs is explained on pp. xiv, 4. But I ought to mention one difficulty here. The whole concept of a conscious art would certainly be strengthened if a certain amount of pacing up and down before revising, or a session devoted to revision, could be shown or inferred in a fair number of particular cases. Unfortunately, though there are slight hints here and there in the manuscripts, I have been unable to find anything substantial enough to be generally significant. Nevertheless, I would think that even revisions made in the course of composition do indicate some degree of conscious art, especially when one can see a systematic scheme of qualification, an effect, for example, being gradually built up or strengthened in this way. And, again, though frequently slight in themselves, such small details do eventually amount to something like a case.

I have used the word 'narrative' fairly broadly to include all in the art of the novel that is involved in the telling of the story. Those readers, who are like myself committed to an organic view of the nature of the novel, will not find my use of the term objectionable. I have also found it impracticable to distinguish between 'art' and 'craftsmanship' (whether the distinction is theoretically valid or not) and those readers who believe I have used one term where I ought to have used the other must make the necessary translation.

This study is based on the thesis for which I was awarded a Ph.D. by the University of Nottingham in 1967 and I wish to thank the University for granting me a post-graduate Student-ship, which enabled me to carry out the necessary research, and Miss Sheila M. Smith, who supervised my research and offered many useful suggestions. I am greatly indebted to Professor James Kinsley of the University of Nottingham for his help and encouragement throughout my research and to Professor K. J. Fielding of the University of Edinburgh, who unsparingly gave me his time and advice while I was pre-paring the book for publication and kindly placed at my disposal his great knowledge of Dickens and Dickens studies; the acknowledgements I have made in footnotes cover only a fraction of my debt to Professor Fielding. Indeed, it would hardly be an exaggeration to add that but for Professor Kinsley this book would never have been written and but for Professor Fielding it would not have been prepared for publication. It goes without saying that the author accepts responsibility for the views that are expressed here and any weaknesses which may occur. Yet, if there are any virtues in the book they may well derive from the expert assistance I have received from others. Parts of Chapter IX, I should point out, have appeared in a slightly different form in *Renaissance and Modern Studies*.

I ought to pay a special tribute to that first and most malign-ed of Dickensians, John Forster, without whose loyalty, public-spiritedness, and foresight, any study of this kind would not have been possible. I must thank the Director, Librarian, and staff of the Victoria and Albert Museum, through whose help and courtesy I am able to quote from manuscripts and corrected proofs in the Forster Collection and to reproduce the extracts from the manuscript of *Bleak House* in the frontispiece, and the Librarian and Trustees of the Wisbech and Fenland Museum for permission to quote from the manuscript of *Great Expectations*.

I would also like to thank Professor W. A. G. Scott and Professor A. King, of Monash University, for their help and understanding during the final stage, Dr. G. G. Hiller for the loan of some first editions and other help, and Mrs. Norma Bolton for typing the final draft of a very trying script. I owe a special word of thanks to Miss E. Smith for several acts of great kindness in Nottingham, to my dear friends Jack and Kathleen Wilson who gave me shelter and much comfort while working on the manuscripts in London, to the late Professor C. S. Lewis, my former tutor, who helped and encouraged me throughout many uncertain years, and to my wife and children who cheerfully endured so much for Dickens's sake.

H. P. S.

November 1968

CONTENTS

ABBREVIATIONS

THE following abbreviations are used for the titles of works by Dickens:

BH	*Bleak House*	*LD*	*Little Dorrit*
BR	*Barnaby Rudge*	*MC*	*Martin Chuzzlewit*
CB	*Christmas Books*	*MHC*	*Master Humphrey's Clock*
CS	*Christmas Stories*	*NN*	*Nicholas Nickleby*
DC	*David Copperfield*	*OCS*	*The Old Curiosity Shop*
D & S	*Dombey and Son*	*OMF*	*Our Mutual Friend*
ED	*The Mystery of Edwin Drood*	*OT*	*Oliver Twist*
GE	*Great Expectations*	*PP*	*Pickwick Papers*
HT	*Hard Times*	*SB*	*Sketches by Boz*
		TTC	*A Tale of Two Cities*

Unless otherwise stated, all references to the above works are to *The New Oxford Illustrated Dickens* (1947–58); I have, however, restored the double inverted commas of the Charles Dickens Edition on which the Oxford Edition is based. Other abbreviations are as follows:

AYR	*All the Year Round* (1859–70)
C	*Letters of Charles Dickens to Wilkie Collins 1851–70*, ed. Laurence Hutton (1892)
Coutts	*Letters from Charles Dickens to Angela Burdett-Coutts 1841–65*, ed. Edgar Johnson (1953)
F	John Forster, *The Life of Charles Dickens* (1872–4)
HD	*The Letters of Charles Dickens 1833–70*, ed. his Sister-in-Law and his Eldest Daughter (1903)
HW	*Household Words* (1850–9)
MP	*Miscellaneous Papers*, ed. B. W. Matz (1908)
N	*The Letters of Charles Dickens*, ed. Walter Dexter, Nonesuch Press (1938)
P	*The Letters of Charles Dickens*, ed. Madeline House and Graham Storey, Pilgrim Edition (Oxford, 1965), vol. i
Speeches	*The Speeches of Charles Dickens*, ed. K. J. Fielding (Oxford, 1960)
W	*Charles Dickens as Editor being Letters Written by Him to William Henry Wills His Sub-Editor*, ed. R. C. Lehmann (1912)

In referring to the manuscripts of the novels, I have followed Dickens's own pagination. The corrected proofs are referred to either by page or column. In the case of both manuscripts and proofs, I have also given chapter number, or book and chapter number, and I have added the corresponding page reference to *The New Oxford Illustrated Dickens* but referred to book or chapter here only when these differ from those in manuscript or proofs. To avoid cumbersome repetition in the footnotes, I have given the location and press marks of manuscripts and corrected proofs only when referring to them for the first time; wherever a manuscript is bound in more than one volume, however, the number of the volume referred to is always given, while the location and press marks of manuscripts and proofs are, of course, listed in the bibliography at the end of this study.

I have used capitals to indicate insertions and second thoughts in the manuscripts and put deletions between angle-brackets. The same system with the addition of underlining is used to indicate revisions in the proofs. Illegible deletions in the manuscripts are indicated thus: ⟨–?–⟩. In the interests of readability, I have occasionally given only significant revisions and I have followed the punctuation of the corrected proofs (or earliest printed version where proofs no longer exist). Spelling has been silently altered to the forms used by Dickens in his later editions and more familiar to the English reader today. In no case do these slight modifications affect any point I have made. On the rare occasion when I have speculated I have said so. Conjectures are indicated thus: ? red, alternative conjectures thus: ? good / ? great.

In quotations from Dickens's notes or memoranda and number plans for the novels, I have indicated words underlined once in the original by italics, words underlined twice by capitals and small capitals, and words underlined three times by capitals and small capitals underlined once.

The place of publication of all printed works cited is London unless otherwise stated.

I

DICKENS AS A CONSCIOUS AND
RHETORICAL ARTIST:
SOME PRELIMINARY DIFFICULTIES

1. *An Initial Obstacle*

An immediate difficulty which stands in the way of a full
understanding and a proper assessment of Dickens as a
narrative artist may be illustrated by two passages of Dickens
criticism. The first is taken from a contemporary review of
A Tale of Two Cities by Sir James Fitzjames Stephen in
The Saturday Review (17 December 1859):

> It would perhaps be hard to imagine a clumsier or more dis-
> jointed framework for the display of the tawdry wares which
> form Mr. Dickens's stock-in-trade. The broken-backed way in
> which the story maunders along from 1775 to 1792 and back
> again to 1760 or thereabouts, is an excellent instance of the
> complete disregard of the rules of literary composition which have
> marked the whole of Mr. Dickens's career as an author. No portion
> of his popularity is due to intellectual excellence ... The two main
> sources of his popularity are his power of working upon the feel-
> ings by the coarsest stimulants, and his power of setting common
> occurrences in a grotesque and unexpected light. In his earlier
> works, the skill and vigour with which these operations were
> performed were so remarkable as to make it difficult to analyse
> the precise means by which the effect was produced on the mind
> of the reader. Now that familiarity has deprived his books of the
> gloss and freshness which they formerly possessed, the mechanism
> is laid bare; and the fact that the means by which the effect is
> produced are really mechanical has become painfully apparent.
> It would not, indeed, be matter of much difficulty to frame from
> such a book as the *Tale of Two Cities* regular recipes for grotesque
> and pathetic writing, by which any required quantity of the
> article might be produced with infallible certainty. The produc-
> tion of pathos is the simpler operation of the two. With a little

practice and a good deal of determination, it would really be as easy to harrow up people's feelings as to poke the fire. The whole art is to take a melancholy subject, and rub the reader's nose in it, and this does not require any particular amount either of skill or knowledge . . . To be grotesque is a rather more difficult trick than to be pathetic; but it is just as much a trick, capable of being learned and performed almost mechanically.

The second passage is taken from a modern critic, Q. D. Leavis:

Dickens stands primarily for a set of crude emotional exercises. He discovered, for instance, the formula 'laughter and tears' that has been the foundation of practically every popular success ever since (Hollywood's as well as the bestseller's). Far from requiring an intellectual stimulus, these are the tears that rise in the heart and gather to the eyes involuntarily or even in spite of the reader, though an alert critical mind may cut them off at the source in a revulsion to disgust.[1]

What is interesting about these two generalizations is not their blatant unfairness but the grounds on which they object to Dickens's novels. They take exception, in fact, to the rhetorical nature of Dickens's art—or rather to what they believe it to be. Both critics regard effects which are induced in the reader as the primary end of Dickens's art; while the means to that end are considered by one critic as crude calculation and as a mechanical trick by the other. Both these writers look down on rhetoric which they judge to be an artificially contrived, unsophisticated and deceitful attempt to capture and play upon the reader's feelings. This view would correspond to the pejorative sense of 'rhetoric' as it has traditionally been defined: 'language designed to persuade or impress (often w. implication of insincerity, exaggeration, etc.)'; 'artificial prose tinged with insincerity'.[2] This is very far from being the only meaning of 'rhetoric'.

These two passages have a further interest. In seeking to depreciate Dickens's rhetoric, they adopt an intellectual attitude of a narrow and aggressive kind which rigorously

[1] *Fiction and the Reading Public* (1932), p. 156. The work was reissued without revision in 1965 and reprinted without revision in 1968.

[2] *The Concise Oxford Dictionary*; Robert C. Whitford, 'Rhetoric', *Dictionary of World Literature*, ed. Joseph T. Shipley (New Jersey, 1960), p. 340.

excludes the emotional standpoint as entirely discreditable. Both critics are conscious of being highbrows and assume a position superior to any emotional contagion. I use the word 'assume' advisedly, for certain tell-tale features betray the fact that the attitude they adopt is only an apparent one. In the contemporary review, for instance, Stephen himself displays the 'vulgarity of mind and of taste' for which on the previous page he censures Dickens. He uses emotive words and degrading images, 'tawdry wares', 'stock-in-trade', 'painfully apparent', 'regular recipes', 'poke the fire', 'rub the reader's nose in it', 'trick', which reveal that he himself is 'working upon the feelings by the coarsest stimulants'. The modern critic, Q. D. Leavis, uses several rhetorical devices to persuade the reader. The novels of Dickens are at once lopped down to the stumps of mere 'exercises'. Emotively loaded words like 'formula', 'popular', 'Hollywood', 'bestseller', which convey an immediate depreciatory connotation to the modern intellectual, are applied directly or indirectly to the novels. What is worse, the work of Dickens is associated with the cheapest products of the American film industry in such a way as to put them both on the same level and confuse their very different values.

Even the most recent Dickens criticism, though much more subtle in its approach, may slip into this particular kind of depreciation. Thus, Robert Garis considers Dickens's art to be on the level of that of a conjurer, 'an illusionist' with his 'version of pulling rabbits out of hats'. While this same critic is prepared to allow Dickens a certain measure of vitality, he still goes on, in however guarded and sophisticated a manner, to imply a kind of mechanical trickery which recalls the accusation made in the contemporary review quoted above.[1]

Fitzjames Stephen was bitterly prejudiced. With regard to the other two critics, we can only conclude that they are deceiving themselves and it does appear that when emotion is not taken into account or is depreciated it may return in another and sometimes virulent form. Dickens understood this principle of intellectual and emotional life very well. He made it the major theme of *Hard Times*: 'In this strife I

[1] *The Dickens Theatre: a Reassessment of the Novels* (Oxford, 1965), pp. 17, 19, 43.

have almost repulsed and crushed my better angel into a demon'.[1]

It is understandable that the intellectual with his hard-won freedom of thought and sense of discrimination should fear the contagion of the rabble, should dread an almost bodily possession by emotions sympathetically induced in him by others. We have only to read Le Bon on the crowd or Freud on group psychology to appreciate how and why this is so. Nevertheless there are already certain indications by the time of Dickens of an uneasy victory for the intellectual standpoint.

Though this is not the place to discuss at length the dangerous one-sidedness of our age about which we were already being warned in certain predictions of Dostoyevsky and more recently by Jung,[2] it should be pointed out how this one-sidedness may prejudice an examination of Dickens as a rhetorical artist right from the outset. Prophetically enough, Dickens himself has warned us against this danger which was beginning to assume a sinister shape in his own day and could be seen most clearly in the development of a particular philosophy:

Utilitarian economists, skeletons of schoolmasters, Commissioners of Fact, genteel and used-up infidels, gabblers of many little dog's eared creeds, the poor you will have always with you. Cultivate in them, WHILE THERE IS YET TIME, the utmost graces of the fancies and affections, to adorn their lives so much in need of ornament; or, in the day of your triumph, when romance is utterly driven out of their souls, and they and a bare existence stand face to face, Reality will take a wolfish turn, and make an end of you!*[3]

* Throughout this study, I have used capitals to indicate insertions and second thoughts in the manuscripts and put deletions between angle-brackets. The same system with the addition of underlining is used to indicate revisions in the proofs. For other signs used in representing manuscripts, proofs, and notes, see above, p. xiv.

[1] *HT*, Bk. II, Chap. XII, p. 217. Cf. C. G. Jung. *Psychological Types*, tr. H. Godwin Baynes (1946), pp. 437-9, 440.
[2] Fyodor Dostoyevsky, 'Memoirs from a Dark Cellar', *A Gentle Creature and Other Stories*, tr. David Magarshack (1960), pp. 119-20, 126, 128; C. G. Jung, *Psychology and Religion: West and East* (1958), p. 534, *Two Essays on Analytical Psychology* (1953), p. 92, *The Archetypes and the Collective Unconscious* (1959), p. 253; all the translations are by R. F. C. Hull.
[3] Corrected proofs of *HT*, Victoria and Albert Museum, Forster Collection, 48. E. 28, Chap. XXII, 14; cf. *HT*, Bk. II, Chap. VI, pp. 162-3.

We should, perhaps, pay special attention to that ominous phrase 'while there is yet time', for it was deliberately added at the proof stage. What the danger was that Dickens and Dostoyevsky had in mind can be seen in certain terrible events of our own time, yet it has less dramatic manifestations. If the thesis of Dickens in *Hard Times* is a valid one, if any abstract study of problems which bear upon human life and human values ignores the affections at its peril, then this holds good also for the study of fiction which is much closer than either economics or philosophy to the very stuff of life, to living in all its concreteness and immediacy.

There is a further, social reason why today in particular the very notion of rhetoric should meet with an immediate and understandable hostility. Even in earlier ages a certain ugly aspect had not passed unnoticed. Quintilian hastened to qualify his definition of rhetoric with the careful proviso that the art should be directed towards an honest and noble end. As late as the time of Dickens, the ablest writer on the subject, Whately, betrays anxiety about this problem. Many writers on rhetoric, including Aristotle, introduce the idea of persuasion into their definition.[1] Now persuasion is a very special anathema of our time when advertising, propaganda, and indoctrination have been pushed to the point of brain washing and mass lunacy. Though Dickens's creation, Slackbridge, the stump orator, addressing an assembly of the United Aggregate Tribunal in the crowded, stuffy, little[2] Hall of Coketown may be a pale preview of certain giant demagogues of our time with their monstrous rallies in vast sports stadiums, still a suggestion of the frightening possibilities is there in *Hard Times*. Dickens, in fact, was so aware

---

[1] Quintilian, *Institutes of Oratory*, ii. xv. 23, tr. Revd. John Selby Watson (1856), ii. xv. 33–8, vol. i, pp. 144–7; Richard Whately, *Elements of Rhetoric* (1828), quoted by Whitford in *Dictionary of World Literature*, p. 342; Aristotle, *The 'Art' of Rhetoric*, i. i. 14–ii. 1, tr. John Henry Freese (1959), pp. 13, 15; Quintilian, op. cit. ii. xv. 3–22, pp. 139–44, gives a very full list of these definitions.

[2] Though he does not mention the size of the hall in Coketown, Dickens almost certainly had in mind the small, stuffy, overcrowded cockpit where he attended the strike meeting in Preston and heard Gruffshaw, the 'original' of Slackbridge, speak; the stuffiness and overcrowding are recalled in the novel. See *HT*, Bk. II, Chap. IV, pp. 138–45, and 'On Strike', *HW*, viii (11 Feb. 1854), reprinted in *MP*, pp. 423–36.

of a false and immoral rhetoric that in his attempt to show its hollowness he has seriously weakened the impact that Slackbridge makes on the reader. In seeking to illustrate the danger of rhetoric, Dickens has failed to indicate its power.

2. *Rhetoric: A Definition*

An open study of Dickens as a rhetorical artist has been discouraged not only by the bad sense to which the idea of rhetoric has often been restricted but also by the absence of an adequate positive definition of the term. A bewildering array of meanings presents itself to the critic today. The convenient summary in *SOED* gives the history of the word as follows:

1. The art of using language so as to persuade or influence others; the body of rules to be observed by a speaker or writer in order that he may express himself with eloquence. b. A treatise on, or 'body' of, rhetoric 1565. 2. †a. Elegance or eloquence of language; eloquent speech or writing. b. Speech or writing expressed in terms calculated to persuade; hence, language characterized by artificial or ostentatious expression. Often *ironical* or *joc.* late ME †c. *pl.* Elegant expressions; rhetorical flourishes. Also rhetorical terms—1628. d. *transf.* and *fig.*, esp. of the persuasiveness of looks or acts 1569. †3. Skill in or faculty of using eloquent and persuasive language—1750.

Thus, the technical, pejorative, and figurative senses have survived. Possibly the most useful list of meanings is given by the *Dictionary of World Literature*:

Rhetoric is the art and science of composition in words. The term has at least 8 restricted meanings. In various modern contexts it carries almost all of the senses which it (or its Gr. original) has borne during the past 24c. It may denominate: (1) a body of principles concerning the composition of persuasive or otherwise effective public speeches, or (a) the speeches themselves, or (b) the skill of an orator; (2) a body of principles applicable in prose composition in general, whether designed for publication or for oral delivery, or (a) the technique of a master of prose style, or (b) artificial prose tinged with insincerity. (3) any classified and systematized body of doctrine about artifices of verbal composition, whether prose or poetry, or (a) the use of such artifices or devices in either prose or verse.[1]

[1] Whitford, 'Rhetoric', *Dictionary of World Literature*, p. 340.

The two most interesting points that emerge from this wide range of definitions are the idea of rhetoric as the art of composition and the stress on the function of rhetoric, which is to produce an effect in the receptor. The use of rhetoric to mean the art of composition, which still survives in the United States, was originally current in Great Britain. In *Elements of Rhetoric* (1828), Richard Whately was anxious to establish the meaning of rhetoric as the art of composition.[1]

It might seem wiser to abandon the word as a modern critical term altogether. Unfortunately, however, no other word in English covers the senses both of composition as an art or technique and as a function directed towards the specific end of producing effects.

Wayne C. Booth has recently defined 'the rhetoric of fiction' as:

the technique of non-didactic fiction, viewed as the art of communicating with readers—the rhetorical resources available to the writer of epic, novel, or short story as he tries, consciously or unconsciously, to impose his fictional world upon the reader.

And in defending his study as a proper one, Booth puts the whole question of rhetoric into a sane perspective:

Regardless of how we define art or artistry, the very concept of writing a story seems to have implicit within it the notion of finding techniques of expression that will make the work accessible in the highest possible degree . . . This first defense of rhetoric does not depend on proving that it is indispensable but rather in showing that in fact it has generally been not only tolerated but embraced by competent writers.[2]

It may, however, be more helpful in examining Dickens's narrative art to define the rhetoric of fiction as *the technical means whereby, through structure, effects are created and vision focused.*

Certain points follow at once from this definition. In the first place, it implies that a study of rhetoric cannot avoid an analysis of structure and vision in addition to effect. Indeed, fiction may be regarded, from the point of view of technique, as a relationship between vision, structure, and effect, a

[1] Ibid., pp. 341–2.
[2] *The Rhetoric of Fiction* (Chicago, 1961), Preface, pp. 105, 106.

triad which roughly corresponds to the relationship between writer, novel, and reader and expresses that relationship within the novel itself. Furthermore, one of the proper studies of fiction is the investigation and evaluation of this relationship and the elements which make it up.

The idea of relationship and the quality of relatedness in my definition is, I believe, essential to any truly productive mode of thinking. The exclusively reductive kind of definition deserves the parody with which Dickens ridicules it since it denies the work of the imagination in arriving at the truth about the world.[1]

A further point might seem to follow from my definition. Wherever there was no vision to focus, effects would flourish as the sole aim of rhetoric. Critics have often accused Dickens of just this weakness. Yet it does seem impossible in practice to avoid focusing some kind of vision through the rhetoric of any story. Even the poorest fiction, the semi-pornography of Reynolds, for example, or the sadistic and cannibalistic fantasies of Prest, or the sensational novels of Rymer, will be found to have a vision of a sort, as Louis James, an authority on the penny press of Dickens's own day, has recently pointed out.[2] What we really object to, here, is not the presentation of effects 'for the sake of effect' at all but the poverty of the vision or its perverseness, its inconsistency, positive untruth, hackneyed character, over-simplified nature, and so on. At such times, the rhetoric forces itself upon our attention because it is exposed. The sentimentality of Dickens, for example, has as much to do with vision and structure as with effect, though sentimentality may be explained in terms of inadequate rhetoric as well as an over-simplified vision.[3] Sometimes, the requirements of rhetoric may seriously restrict vision, as in the case of Mr. Dick.[4] Sometimes, the converse is true and a vision which is insisted on will ruin a rhetorical effect; Little Nell's death is a good example.[5] I wish to stress throughout this study that rhetoric may often be a limiting factor in Dickens's narrative art and is always

---

[1] *HT*, Bk. I, Chap. II, p. 5.
[2] *Fiction for the Working Man 1830–1850* (1963), pp. 166, 163–4, 115.
[3] See below, pp. 277–89. [4] See below, pp. 37–40.
[5] See below, pp. 284–7

a factor to be taken into account in his best as well as his less happy achievements. Rhetoric, that is, would be as much responsible for the success of, say, Mr. Micawber in *David Copperfield* as it would for the failure of Martha in the same novel.

3. *Dickens as a Conscious Artist*

It is significant that those scholars who have consulted Dickens's manuscripts have treated him as a conscious artist and stressed the care with which he worked. Nevertheless, relatively little use has been made of the manuscripts of the novels other than Dickens's notes for them.[1] The neglect of the manuscripts certainly helps to explain the long-held view that Dickens was an instinctive or intuitive novelist, or a writer under a spell of various kinds, a view which still persists.[2]

Other factors have contributed to the view of Dickens as an unconscious artist. The haphazard origin of *Pickwick Papers* and the lucky stroke of fortune on which Dickens's career was founded have lent some substance to the view. So has the distant survey of post-Jamesian critics as they have looked back at what they have conceived to be 'large loose baggy monsters'.[3] In more recent years Dickens has also

[1] See 'Dickens's Number Plans for *The Mystery of Edwin Drood*', *The Dickensian*, xxvii (1931), 184–5, 200–1, 268–9, 284–5, 300–1; Ernest Boll, 'The Plotting of *Our Mutual Friend*', *Modern Philology*, xlii (1944), 96–122; John Butt, '*David Copperfield* from Manuscript to Print', *Review of English Studies*, NS., i (1950), 247–51; Sylvère Monod, *Dickens romancier* (Paris, 1953); K. J. Fielding, *Charles Dickens*, revised edition (1954); John Butt and Kathleen Tillotson, *Dickens at Work* (1957); H. P. Sucksmith, 'Dickens at Work on *Bleak House*: A Critical Examination of his Memoranda and Number Plans', *Renaissance and Modern Studies*, ix (1965), 47–85; Paul D. Herring, 'Dickens' Monthly Number Plans for *Little Dorrit*', *Modern Philology*, lxiv (1966), 22–63.

[2] See *A New Spirit of the Age*, ed. R. H. Horne (1844), vol. i, p. 76; 'Modern Novelists: Charles Dickens', *The Westminster Review*, lxxxii (Oct. 1864), 414–41, quoted in Fred G. Kitton, *Dickensiana* (1886) [henceforth referred to as *Dickensiana*], pp. 124–5; G. H. Lewes, 'Dickens in Relation to Criticism', *Fortnightly Review*, xvii (1 Feb. 1872), 141–54, quoted in *The Dickens Critics*, ed. George H. Ford and Lauriat Lane, Jnr. (New York, 1961) [henceforth referred to as *The Dickens Critics*], pp. 59–61, 69; H. A. Taine, *History of English Literature*, tr. H. Van Laun (1907), vol. i, p. 124; A. O. J. Cockshut, *The Imagination of Charles Dickens* (1961), p. 14; Taylor Stoehr, *Dickens: The Dreamer's Stance* (New York, 1965), p. 89.

[3] Henry James originally applied the phrase to Tolstoy's *War and Peace* and Thackeray's *The Newcomes*, 'Preface to *The Tragic Muse*', *The Art of the*

suffered from the general delusion, even among academic critics, that early Victorian novelists were without a theory of the novel and therefore wrote purely as instinctive entertainers, a delusion weakened by Richard Stang's *The Theory of the Novel in England 1850–1870* (1959) and now being steadily undermined still further.

Apart from all that is implied by a study of the novels themselves, there are, in fact, two main sources for the view that Dickens was a conscious artist. One is to be found in his own pronouncements about narrative art in letters, prefaces, his fiction, and occasionally in his journalism,[1] the other in his notes and the revisions in his manuscripts, corrected proofs, and various editions of the novels which show him consciously practising his art.

Thus, the very preface which admits the haphazard origin of *Pickwick* also goes on to show how quickly Dickens set about establishing his artistic authority over the direction the book was to take; and what Dickens says here, admittedly a dozen years later, is confirmed by the earliest preface.[2] An even earlier address to the reader, which appeared when only half of *Pickwick* had been published, confirms more strikingly still the deliberate artistic integrity of Dickens and his conscious sense of responsibility:

He has long been desirous to embrace the first opportunity of announcing that it is his intention to adhere to his original pledge of confining this work to twenty numbers. He has every temptation to exceed the limits he first assigned to himself, that brilliant success, an enormous and increasing sale, the kindest notice, and the most extensive popularity, can hold out. They are, one and all, sad temptations to an author, but he has determined to resist them; firstly, because he wishes to keep the strictest faith with his readers; and, secondly, because he is most anxious that when the *Posthumous Papers of the Pickwick Club* form a complete work, the book may not have to contend against the heavy disadvantage of being prolonged beyond his original plan.[3]

Novel, ed. R. P. Blackmur (New York, 1934), p. 84. Cf. George H. Ford, *Dickens and His Readers* (New York, 1965), pp. 207, 225.

[1] For an example from his journalism, see below, p. 11. Examples from his fiction are given throughout this study.

[2] Prefaces to the First Cheap Edition of *PP* (1847) and the First Edition of *PP* (1837).

[3] Address which appeared in *PP*, Part X (Jan. 1837). It is dated Dec.

The following example, which is by no means untypical,
illustrates what the manuscripts can tell us about the conscious
artistry of Dickens. In *Household Words*, Dickens ably refuted
an accusation, made by the highbrow *Edinburgh Review*, that
he was a sheer opportunist in the matter of plot:

'Even the catastrophe in *Little Dorrit* is evidently borrowed
from the recent fall of houses in Tottenham Court Road, which
happens to have appeared in the newspapers at a convenient
period.'

Thus the Reviewer. The Novelist begs to ask him whether there
is no License in his writing those words and stating that assumption as a truth, when any man accustomed to the critical examination of a book cannot fail, attentively turning over the pages of
Little Dorrit, to observe that that catastrophe is carefully prepared for from the very first presentation of the old house in the
story; that, when Rigaud, the man who is crushed by the fall of
the house, first enters it (hundreds of pages before the end), he is
beset by a mysterious fear and shuddering; that the rotten and
crazy state of the house is laboriously kept before the reader,
whenever the house is shown; that the way to the demolition of
the man and the house together, is paved all through the book
with a painful minuteness and reiterated care of preparation, the
necessity of which (in order that the thread may be kept in the
reader's mind through nearly two years), is one of the adverse
incidents of that serial form of publication?[1]

That Dickens had been conscious of and deliberate about this
preparation from the outset and was not now simply reading
what happened to be convenient into his work can be seen by
examining his notes for *Little Dorrit* where we find:

'Begin (with a view to Rigaud catastrophe) the mysterious
sounds in the old house' (I, Chap. XV); 'Arrival of Rigaud to
close the chapter. *Mysterious sounds again, as he enters*' (I, Chap.
XXIX); 'Pave the way. Both with the noises—to impress them

1836. Contrast G. W. M. Reynolds who kept *The Mysteries of the Court of
London* running from 1849 to 1856 and is said to have used 'ghost' writers;
this extended performance has been estimated at four and a half million
words or the equivalent of forty-eight modern novels. See Louis James,
op. cit., p. 41.

[1] 'Curious Misprint in the *Edinburgh Review*', *HW*, xvi (1 Aug. 1857),
97–100, quoted in *MP*, p. 629; Sir James Fitzjames Stephen, 'The Licence of
Modern Novelists', *The Edinburgh Review*, cvi (July 1857), 124–56, quoted in
Dickensiana, p. 277.

again, for their connexion from the first with the catastrophe there: and with Affery—for the telling of her dreams' (II, Chap. XXIII).[1]

Furthermore, the original manuscript of *Little Dorrit* shows Dickens at work, in those very passages which prepare the catastrophe, carefully adding small details which point all the more significantly to the catastrophe and bring out its ironic structure. In the first description of the house an important dimension of time is carefully introduced:

⟨It⟩ MANY YEARS AGO, IT had had it in its mind to tumble down sideways; it had been propped up, however, and was leaning on some half dozen gigantic crutches: which GYMNAZIUM FOR THE NEIGHBOURING CATS, weather-stained, smoke-blackened, and overgrown with stone crop and weed, appeared IN THESE LATTER DAYS to be no very sure reliance.

The words, 'Many years ago' and 'in these latter days', were a second thought of Dickens and clearly stress the long period the house has been in a state of collapse and make all the more ominous the present state of affairs, to which attention is also drawn; while the phrase, 'gymnazium for the neighbouring cats', which was also added, conveys a strikingly concrete impression of the perilous space that yawns beneath the huge props. Again, the ominous warning Rigaud receives when he first enters the house which is later to crush him is intensified by the two tiny details, 'A tremble' and 'light', that Dickens inserted in what he had first written:

The strangest of sounds. Evidently close at hand from the peculiar shock it communicated to the air, yet subdued as if it were far off. A TREMBLE, A ⟨A⟩ rumble, and a fall of some LIGHT dry matter.

'A tremble' adds the specific impression of movement to the threat implied by the sound while, at the same time, it communicates the physical sensation of fear, a forceful identity of object and subject which is already present in Dickens's outline notes for this chapter (I, XXIX) above. The word 'light' is a superb ironical touch. Under the appearance of the fall of the unsubstantial and harmless, it conceals

---

[1] Original MS. of *LD*, Victoria and Albert Museum, Forster Collection, 47. A. 32 (Vol. IA), 47. A. 34 (Vol. IIA).

a specific reference to the crumbling weakness into which the original strength of the building is being so dangerously changed. Finally, Dickens is always careful to make appearance as convincing as possible while he is, at the same time, hinting ominously at a specific reality. Thus, when Affery Flintwinch describes the strange disturbances in the kitchen, a warning which her husband scornfully rejects, Dickens adds the words, 'rustle and a sort of':

"No, Jeremiah; I have felt it before. I have felt it up-stairs, and once on the staircase as I was going from her room to ours in the night—a RUSTLE AND A SORT OF trembling touch behind me."[1]

At first, he had simply described the movement; then he makes this movement much vaguer and he adds the less frightening sound which, at the same time, describes so accurately the deadly fall of crumbling masonry. Dickens, that is, does not concern himself simply with preparation but with ironic preparation, which simultaneously works towards surprise and inevitability. He was, in fact, so anxious not to give away too much by his preparation that earlier in the same chapter (II, XV) he cancelled at the proof stage the following passage which had stood as the second paragraph in the manuscript:

So disused was the spot, and so long was it since it had known repair, that the whole concern seemed to be resolving itself into the city mud and dust, the showers, fogs, and winds. The outer surface of the bricks turned to powder under the hands; the painted wood peeled off in layers; the iron of the railings was in rusty rags. The twigs broke when they were touched, and the patch of grass was little better than green mildew on the ground. What manner of worms were underneath it, Heaven knows; but those that occasionally died upon the surface were as black as the twigs, and as brittle, and assumed their forms, and crumbled like them, and cast their undistinguishable mites of rottenness into the general bank.[2]

[1] Ibid., Vol. IA, Bk. I, Chap. III, p. 23 (proofs read 'slide' after 'mind to', omit 'stone crop and' and read 'weeds'), 47. A. 33 (Vol. IB), Bk. I, Chap. XXIX, p. 28, Vol. IA, Bk. I, Chap. XV, p. 7; cf. *LD*, pp. 31, 346, 185.

[2] Corrected proofs of *LD*, Victoria and Albert Museum, Forster Collection, 48. B. 17, Bk. I, Chap. XV, p. 129; cf. *LD*, p. 178. A French translation of part of this deleted paragraph was given in Sylvère Monod, op. cit., p. 406.

4. *Dickens's Concept of Narrative Art*

Despite statements to the contrary,[1] there is a substantial body of remarks on the art of fiction in Dickens's prefaces, letters, and novels. What, if anything, does all this wealth of material amount to? The answers other scholars have given are obviously true of the material they have selected yet appear unsatisfactory when put side by side. Thus, W. C. Phillips sees Dickens as primarily concerned with creating a very special kind of fiction, the dramatic sensation novel; he ignores the importance of all Dickens has to say about probability or unity. Richard Stang is content to present an amorphous mass of material in one section of his book simply to make his general point that Dickens considered diverse problems of technique; in a further section he rakes over the material Phillips had already worked through but sees it as Dickens's contribution to 'the disappearance of the author' which constitutes for him the most significant development in the technique of the novel. George H. Ford considers Dickens's views on probability and unity, that is, the material which Phillips had ignored, and it is the views on probability which are for Ford the most important part of Dickens's thinking on narrative art: 'Some of these comments deal with the problem of unity and serial publication, but most of them are concerned with aspects of the problem of probability.'[2]

My own view is that, although Dickens does not formulate a complete theory of the novel in so many words, yet there is a fundamental principle underlying both his theory and his practice of fiction which does bring together the fragments of his various opinions on narrative art into something like a single view. That principle is rhetoric in the sense in which I have defined it above.

Whatever modern critics or writers on aesthetics may think about rhetoric as a factor in literary art, whether like Croce and Collingwood they regard it as irrelevant to true art or like Wimsatt and Beardsley they consider other objective

---

[1] An extreme case is cited by Ford, op. cit., p. 130.

[2] W. C. Phillips, *Dickens, Reade, and Collins: Sensation Novelists* (New York, 1919), pp. 129–35; Richard Stang, *The Theory of the Novel in England 1850–1870* (1959), pp. 19–28, 99–103; Ford, op. cit., pp. 122–8, 129–45, 130.

qualities as distinguishing art or like Richards they do accept a psychological and subjective theory of values,[1] Dickens, like Tolstoy,[2] never doubted that fiction above all involved communication: 'You write to be read, of course,' he warns a contributor to his periodical before proceeding to give detailed advice.[3] This remark is the core of Dickens's concept of narrative art. He never falters in his belief that effect is of paramount importance. Moreover, this principle welds together the various fragments of his opinions on different topics of narrative art, since Dickens can be shown to subordinate each technical problem to rhetorical considerations and to work out the problem in terms of effect. Nor is the principle, in the hands of Dickens, necessarily simple or disreputable.

To begin with what Dickens in his letters regarded as a basic matter, characterization. Invariably, characters must make an impact on the reader, an impact which Dickens narrows down to a specific emotional effect. It is absolutely essential that the writer creates either a strong sympathy for a character or a violent antipathy against him: 'You cannot interest your readers in any character unless you have first made them hate, or like him.' Improbability in characterization is to be avoided precisely because it inhibits the reader's sympathy:

The father is such a dolt, and the villain *such* a villain, the girl so especially credulous and the means used to deceive them so very slight and transparent, that the reader *cannot* sympathize with their distress. Action too is terribly wanting, and the characters not being strongly marked (except in improbabilities) the dialogues grow tedious and wearisome.[4]

---

[1] Benedetto Croce, *Aesthetic*, tr. D. Ainslie (1909), esp. pp. 109–20; R. G. Collingwood, *The Principles of Art* (Oxford, 1963); esp. W. K. Wimsatt, Jr. and Monroe C. Beardsley, 'The Affective Fallacy', *Sewanee Review*, lvii (1949), 52, 'The emotions correlative to the objects of poetry become a part of the matter dealt with—not communicated to the reader like an infection or disease . . . but presented in their objects and contemplated as a pattern of knowledge'; I. A. Richards, *The Principles of Literary Criticism*, esp. pp. 44–57.

[2] Leo Tolstoy, 'What is Art ?', *Tolstoy on Art*, tr. Aylmer Maude (1925).

[3] To Miss Emily Jolly (17 July 1855), *HD*, p. 374. Dickens, of course, like Thackeray and other Victorian writers, not only came to fiction from journalism but retained many of the journalist's attitudes and attributes.

[4] To J. A. Overs (12 Apr. 1840, 27 Sept. 1839), *N*, vol. i, p. 255, *P*, vol. i, pp. 587–8.

Vitality is desirable in fiction because it excites a certain kind of sympathy.[1] This explains why Dickens insists on this quality in characters. In the absence of vitality, no amount of ingenuity in construction or plot will redeem a story; it will appear mere heartless machinery:

> Your MS. . . . has interest, but it seems to me to have one great want which *I* cannot overcome. It is all working machinery, and the people are not alive. I see the wheels going and hear them going, and the people are as like life as machinery can make them— but they don't get beyond the point of the moving waxwork.[2]

One critic of Dickens has shrewdly observed that verisimilitude in Dickens's fiction is not pursued as an end in itself but as a means to an end.[3] Baker, however, does not point out that Dickens sees probability as an effect, a kind of illusion imposed on the reader. Thus, Dickens does not advise the writer to present the probable directly but to overcome improbability through rendering the scene dramatically. The secret here is vitality and immediacy which the dramatic method makes possible:

> Consider if you had been outside that coach, and had been suddenly carried into the midst of a Torchlight meeting of that time, whether you would have brought away no other impression of it than you give the reader. Imagine it a remembrance of your own, and look at the passage. And exactly because that is not true, the conduct of the men who clamber up is in the last degree improbable. Whereas if the scene were truly and powerfully rendered, the improbability more or less necessary to all tales and allowable in them, would become a part of a thing so true and vivid, that the reader must accept it whether he likes it or not.

Dickens had made exactly the same point in a letter to Miss Emily Jolly.[4]

Dickens often criticizes unnatural dialogue[5] but considerations of probability or realism may be outweighed by the need to create an effect. Thus the need for idealization, which is

---

[1] See below, p. 132.

[2] To W. H. Wills (13 Apr. 1855), *W*, p. 160.

[3] Ernest A. Baker, *The History of the English Novel*, vol. vii (1936), pp. 329–30.

[4] To W. H. Wills (13 Apr. 1855), *W*, p. 161; Miss Emily Jolly (30 May 1857), *HD*, pp. 427–8.

[5] To Mrs. Gaskell (3 May 1853), Miss King (24 Feb. 1855), *HD*, pp. 288, 360.

calculated to arouse the special kind of sympathy that we call approval,[1] may overrule verisimilitude:

I know the kind of boyish slang which belongs to such a character in these times; but, considering his part in the story, I regard it as the author's function to elevate such a characteristic, and soften it into something more expressive of the ardour and flush of youth, and its romance.

Commenting on this letter, Monroe Engel points out:

This had obvious bearing on the often repeated complaint that Dickens' lower class characters speak as uneducated people could not speak. There is also an essay in *Household Words* on slang that emphasizes the undesirable features of the expansion of the language.

And in a footnote Engel also refers us to the preface to the third edition of *Oliver Twist* (1841) where Dickens deals with a similar problem in the same way. To Engel's comments might be added the fact that Dickens went to some pains to have a young woman prosecuted for using bad language in the street.[2] What should be noted, here, is how a moral purpose may be expressed in a novel through an effect and how, in practice, the aesthetic and the moral may overlap, become blurred and may even fuse into a single purpose.[3]

Indeed, a moral purpose may be best achieved through a strong effect. Thus, the Victorian prejudice against the fallen woman, which makes rehabilitation so difficult, may be softened through the pathetic spectacle of a victim.[4] On the other hand, a certain kind of effect may stand in the way of the moral purpose. Too painful a catastrophe, for instance,

---

[1] See below, pp. 132–3, 134.

[2] To Miss King (9 Feb. 1855), *HD*, p. 357; Monroe Engel, *The Maturity of Dickens* (Cambridge, Mass., 1959), p. 18; G. A. H. Sala, 'Slang', *HW*, viii (24 Sept. 1853), 73–8; 'The Ruffian', *AYR*, xx (10 Oct. 1868), 421–4; see K. J. Fielding, 'Charles Dickens and "The Ruffian"', *English*, x (1954), 89–92; Philip Collins, *Dickens and Crime* (1962), pp. 112–13, argues that Dickens's action was 'sensible and public-spirited'.

[3] The overlapping of the moral and the aesthetic is a fact of common human experience. 'Bad' language is also 'foul'. Beauty is readily associated with goodness and ugliness with evil. Such deep-rooted associations persist in flying in the face of reality.

[4] To M. De Cerjat (29 Dec. 1849), *HD*, pp. 208–9. The relevant section of this letter is quoted below, p. 30.

may thwart the aim of the writer. The effect may, however, be modified by adjusting the plot:

The close of the story is unnecessarily painful—will throw off numbers of persons who would otherwise read it, and who (as it stands) will be deterred by hearsay from so doing, and is so tremendous a piece of severity, that it will defeat your purpose. All my knowledge and experience, such as they are, lead me straight to the recommendation that you will do well to spare the life of the husband, and of one of the children. Let her suppose the former dead, from seeing him brought in wounded and insensible—lose nothing of the progress of her mental suffering afterwards when that doctor is in attendance upon her—but bring her round at last to the blessed surprise that her husband is still living, and that a repentance which can be worked out, *in the way of atonement for the misery she has occasioned to the man whom she so ill repaid for his love, and made so miserable,* lies before her. So will you soften the reader whom you now as it were harden, and so you will bring tears from many eyes, which can only have their spring in affectionately and gently touched hearts. I am perfectly certain that with this change, all the previous part of your tale will tell for twenty times as much as it can in its present condition.[1]

Alongside the change in effect, here, there is also a change in the quality of the moral vision which has shifted towards a more charitable view of penance.

Not only minor details but the major elements of structure are carefully judged by their effect. The climax of a novel is seen as an effect, towards which a good deal, if not the whole of the book, has been building up. Thus, Dickens expresses his own excited involvement in a climax which he has been anticipating with relish for some time:

I am three parts mad, and the fourth delirious, with perpetual rushing at *Hard Times.* I have done what I hope is a good thing with Stephen, taking his story as a whole; and hope to be over in town with the end of the book on Wednesday night ... I have been looking forward through so many weeks and sides of paper to this Stephen business, that now—as usual—it being over, I feel as if nothing in the world, in the way of intense and violent rushing hither and thither, could quite restore my balance.

Furthermore, Dickens wanted to communicate this powerful effect he had experienced for, in the prominent right-hand

[1] To Miss Emily Jolly (17 July 1855), *HD*, p. 374.

corner of his notes for Weekly No. 19, he carefully labelled the outlines for Chapters XXXIII and XXXIV, 'The great effect', and underlined the words twice.[1] This note is particularly interesting since not only does it show Dickens thinking along the rhetorical lines I have indicated but also using the same basic term.

Again, plot exists for the sake of the effect it produces. Critics[2] sometimes speak as if a growing mastery of the complex and highly unified plot by Dickens was pursued as an end in itself, as if he wished to make up for his earlier trifling with the episodic and picaresque structure of *Pickwick* or *Nicholas Nickleby* by a kind of virtuoso performance in complication. On the contrary, Dickens comes down heavily on the cleverest and most intricate construction which he believes is pursued for its own sake with a disregard of the reader's proper reaction: 'I quite agree with you about the "Moonstone." The construction is wearisome beyond endurance, and there is a vein of obstinate conceit in it that makes enemies of readers.' Originality or ingenuity of plot is always commended in terms of its effect on the reader. Thus he, records with delight the gripping effect of a well-constructed novel on himself. Or he praises the tantalizing maze into which Bulwer-Lytton has cunningly shepherded him:

I received your revised proofs only yesterday, and I sat down to read them last night. And before I say anything further I may tell you that I COULD NOT lay them aside, but was obliged to go on with them in my bedroom until I got into a very ghostly state indeed . . . I am burning to get at the whole story ;—and you inflame me in the maddest manner by your references to what I don't know.[3]

Effect was so important to Dickens that a failure to exploit a potential effect in his material made him uneasy:

'As to the story I am in the second number, and last night and

---

[1] *F*, vol. iii, p. 48, footnote ; original MS. of *HT*, Victoria and Albert Museum, Forster Collection, 47. A. 31.

[2] For some examples see George H. Ford, op. cit., pp. 123–8.

[3] To W. H. Wills (26 July 1868), p. 386 ; *W*. but contrast a very favourable impression of *The Moonstone* in an earlier letter to Wills (30 June 1867), *W*, p. 360; to Henry F. Chorley (3 Feb. 1860); Sir Edward Bulwer-Lytton (12 May, 17 Sept. 1861), *HD*, pp. 493, 517, 526.

this morning had half a mind to begin again, and work in what I have done, afterwards. It had occured to him, that, by making the fellow-travellers at once known to each other, as the opening of the story stands, he had missed an effect, 'It struck me that it would be a new thing to show people coming together, in a chance way, as fellow-travellers, and being in the same place, ignorant of one another, as happens in life; and to connect them afterwards, and to make the waiting for that connection a part of the interest.' The change was not made.

These remarks about the opening of *Little Dorrit* are confirmed by the author's notes:

People to meet and part as travellers do, and the future connexion between them in the story, not to be shewn to the reader but to be worked out as in life. *Try this uncertainty and this not-putting of them together, as a new means of interest.* Indicate and carry through this intention (memoranda for No. I).[1]

If we compare the plan with the novel, it is clear that Dickens has not pursued his original intention. Yet these passages do give some idea of the care, in planning and revision, which Dickens believed an effect might merit. They also indicate that he thought about the relationship between structure and effect and recognized that effect might help to shape plot.

Dickens's use of the phrase 'the great effect' shows that he gauges an effect by its power. So does his comment on the effect of the 'curtain' which falls on David's nostalgic vision of his dead mother:

Get a clean pocket-handkerchief ready for the close of "Copperfield" No. 3 [Chap. IX]; 'simple and quiet, but very natural and touching.'

Yet an effect may be so powerful as to produce not an artistic emotion but an impression of the very pain of life itself and so rule out a story whatever its merits:

I have been so very much affected by the long story without a title—which I have read this morning—that I am scarcely fit for

---

[1] *F*, vol. iii, p. 132; Victoria and Albert Museum, Forster Collection, 48. E. 1.

a business letter. It is more painfully pathetic than anything I
have read for I know not how long . . . So many unhappy people
are, by no fault of their own, linked to a similar terrible possibility
—or even probability—that I am afraid it might cause prodigious
unhappiness, if we could address it to our large audience. I shrink
from the responsibility of awakening so much slumbering fear and
despair.

It would be easy, here, to see simply the mercenary editor
with an eye on his circulation, anxious not to disturb his
complacent readers. Yet the matter goes deeper. In the first
place, Dickens scrupulously refuses to tamper with either the
effect or construction of the tale which he considers all of a
piece:

I am not at all of your opinion about the details. It seems to me
to be so thoroughly considered, that they are all essential and in
perfect keeping. I could not in my conscience recommend the
writer to cut the story down in any material degree. I think it
would be decidedly wrong to do so; and I see next to nothing in
the MS., which is otherwise than an essential part of the sad
picture . . . I honestly think it a work of extraordinary power.[1]

In the second place, Dickens has experienced the disturbing
effect himself. He senses an aesthetic as well as a commercial
difficulty. This is, in fact, the problem of 'distancing', a
problem which Dickens often solves in his own work.[2]

The relationship between writer and reader is not simple,
even at its most superficial. True, a narrative for Dickens
must always pass the most obvious tests of readability. It
must avoid jerkiness, there must be smooth transitions from
one narrative form to the next: 'Also, when you change from
narrative to dialogue, or *vice versa*, you should make the
transition more carefully.' Shorter chapters or more sub-
division may be required; there is a limit to what the reader
can take at each bite as well as digest at each sitting. A lengthy
retrospect must not hold up the steady march of the narrative:
'that long stoppage and going back to possess the reader with
the antecedents of the clergyman's biography, are rather

---

[1] To Mark Lemon (25 June 1849), *HD*, pp. 198–9; to W. H. Wills (22 July
1855), *W*, pp. 168–9

[2] See, for example, the discussion on Merdle's suicide, below, pp. 300–1.

crippling'. The effect on the reader prompts Dickens's belief that prefaces, notes, and other forms of explanation outside the narrative are inadvisable. Thus, Dickens advises Bulwer-Lytton to avoid notes in *A Strange Story* since these would be regarded by readers 'as interruptions of the text' and ignored. Similarly, Dickens tells the author of *Basil* that 'the prefatory letter would have been better away, on the ground that a book (of all things) should speak for and explain itself' and in his own prefaces he constantly affirms that the author should not stand between the reader and the book.[1] Yet this concern for readability is not simply a case of tailoring the narrative to fit the reader's crudest needs since all these demands for smoothness, proportion, steady development, and objectivity which characterize readability turn out to be aesthetic qualities that a fastidious critic would require.

The immense popularity of Dickens's novels, which always delighted him, was one standard by which he judged their success. This was true of his first novel: 'The almost un-exampled kindness and favour with which these papers have been received by the public will be a never-failing source of gratifying and pleasant recollection while their author lives.' It remained true of his most mature works:

You will be glad to hear, I know, that "Copperfield" is a great success. I think it is better liked than any of my other books . . . In the Preface to "Bleak House" I remarked that I had never had so many readers. In the Preface to its next successor, "Little Dorrit," I have still to repeat the same words . . . Pray read "Great Expectations." I think it is very droll. It is a very great success, and seems universally liked.[2]

Yet this standard of judging by popularity cannot be explained simply in terms of finance or personal vanity. It is a case rather of a sincere and intimate bond with the reader: 'Deeply sensible of the affection and confidence that have grown up between us, I add to this Preface, as I added to that

---

[1] To Mrs. Brookfield (20 Feb. 1866), Miss King (9 Feb. 1855), Sir Edward Bulwer-Lytton (20 Nov., 18 Dec. 1861), Wilkie Collins (20 Dec. 1852), *HD*, pp. 600, 357, 532, 536, 281; Prefaces to the First Editions of *MC* (1844), *DC* (1850), and *LD* (1857).

[2] Preface to the First Edition of *PP* (1837); to M. De Cerjat (29 Dec. 1849), *HD*, p. 209; Preface to the First Edition of *LD* (1857); to Miss Mary Boyle (28 Dec. 1860), *HD*, p. 510.

[of *Bleak House*], May we meet again!'[1] Such a bond obviously encourages a nice calculation of effect and its success is
then judged by popular response and acclaim. Thus, Dickens
thinks the end of *A Tale of Two Cities* 'is certain to make a
still greater sensation'. He gives the following reason for the
immediate success of *Great Expectations*: 'I suppose because
it opens funnily, and with an interest too'. From the earliest
days of his career, he would anticipate the effect of a character
on the reader and congratulate himself in advance: 'a very
different character from any I have yet described, who I
flatter myself will make a decided hit'.[2] From an early display
of integrity,[3] Dickens continued to show the attitude not of a
huckster but of a responsible artist. In any case, the circulation of Dickens's fiction, large though it was by contemporary standards, has perhaps been exaggerated. When, for
example, the circulation of his work had risen to 32,000,
from an earlier slump to 20,000, the circulation of Reynolds's
Mysteries of London had reached 40,000; and, a little later, a
Manchester bookseller reported that he was selling a thousand
copies of Reynolds's *Mysteries* as compared with 250 of
Dickens's novels.[4] Yet Dickens was certainly not prepared to
emulate Reynolds, of whose work he disapproved,[5] in order to
capture more of the working-class market. Moreover, the view
that Dickens was simply using popularity as an additional
yardstick to test his own personal judgement of a novel's
effectiveness can be verified by his reaction to the drastic and
alarming fall in circulation when *Chuzzlewit* was originally
serialized. Although he did take some steps to make the novel
more attractive, he did not hesitate to back his own judgement
which was subsequently vindicated when the book version
became one of his most appreciated novels and very best
sellers:

You know, as well as I, that I think *Chuzzlewit* in a hundred
points immeasurably the best of my stories. That I feel my power

---

[1] Preface to the First Edition of *LD* (1857).
[2] To M. Regnier (15 Oct. 1859), Miss Mary Boyle (28 Dec. 1860), *HD*,
pp. 488, 510; to Miss Kate Hogarth (21 Feb. 1836), *P*, vol. i, p. 133.
[3] See above, p. 10.
[4] See George H. Ford, op. cit., pp. 78–81; see *F*, vol. ii, pp. 269, 41–2;
Louis James, op. cit., p. 41; John W. Dodds, *The Age of Paradox* (1953),
pp. 126–8.   [5] See Ford, op. cit., p. 79.

now, more than I ever did. That I have a greater confidence in myself than I ever had. That I *know*, if I have health, I could sustain my place in the minds of thinking men, though fifty writers started up to-morrow. But how many readers do *not* think! How many take it upon trust from knaves and idiots, that one writes too fast, or runs a thing to death! How coldly did this very book go on for months, until it forced itself up in people's opinion, without forcing itself up in sale! If I wrote for forty thousand Forsters, or for forty thousand people who know I write because I can't help it, I should have no need to leave the scene.[1]

Obviously, Dickens can only judge his work by estimating its effect on an ideal reader. He can never be certain in advance of the impact the work will make on a mass public. Sometimes, he seeks to confirm his own impression by trying out the effect on a single reader, his wife say, or John Forster:

Nancy is no more. I showed what I have done to Kate last night, who was in an unspeakable *"state:"* from which and my own impression I augur well. When I have sent Sikes to the devil, I must have yours [your impression].

Sometimes, he tries the effect on a small circle of friends:

To finish the topic of "Bleak House" at once, I will only add that I like the conclusion very much and think it *very pretty indeed* . . . We had a little reading of the final double number here the night before last, and it made a great impression I assure you.

Yet his judgement of effect remains very largely a personal one,

At any rate, if my readers have derived but half the pleasure and interest from its perusal, which its composition has afforded me, I have ample reason to be gratified . . . I foresee, I think, some very good things in "Bleak House." . . . I behold them in the months ahead and weep,[2]

which is encouraged by his strong identification with his characters and their experience.[3]

[1] *F*, vol. ii, pp. 42–9.

[2] Ibid., vol. i, p. 131; to the Hon. Mrs. Watson (27 Aug. 1853), *HD*, p. 293; Preface to the First Edition of *MC* (1844); to Miss Mary Boyle (22 July 1852), *HD*, p. 271.

[3] For example, Dickens writes in the preface to the First Edition of *TTC* (1859): 'A strong desire was upon me then, to embody it in my own person . . .

Not only his own work but that of other writers is judged in terms of effect. Thus, he commends the tenderness of *The Woman in White*. Another story is judged very highly on account of its unusual passion and power: 'I think there is a surprising knowledge of one dark phase of human nature throughout this composition; and that it is expressed, generally, with uncommon passion and power.'[1]

Dickens was ready to censure the two major weaknesses of effect that critics have attacked most often in his work. Thus, he explains why the forced and artificial should be avoided: 'Eleonor, I regard as forced and overstrained. The natural result is, that she carries a train of anticlimax after her.' In the same letter to Miss Jolly, Dickens also condemns wild and emotional outpourings in fiction of which he confesses he too has been guilty:

I have no means of knowing whether you are patient in the pursuit of this art; but I am inclined to think that you are not, and that you do not discipline yourself enough. When one is impelled to write this or that, one has still to consider: "How much of this will tell for what I mean? How much of it is my own wild emotion and superfluous energy—how much remains that is truly belonging to this ideal character and these ideal circumstances?" It is in the laborious struggle to make this distinction, and in the determination to try for it, that the road to the correction of faults lies. (Perhaps I may remark, in support of the sincerity with which I write this, that I am an impatient and impulsive person myself, but that it has been for many years the constant effort of my life to practise at my desk what I preach to you.)[2]

Dickens's claim that the progress of his own narrative art has been towards a consciously directed rhetoric is substantially true. For example, the following note for *Little Dorrit*, written only a few months before the letter to Miss Jolly, shows him

I have so far verified what is done and suffered in these pages, as that I have certainly done and suffered it all myself.' The basic situation in the novel had developed from Wilkie Collins's play *The Frozen Deep* (1857) in which Dickens had acted the part of the lover who sacrifices his life to save his rival, a role with which he strongly identified himself; see Robert Ashley, *Wilkie Collins* (1952), pp. 43–4, Edgar Johnson, *Charles Dickens: His Tragedy and Triumph* (1953), vol. ii, p. 972.
   [1] To Wilkie Collins (7 Jan. 1860), *HD*, p. 492; to W. H. Wills (12 July 1855), *W*, p. 167.
   [2] To Miss Emily Jolly (30 May 1857), *HD*, pp. 427, 428.

in the act of dealing with the kind of problem of characterization he later discusses with her: 'Delicately trace out the process of Fanny's engagement to Sparkler; shewing how it comes about, and how such a mind in such a person naturally worked that way' (II, Chap. XIV). A careful control of emotion is indicated in a further note: 'Clennam on the Summer Evening—Scene with Pet, delicately shewing that the father and mother have been for him, and that they all know of his affection. VERY DELICATE. The dead daughter AND THE ROSES FLOATING AWAY' (I, Chap. XXVIII).[1] The notes and the letter show that Dickens does not rule out either rhetoric or emotion. The qualifications, 'wild', and 'superfluous', in his letter show that other kinds of emotion and energy may be acceptable. His insistence on discipline, on the conscious direction of emotion and energy do not indicate the romantic concept of art as self-expression but rather the traditional view of art as rhetoric. Dickens is, in fact, advocating an ideal rhetoric, a responsible striving not simply for effect but for the best effect.

What precisely would he have understood by the best effect? What, in fact, would the term 'effect' have meant to him? Most of the examples above suggest that Dickens was preoccupied with strongly emotive effects and this suggestion is perhaps confirmed by a book on literary technique which he had in his library.

Unfortunately, it is impossible to determine when this interesting work, *Essays on the Sources of the Pleasures Received from Literary Compositions*[2] was added to Dickens's library, though since it was published in 1809 it may have been in his possession from the beginning of his career. The contents of this book, overlooked by critics and scholars, are most revealing. It is, in essence, a textbook on how to use effects in literary composition. It includes separate essays entitled, 'On the Sublime', 'On Terrour [*sic*]', 'On Pity', 'On the Tender Affections', 'On the Ludicrous'. Even if the book were added at a late date in Dickens's career and did not

---

[1] Original MS. of *LD*, Vols. IIA, IA. No. XIV, which contained Chap. XIV, was published Jan. 1857.

[2] Edward Mangin, *Essays on the Sources of the Pleasures Received from Literary Compositions* (1809); see *Catalogue of the Library of Charles Dickens*, ed. J. H. Stonehouse (1935), p. 43.

therefore influence his development, it still tends to show what may have interested Dickens about narrative technique and to confirm that he saw his art as a rhetorical one, concerned with producing emotive effects, like terror, pity, and the ludicrous, in the reader. In later chapters of the present study, some of the remarkably significant ways in which this book may have influenced, or at least interested, Dickens will be pointed out.

By the best effect, Dickens would almost certainly have understood one which included the most *powerful* emotive reaction in the reader that could be successfully produced under the circumstances. Referring to the number of *David Copperfield* which contains the great storm scene at Yarmouth and the deaths of Steerforth and Ham, Dickens remarks: 'I am in that tremendous paroxysm of Copperfield—having my most powerful effect in all the Story on the Anvil.'[1] Magnitude and quality are not necessarily irreconcilable factors in the aesthetic experience and there are clearly points at which they become interrelated. The size of an audience may sometimes have fascinated Dickens but unlike contemporary writers such as G. W. M. Reynolds he was not simply counting heads or glorying in output[2] as a measure of success. Dickens's final criterion seems rather to have been the magnitude of the effect in an ideal reader.

The term 'emotive' needs handling with considerable caution. Readers of Dickens are well aware that he does not necessarily deal in crude emotions or crudely with emotion. In any case, emotion may very well range from *affect*, in which sensation predominates and the subject is possessed by the emotion, to that kind of feeling which becomes a directed function and forms the basis of all our value judgements.[3] Feeling, therefore, in life and in literature, may help us to evaluate experience and so the critic cannot afford to dismiss emotive effects as beneath his notice. Irony, for example, is partly emotive and recognized by Dickens as an effect which may have great power: 'I have a grim pleasure upon me

---

[1] To W. H. Wills (17 Sept. 1850), *W*, p. 41.
[2] See Louis James, op. cit., p. 41; E. S. Turner, *Boys Will Be Boys* (1948), p. 31.
[3] See C. G. Jung, *Psychological Types*, pp. 544, 546.

to-night in thinking that the Circumlocution Office sees the light, and in wondering what effect it will make.'[1] Yet irony may release a critical and intellectual awareness.[2]

5. *Intention and Effect in Dickens's Narrative Art: A Further Problem*

Dickens's fiction can be examined in terms of the kind of art I believe he was trying to create only if we accept the study of conscious rhetoric as legitimate. Yet the study of intention and effect in literature has recently been declared invalid. The question raised by the so-called 'intentional' and 'affective fallacies' I have answered in some detail elsewhere.[3] Very briefly it can be said here that the critical theory, expounded by Wimsatt and Beardsley, Wellek and Warren, derives from an *a priori* assumption. Yet we may start from a different assumption (close to that adopted by Hegel and others), which is no easier to refute, and go on to argue that the significance of a literary work can ultimately be exhausted only by the study both of the work and its relationship with the author and the reader, with a world in which it has both origin and function.

The method of 'nothing but the words on the page' may have its place in literary criticism yet it cannot fully explain what has gone wrong with scenes like the death of Little Nell or the interview between Rosa Dartle and Little Em'ly which have embarrassed many critics for over a century.[4]

[1] *F*, vol. iii, p. 136.

[2] See below, pp. 160–1.

[3] W. K. Wimsatt, Jr., and M. C. Beardsley, 'The Intentional Fallacy', 'The Affective Fallacy', *Sewanee Review*, liv (1946), 468–88, lvii (1949), 31–55; René Wellek and Austin Warren, *Theory of Literature* (1963), esp. pp. 142–57. George Watson, 'A Modern Literary Heresy', *The Listener*, lx (1958), 595–6, summarizes much of the case against this school of criticism; see also H. P. Sucksmith, 'The Narrative Art of Charles Dickens: the Rhetoric of Sympathy and Irony in his Novels', unpublished Ph.D. thesis (University of Nottingham, 1967), pp. 39–41.

[4] A fair sample of criticism which fails to explain adequately what has gone wrong with Nell's death might include James Fitzjames Stephen, *Cambridge Essays* (1855), p. 175; G. H. Lewes, 'Dickens in Relation to Criticism', *Fortnightly Review*, xvii (1872), and Aldous Huxley, *Vulgarity in Literature* (1930), both quoted in *The Dickens Critics*, pp. 73–4, 155; Lord David Cecil, *Early Victorian Novelists* (1934), p. 30. George H. Ford, op. cit., p. 127, cites criticism of the scene between Rosa Dartle and Little Em'ly.

An analysis of the death of Little Nell, which finds it necessary to take intention and effect into account, is given below.[1]

The scene between Rosa Dartle and Little Em'ly has been widely regarded as melodramatic and the dialogue in particular criticized as stilted[2]. Yet these criticisms do not completely explain why the scene is so unsatisfactory. The situation is full of promise. We have only to compare it with the situation in the scene between Nancy and Rose Maylie in Chapter XL of *Oliver Twist* to appreciate this. In *Oliver Twist*, a prostitute is awakened to remorse for her way of life in the presence of idealized purity. In *David Copperfield*, a professed virtue is on trial for its attitude towards the fallen woman, abandoned and remorseful. One can imagine what Dostoyevsky would have made of such material. Why is Dickens unsuccessful?

There is nothing naïve about the characterization of Rosa Dartle. To the post-Freudian reader, this portrait of a deeply passionate, sexually frustrated nature is psychologically true in every detail. In a subtle way, the physical result of the hammer attack on her, which is carefully recalled in this scene, symbolizes her traumatic experience at the hands of Steerforth with its strong sexual character and sado-masochistic undertones. It has become a symbolic rape, expressing her deepest longings, her sense of humiliation and outrage, and her hatred:

> The resolute and unrelenting hatred of her tone, its cold stern sharpness, and its mastered rage, presented her before me, as if I had seen her standing in the light. I saw the flashing black eyes, and the passion-wasted figure; and I saw the scar, with its white track cutting through her lips, quivering and throbbing as she spoke.

Paradoxically, Em'ly's abject defeat excites Rosa's darkest and most insatiable fury because it is bound to remind Rosa of her own humiliation at the same man's hands and, though the situation offers her a crumb of consolation in a feeling of moral superiority to Em'ly, it also stings her with the thought of all that Em'ly has enjoyed. So the refined Victorian lady's companion describes the affair between Em'ly

[1] See below, pp. 284–7.
[2] See, for example, John Butt and Kathleen Tillotson, op. cit., pp. 149, 164.

and Steerforth as coarsely as she can and, while she revels in her own smug sense of decency, she also associates together thoughts of humiliation and the crudest sexuality. Significantly, the crisis of her outburst takes the form of a punishment fantasy which is not only vicious and perverse but blatantly sexual: a series of girls like Em'ly are to be savagely flogged.[1]

A modern reader might be forgiven for concluding that the intention of this scene was to expose the sexual envy which lies behind the moral indignation of the half-demented Rosa. Yet we can deduce, from Dickens's declared conscious intention as regards Little Em'ly, that the main stress in the scene was probably intended to fall on Em'ly's sufferings and that the chief purpose of the scene was a social one:

> I had previously observed much of what you say about the poor girls. In all you suggest with so much feeling about their return to virtue being cruelly cut off, I concur with a sore heart. I have been turning it over in my mind for some time, and hope, in the history of Little Em'ly (who *must* fall—there is no hope for her), to put it before the thoughts of people in a new and pathetic way, and perhaps to do some good.

We know that the rehabilitation of fallen women deeply concerned Dickens and that he was helping Miss Coutts to organize a home for them while he was writing *David Copperfield*.[2] Yet the way Rosa Dartle's character is developed throughout the scene not only fails to help this strong avowed purpose but actively contradicts it.

Certainly Rosa Dartle's cruelty should intensify even more than Minnie Joram's callousness the pathos of Em'ly's predicament. Yet Rosa's cruelty cannot represent the general Victorian attitude towards the rehabilitation of fallen women, not at least as it was consciously expressed. Rosa Dartle is a special, pathological case. As such, she cannot stand for all the cooler, less emotive censure, the lower-class prejudice of Minnie Joram, for example, or the selfish class-conscious point of view of Mrs. Steerforth which is not devoid of a

---

[1] *DC*, Chap. L, pp. 718, 721.

[2] To M. De Cerjat (29 Dec. 1849), *HD*, pp. 208–9; see Phillip Collins, *Dickens and Crime*, pp. 94–116, and *Coutts, passim*.

certain heartless rationality.[1] Had Dickens been able to put the attitude in a more reasonable form and still shown it to be cruel, then he would have made his point.

Yet the more successfully does Dickens convey Rosa Dartle's character, the more she hinders and obscures the social purpose of the scene. Indeed, the very improvements Dickens sought to add in revision only make matters worse. Perhaps the finest piece of dialogue in the whole scene, one which does ring true and is far above mere melodrama in its shocking intensity—the whipping fantasy of Rosa Dartle— was added in proof:

"And tell that to *me*," she added, "with your shameful lips? Why don't they whip these creatures? If I could order it to be done, I would have this woman whipped to death."

On the other hand, the stereotyped Victorian sentiments against illicit sexuality which Dickens crams into the mouth of Miss Dartle seem all the more artificial by contrast with her genuine individual passion. Thus, in a final passage, which was also added in proof, Rosa, with her cruel sarcasm, does bring out all the irony in the plight of the girl who had sought to become a lady through Steerforth; and yet, in a final alliterative anti-climax, Rosa can only consign Em'ly to the conventional fate of the Victorian fallen woman and her corpse to that Victorian bowdlerized version of a dung hill, the 'dust heap'. So uneasy does Dickens feel about the success of his intention to create pity for Em'ly in this scene that he felt driven to add in proof at the end of the scene a clumsy appeal for some proper sentiment on the part of the reader:

"Oh me, oh me!" exclaimed the wretched Emily, in a tone that might have touched the hardest heart, I should have thought.[2]

What is true of intention also holds true of effect. A full appreciation of Dickens's fiction may only be arrived at by taking into account its function as well as its origin. Consider, for example, the comment on Little Dorrit:

At what period of her early life, the little creature began to

---

[1] *DC*, Chap. XXXII, pp. 468–70.
[2] Corrected proofs of *DC*, Victoria and Albert Museum, Forster Collection, 48. B. 14, Chap. L, pp. 511 (First Edition reads 'girl' after 'this'), 512; cf. *DC*, pp. 721, 722.

perceive that it was not the habit of all the world to live locked up in narrow yards surrounded by high walls with spikes at the top, would be a difficult question to settle. But she was a very, very little creature indeed, when she had somehow gained the knowledge, that her clasp of her father's hand was to be always loosened at the door which the great key opened; and that while her own light steps were free to pass beyond it, his feet must never cross that line. A pitiful and plaintive look, with which she had begun to regard him when she was still extremely young, was perhaps a part of this discovery.[1]

If we regard this passage from a purely 'objective' and cognitive point of view, we must acknowledge that its subject is Little Dorrit's dawning awareness that her father is a prisoner and we must restrict the feeling in the passage to the child's concern for her father's predicament. In that case, what are we to make of Dickens's insistence on the childhood qualities which make Little Dorrit vulnerable, her smallness, extreme youth, and helplessness? If, however, we examine our reaction to the passage honestly, we find that our feelings are primarily directed not towards the father but the child. This is as it should be, for the chapter in which the passage occurs presents a pathetic spectacle of 'the Child of the Marshalsea'; it was the preceding chapter which centred on 'the Father of the Marshalsea'. If we consider the helpless predicament of the child and her painful concern solely as inherent properties of the passage, they appear to have little connection. Yet they are, in fact, there because together they create the effect of pathos, a compound emotion which, as we shall see later, requires both these elements of pain and helplessness. Separate details in the text may acquire their full meaning only when they are referred to the effect which the text produces on the reader.

Wellek and Warren argue that the study of effect does not belong to the province of literary criticism. They base their case on two further objections. First, the effect on the reader cannot be known with the certainty which cognitive perception of the work offers. Secondly, judgement by effect leads to relativism and subjectivism. Both these arguments are fallacies. The report of feeling judgements is neither more nor

---

[1] *LD*, Bk. I, Chap. VII, pp. 68–9.

less a 'subjective' process than the report of cognitive percep-
tions. In fact, the history of philosophy shows how indecisive
and contradictory cognitive attempts to arrive at truth may
be. The history of traditional criticism shows how comparatively stable and universal, within certain major shifts of
taste, the report of feelings has been, even though feeling
labours under the grave disadvantage of an imprecise language. Feeling has its own absolute laws and works according
to patterns which are as reliable and predictable as the laws
of logic. Some have even gone so far as to speak of the logic of
feeling and to describe certain kinds of feeling as rational.
Cognition can only yield knowledge; it cannot participate
directly in experience and it would seem axiomatic to me that
one cannot fully judge what one has never experienced.
Joseph Conrad forcefully expressed this credo as an article of
aesthetic faith:

The changing wisdom of successive generations discards ideas,
questions facts, demolishes theories. But the artist appeals to that
part of our being which is not dependent on wisdom; to that in us
which is a gift and not an acquisition—and, therefore, more
permanently enduring. He speaks to our capacity for delight and
wonder, to the sense of mystery surrounding our lives; to our
sense of pity, and beauty, and pain; to the latent feeling of fellowship with all creation.[1]

A simple instance from *The Old Curiosity Shop* will illustrate the point. At the beginning of Chapter XXII, Kit is
expressing his detestation of Little Bethel. The guilty asceti-
cism and the perverse gloom offends him because it denies his
own vision of joy:

"Unless you want to make me feel very wretched and uncomfortable, you ⟨won't take⟩ 'LL KEEP that bow ⟨off⟩ ON your
bonnet, which you'd more than half a mind to pull off last week.
Can you suppose there's any harm in looking as cheerful AND
BEING AS CHEERFUL as our poor circumstances will permit?

[1] René Wellek and Austin Warren, op. cit., pp. 146–7, 154, 156; C. G. Jung,
Psychological Types, p. 545; as M. H. Abrams, *The Mirror and the Lamp*
(New York, 1958), pp. 20–1, points out, 'The pragmatic orientation, ordering
the aim of the artist and the character of the work to the nature, the needs,
and the springs of pleasure in the audience . . . has been the principal aesthetic
attitude of the Western World'; F. Paulham, *The Laws of Feeling*, tr. C. K.
Ogden (1930), p. 153; Preface to *The Nigger of the Narcissus* (1897).

Do I see anything in the way I'm made, which calls upon me to be a snivelling, solemn, whispering chap, sneaking about as if I couldn't help it, and expressing myself in a most unpleasant snuffle ? on the contrairy, don't I see every reason why I shouldn't ?''

Kit's vision here is either expressed in negative terms or offered as a statement, presented either as knowledge or as an argument with an appeal to reason at the end. But in going on to vindicate the natural animal joy in man, Kit jumps from cognition, 'see every reason', to sensation, 'hear', since he can only communicate his vision in its fullness as an experience of joy which his own immediate audience and the reader are instinctively compelled, through the sympathetic induction of emotion, to share:

"Just hear this! Ha ha ha! An't that as nat'ral as walking, and as good for the health ? Ha ha ha! An't that as nat'ral as a sheep's bleating, or a pig's grunting, or a horse's neighing, or a bird's singing ? Ha ha ha! Isn't it, mother ?''

There was something contagious in Kit's laugh, for his mother, who had looked grave before, first subsided into a smile, and then fell to joining in it heartily, which occasioned Kit to say that he knew it was natural, and to laugh the more. Kit and his mother, laughing together in a pretty loud key, woke the baby, who, finding that there was something very jovial and agreeable in progress, was no sooner in its mother's arms than it began to kick and crow and laugh, most vigorously. This new illustration of his argument so tickled Kit, that he fell backward in his chair in a state of exhaustion, pointing at the baby and ⟨–?–⟩ing at the very top of his –?–⟩ SHAKING HIS SIDES TILL HE ROCKED AGAIN.[1]

Thus, the vision here is sharply focused by the effect. An irresistible conviction is lent to assertion; power is added to knowledge. And, as we can see in the original manuscript, Dickens was so eager to reproduce the sheer physical experience of laughter that he had substituted the infectious[2]

---

[1] Original MS. of *OCS*, Victoria and Albert Museum, Forster Collection, 47. A. 6 (Vol. IB), Chap. XXI, pp. 14–15 (First Edition of *MHC* omits 'and crow'); cf. *OCS*, Chap. XXII, p. 167. For a fuller explanation of the term 'sympathetic induction of emotion', see below, pp. 120–4.

[2] See William McDougall, *An Introduction to Social Psychology* (1960), pp. 80–1: 'Laughter is notoriously infectious all through life, and this . . . affords the most familiar example of sympathetic induction of an affective state.'

climax of his account, 'shaking his sides till he rocked again', as a second thought for what would appear to be a much vaguer and weaker statement, '–?–ing at the very top of his ?voice'.

In this respect, Dickens is not in some special category. The reader may recall how Joyce expresses a final affirmation of life in *Ulysses* through the closing lines of Molly Bloom's soliloquy. Joyce's vision here is, of course, more complex than that of Dickens yet when Joyce comes to his final expression of that affirmation he resorts to the same kind of physiological accompaniment as Dickens. Just as Dickens had induced an inner laughter in his reader, so Joyce does not describe the sexual surrender of Molly Bloom in vague terms but through the powerful rhythm and the repetition of 'Yes' he conveys something very like the mounting excitement, the breathlessness, and the reiterated cry of orgasm. A vision of joyful affirmation is not only stated as an idea by the word 'Yes', it is focused as a powerful 'memory image' of experience through the effect evoked in the reader.[1]

Even when such a vision is presented as a philosophical idea, it may well take on a form which aims to persuade through effect. Thus 'The Everlasting Yea' of Carlyle's *Sartor Resartus*, which comprehends a view of life no less positive than that of Joyce or Dickens, finds expression at one point in a curious parallel to Dickens's vision:

We gladly recall to mind that once we saw him *laugh*; once only, perhaps it was the first and last time in his life; but then such a peal of laughter, enough to have awakened the Seven Sleepers! . . . gradually a light kindled in our Professor's eyes and face, a beaming, mantling, loveliest light; through those murky features, a radiant, ever-young Apollo looked; and he burst forth like the neighing of all Tattersall's,—tears streaming down his cheeks, pipe held aloft, foot clutched into the air,—loud, long continuing, uncontrollable; a laugh not of the face and diaphragm only, but of the whole man from head to heel.[2]

It is also interesting to see in the passage from the manuscript of *The Old Curiosity Shop* that Dickens is so anxious to

---

[1] James Joyce, *Ulysses* (1947), pp. 740–2. The passage begins 'I love flowers' and continues to the end of the novel.

[2] Thomas Carlyle, *Sartor Resartus* [1833–4], People's Edition (1872), Bk. II, Chap. IX, pp. 126–36, Bk. I, Chap. IV, p. 22.

present a vision of affirmation that he even alters the negative form, 'you won't take that bow off your bonnet' to the positive form, 'you'll keep that bow on your bonnet', and he is careful to insert the phrase, 'and being as cheerful', after 'looking as cheerful', thus adding the actuality of cheerfulness to its mere semblance.

It is worth considering what may happen when effect is ignored and another criterion, say probability, substituted. The dispute, for instance, between Dickens and G. H. Lewes about Spontaneous Combustion misses the only point that matters. Even if Dickens had been correct that such a phenomenon was possible, it would not make the slightest difference. The idea of Spontaneous Combustion as the cause of Krook's death produces the kind of farcical anticlimax which Dickens had already recognized in *Martin Chuzzlewit*. It cannot therefore carry the grave weight which Dickens expects it to bear as the conclusion of the tenth monthly number of *Bleak House*. The careful build-up of tension throughout the chapter only increases the ludicrous effect of the anticlimax. A cognitive type of criticism might point out that, as a symbol of organic corruption which brings about its own dissolution, the idea of Spontaneous Combustion contributes to the theme of the novel. It is all of no avail. A description of the stages of human disintegration or of recognizable human remains may awaken horror but the sudden evaporation of a man into soot and effluvium is not serious. The intrinsic quality of humour in such an idea is confirmed by the anticlimax that ruins the effect of a similar catastrophe in a novel by Bram Stoker. Oddly enough, a wretched production from the Victorian penny press, which uses the idea, avoids anticlimax and creates something like horror by describing the burning that precedes death and dissolution.[1]

Failure to take effect into account may lead to serious misjudgements. Thus, critics have not distinguished between

---

[1] Preface to the First Edition of *BH* (1853); G. H. Lewes, *The Leader* (11 Dec. 1852, 15 Jan., 5, 12 Feb. 1853); Gordon S. Haight, 'Dickens and Lewes on Spontaneous Combustion', *Nineteenth-Century Fiction*, x (1955), 53–63; *BH*, Chap. XXII, pp. 443–56; *MC*, Chap. XI, p. 185; Bram Stoker, *The Jewel of the Seven Stars* (1962), Chap. XIX, pp. 250–4; *The Darling of Our Crew* (1880) [the relevant passage is quoted in E. S. Turner, op. cit., pp. 27–8].

the ironic and non-ironic forms of coincidence which need to be judged separately.[1]

Again, effect must be treated as an important factor in Dickens's narrative art since it may seriously limit his vision. His handling of Mr. Dick in *David Copperfield* is a case in point. The manuscript of the novel shows that Dickens originally intended to give a realistic portrait of lunacy; he subsequently modified this picture in proof. It has been pointed out that Dickens thereby avoided the disgust which Wordsworth has occasionally aroused in his picture of the Idiot Boy.[2] Yet was Dickens only avoiding disgust or was he concerned with a more positive programme?

Dickens had touched on the ill treatment of the insane in two earlier novels and we gather from Forster that in *David Copperfield* he wanted to recommend humane treatment.[3] It was important, therefore, that Mr. Dick should win the sympathy, even the affection, of the reader and that he should justify the kindly domestic treatment of lunacy which Dickens was recommending. The changes which Dickens made in proof confirm that he was seeking to create a picture of Mr. Dick which would further this policy. Moreover, Mr. Dick's entrance into the story coincides with a change for the better in David's fortunes and the mood of the novel shifts from unpleasant to pleasant. Certainly, the starkly realistic face and grimaces at the window of Aunt Betsey's house on Mr. Dick's first appearance in the manuscript are apt to disgust the reader. If Dickens had simply wished to eliminate disgust he might have cut the incident altogether. Mr. Dick would still have been able to make his formal entrance into the story later in the chapter. But Dickens does not do this. Instead he substitutes another portrait at the proof stage. This portrait is a positive one; it is calculated to win sympathy for Mr. Dick right from the start:

I lifted up my eyes to the window above it, where I saw a florid, pleasant-looking gentleman, with a grey head, ⟨putting his tongue out against the glass, and carrying it across the pane and back again; who, when his eye caught mine, squinted at me in a

---

[1] See below, pp. 235–9.
[2] Butt and Tillotson, op. cit., p. 130.
[3] *OCS*, Chap. XXIV, p. 180; *BR*, Chap. XLVII, p. 357; *F*, vol. iii, p. 18.

most terrible manner, laughed, and went away.⟩ WHO SHUT UP ONE EYE IN A GROTESQUE MANNER, NODDED HIS HEAD AT ME SEVERAL TIMES, SHOOK IT AT ME AS OFTEN, LAUGHED, AND WENT AWAY.[1]

The epithet, 'pleasant-looking', is now no longer contradicted by the rest of the sentence. The squint has become a wink and the expression and gestures are no longer repulsively inane but attractively knowing and amusing while the laugh from what seemed a horrible mad outburst has become agreeable.

Dickens does not stop here. The manuscript and the corrected proofs show that he tries on every possible occasion to intensify sympathy for Mr. Dick. In Chapter XIV, for example, when David first encounters the insane delusions of Mr. Dick about the memorials and the kite, Dickens modifies the evidence of lunacy with a most attractive series of touches:

His face was so very MILD AND pleasant, and had something so reverend in it, though it was hale and hearty, that I was not sure but that he was having a good-humoured jest with me. So I laughed, and he laughed, and we parted the best friends possible.[2]

The manuscript shows that the words, 'mild and', which are calculated to steer the reader away from any association of lunacy and obsession with passion and violence, were inserted as a second thought and strengthen what is already a sympathetic portrait.

Again, the very attractive development of Mr. Dick's character in Chapter XVII is carried even further in the manuscript than in the printed text. A rather gratuitous passage of explanation, which was cut in proof for reasons of space, also contained a warm-hearted approval of Mr. Dick's honesty, his frankness, and his eager persistence in holding to an exact truth. All these qualities are intended to win over the reader from the conventional unsympathetic view of the madman as shifty and cunning, apathetic and feather-

---

[1] Corrected proofs of *DC*, Chap. XIII, p. 136; cf. *DC*, p. 190.
[2] Original MS. of *DC*, Victoria and Albert Museum, Forster Collection, 47. A. 23 (Vol. IA), Chap. XIV, p. 15; cf. *DC*, p. 203.

brained, vague and with little respect for consistency or
reality:

but when I observed the straightforward earnestness with which
he told it, in the openness of his heart towards me, and the un-
varying way in which, both on that and succeeding occasions, he
described the circumstances and the man, I began to think there
must be something in it, though how much of it might be true, and
how much fanciful, I could not guess.

Finally, in Chapter XLIX, Micawber's eulogy on Mr. Dick's
amiability and kindly optimism was inserted in proof:

"The friendliness of this gentleman," said Mr. Micawber to my
aunt, "if you will allow me, ma'am, to cull a figure of speech from
the vocabulary of our coarser national sports—floors me." . . .
Mr. Micawber was quite overcome by these friendly words, and
by finding Mr. Dick's hand again within his own. "It has been my
lot," he observed, "to meet, in the diversified panorama of human
existence, with an occasional oasis, but never with one so green,
so gushing, as the present!"[1]

It is clear from his earliest repelling picture of Mr. Dick that
Dickens was well aware of the ugly side of madness. Indeed,
he knew that the truth could be even uglier. He was interested
in Dr. John Connolly's work with the insane, had visited
asylums abroad, and an article he wrote in collaboration with
W. H. Wills shows he was well aware how horrible real idiots
could appear: 'a miserable monster, whom nobody may put
to death, but whom every one must wish dead, and be dis-
tressed to see alive.'[2] Yet this ugly side is carefully excluded
from the portrait of Mr. Dick. Dickens's compassionate view
of life demands an effect of sympathy through which to work;
the vision of the real world is correspondingly restricted. One
might argue that only the full horror of lunacy would test
true compassion. Yet this was not Dickens's way. He was
essentially the practical man, here, who realized that most

[1] Corrected proofs of *DC*, Chap. XVII, p. 179, Chap. XLIX, p. 502 (First
Edition omits 'very' after 'reception is'); cf. *DC*, pp. 250, 708–9. The deleted
passage followed the words, 'ill-fated Prince who occasioned him so much
difficulty'. The entire passage from 'The friendliness of this gentleman' to 'so
gushing, as the present!' was inserted in proof.
[2] 'Idiots', *HW*, vii (4 June 1853), 313; cf. 'Idiots Again', *HW*, ix (15 Apr.
1854), 197–200.

men cannot bear too much reality and that the way to progress might have to fall short of the whole truth. A harsh critic might condemn this as myopia or a kind of artistic machiavellianism. Yet it could also be regarded as wise policy and, in so far as an artist seeks to impose a moral view which aims at reform, he must consider what is politic.

The case of Mr. Dick also throws some light on the problem of intention. Examination of the treatment of this character in the manuscript and corrected proofs of *David Copperfield* shows that Dickens is a conscious artist, prepared to consider two alternatives but then determined to prosecute his final decision with the utmost vigour. It also shows that he is a responsible artist, knowing exactly what he is about, able to weigh the consequences of a decision, not shirking the difficult conflict between truth and goodness and able to decide between absolute values in the only way he can—as an artist seeking to *communicate* a vision of life rather than to instruct or preach.

II

DICKENS'S USE OF LANGUAGE AS
A NARRATIVE MEDIUM

1. *Surface Wit and Structural Rhetoric*

THE very obviousness of Dickens's rhetorical manner may
be a further obstacle to a proper appreciation of his narrative
art. Yet an understanding of why this is so will uncover an
important element in Dickens's narrative technique.

Dickens has a style which varies from a surface of dazzling
brilliance to one of heavily laboured mannerisms. As A. W.
Ward comments:

> His more important mannerisms were, like many really dangerous
> faults of style, only the excess of characteristic excellences. Thus
> it was he who elaborated with unprecedented effect, that humorous
> species of paraphrase which, as one of the most imitable devices of
> his style, has also been the most persistently imitated . . . but
> in the end the device becomes a mere trick of circumlocution.
> Another mannerism which grew upon Dickens, and was faithfully
> imitated by several of his disciples, was primarily due to his habit
> of turning a fact, fancy, or situation round on every side. This
> consisted in the reiteration of a construction, or of part of a
> construction, in the strained rhetorical fashion to which he at last
> accustomed us in spite of ourselves, but to which we were loth to
> submit in his imitators. These and certain other peculiarities,
> which it would be difficult to indicate without incurring the charge
> of hypercriticism, hardened as the style of Dickens hardened; and,
> for instance, in the *Tale of Two Cities* his mannerisms may be seen
> side by side in glittering array.

Formal rhetorical figures occur in many of the brilliant
passages of Dickens's fiction and in many of those which
appear forced and artificial. Indeed, Dickens uses an excep-
tionally wide range of these figures and he uses them frequently. Yet why should Dickens's use of traditional rhetorical
figures produce such a striking variation in his style between

the scintillating and the banal? Surprisingly, the criticism that sets out to deal with Dickens's style does not ask, let alone try to answer, this question even when it notes the variation.[1] The reason is, I think, that criticism of this kind makes a fundamental assumption about the nature of style in general and Dickens's in particular which is superficial and limiting. It is here that the obviousness of Dickens's rhetorical manner becomes an obstacle.

In the passage quoted above, style tends to be treated as if it could be detached and considered in isolation. This practice of treating style as a separable element in a writer's work is, of course, characteristic of a certain traditional approach which may seem old-fashioned today but which may re-appear, as I shall show later, in a modern disguise. Obviously, such a practice encourages, and is encouraged by, a view of rhetorical figures as something ornamental, something added as mere embellishment, something which may in the end come to be described as 'airs and graces'. Again, Professor Ward's illustrations are revealing. Only two examples are given and they illustrate only the happy side of Dickens's style. Paucity of illustration is typical of this kind of critical approach. Yet, whether instances of Dickens's happier rhetorical style are chosen, as in Professor Ward's study or that of Alice Meynell, or Dickens's less happy style, as in the case of the Fowlers,[2] the significant fact is that the examples are treated as if they could be considered quite apart from their immediate context. This fact is not really so surprising since it follows naturally from the assumption, whether conscious or unconscious, that the style is a separable element or at least one which may be abstracted and considered in isolation.

It might be thought that the advent of 'close reading' and 'practical criticism' had put an end to this traditional approach to style. Yet the assumption behind the traditional approach has sometimes only made concessions to a newer

---

[1] A. W. Ward, *Dickens* (1882), pp. 206–7; see also Alice Meynell, 'Charles Dickens as a Man of Letters', *Atlantic Monthly* (Jan. 1903), 52–9, reprinted in *The Dickens Critics*, pp. 95–108, esp. p. 96.

[2] H. W. and F. G. Fowler, *The King's English* (Oxford, 1940), pp. 180–2, 222, 225, 304; H. W. Fowler, *A Dictionary of Modern English Usage* (Oxford, 1944), p. 622.

fashion. Consider, for example, the method which Q. D. Leavis lays down for the study of a novel when she rejects the technical approach of E. M. Forster and Percy Lubbock:

> To take *Madame Bovary* or *Vanity Fair* to pieces does not help; a discussion of the mechanics of successful novels (except for professional novelists) is pointless and profitless. The essential technique in an art that works by using words is the way in which words are used . . . The soundest method for the critic of the novel would be to reinforce a general impression by analysis of significant passages.

But, if a general impression of a novel is to dictate the selection of passages for 'close reading', may not this kind of scrutiny simply lead to the confirming in detail of a vague, eccentric, or even wild judgement? May not the whole question of what is truly significant be begged by this method? Certainly, if we test the method in use by Mrs. Leavis herself we find that in the same book in which she formulates her method she prefers Mrs. Aphra Behn to most of the Victorian novelists in whose hands she believes the novel began its deterioration; she compares Dickens unfavourably with Mrs. Radcliffe; and she equates Dickens quite seriously with Marie Corelli and Edgar Wallace.[1] Again, if the context of a passage or even a phrase may very well be an entire book, does not an entire book consist, among other things, of its total structure? Some of the titles of Dickens's novels, for example, only gain their full significance when they are related to the complete structure of the book.

The method of Mrs. Leavis appears to set up a claim for what we might call texture as against structure. This is also what Professor Ward, Alice Meynell, and the Fowlers were doing when they set out to criticize Dickens's style. Preoccupation with texture will, in fact, encourage a view of style as an element which can be detached, in critical practice if not in theory, and a view of rhetorical language as surface—though not necessarily superficial—ornament. Of course, in a truly organic piece of work, texture and structure cannot be separated except through a process of abstraction but it is

[1] Q. D. Leavis, *Fiction and the Reading Public*, pp. 232–3; pp. 253, 153–4, 185, 168.

important to make a theoretical distinction if only to recognize the claims of each. I would regard structure as the principle, idea, or design which organizes, or tries to organize, texture into a pattern that has more meaning, power, or effect than the texture by itself would possess; structure would therefore range in my view from syntax to plot and form. It is true that modern critics who show a preoccupation with texture do not as a rule in practice completely ignore structure; instead, they treat structure as a purely local matter. This can, for instance, be seen at its best in a more recent criticism of a passage from Dickens's *Little Dorrit* by Mrs. Leavis.[1]

As against the critic who concerns himself with texture, we must set the critic who is preoccupied with structure. Critics who concern themselves with over-all structure tend to neglect the relationship between texture and structure. This is true of Aristotle, of Dryden, and more recently of Percy Lubbock in *The Craft of Fiction* (1921).

On the other hand, what a preoccupation with texture may lead to can be seen in the view of two recent critics that the characterization of Dickens is almost entirely an attribute of his style or verbal dexterity. Miriam Allott claims:

What neither James nor Trollope possesses, however, is Dickens's brilliant conversational fantasy. This depends on the verbal inventiveness which is the gift finally separating his genius from that of almost all other novelists (Joyce, perhaps, apart). On examination, Dickens's characters are found to exist very largely through their speech. Jingle, Chadband, Pecksniff, Micawber, above all Mrs. Gamp, live through the words which are put into their mouths . . . This verbal ingenuity secures Dickens our forgiveness for the quite terrible things he can perpetrate in sentimental or moral dialogue.

Quoting from *Martin Chuzzlewit*, 'His enemies asserted, by the way, that a strong trustfulness in sounds and forms, was the master-key to Mr. Pecksniff's character', W. A. Ward comments:

Such a trustfulness is, in fact, the key to most of Dickens's characters. They are misled by language. Their views of reality

---

[1] 'A Note on Literary Indebtedness: Dickens, George Eliot, Henry James', *The Hudson Review*, viii (1955), 423–8; see esp. p. 425.

are shaped by their command of grammar, syntax, and vocabulary and a critique which seeks to account for the vitality of the prose and the inclusiveness of the vision would most profitably start in working out the extent of Dickens's virtuosity in representing such a complex variety of idioms . . . Mr. Pecksniff, in fact, is not a character in any real sense. He is a device that enables Dickens to exhibit his ability to imitate the speaking voice and to catch thereby the precise tone of a wealth of attitudes.[1]

I think there is a strong analogy between the view of Dickens's style as a display of verbal fireworks, sometimes spectacular, at other times garish, but always exploding into momentary patterns only, and the view of most of his characters as 'flat',[2] their vitality contrived only through the ventriloquism of their master's voice with its wonderful verbal dexterity. Both these views ignore the element of structure in Dickens's rhetorical use of language and in his characterization. By stressing surface they tend to deny any great depth and may end in attributing a superficial brilliance and vitality to all Dickens's work.[3]

It is true that Dickens often depicts men and women who are completely identified with their own *personae*, who appear at a first glance to possess no inner lives. Yet as Jung, who introduced the idea of the *persona* to modern psychology, has insisted frequently, most people in the world belong to this class.[4] The true individual who is conscious of the richness of his inner life is a very rare and gifted exception. Whether literature should restrict itself to such individuals as characters and ignore the rest of humanity is a very debatable point. Since several authorities have noted the extraordinary medical

[1] Miriam Allott, *Novelists on the Novel* (1960), pp. 210, 211–12; W. A. Ward, 'Language and Charles Dickens', *The Listener*, lxix (23 May 1963), 871, 874.

[2] This glib and misleading term was introduced into criticism in 1927 by E. M. Forster, *Aspects of the Novel* (1958), pp. 65–70, and is applied by him to Dickens's characterization, pp. 68–9; Edwin Muir, *The Structure of the Novel* (1928), exposes some of the shortcomings of the term, 'flat', in general and as applied to Dickens's characterization, pp. 25–6, 134–46.

[3] E. M. Forster, Miriam Allott, and W. A. Ward have all made this mistake. Robert Garis is the most recent instance; see below, pp. 48–9.

[4] The best description of the *persona* is to be found in C. G. Jung, *Psychological Types*, pp. 590–6; here, Jung insists on the collective nature of the *persona*, the extent to which a man may become identified with the *persona* and its rigidity throughout life. For true individuality as a rarity, see also Jolande Jacobi, *The Psychology of C. G. Jung* (1962), p. 104.

and psychological accuracy in so much of Dickens's minor characterization, I will only draw attention to a few characters, usually regarded as 'flat', whose psychological validity has not been pointed out. Manic-depressive phases, for example, explain the remarkable alternations of elation and despair in Mr. Micawber. Psychic masochism accounts for the main idiosyncratic trait of Mark Tapley. A careful social psychology underlies the motivation of Uriah Heep.[1] The relationship between so many of the masterful females and submissive males in Dickens's work is based upon a sado-masochistic relationship presented with such accuracy that the full shape of a classic sexual perversion almost breaks the surface in the cases of Miss Abbey Potterson and her docile customers, Jenny Wren and her naughty child of a father, Mrs. Wilfer and her cupid of a husband whose youthful and chubby appearance seems to invite a caning.[2] Again, many of Dickens's characters indulge in paranoiac projections.[3] The fact that Dickens uses this realist psychological material for the purpose of comedy should not blind us to the deep human truths incarnated in these characters. It is in fact Dickens's comic genius here that enables him to get across certain truths about human personality which no other early or mid-Victorian novelist dared to handle so openly and only those critics who do not understand, who deny, or ignore these deep layers of human character will describe such traits when they are presented by Dickens as exaggerated or unreal. Often Dickens represents the inner life of a character through the activity of the *persona*, a process which is not only psychologically accurate but typical of the way most people do express an inner life of which they are unconscious.[4] Thus, both

[1] *DC*, Chaps. XI, XVII, pp. 159, 163, 165, 263–4; *MC*, Chap. V, pp. 66–9; *DC*, Chap. XXXIX, pp. 574–5.

[2] *OMF*, Bk. I, Chap. VI, pp. 63, 65–6; Bk. II, Chap. II, pp. 240–2; Bk. I, Chap. IV, p. 32; Bk. IV, Chap. V, pp. 684–5. Dickens was fully aware of the nature of sadism; see 'Proposals for Amusing Posterity', *HW*, vi (12 Feb. 1853), reprinted in *MP*, p. 367. He defines masochism with great exactness in *OCS*, Chap. LXII, p. 463.

[3] See below, pp. 256–7.

[4] Cf. C. G. Jung, *Psychological Types*, p. 596: 'Identity with the persona automatically conditions an unconscious identity with the soul . . . The man who is unconditionally his outer role therewith[delivers himself over unquestion-ingly to the inner processes, i.e. he will even frustrate his outer role by absolute inner necessity, reducing it *ad absurdum*.' Only someone ignorant of these

Mrs. Joe Gargery and Mrs. MacStinger express their anal sadism not only in the corporal punishment of children but also in the physical subjection of their menfolk and the frequent ritual and punitive cleansings by which they purify their households; it is not a case of one detail but of many which build up a convincing psychological picture. In a flood of fantasy, Quilp and Jenny Wren release quite a range of the 'polymorphous perversions' normally locked up, according to Freud and Melanie Klein, in the infantile unconscious.[1] Nor is all this simply the peculiar unconscious feelings of Dickens[2] streaming forth indiscriminately for it is related precisely to a certain carefully differentiated type in each case and a specific situation in which the character is placed.

'What is life but language?' W. A. Ward concluded his article.[3] The truth is that life is much more, though it is perhaps understandable that the literary critic should be inclined to overestimate the part which language plays in life and literature. How little Dickens's narrative art may depend on sheer virtuosity of language can be seen in a short passage from *Little Dorrit*:

> They adjourned to the pump. Mr. Pancks, instantly putting his head under the spout, requested Mr. Rugg to take a good strong turn at the handle. Mr. Rugg complying to the letter, Mr. Pancks came forth snorting and blowing to some purpose, and dried himself on his handkerchief.

mental processes can maintain that Dickens fails to give characters of this type a valid inner life. If Robert Garis, *The Dickens Theatre*, p. 51, is suggesting that a character must be conscious of his own inner life as a field for moral scrutiny, then clearly serious literature, as he defines it, cannot deal with the greater part of mankind at all. I must also question his view, ibid., p. 161, that Dickens is only successful in rendering unusual states of mind; in fact, Dickens's remarkable psychological insight enables him to represent accurately the unconscious life which is reflected in surface traits of character common to much of humanity.

[1] *GE*, Chaps. II, IV, pp. 6–7, 10, 19–20; *D & S*, Chap. XXIII, pp. 328–30, cf. Chap. LX, pp. 857–8; *OCS*, Chaps. IV, V, XXI, pp. 37, 41–2, 160; *OMF*, Bk. II, Chap. II, pp. 241, 242, 243; Bk. III, Chap. X, p. 533.

[2] An element in Dickens's own character may have given him an insight into some of the above traits; see Humphry House, *The Dickens World* (1944), pp. 202–3. The preoccupation with sanitation, which he shared with his age, may also have turned his attention towards this side of life; see *Speeches*, pp. 104, 110, 127–32.

[3] 'Language and Charles Dickens', *The Listener*, lxix (23 May 1963), 874.

"I am the clearer for that," he gasped to Clennam standing astonished. "But upon my soul, to hear her father making speeches in that chair, knowing what we know, and to see her up in that room in that dress, knowing what we know, is enough to—give me a back, Mr. Rugg—a little higher, sir,—that'll do!"

Then and there, on that Marshalsea pavement, in the shades of evening, did Mr. Pancks, of all mankind, fly over the head and shoulders of Mr. Rugg, of Pentonville, General Agent, Accountant, and Recoverer of Debts. Alighting on his feet, he took Clennam by the button-hole, led him behind the pump, and pantingly produced from his pocket a bundle of papers.[1]

The words here act as a clear medium; they do no more than convey a picture of an action, which is itself significant, and the words have no other merit or function. It would be true to say that the action might be successfully translated into another medium, if Dickens's narrative were treated as stage or camera directions without losing any of the vitality of the original. Although a structural irony is hinted at in the dialogue of this passage, the action described by the narrative creates an effect of sympathy with Pancks's elation at his discovery and his consequent vitality. Actor and director, on the stage or screen, might achieve the same effect with an equal quality and significance.

A very different picture of Dickens's style is presented by Robert Garis in *The Dickens Theatre*. Garis claims that Dickens fails to pass the test of relevancy and of the high degree of organic structure to be found in novelists like Conrad or George Eliot; that he never ceases to draw attention to himself as narrator and the effect he seeks in the reader is applause for his virtuoso performance. Since Garis does not seek to deny Dickens's genius, so he says, and yet the method of Dickens is not that of the great mature novelists, there is a genuine 'Dickens problem' which has been neglected hitherto and which can only be solved by formulating a special category for Dickens that will do equal justice to his genius and to the limits within which he works:

The kind of art Dickens practises I propose to call 'theatrical art' . . . There is the constant and overt intention to dazzle us with verbal devices, leading us through our impulse to applaud to a

[1] *LD*, Bk. I, Chap. XXXII, p. 387.

continual awareness of the artificer responsible, a self-exhibiting master of language . . . there is the fact that the several effects or 'points' made by the artist are not 'integrated' into a 'continuity' as we ordinarily understand the word, and do not need to be, since each one is sponsored directly by the artist to achieve his obvious moment by moment plans and purposes, one of which is self-display.[1]

Garis deserves special attention as the latest and possibly the most subtle of those critics who have become preoccupied with the texture of Dickens's style. Garis *is* subtle because he admits the brilliance of Dickens's genius but tries to account for it by distinguishing Dickens as a special case. In fact, Garis has selected from the evidence only that which supports his argument by showing Dickens at work solely in the way he defines as 'theatrical'. He then transfers the general impression of Dickens's genius (which no serious critic has ever really been able to deny) to these carefully selected examples. Yet, in my view, Dickens is not consistent in his artistic practice and when he is successful his genius, apart from the unique quality which stamps all art of merit, does not differ fundamentally from the genius of other great mature novelists. Certainly, Dickens's work does not always pass the test of relevancy, but it frequently does. Garis's major mistake has been to assume without any qualification that Dickens's manner is consistent and to assert his view so emphatically as this: 'He is always the self-conscious virtuoso and we never lose sight of him for a moment.'[2] The example of Dickens's plain narrative style, which I quoted above, shows that this statement is not completely true. Only a comprehensive survey of Dickens's use of rhetorical language, however, can decide this issue.

2. *A Comprehensive Survey*

Without doubt, Dickens does sometimes write in the 'theatrical' manner that Garis describes. It is no exaggeration to say that, at various times, Dickens uses all the commonest rhetorical figures without regard to their structural relevancy.

[1] Robert Garis, op. cit., pp. 9–12, 17–18, 31, 3, 28, 24.
[2] Ibid., pp. 5, 39.

Yet for every occasion when he uses a figure in this way, there are many instances in which he does precisely the reverse.

In *Pickwick Papers*, Dickens resorts much more frequently to rhetorical figures with little if any structural relevance whenever his invention flags, as in the tedious moments of the Bath interlude. Thus, of the six instances of syllepsis in the novel no less than four are concentrated into little more than half a dozen pages of this interlude: 'Miss Bolo rose from the table considerably agitated, and went straight home, in a flood of tears, and a sedan-chair'; 'Mr. Pickwick . . . went to bed, and to sleep, almost simultaneously'; 'This was no other than Prince Bladud himself, in honour of whose happiness a whole people were at that very moment, straining alike their throats and purse-strings'; 'He knew not on whom to vent his grief and wrath, until fortunately bethinking himself of the Lord Chamberlain who had brought him home, he struck off his pension and his head together'. In this section of the novel, we can find two other figures used with little structural relevance. Thus, of the three malapropisms used in this way throughout the novel one occurs here: "Servants is in the arms o'Porpus, I think," said the short chairman'; and of the two clichés used consciously one also occurs here: 'If he played a wrong card, Miss Bolo looked a small armoury of daggers'. This section of the novel also contains one of the most feeble of the interpolated stories and it is significant, I think, that where the over-all structure of the novel is weakest there is also a striking failure to integrate rhetorical figures; both cases show a failure in 'structural thinking'.[1]

Yet in other more lively, more tightly organized parts of the novel Dickens is strikingly successful in integrating rhetorical figures. Thus, many different figures are used for the purpose of deflation and, as such, are part of the gentle mock-heroic vein which runs through much of the book. A simile, for example, in the account of the attack on the citadel

[1] *PP*, Chaps. XXXV, XXXVI, pp. 504, 509, 510 (for the two instances of syllepsis which I do not discuss, see Chaps. XX, XLI, pp. 268, 585); Chap. XXXVI, p. 513 (the other two malapropisms occur in Chaps. XXIV, XXXIX, pp. 333, 558); Chap. XXXV, p. 503 (the other example occurs in Chap. XXVII, p. 370); Chap. XXXVI, pp. 507–11 (the story referred to is 'The True Legend of Prince Bladud').

during the field day brings home to us with a fine irony the slightly ridiculous appearance which the mere pretence of war creates: 'Then there was such a ramming down of the contents of enormous guns on the battery, with instruments like magnified mops'; the alliteration, here, emphasizes the ludicrous effect. The hero of the story and his followers are held at an ironic distance from us for much of the book and this effect may be helped by hyperbole, 'If any dispassionate spectator could have beheld the countenance of the illustrious man . . . he would have been almost induced to wonder that the indignant fire which flashed from his eyes, did not melt the glasses of his spectacles—so majestic was his wrath', or by a simile which combines with the irony of understatement and points particularly to Tupman's portly stature, 'As brisk as bees, if not altogether as light as fairies, did the four Pickwickians assemble on the morning of the twenty-second day of December.' Again, the heroic pretensions of two village cricket teams are deflated by the use of an analogy drawn from the famous interview between Diogenes and Alexander the Great.[1]

Paradoxically, the same rhetorical figure may help to set a character at an ironic distance from us and yet at the same time draw our sympathies towards him. Thus, a comparison of Mr. Pickwick with the rising sun is carefully calculated as part of the general mock-heroic effect yet, through the simile, we are also made to feel and sympathize with the vitality of the comic hero:

That punctual servant of all work, the sun, had just risen, and begun to strike a light on the morning of the thirteenth of May, one thousand eight hundred and twenty-seven, when Mr. Samuel Pickwick burst like another sun from his slumbers, threw open his chamber window, and looked out upon the world beneath.[2]

This is an example of what I shall refer to later as 'the complex effect'. This effect focuses a double vision of a character so that we are able to view him both sympathetically and critically. Here, the complex effect and vision are also helped by the use of personification. The idea of the sun as a maid of

[1] Ibid., Chaps. IV, X, XXVIII, VII, pp. 52, 130, 374, 94.
[2] Ibid., Chap. II, p. 6.

all work adds an element of 'low burlesque' and so aids the effect of ironic distance. But it also makes much smoother the transition to the image of Pickwick as another sun and so strengthens both Pickwick's identity with the sun's energy and vitality and the effect of this vitality on the reader.

Rhetorical figures may be used to draw attention to the irony in a situation. When Sam Weller arranges to have himself arrested for debt at the suit of his father, the whole situation is commented on, with either a deliberate or an unconscious irony, in a malapropism used by Tony Weller:

"Wot a game it is!" said the elder Mr. Weller, with a chuckle. "A reg'lar prodigy son!"
"Prodigal, prodigal son, sir," suggested Mr. Pell, mildly.

Sam is a feigned 'prodigal son' but the superb ruse devised by him so that he can remain with his master, Mr. Pickwick, in the Fleet Prison pronounces him a 'prodigy'. Again, Tupman's courtship of Rachael Wardle with its romantic pretensions is deflated ironically by the use of an apt simile:

"Miss Wardle," said Mr. Tupman, "you are an angel."
"Mr. Tupman!" exclaimed Rachael, blushing as red as the watering-pot itself.[1]

The prosaic image reminds the reader of the reality underlying the delusions of the couple—Rachael is a middle-aged spinster and certainly no angel in the long tradition of romantic and courtly love.

Perhaps the most striking instance of a rhetorical figure used structurally in *Pickwick* is a humorous example of synecdoche which helps in the development of the story. As bootboy at the White Hart, Sam Weller uses the figure naturally. It is more than a flourish of wit, it is an organic part of his thinking and this professional manner of identifying people by their footwear is skilfully used as the means by which Rachael is identified:

"Who there is in the house!" said Sam, in whose mind the inmates were always represented by that particular article of their costume, which came under his immediate superintendence. "There's a wooden leg in number six; there's a pair of Hessians in

[1] *PP*, Chaps. XLIII, VIII, pp. 612, 97.

thirteen; there's two pair of halves in the commercial; there's these here painted tops in the snuggery inside the bar; and five more tops in the coffee-room."

"Nothing more?" said the little man.

"Stop a bit," replied Sam, suddenly recollecting himself. "Yes; there's a pair of Wellingtons a good deal worn, and a pair o' lady's shoes, in number five."

"What sort of shoes?" hastily inquired Wardle, who, together with Mr. Pickwick, had been lost in bewilderment at the singular catalogue of visitors.

"Country make," replied Sam.

"Any maker's name?"

"Brown."

"Where of?"

"Muggleton."

"It *is* them," exclaimed Wardle. "By Heavens, we've found them."[1]

Finally, rhetorical figures may be used to focus the vision of a character and, through his attitude, the vision of the book. Thus, a critical view of a narrow nonconformism is focused through Tony Weller's ironic comment on Stiggins when the shrewd old coachman neatly caps a metaphor used by the hypercritical and canting minister of religion:

"Benighted man!" said the reverend Mr. Stiggins.

"If I don't get no better light than that 'ere moonshine o' yourn, my worthy creetur," said the elder Mr. Weller, "it's wery likely as I shall continey to be a night coach till I'm took off the road altogether."

The dead image used by Stiggins, which aptly sums up his sterile religious pose, is brought into sharp contrast with a living extension of the same image by Tony Weller, which reflects his genuine and positive attitude to life, his acceptance of its laughter and pleasures as well as its gloom and sorrows. Similarly, when Sam Weller wants to enlighten the inexperienced Mr. Pickwick about the plight of the homeless poor in London, he uses a euphemism with a fine compact irony:

"I had unfurnished lodgin's for a fortnight."

"Unfurnished lodgings?" said Mr. Pickwick.

"Yes—the dry arches of Waterloo Bridge."[2]

---

[1] Ibid., Chap. X, pp. 125–6.   [2] Ibid., Chap. XLV, XVI, pp. 637, 209–10.

This figure conveys, in a perfectly natural manner, Sam's ironic view of life, that of the shrewd servant who instinctively resorts to the weapon of the dependent and criticizes with a sly indirectness. But, through him, it also focuses the general ironic vision in the book with an economy and understatement which makes that vision seem all the more powerful.

If the effect of 'theatrical' style (as Garis defines it) is to draw the attention and applause of the reader solely to the narrator's verbal dexterity then the effect of the passages quoted above is quite different. The rhetorical figures used in these passages may have an immediate impact on the reader but they also refer to a wider context. They help to direct an attitude in the reader towards the characters and events. They help to focus a vision which may be critical or sympathetic.

What is true of the style of the loosely constructed *Pickwick Papers* is true of Dickens's maturing art. Even in his most mature novels he can still resort to occasional rhetorical flourishes which are no more than surface wit; but much, and on the whole an increasing proportion, of his rhetorical style comes to have structural relevance. By this, I do not mean that Dickens progresses in a straight line. On the contrary, as he tries to adjust his style so as to grapple with new narrative problems, he often lapses into earlier bad habits and falls into new ones. This is one of the prices Dickens and his readers have had to pay for his development as a novelist; had he continued to write or even perfect a series of *Pickwicks*, we should have greater cause for complaint.

In *Oliver Twist*, for example, the problem of assuming a new tone sometimes results in considerable clumsiness. In *Pickwick*, the irony had been fairly mild, on the whole, and often gentle; the vision was critical but, at the same time, intensely compassionate. In *Oliver Twist*, the ironic vision of certain social spheres was to be a very savage one indeed while the compassionate vision tends to deteriorate into a sentimental view of life.[1] If Dickens was influenced by Fielding as well as Smollett, then we might say that, whereas *Tom Jones* provided

[1] Whereas, on the whole, the world of *Pickwick* remains one, the world of *Oliver Twist* tends to fragment into three spheres which are viewed with a separate vision.

a model in certain respects for *Pickwick*, in *Oliver Twist* it is as though Dickens tried to take over the savage mock-heroic style of *Jonathan Wild*. Even so, the fault of the ironic language Dickens uses in *Oliver Twist* is that it *is* obtrusive but *not* that it is irrelevant. We might even say that its relevance is sometimes painfully laboured.

Dickens sets out to dispel romantic illusions about the squalid world of crime, as he claims in the preface to the third edition (1841), and to deflate the delusions of grandeur indulged in by the petty world of Bumbledom, to expose the cruelty and acquisitiveness behind its masquerade of charity. And even when the author comments in his own person on the narrative, the ironic tone, though heavy, is strictly relevant. Indeed, the manuscript shows how deliberately Dickens could insist on a mock-heroic effect and how the very insistence on a strict and powerful relevance could betray him into a heavy style:

> As it would be, by no means, seemly in a humble author to keep so ⟨great⟩ MIGHTY a personage as a beadle waiting, . . . the faithful historian whose pen traces these words—trusting that he knows his place, and entertains a becoming reverence for those upon earth to whom high and important authority is delegated—hastens to pay them that respect which their position demands, and to treat them with all that duteous ceremony which their exalted rank, and (by consequence) great virtues, imperatively claim at his hands. Towards this end, indeed, he had purposed to introduce, in this place, a dissertation touching the divine right of beadles, and elucidative of the position, that a beadle can do no wrong.[1]

Occasionally, the sheer exuberance of Dickens's wit does escape into a mere flourish as in the instance of syllepsis when Mr. Gamfield, the sweep, is described as 'alternately cudgelling his brains and his donkey'. But a wide range of other figures, which include hyperbole, euphemism, parody, and anticlimax, is not used irrelevantly but helps to build up the general ironical tone. Bathos, for example, is used to betray the

[1] Original MS. of *OT*, Victoria and Albert Museum, Forster Collection, 47. A. 1 (Vol. IA), Bk. II, Chap. V, p. 30 (from the 1846 edition onwards the text omits 'faithful' and reads 'and that he entertains'); cf. *OT*, Chap. XXVII, p. 196.

true quality of Mrs. Corney as a potential wife and so predicts the fate of Bumble as her second husband:

The small teapot, and the single cup, had awakened in her mind sad recollections of Mr. Corney (who had not been dead more than five-and-twenty years); and she was overpowered.

"I shall never get another!" said Mrs. Corney, pettishly; "I shall never get another—like him."

Whether this remark bore reference to the husband, or the teapot, is uncertain. It might have been the latter; for Mrs. Corney looked at it as she spoke: and took it up afterwards.[1]

There is a really fine structural use of malapropisms in the great comic scene of the Dodger's trial. The malapropisms, here, stand in sharp ironical contrast to the pose of the petty thief in court as an important, knowledgeable person, well connected and much to be reckoned with. The ground has already been prepared earlier in the chapter for the Dodger's deflation in the reader's eyes, though not in his own. The criminal is viewed throughout the novel as a deluded creature, victim of his own vanity even when, as here, his bravado expresses itself with a vitality we cannot help but admire. Such a vision is at its sharpest throughout this scene and the Dodger's illiterate mistakes are among the finest things in this burlesque of grandeur. That Dickens was deliberately seeking his effect through the careful repetition of a rhetorical figure can be seen in the manuscript which shows that the only correction is the addition of a malapropism. Dickens had started to write 'a case of defamation of character', got as far as the 't' in 'defamation', erased the word and substituted 'deformation'. The conscious use of figures can also be illustrated by another example from the manuscript. When Dickens wanted to expose Saffron Hill, a resort of thieves and receivers, for the sordid and squalid place it was in the London of his day, he inserted a periphrasis in the mockingly inflated style, 'the emporium of petty larceny', only as a second thought.[2]

The comic exuberance in *Martin Chuzzlewit* is probably

[1] *OT*, Chap. III, p. 15; Chap. II, p. 14; Chap. V, p. 34; Chap. XXV, p. 180; Chap. XXVI, p. 185; Chaps. IV, V, XXVIII, pp. 26, 31, 210; Chap. XXIII, p. 166.

[2] Original MS. of *OT*, Victoria and Albert Museum, Forster Collection, 47. A. 4 (Vol. IIB), Bk. III, Chap. VI, p. 83, Vol. IA, Bk. II, Chap. IV ,p. 3; cf. *OT*, Chap. XLIII, p. 334, Chap. XXVI, p. 184.

greater than in any other novel of Dickens's. Some of it is
surface wit. Much more is brought under control and made to
serve the book's larger structural ends. The two greatest
comic triumphs in *Martin Chuzzlewit* are Pecksniff and Mrs.
Gamp and it is interesting to compare them with regard to
rhetorical language.

As a study in the selfishness and hypocrisy which often
characterized the nursing profession of the period, Mrs. Gamp
may be regarded as relevant to the novel's main theme.[1] But
her wit usually has nothing more than an immediate, though
brilliant, comic effect. In the following typical example,
alliteration only emphasizes this effect and the use of synecdoche, here, should be contrasted with the structural use of the
same figure illustrated from *Pickwick* earlier:

"And as to husbands, there's a wooden leg gone likeways home
to its account, which in its constancy of walkin' into wine vaults,
and never comin' out again 'till fetched by force, was quite as
weak as flesh, if not weaker."[2]

Pecksniff's case is very different. The hypocrisy of this character creates effects which focus the subtlest and most profound
vision in *Martin Chuzzlewit*. The power of this vision derives
partly from the bold attack on the precise shape which the
vice assumed, and the high place which it occupied, in Victorian England. But the power of the vision also derives from
the rhetoric with which it is presented. Possibly one of the
subtlest uses of rhetorical language is to exploit the very
artificiality which may be its gravest defect. Dickens shows in
a letter that he is well aware how artificial rhetorical language
may be. In *Martin Chuzzlewit*, he deliberately resorts to
forced rhetorical figures to betray the insincerity which lies
behind the various poses of Pecksniff. When, for instance,
Pecksniff assumes a virtuous posture in preparing to dismiss
young Martin, Dickens uses an accumulation of pompous
clichés the stale and empty imagery of which brings out
ironically all the hypocrisy of Pecksniff's thoughts:

But Mr. Pecksniff, dismissing all ephemeral considerations of
social pleasure and enjoyment, concentrated his meditations on
the one great virtuous purpose before him, of casting out that

[1] Preface to the First Cheap Edition of *MC* (1849), *F*, vol. ii, p. 30.
[2] *MC*, Chap. XL, p. 625.

ingrate and deceiver, whose presence yet troubled his domestic hearth, and was a sacrilege upon the altars of his household gods.

The language of Stiggins and Chadband, as House has pointed out, is a deliberate parody on the stilted imagery which characterized so much of early Victorian religious expression and came to colour everyday speech. Pecksniff's language, however, has an originality and even a kind of freshness in its very artificiality which carries the stamp of the highest imaginative genius. Thus, when Pecksniff is caught in a typical moralizing posture, he strains an allegory in such a way that it displays his wonderful vitality and resilience yet reveals his hypocrisy with a fine irony:

"Some of us, I say," resumed her parent with increased emphasis, "are slow coaches; some of us are fast coaches. Our passions are the horses; and rampant animals too!"—

"Really, Pa!" cried both the daughters at once. "How very unpleasant."

"And rampant animals too!" repeated Mr. Pecksniff with so much determination, that he may be said to have exhibited, at the moment, a sort of moral rampancy himself: "and Virtue is the drag. We start from The Mother's Arms, and we run to The Dust Shovel."[1]

By *Dombey and Son*, Dickens is thinking so much in terms of over-all structure that his rhetorical figures and imagery repeatedly hint at the drift of the story and often comment ironically on present events by placing them in the context of the future. A simile foreshadows the fate of Paul Dombey at Dr. Blimber's school; the servant, who opens the door on the small boy's arrival, 'looked at Paul as if he were a little mouse, and the house were a trap'. Although the analogy, drawn between Carker's handling of the business correspondence at 'Dombey and Son's' and a man engaged in a game of cards, tends to clash with the elaborate comparison of the Manager to a watchful cat in the following paragraph, both images look ahead to the sinister role Carker will play in the story.[2]

If a single theme in *David Copperfield* is worked out through

[1] To Miss Emily Jolly (30 May 1857), *HD*, p. 427 [cf. a letter to Mrs. Gaskell (3 May 1853), *HD*, pp. 287–8]; *MC*, Chap. XI, p. 190; Humphry House, *The Dickens World*, pp. 114–16; *MC*, Chap. VIII, pp. 116–17.
[2] *D & S*, Chap. XI, p. 144; Chap. XXII, pp. 298–9.

the structure of the novel, then it is 'the first mistaken impulses of an undisciplined heart'. The novelist shows how
David grows through various stages of self-deception towards
a mature experience of love. Many readers have found the
final stage of David's development unsatisfactory[1] but I think
no reader would deny the accuracy and power with which
Dickens presents his vision of the silly romantic charm of
earlier love-affairs. Perhaps the most apt rhetorical figure
through which to focus this vision is hyperbole used so as to
produce an ironic effect. The exaggerated claims made by
this figure can adequately mirror the extravagant, if charming,
attitudes of infatuation, while the ironic gap which the sheer
extravagance of the figure opens up between the romantic
illusion and reality will expose all the silliness in such attitudes. We, therefore, find many instances of hyperbole used
for this purpose in appropriate sections of the novel. The calf
love of David, in his early schooldays, for Miss Shepherd, 'a
little girl, IN A SPENCER, with A ROUND FACE AND
CURLY flaxen hair', is described in such high-flown language
as this: 'a transport of love'; 'ECSTASY!'; 'the one pervading
theme and vision of my life'; 'Miss Shepherd and myself live
but to be united'; 'All is over. The ⟨love of years⟩ DEVOTION
OF A LIFE—it seems ⟨years⟩ A LIFE, it is all the same—is
at an end.' With what deliberate irony Dickens was using this
kind of language, here, can be seen in the manuscript, for he
inserted the words, 'in a spencer', 'a round face and curly',
and 'Ecstasy!' as afterthoughts while 'devotion of a life' was
also a second thought in place of 'love of years' which he
cancelled.[2] The adolescent passion of David, at seventeen, for
the eldest Miss Larkins is described in similar language: 'My
passion for her is beyond all bounds'; 'I could be content to
make a figure before Miss Larkins, and expire'; 'I waltz with
the eldest Miss Larkins! I don't know where, among whom,
or how long. I only know that I swim about in space, with a
blue angel, in a state of blissful delirium.'[3] In addition, the

[1] Cf. A. O. J. Cockshut, *The Imagination of Charles Dickens*, pp. 122–3,
George Orwell, 'Charles Dickens', *Critical Essays* (1946), p. 54, quoted in *The
Dickens Critics*, p. 169.
[2] Original MS. of *DC*, Victoria and Albert Museum, Forster Collection, 47.
A. 24 (Vol. IB), Chap. XVIII, p. 24; cf. *DC*, pp. 265–6.
[3] Ibid., Chap. XVIII, pp. 268, 269, 270.

corrected proofs of the novel show that a powerful instance
of hyperbole in this episode was deleted whether for reasons
of space or because it was thought to be too extreme: 'If the
eldest Miss Larkins would drive a triumphal car down the
High Street, and allow me to throw myself under the wheels
as an offering to her beauty, I should be proud to be trampled
under her horses' feet.'[1]

Many of the expressions Dickens uses in the early love
episodes of the novel are clichés of language and feeling and
this is perhaps necessary since he is describing experiences
common to all mankind; the originality lies in the ironic way
he uses these expressions. Nevertheless, when he comes to
relate David's first adult love affair, Dickens manages to add
to the conventional expressions phrases of such striking
originality that they convey in a marvellous manner the *very
quality* of David's experience *as it appeared to him at the time*;
beside a common experience, slightly absurd in retrospect,
such phrases set all the wonderful freshness and intensity of
what at the time does appear a unique experience, the lover's
feeling that no one has ever loved in this way. When David
first meets Dora Spenlow, we find this mixture of cliché and
originality: 'I had fulfilled my destiny. I was a captive and a
slave. I loved Dora Spenlow to distraction! She was more than
human to me. She was a Fairy, a Sylph, I don't know what
she was—anything that no one ever saw, and everything that
everybody ever wanted. I was swallowed up in an abyss of
love in an instant'; 'I have not the least idea what we had for
dinner, besides Dora. My impression is, that I dined off Dora
entirely'; 'I was wandering in a garden of Eden all the while,
with Dora'; 'To be allowed to call her "Dora", to write to her,
to dote upon and worship her, to have reason to think that
when she was with other people she was yet mindful of me,
seemed to me the summit of human ambition'; 'I heard her
sing, and the congregation vanished. A sermon was delivered—
about Dora, of course.' The progress of David's infatuation is
described with a similar technique: 'I was steeped in Dora. I
was not merely head and ears in love with her, but I was
saturated through and through'; 'He stood up sometimes,

---

[1] Corrected proofs of *DC*, Chap. XVIII, p. 192; cf. *DC*, p. 268 (the deleted
passage followed 'My passion for her is beyond all bounds').

and asked me what I thought of the prospect. I said it was delightful, and I dare say it was; but it was all Dora to me. The sun shone Dora, and the birds sang Dora. The south wind blew Dora, and the wild flowers in the hedges were all Doras, to a bud'; 'we all seemed, to my thinking, to go straight up to the seventh heaven. We did not come down again. We stayed up there all the evening'; 'as enraptured a young noodle as ever was carried out of his five wits by love'. When the progress of infatuation is frustrated, hyperbole is strained even further: 'I . . . implored Miss Mills to interpose between us and avert insanity'; 'I . . . was a long way beyond the end of my wits when Miss Mills came into the room'; 'I informed her that my reason was tottering on its throne, and only she, Miss Mills, could prevent its being deposed.'[1]

In the novels of Dickens's maturity, there is an increasing subtlety and complexity in the way he uses language to serve the purposes of his story and his vision. *Great Expectations* is a masterpiece of the story-teller's art and we can find the tale's remarkable ironic structure reflected in the very figures of the language by which it progresses. Pip's mistaken belief that Miss Havisham is his secret patron is mirrored in an image which is charged with structural irony: ' "This is a gay figure, Pip," said she, making her crutch stick play round me, as if she, the fairy godmother who had changed me, were bestowing the finishing gift.' It is true that this kind of irony may become apparent only on rereading the book, yet this provides one of the pleasures of rereading and accounts for some of the extraordinary richness we find in Dickens's narrative. When Pip expects the lawyer, Jaggers, to tell him at last who his patron is, an analogy recalls a previous incident in the story: 'As I sat down, and he [Jaggers] preserved his attitude and bent his brows at his boots, I felt at a disadvantage, which reminded me of that old time when I had been put upon a tombstone.' It was in fact Magwitch, the convict, Pip's real though unsuspected patron, who had held him on the tombstone as a small boy and it was out of this incident that Magwitch's decision to become Pip's benefactor had arisen; but Jaggers does not reveal the truth and the ironic

---

[1] *DC*, Chap. XXVI, pp. 390–6; Chap. XXXIII, pp. 474–87: Chaps. XXXIII, XXXVII, XXXVIII, pp. 490, 542, 554.

effect is sustained. When Magwitch tries to disguise himself in preparation for his escape from London, an analogy used in describing him foreshadows his detection and death with an ominous irony:

> It had been his own idea to wear that touch of powder . . . But I can compare the effect of it, when on, to nothing but the probable effect of rouge upon the dead; so awful was the manner in which everything in him, that it was most desirable to repress, started through that thin layer of pretence, and seemed to come blazing out at the crown of his head.[1]

Similes and metaphors are used to foreshadow events throughout the later work of Dickens in a less obvious or a more strikingly original manner than in *Dombey and Son*. When the sinister figure, Rigaud, in *Little Dorrit* signs his name beneath those of the other visitors at the inn, we are told that he ended his complicated inscription 'with a long lean flourish, not unlike a lasso thrown at all the rest of the names'. In the same novel, when Dickens tells us about Mr. Merdle's absence from the dinner party, the comparison drawn from *Macbeth* seems to apply to the immediate context only, a mere flourish of Dickens's wit at the expense of the great financier's failure to shine in society: 'Mr. Merdle's default left a Banquo's chair at the table; but, if he had been there, he would have merely made the difference of Banquo in it, and consequently he was no loss.'[2] Yet the subtle structural irony, here, becomes apparent on the discovery that Merdle has committed suicide and that, like the murdered Banquo, he could only have attended the banquet as a ghost.

Even puns and polysyllabic wit[3] may be used with some feeling for structure and in this respect the device of repetition undergoes considerable development in Dickens's hands. True, he can use this device in a very embarrassing manner, particularly in his early work and especially where he uses the repetition of words and syntax in a passage of dialogue to attempt a high-flown burst of noble or pathetic sentiment. Thus, in *Martin Chuzzlewit*, he tries to raise the tone of

[1] *GE*, Chap. XIX, p. 149; Chap. XXXVI, p. 272; Chap. XL, p. 319.
[2] *LD*, Bk. II, Chap. I, p. 446; Chap. XXV, p. 703.
[3] Ibid., Bk. II, Chap. XV, pp. 599–600; *OMF*, Bk. I, Chap. V, p. 54; *LD*, Bk. I, Chap. XVII, p. 206.

idealistic thoughts and feelings but succeeds only in giving to Tom Pinch's speech an artificial and stilted effect which appears to the reader excessively contrived and pompous; in a similar vein are the various apostrophes to Tom Pinch. Later, Dickens came to recognize the comic possibilities of repetition in dialogue and he uses it as the basis of Mrs. Chivery's speech while a parody of Hebraic parallelism becomes the basis of Chadband's mannerisms. Fairly early in his career, Dickens had recognized the ironic use to which he could put the repetition of a single word in a passage of description. He uses this device to deflate the pretensions of Little Bethel in *The Old Curiosity Shop* and the vulgar megalomania displayed by the house of the wealthy brass and copper founder in *Martin Chuzzlewit*. As distinct from this direct satirical use, Dickens puts the device to work in a more mature and structurally relevant way. Thus, the repetition of the word 'dead' in the description of Miss Wade's house at Calais in *Little Dorrit* makes its own comment on the sterility, the spiritual death of Miss Wade, and prepares us for the recital of her narrative, 'The History of a Self Tormentor', in the following chapter. Again the repetition of 'stone' in the description of the Marquis's chateau at the beginning of Chapter IX in the second book of *A Tale of Two Cities* ironically foreshadows the discovery of the murdered Marquis which concludes the chapter. The device can occasionally revert to something worse than a mannerism. When Dickens describes Rob the Grinder, for example, in *Dombey and Son*, the repetition of the epithet 'round' only produces an effect of caricature. If we compare with this picture only the rather flat portrait of Miss Peacher in *Our Mutual Friend*, we see that the repetition of 'little' which creates a pathetic impression of a colourless character does prepare us for the role the schoolmistress is to play in the story: the ineffectual spinster with her day-dreams and unrequited love.[1] The earliest description of Bradley Headstone is more impressive:

Bradley Headstone, in his decent black coat and waistcoat, and

[1] *MC*, Chap. XLVIII, p. 734; Chaps. V, LIV, pp. 63–4, 836–7; *LD*, Bk. I, Chap. XXII, p. 258; *BH*, Chap. XXV, pp. 358–61; *OCS*, Chap. XLI, p. 305; *MC*, Chap. IX, p. 134; *LD*, Bk. II, Chap. XX, p. 654; *TTC*, Bk. II, Chap. IX, pp. 112, 122; *D & S*, Chap. XXII, p. 303; *OMF*, Bk. II, Chap. I, p. 219.

decent white shirt, and decent formal black tie, and decent pantaloons of pepper and salt, with his decent silver watch in his pocket and its decent hair-guard round his neck, looked a thoroughly decent young man of six-and-twenty. He was never seen in any other dress, and yet there was a certain stiffness in his manner of wearing this, as if there was a want of adaptation between him and it, recalling some mechanics in their holiday clothes. He had acquired mechanically a great store of teacher's knowledge. He could do mental arithmetic mechanically, sing at sight mechanically, blow various wind instruments mechanically, even play the great church organ mechanically. From his early childhood up, his mind had been a place of mechanical stowage. The arrangement of his wholesale warehouse, so that it might be always ready to meet the demands of retail dealers . . . had imparted to his countenance a look of care; while the habit of questioning and being questioned had given him a suspicious manner, or a manner that would be better described as one of laying in wait. There was a kind of settled trouble in the face. It was the face belonging to a naturally slow or inattentive intellect that had toiled hard to get what it had won, and that had to hold it now that it was gotten . . . Suppression of so much to make room for so much, had given him a constrained manner, over and above. Yet there was enough of what was animal, and of what was fiery (though smouldering), still visible in him, to suggest that if young Bradley Headstone, when a pauper lad, had chanced to be told off for the sea, he would not have been the last man in a ship's crew. Regarding that origin of his, he was proud, moody, and sullen, desiring it to be forgotten. And few people knew of it.[1]

With what penetration this study of the new kind of schoolmaster, rising from a humble origin to staff the national schools of Dickens's time, analyses the interaction between certain social conditions[2] and the psychological make-up of an individual. By repeating 'mechanical', Dickens draws attention to the way the instinctive man in Bradley Headstone has been repressed beneath a difficultly acquired veneer of culture; by repeating 'decent', the novelist stresses that the professional *persona* of the schoolmaster is overcompensating

[1] *OMF*, Bk.II, Chap. I, pp. 217–18.

[2] Philip Collins, *Dickens and Education* (1963), pp. 159–71; see esp. p. 160: 'Dickens's presentation of these teachers, though unsympathetic and incomplete, is a notable piece of social analysis, shrewd and original in its study of that part of the truth on which he has chosen to concentrate.'

for his social origin. It is only later, however, that we come to appreciate the full irony so carefully prepared by this repetition. When the instinctive man begins to break through the outward shell of cultivation and decency and Bradley Headstone becomes a would-be-murderer, the very antithesis of all that has been insisted on, Dickens takes care to recall the earlier picture and even the verbal formula which had insisted with such deep irony:

> Up came the sun to find him washed and brushed, methodically dressed in decent black coat and waistcoat, decent formal black tie, and pepper and salt pantaloons, with his decent silver watch in its pocket, and its decent hair-guard round his neck: a scholastic huntsman clad for the field, with his fresh pack yelping and barking around him.
>
> Yet more really bewitched than the miserable creatures of the much-lamented times, who accused themselves of impossibilities under a contagion of horror and the strongly suggestive influence of Torture, he had been ridden hard by Evil Spirits in the night that was newly gone. He had been spurred and whipped and heavily sweated. If a record of the sport had usurped the places of peaceful texts from Scripture on the wall, the most advanced of the scholars might have taken fright and run away from the master.

After the murderous attack on Eugene Wrayburn, a small action of Bradley's enacts almost symbolically the final rejection of his decent *persona* and again the reiteration of the word brings home all the irony: 'He made a little parcel of his decent silver watch and its decent guard, and wrote inside the paper: "Kindly take care of these for me.' "[1]

Quotations from the manuscript of *Oliver Twist* have already shown that early in his career Dickens was deliberately using rhetorical language with an eye to its structural relevance. Examples from the manuscripts of two later novels illustrate that Dickens increasingly made a conscious effort to use his rhetorical style as an integral part of his narrative. *Bleak House* and *Little Dorrit* are usually considered today to be both mature and complex novels. It is perhaps not surprising therefore that the attempt at a complex view of society, together with Dickens's maturing as artist and storyteller, should not only be realized in an over-all structure, which is

---

[1] *OMF*, Bk. II, Chap. XI, p. 555; Bk. IV, Chap. XV, p. 795.

intricate and organic, but that the concern for a complex unity should be reflected in a rhetoric, which consciously works for structural effects.

In the manuscript of *Bleak House*, to give one example, a mocking periphrasis which ironically deflates the pretensions of the legal small fry, Guppy, Jobling, and Smallweed, was a second thought of Dickens. He had originally described the two clerks and the office boy, who have met to conspire against their betters and are trying to cut a figure in the restaurant, as 'the legal gentlemen'. This Dickens emended to 'the legal triumvirate'. Again, when the legal shark, Vholes, is commending his professional services to his client, Richard Carstone, Dickens's revised version is a striking improvement:

"This desk is your rock, sir!"
⟨There is encouragement in the sounding rap that⟩ Mr. Vholes gives it⟨. Perhaps Mr. Vholes knows there is.⟩ A RAP, AND IT SOUNDS AS HOLLOW AS A COFFIN. NOT TO RICHARD, THOUGH. THERE IS ENCOURAGEMENT IN THE SOUND TO HIM. Perhaps Mr. Vholes knows there is.[1]

The simile, which has been inserted, certainly draws attention to the hollowness of Mr. Vholes's assurance. The image of the coffin, however, adds much more to the irony of the situation. It hints grimly at catastrophe and catastrophe does follow from the desperate trust Richard puts in Vholes that the great Chancery suit will be settled in his favour. Admittedly, Dickens can revert even as late as this in his career, to a figure which is not only stale and artificial but has little relevance since it draws the mind away from his story to the world of classical legend: 'Presently came Charley, lightly winding among the bushes, and tripping along the paths, as rosy and pretty as one of Flora's attendants instead of my maid.'[2] Yet Dickens can use a classical reference in a relevant manner. For example, when Richard Carstone had been showing a gloomy impatience at the progress of 'Jarndyce and Jarndyce', Vholes had tried to sooth him with platitudes:

"A good deal is doing, sir. We have put our shoulders to the wheel, Mr. Carstone, and the wheel is going round."

[1] Original MS. of *BH*, Victoria and Albert Museum, Forster Collection, 47. A. 28 (Vol. IB), Chap. XX, p. 4, 47. A. 29 (Vol. IIA), Chap. XXXIX, p. 4; cf. *BH*, pp. 276, 551.   [2] Ibid., Chap. XLV, p. 614.

"YES, WITH IXION ON IT. How am I to get through the next four or five accursed months?" exclaims the young man, rising from his chair and walking about the room.

The manuscript does not contain the sentence, ' "Yes, with Ixion on it" '. It was added in proof. Vholes's remark about putting one's shoulder to the wheel suggests Sisyphus as well as Ixion; the two damned and tortured souls were always closely associated and represented side by side in Tartarus. The momentary sarcasm of Richard has a deeper irony than he knows; his case is to be an exact parallel to that of Ixion and Sisyphus. All his schemes are to come to nothing, he is to be involved in an impossible punitive task and his life will become a hell of endless torment. Moreover, the classical reference is perfectly natural in Richard's mouth since his exclusively classical education at a public school has been insisted upon early in the novel.[1]

The manuscript of *Little Dorrit* shows a similar deliberate care for structure when rhetorical figures are introduced into an earlier version. For instance, the imagery which compares the two inmates of the prison in Marseilles to captive birds was sustained by a conscious effort and the precise idea of the cage was added as an afterthought. Consider the following passage from this episode as it appears in the manuscript:

"Poor birds!" said the child.
The fair little face, touched with divine compassion, as it peeped shrinkingly through the grate, was like an angel's in the prison. John Baptist rose and moved towards it, as if it had a good attraction for him. The other ⟨man⟩ BIRD remained as before, except for an impatient glance at the basket.
"Stay!" said the jailor, standing his little daughter on the outer ledge of the grate, "she shall feed the birds. This big loaf is for Signor John Baptist. We must break it to get it through INTO THE CAGE. So, there's a ⟨good⟩ TAME bird, to kiss the little hand!"[2]

Dickens had originally begun the final sentence of the second paragraph, 'The other man remained as before', the phrase

[1] Original MS. of *BH*, Vol. IIA, Chap. XXXIX, p. 3, corrected proofs of *BH*, Victoria and Albert Museum, Forster Collection, 48. B. 15, Chap. XXXIX, p. 385; cf. *BH*, p. 550. Ibid., Chap. XIII, pp. 167–8.
[2] Original MS, of *LD*, Vol. IA, Bk. I, Chap. I, p. 4 (proofs read 'putting' after 'jailor,'); cf. *LD*, p. 5.

'into the cage' was inserted as a second thought, and the epithet 'tame' was substituted for 'good'. The imagery in this passage is calculated to create an effect of grim irony with a touch of pathos and the purpose of the revisions is to maintain, if not increase, this effect. The effect has some structural relevance for it focuses the child's compassionate view of the prisoner and so prepares a suitable emotive climate for Little Dorrit's vision of her father in the Marshalsea; but, in addition, the irony enables the mind to escape to a more distanced view, to see one world in terms of another, a view which finds its ultimate expression in the vision of society as a kind of prison. Again, some of the finest strokes of rhetoric which reduce Flora Finching to such a marvellously absurd spectacle were, in fact, second thoughts by Dickens. For instance, when Flora is describing Mr. F's courtship, the printed text gives this version:

"As I openly said to Mr. F when he proposed to me and you will be surprised to hear that he proposed seven times once in a hackney-coach once in a boat once in a pew once on a donkey at Tunbridge Wells and the rest on his knees."

The manuscript, however, reveals that the wonderful bathos of this ending would have been lost in the earlier version since the conventional mode of proposal was first intended to follow after 'boat' instead of after the complete list of bizarre proposals; neither would the marvellous climax of bizarre proposals quite have been managed for 'on a donkey at Tunbridge Wells' was a revision for a weaker idea. A few pages later the final text describes the death of Mr. F as follows:

"We returned to the immediate neighbourhood of Number Thirty Little Gosling Street London Docks and settled down, ere we had yet fully detected the housemaid in selling the feathers out of the spare bed Gout flying upwards soared with Mr. F to another sphere."

Yet the manuscript reveals that Dickens's first idea, which is heavily scored, was to extend the personification at the end in a rather strained manner. In this version, Gout 'dolefully clipped the wings ⟨– ? –⟩ of Hymen'. The elegant euphemism, 'flying upwards soared with Mr. F to another sphere', which brings the whole passage crashing down into bathos was a substitution for something immeasurably weaker.[1] By such details of rhetoric as these Dickens focuses an ironic vision of romantic love, the early infatuation between Arthur Clennam and Flora which collapses into farce and is so aptly burlesqued in the courtship and marriage of Flora and Mr. F.

Dickens, I think we must conclude, does not invariably use rhetorical language in a structurally irrelevant manner. Even less does he treat language as a means of mesmerizing the reader while he persuades him to accept as a novel what is, in fact, only a mechanical and conventional plot, a gallery of eccentric characters and a histrionic performance on the part of the author. Certainly there are lapses, occasionally bad ones, and the lapses are more obvious than cases in which the language is working smoothly and efficiently. But more often than not Dickens is using language as an adequate, and some-times as a subtle, narrative medium which helps to build and unfold his story, to give an organic impression of a world, its events and its characters, and to convey the significance of his vision. Moreover, as the manuscripts show, Dickens uses language in this way as the instrument of a *conscious* narrative art.[2]

[1] Original MS. of *LD*, Vol. IB, Bk. I, Chap, XXIV, pp. 12, 14; cf. *LD* pp. 283, 285.

[2] Randolph Quirk, *Charles Dickens and Appropriate Language* (1959), pp. 9 ff., 'Some observations on the Language of Dickens', *A Review of English Literature*, ii (1961), 22–3, touches on the structural manner in which Dickens uses the verb throughout his work; Professor Quirk does not, however, discuss the relationship between structure, effect, and vision, nor does he particularly concern himself with rhetorical language as such. Further interesting points about Dickens's use of language are made in G. L. Brooks, 'The Language of Dickens', *Bulletin of the John Rylands Library*, xlvii (1964), 32–48, Stanley Gerson, 'Dickens's Use of Malapropisms', *The Dickensian*, lxi (1965), 40–5, Sylvère Monod, *Dickens romancier*, *passim*, Sheila M. Smith, 'Anti-Mechanism and the Comic in the Writings of Charles Dickens', *Renaissance and Modern Studies*, iii (1959), 131–44.

III

THE SIMPLE EFFECT

1. *Dickens and Poe: Unity of Effect*

THE significance of what Edgar Allan Poe and Dickens probably discussed when they met in Philadelphia has escaped notice. True, precise details of the discussions in Philadelphia are a matter of speculation. Nevertheless, a number of clues point towards a certain possibility. In his reviews of Dickens's sketches, stories, and novels, Poe repeatedly stresses one feature of Dickens's art. He praises the way Dicken's material is organized so as to create unity of effect. Thus, in his review of a pirated edition of *Sketches by Boz*, Poe writes: 'Unity of effect, a quality not easily appreciated or indeed comprehended by an ordinary mind . . . is indispensable in the "brief article" '; and he praises Dickens for putting the principle into practice: 'Sketches by Boz are all exceedingly well managed, and never fail to tell as the author intended'. Poe particularly admires 'The Black Veil', and of 'The Pawnbroker's Shop' he writes: 'We are enveloped in its atmosphere of wretchedness and extortion—we pause at every sentence, not to dwell upon the sentence, but to obtain a fuller view of the gradually perfecting picture.' Again, Dickens earns Poe's approval because he observes the principle of unity in building up his effect: 'To the illustration of this one end all the *groupings* and *fillings in* of the painting are rendered subservient—and when our eyes are taken from the canvass, we remember the personages of the sketch not at all as independent existencies, but as essentials of the one subject we have witnessed—as a part and portion of the *Pawnbroker's Shop*.' For the same reason, he commends an episode in *The Old Curiosity Shop*: 'every thing' is 'in rigid consonance with the one impression to be conveyed'.[1] When

[1] Edgar Allan Poe, 'Watkins Tottle and Other Sketches', *Southern Literary Messenger*, ii (June 1836), reprinted in *The Complete Works of Edgar Allan*

he believes Dickens has failed in *Barnaby Rudge*, Poe analyses that failure partly in terms of effect.[1]

By the time they met in early March 1842, Poe had been considering his theory of the unity of effect for at least seven years. As early as 1835, he was advocating strong effects as the secret of success:

> The history of all Magazines shows plainly that those which have attained celebrity were indebted for it to articles *similar in nature—to Berenice*—although, I grant you, far superior in style and execution. I say similar in *nature*. You ask me in what does this nature consist? In the ludicrous heightened into the grotesque: the fearful coloured into the horrible: the witty exaggerated into the burlesque: the singular wrought out into the strange and mystical . . . To be appreciated you must be *read*, and these things are invariably sought after with avidity.

His definitive version of the theory, as applied to fiction, was published only a month after the meeting with Dickens:

> A skilful literary artist has constructed a tale. If wise, he has not fashioned his thoughts to accommodate his incidents; but having conceived, with deliberate care, a certain unique or single *effect* to be wrought out, he then invents such incidents—he then combines such events as may best aid him in establishing this preconceived effect. If his very initial sentence tend not to the outbringing of this effect, then he has failed in his first step. In the whole composition there should be no word written, of which the tendency, direct or indirect, is not to the one pre-established design. And by such means, with such care and skill, a picture is at length painted which leaves in the mind of him who contemplates it with a kindred art, a sense of the fullest satisfaction.

This was probably written shortly before or after the meetings with Dickens. Poe may even have been in the course of writing it when he met Dickens.[2] At the time of the meeting,

---

Poe, ed. James A. Harrison (New York, 1965), vol. ix, pp. 46, 48 ; *Graham's Magazine* (May, 1841) quoted in *The Dickens Critics*, pp. 23–4.

[1] See below, pp. 73–4.

[2] To Thomas W. White (30 Apr. 1835), *The Letters of Edgar Allan Poe*, ed. John Ostrom (Cambridge, Mass., 1948), vol. i, pp. 57–8. Poe 'Twice-Told Tales', *Graham's Magazine* (May 1842), quoted in *Edgar Allan Poe*, ed. Margaret Alterton and Hardin Craig (New York, 1935), pp. 359–60. The May number of *Graham's* was published in mid April. In the opening sentence of the review, Poe recalled a notice in the previous number of *Graham's* and made it clear that the review had already been intended for the May number at least

therefore, Poe's theory of the 'single effect' in fiction was fresh in his mind. Further, he no doubt recalled that he had repeatedly praised Dickens's skill in putting this theory into practice and that the review of *Barnaby Rudge*, at the moment in Dickens's hands, criticized Dickens's failure in this respect.

There are two main sources for what we know with absolute certainty about the 'two long interviews'. The first source is a letter of Dickens's, dated 6 March 1842, in reply to one from Poe which was unfortunately lost; from Dickens's letter, however, the gist of Poe's letter can be gathered:

I shall be very glad to see you whenever you will do me the favor to call. I think I am more likely to be in the way between half-past eleven and twelve, than at any other time. I have glanced over the books you have been so kind as to send me, and more particularly at the papers to which you called my attention. I have the greater pleasure in expressing my desire to see you on this account. Apropos of the "construction" of "Caleb Williams," do you know that Godwin wrote it *backwards*,—the last volume first,—and that when he had produced the hunting down of Caleb, and the catastrophe, he waited for months, casting about for a means of accounting for what he had done?

Scholars are agreed that the books and papers referred to were Poe's *Tales of the Grotesque and Arabesque* (2 vols.) and his review of *Barnaby Rudge*. The reference to Godwin may well have been prompted by the concluding sentences of Poe's review. The second source for what occurred at the interviews is a letter from Poe to Lowells in which Poe mentions that he and Dickens exchanged ideas about literature:

I still adhere to Dickens as either author, or dictator, of the review. My reasons would convince you, could I give them to you— but I have left myself no space. I had two long interviews with Mr. D[ickens]. when here. Nearly everything in the critique, I heard from him or suggested to him, personally. The poem of Emerson I read to him.[1]

as early as mid March 1842 when the April number was published. The meetings with Dickens took place about 6 Mar. 1842.

[1] To Edgar Allan Poe (6 Mar. 1842), *The Complete Works of Edgar Allan Poe*, ed. James A. Harrison, vol. xvii, p. 107; to James Russell Lowell (2 July 1844), *The Letters of Edgar Allan Poe*, ed. J. Ostrom, vol. i, p. 258 (the review referred to was an article on 'American Poetry' in the *London Foreign Quarterly*).

It seems reasonable to suppose that Dickens and Poe discussed the business of 'plotting backwards' to which Dickens refers in his letter; Dickens gives the impression he is particularly looking forward to discussing this matter with Poe. What then did this topic involve? Fortunately, there is a gloss on this part of Dickens's letter in an article of Poe's:

Charles Dickens, in a note lying before me, alluding to an examination I once made of the mechanism of "Barnaby Rudge", says—"By the way, are you aware that Godwin wrote his 'Caleb Williams' backwards? He first involved his hero in a web of difficulties, forming the second volume, and then, for the first, cast about him for some mode of accounting for what had been done." . . . Nothing is more clear than that every plot, worth the name, must be elaborated to its *dénouement* before anything be attempted with the pen. It is only with the *dénouement* constantly in view that we can give a plot its indispensable air of consequence, or causation, by making the incidents, and especially the tone at all points, tend to the development of the intention.

The whole point of 'The Philosophy of Composition' is the rigid control which unity of effect exercises on the structure of 'The Raven'. In other words, 'plotting backwards' involves two things: the systematic organization of the material to produce a unity of effect and the intimate relationship which this principle sets up between effect and structure. In the review of *Barnaby Rudge*, Poe is making a similar point. He is criticizing Dickens for failing to bring his construction into line with his effect:

The soul of the plot, as originally conceived, was the murder of Haredale, with the subsequent discovery of the murderer in Rudge—but that this idea was afterwards abandoned, or rather suffered to be merged in that of the Popish Riots. The result has been most unfavourable. That which, of itself, would have proved highly effective, has been rendered nearly null by its situation. In the multitudinous outrage and horror of the Rebellion, the *one* atrocity is utterly whelmed and extinguished.

The reasons of this deflection from the first purpose appear to us self-evident. One of them we have already mentioned. The other is that our author discovered, when too late, that *he had anticipated, and thus rendered valueless, his chief effect*. This will be readily understood. The particulars of the assassination being withheld, the strength of the narrator is put forth, in the beginning of the story, to *whet curiosity* in respect to these particulars; and, so far, he is but in proper pursuance of his main design. But from this intention he unwittingly passes into the error of *exaggerating anticipation* . . . He had placed himself in a dilemma from which even his high genius could not extricate him. He at once shifts the main interest—and in truth we do not see what better he could have done. The reader's attention becomes absorbed in the riots, and he fails to observe that what should have been the true catastrophe of the novel, is exceedingly feeble and ineffective.[1]

Considering that Poe had been bold enough to send Dickens his review of *Barnaby Rudge* and ask for an interview and that Dickens had shown interest in his views, it would be surprising if Poe did not then go on to press his theories about plotting and effect very forcefully on Dickens when they met. Also considering that his theory of unity of effect was fresh in Poe's mind and the interviews were with a writer he had often instanced as putting this theory into practice, it would be equally surprising if he did not give the theory a vigorous airing.[2]

2. *Dickens and Edward Mangin: Intensity of Effect and Narrative Power*

It is certainly worth noting that the manuscripts of Dickens's novels written before his meeting with Poe show only slight traces of any *conscious* attempt to build up unity of effect. Yet from *Martin Chuzzlewit*, which followed immediately on Dickens's first American tour, the manuscripts reveal an increasing, deliberate concern to exploit this principle. This partly arises from Dickens's general development as a novelist; yet it is probably more than a coincidence that Dickens certainly knew of the principle from another source. It is elaborated in Mangin's *Essay on the Sources of the*

---

[1] 'The Philosophy of Composition' and 'Barnaby Rudge', *Graham's Magazine* (Apr. 1846, Feb. 1842), quoted in *Edgar Allan Poe*, ed. M. Alterton and H. Craig, pp. 365, 336–8.

[2] Since Poe had sent Dickens a copy of his *Tales of the Grotesque and Arabesque*, hoping to enlist his help in finding an English publisher, Poe may even have drawn attention to the theory he was practising in these stories and compared them in this respect with 'The Black Veil'.

Pleasures Received from Literary Compositions, the book on literary theory that Dickens had in his library:

We may observe, in the first place, how much depends on the selection of circumstances. In real life our attention is distracted by the variety of objects, which all equally affect our senses, but which produce various and contrary effects on the mind. In the same manner, also, every individual object has a variety of qualities or circumstances, which raise emotions of different and perhaps opposite natures.

Now when any object or any scene is presented to the imagination, although it may not appear so distinct or so lively as it does to the eye, yet it may be presented in that point of view, which will conduce in the highest degree to some particular effect; all the qualities and circumstances which are favourable to the effect being forced on our attention, while such as are unfavourable or indifferent are concealed and overlooked. The finest landscape is interspersed with objects which either have no beauty or are positively disagreeable. But these are neglected by the poet, who selects only what is sublime, picturesque, or beautiful, and thus by his description rouses the imagination to contemplate a scene, not so distinct or lively, but more conducive to his particular purpose than that which is exhibited by nature.

Or to take an instance of a different kind: in the mortality of a plague on shipboard, how many things would occur to overwhelm the spectator with terrour and disgust, as *well* as to melt him with the kindlier sympathies of pity! But in Thomson's description of a scene of this kind on the coast of Carthagena, that engaging poet has omitted every loathsome circumstance, and touched the terrible but with a gentle hand, while he holds up to view the particulars which are calculated to awaken our tenderest compassion . . .

We are next to observe, that as in real life we frequently see too much, so on the other hand, we frequently see too little, to raise a particular emotion to it's greatest height. Thus in the distress as of our fellow-creatures, it is but rarely that we are witnesses of the whole series of calamitous events, and that only at intervals both of time and place. It is but seldom that we are acquainted with the character of the sufferer, that we know how much he has lost, his sensibility to his losses, and the patience and fortitude with which he endures his afflictions. On the other hand, in those distressful scenes which we form in our imagination, or which are represented to us by the novelist or dramatic poet, the whole story is brought at once before us, and all the pathetic circumstances, which are unknown or overlooked in real life, may be exhibited in their full force . . .

These observations on the vivacity of the emotions produced by the imagination suggest the general principles which a composer ought to keep in view for exciting and regulating its influence according to his particular purpose.

He ought, in the first place, to be extremely careful in selecting and bringing forward the circumstances which are conducive to his purpose, and concealing as much as may be those which are unfavourable, or even superfluous.[1]

This version of the principle would have particularly commended itself to Dickens since it stresses intensity of effect as much as unity. A mind like Dickens's, which is very practical, will look at the subject of the unity of effect in a different way from a mind like Poe's, which is strongly analytical. Whereas Poe stresses the *idea* of unity, an absolute mystical principle to which the method of composition must subscribe, Dickens rarely mentions the idea of the unity of effect. He is preoccupied with the practical result of the *method*, the increase in power which the narrative gains. What he writes about constantly is the *intensity* of effect.[2]

The method of intensifying effects in this way is as much the basis of Dickens's outstanding power as a narrative artist as it is of Poe's. Fortunately, a letter from Dickens to Wilkie Collins, the significance of which has escaped notice, indirectly throws some light on Dickens's practice of this method:

You have guessed right! The best of it was that she [Mrs. Gaskell] wrote to Wills, saying she must particularly stipulate not to have her proofs touched, "even by Mr. Dickens." That immortal creature had gone over the proofs [*North and South*] with great pains—had of course taken out the stiflings—hard-plungings, lungeings, and other convulsions—and had also taken out her weakenings and damagings of her own effects. "Very well," said the gifted Man, "she shall have her own way. But after it's published show her this Proof, and ask her to consider whether her story would have been the better or the worse for it."

---

[1] Edward Mangin, *Essays on the Sources of the Pleasures Received from Literary Compositions* (1809), pp. 24–6, 32–3.

[2] See above, pp. 20–1, 34.

Dickens plainly implies, here, that the method which he wished to apply to Mrs. Gaskell's work was the common practice of both Collins and himself. It was so usual and sensible a method of revision that he is quite indignant, beneath his evident amusement, that Mrs. Gaskell should object to it. Dickens's complaint also suggests how consciously and with what deliberate care he had come to revise his own work by this time, so as to intensify effects and to erase weaknesses of effect. Interestingly enough, this deliberate method of revision so as to increase the power of effects had been recommended by Edward Mangin:

When the glow of composition has subsided, let him calmly revise his work and prune it not only of what is unfavourable to the emotions which he wishes to communicate, but even of what is indifferent . . . The great care of this selection ought to be, not in the time of composing, but both before and after; that is to say, when the author forms, or at least when he corrects his plan, and above all in the revisal of what he has finished.[1]

In the case of Mrs. Gaskell's work, Dickens of course could only revise at the proof stage but in the case of his own work it is only reasonable to suppose that he applied the same method at the manuscript stage. We should expect to find evidence of this kind of revision in both manuscripts and corrected proofs and, in fact, this is what we do find.

3. *Immediacy and the Appeal to the Senses: Dickens's Debt to the Tale of Terror in* Blackwood's Edinburgh Magazine

Since immediacy goes far towards explaining the remarkable power of Dickens's narrative, its secret is worth investigating. Dickens's practice of piling up concrete details partly accounts for his success here but he also achieves a strong impression of immediacy by appealing to the reader's senses. The Dickens world appears sensuous and tangible because it is evoked either directly through the reader's own memory images of sensations, a reflection of the manner in which he apprehends the real world, or indirectly through the sense-impressions of a character with whom he is invited to identify himself.

[1] To Wilkie Collins (24 Mar. 1855), *C*, pp. 29–30; Mangin, op. cit., pp. 34–5.

What, however, ensures the final success of this method is the intensity with which the sense-impressions are presented; once again, it is a case of unity of effect, the practical result of which is a powerful immediacy.

Dickens may be correctly described as a 'sensation novelist' but the term should be given a wider meaning than W. C. Phillips gives it, a meaning closer to Conrad's:

> Such an appeal to be effective must be an impression conveyed through the senses; and, in fact, it cannot be made in any other way . . . All art, therefore, appeals primarily to the senses, and the artistic aim when expressing itself in written words must also make its appeal through the senses, if its high desire is to reach the secret spring of responsive emotions.

Even within the narrow limits in which Phillips uses the term 'sensation novelist' he is mistaken, I believe, in trying to trace the development of Dickens exclusively from Mrs. Ann Radcliffe and the Gothic tale through Byron and Bulwer-Lytton.[1] Apart from Shakespeare's influence, especially that of *Macbeth*, there was probably a stronger and more important influence on Dickens which has been overlooked. I refer to a series of tales in *Blackwood's* which includes Henry Thomson's 'Le Revenant' (1827) and Samuel Warren's 'Passages from the Diary of a Late Physician' (1830–7).

What distinguishes these tales of terror from the traditional Gothic tale is a completely revolutionary technique. The Gothic tale arouses a purely romantic terror through vagueness and suggestion. But the Blackwood tale creates a realistic terror through precision. Objects which arouse horror are described with a meticulously scientific accuracy and detail and the sensations of horror are analysed with an almost medical thoroughness; indeed, this new method of description derived, in part, from observing the powerful impressions of terror produced by a certain kind of medical report.

I have argued the case for this influence on Dickens's

---

[1] W. C. Phillips, *Dickens, Reade, and Collins: Sensation Novelists*; Joseph Conrad, Preface to *The Nigger of the Narcissus*; Phillips, op. cit., pp. 152–81 (this influence almost certainly explains both the name and melodramatic posturing of Monks in *OT*).

fiction elsewhere[1] and can give only a brief summary of my findings here. There is a striking parallel between several unusual situations in Dickens and Warren[2] and Henry Thomson's 'Le Revenant' almost certainly provided the source for Dickens's 'Criminal Courts', the episode which concludes 'A Visit to Newgate', and the penultimate chapter of *Oliver Twist*; thus, in a passage of 'Le Revenant' and of 'Criminal Courts', in each case of little more than a page, there are no less than seven similar incidents which contain close verbal echoes.[3]

Although 'Criminal Courts' appeared in *Sketches by Boz*, Second Series (December 1836), it was one of the very earliest sketches Dickens wrote and was published under another title, 'The Old Bailey', in the *Morning Chronicle* (23 October 1834). Dickens's debt to 'Le Revenant', therefore, dates from the very beginning of his career. Since Dickens published his first work of fiction in December 1833, we may conclude that the realistic Blackwood tale of terror, which was making an impact on him just eleven months later (when he had published only the first ten of the fifty-six pieces that were to make up *Sketches by Boz*), was one of the earliest influences on his career and may well have been decisive in indicating an important direction his narrative art was to take.

The method which Dickens was mastering in the early stories and in *Oliver Twist* has important consequences which go far beyond the evocation of terror. This method partly explains the extraordinary power of many scenes and descriptions in Dickens's work, the amazing tangibility of the

---

[1] H. P. Sucksmith, 'The Narrative Art of Charles Dickens: The Rhetoric of Sympathy and Irony in His Novels', unpublished Ph.D. thesis (University of Nottingham, 1967), pp. 105–17; see also my forthcoming article, 'The Secret of Immediacy: Dickens's Debt to the Tale of Terror in *Blackwood's Edinburgh Magazine*', *Nineteenth-Century Fiction*.

[2] Cf. 'The Black Veil', *SB*, pp. 371–81, with 'Early Struggles', 'Grave Doings', 'The Thunder-Struck—The Boxer', "Passages from the Diary of a Late Physician", *Blackwood's Edinburgh Magazine*, xxviii (1830), 322–38, xxix (1831), 960–7, xxxii (1832), 279–84; cf. 'A Madman's Manuscript', *PP*, Chap. XI, pp. 139–47, with 'The Spectre-Smitten', "Passages", *Blackwood's*, xxix (1831), 361–75; cf. the case of Merdle in *LD* with 'The Forger', "Passages", *Blackwood's*, xxviii (1830), 786–93.

[3] Cf. *OT*, Chap, LII, pp. 404–5, 406–7, with 'Le Revenant', *Blackwood's*, xxi (1827), 410–11, 414–15, 413–14; cf. 'Criminal Courts', *SB*, pp. 198–9, with 'Le Revenant', *Blackwood's*, xxi (1827), 410–11.

Dickens world. One thinks of the gay happy atmosphere at the wedding of Trundle and Isabella, the comfortable inn in 'The Bagman's Tale', or the summer delights which Mr. Pickwick experiences on the journey to Bury St. Edmund's. The method accounts for the effectiveness in *Oliver Twist* of much of the realistic background, the picture of the awakening Metropolis, for example, as Sikes makes his way with Oliver from Bethnal Green to Shoreditch, the graphic description of Smithfield Market with all its squalid bustling congestion, or the sketches of the sordid poverty and delapidation in a dockland district. The account of the odyssey of Nell and her Grandfather is in a loose episodic form but many of the episodes which make it up are very tightly constructed so as to create a unified impression. Thus, the description of the flight from London through the suburbs consists of a series of tableaux, the early morning quietness and stillness, then the later morning bustle, the shabby genteel locality followed by the poverty-stricken slum. Later on, the picture of the dirty busy industrial town in the Black Country, the nightmarish wasteland of a contemporary industrial landscape, and then by contrast the accounts of the pleasures of travelling by wagon and the delights of settling into a new home, give the impression of an archetypal journey through hell and purgatory towards paradise, and this mythical depth to the story owes a great deal of its effectiveness to the method I have described. In *Martin Chuzzlewit*, similarly effective pen-pictures record the dull drowsy comfort of the best room at the Blue Dragon, the dingy establishment of Anthony Chuzzlewit and Son, and the immortal seediness of Todgers's. Sometimes, the method may be applied without freshness or inspiration and then Dickens is apt to produce lifeless or strained descriptions such as the picture of nautical compactness at the Wooden Midshipman's with its rather strained picturesqueness in *Dombey and Son* or, worse still, the dull mechanical account of the dusty church where Walter and Florence are married.[1]

[1] *PP*, Chaps, XXVIII, XIV, XVI, pp. 383–9, 180–1, 208–9; *OT*, Chaps. XXI, L, pp. 152–3, 381–2; *OCS*, Chaps, XV, XLIII, XLV, XLVI, LII, pp. 114–15, 325, 334–6, 345–6, 387–8; *MC*, Chaps. III, XI, VIII, pp. 28, 176, 123–4, 126 (cf. Chap. IX, pp. 129–30); *D & S*, Chaps. IV, LVII, pp. 32–3, 806–7.

Many instances from the later novels suggest themselves, the very impressive description of the hottest long vacation for years in *Bleak House*, or the effective little sketch of Casby's quiet house and the panoramic views of the Great St. Bernard landscapes in *Little Dorrit*, or the gripping account of the mist-bound mail coach toiling up Shooter's Hill on the Dover Road in *A Tale of Two Cities*. Perhaps not quite so effective are the descriptions in *Our Mutual Friend* of Mortimer Lightwood's dismal office and the picturesque Six Jolly Fellowship Porters whose various qualities are elaborated in a series of unified impressions.[1]

The manuscripts confirm that Dickens was *consciously* setting out to build up powerful impressions with a striking quality of immediacy and that he intensified his effects by rigorously applying the principle of unity. Through various revisions, all the possible material is gradually assimilated by the central theme, so contributing to a single effect. As early as *Oliver Twist*, we find the occasional revision of this kind. In the account of the bitter night which the homeless poor face, for example, Dickens has added the words, 'dark and', to the phrase, 'Bleak, DARK, AND piercing cold'.[2] In later manuscripts, this kind of revision is more frequent and on a much greater scale. Thus, in the description of Montagu Tigg's murder and Jonas Chuzzlewit's guilty recollections of it, Dickens deliberately intensifies the terror and the horror in the manner he had learned from the Blackwood tale:

The body of a murdered man. In one thick solitary spot, it lay among the last year's leaves of oak and beech, just as it had fallen headlong down. It had never moved since the striking of the first blow he had dealt at it from behind. Sopping and soaking in among the leaves that formed its pillow; oozing down into the boggy ground, as if to cover itself from human sight; FORCING ITS WAY BETWEEN AND THROUGH the curling leaves, as if those senseless things rejected and foreswore it, and were coiled up in abhorrence; went a ⟨deep red stream⟩ DARK, DARK STAIN that ⟨stained the⟩ DYED AND SCENTED the whole summer night from earth to heaven.

[1] *BH*, Chap. XIX, pp. 259–60; *LD*, Bk. I, Chap. XIII, p. 145, Bk. II, Chap. I, pp. 431–2; *TTC*, Bk. I, Chap. II, pp. 4–8; *OMF*, Bk. I, Chap. VIII, p. 86; Bk. I, Chap. VI, pp. 61–2.

[2] Original MS, of *OT*. Vol. IA, Bk. II, Chap. I, p. 2; cf. *OT*, Chap. XXIII, p. 165.

The doer of this deed came leaping from the wood so fiercely, that he cast into the air a shower of fragments of young boughs, TORN AWAY IN HIS PASSAGE, and fell with violence upon the grass . . . He thought—of his own controlling power and direction he thought—of the one dread question only. When they would find the body in the wood.

He tried—he had never left off trying—not to forget it was there, for that was impossible, but to forget to weary himself by drawing vivid pictures of it in his fancy: by going softly about it and about it among the leaves, approaching it nearer and nearer peeping through a gap in the boughs, and startling the very flies that were ⟨gathered there⟩ THICKLY SPRINKLED ALL OVER IT, LIKE HEAPS OF DRIED CURRANTS.[1]

The manuscript of *David Copperfield* shows Dickens intensifying the desolate impression of the schoolroom at Salem House:

Scraps of old copybooks and exercises, litter the dirty floor. Some silkworms' houses, made of the same materials, are scattered over the desks. Two MISERABLE LITTLE white mice, left behind by their owner, are running up and down in a FUSTY castle made of pasteboard and wire, looking in all the corners with their red eyes for anything to eat. A bird, in a cage a very little bigger than himself, makes a MOURNFUL rattle now and then in hopping on his perch, two inches high, or dropping from it; but neither sings nor chirps. There is a strange unwholesome smell upon the room, like mildewed corduroys, SWEET APPLES WANTING AIR, and rotten books.[2]

In his notes for the opening of *Little Dorrit*, Dickens indicates that he was aiming at two strong contrasting effects: 'Hot dusty picture Cold, shaded prison' (I, Chap. I). The result in the novel is a powerful assault on the senses and the following revisions in the manuscript show with what rigorous care Dickens worked to intensify what was already a striking impression of heat:

Thirty years ago, Marseilles lay broiling in the sun, one day.
A blazing sun upon a fierce August day was no greater rarity in southern France then, than at any other time, before or since.

[1] Original MS. of *MC*, Victoria and Albert Museum, Forster Collection, 47. A. 18 (Vol. IIB), Chaps. XLVII, LI, pp. 38 (First edition omits 'It had never . . . behind'), 2 (First Edition omits 'peeping'); cf. *MC*, pp. 725, 774.
[2] Original MS. of *DC*, Vol. IA, Chap. V, p. 24; cf. *DC*, pp. 77–8.

Everything in Marseilles, and about Marseilles, had stared at the fervid sky, and been stared at in return, until a staring habit had become universal there. Strangers were stared out of countenance by staring white houses, staring white walls, staring white streets, staring tracts of arid road, staring hills from which verdure was burnt away. The only things to be seen not FIXEDLY staring and glaring were the vines drooping under their load of grapes. These did occasionally wink a little, as the hot air barely moved their faint leaves.

There was no wind to make a ripple on the foul water within the harbour, or on the beautiful sea without. The line of demarcation between the two colours, black and blue, showed the point which the pure sea would not pass; but it lay as quiet as the abominable pool, with which it never mixed. Boats without awnings were too hot to touch; ships blistered at their moorings; the stones of the quays ⟨were like heated ovens⟩ HAD NOT COOLED, NIGHT OR DAY, FOR MONTHS. Russians, Hindoos, Chinese, Spaniards, Portuguese, Englishmen, Frenchmen, Genoese, Neapolitans, Venetians, Greeks, Turks, descendants from all the builders of Babel, come to trade at Marseilles, sought the shade alike— taking refuge in any hiding-place from a sea too intensely blue to be looked at, and a sky of purple, set with one great flaming jewel of fire.

The universal stare made the eyes ache. Towards the distant line of Italian coast, indeed, it was a little relieved by light clouds of mist, slowly rising from the evaporation of the sea; but it softened nowhere else. Far away the staring roads, deep in dust, stared from the hill-side, stared from the hollow, stared from the interminable plain. Far away the dusty vines overhanging way-side cottages, and the monotonous wayside avenues of parched trees without shade, drooped beneath the stare of earth and sky. So did the horses with drowsy bells, in long files of carts, creeping slowly towards the interior; so did ⟨the⟩ THEIR RECUMBENT drivers, when they were awake, which rarely happened; SO DID THE EXHAUSTED LABOURERS IN THE FIELDS. Every-thing that lived or grew, was oppressed by the glare; except the lizard, passing like a swift shadow over rough stone walls, and the cicala, chirping his dry hot chirp, like a rattle up in the scorched trees. The very dust was baked brown, and something quivered in the atmosphere as if the air itself were panting.

Blinds, shutters, curtains, awnings, were all closed and drawn to keep out the stare. Grant it but a chink or key hole, and it shot in like a ⟨?red⟩ WHITE-hot arrow. The churches were the freest from it. To come out of the twilight of pillars and arches—dreamily dotted with winking lamps, dreamily peopled with ugly old shadows piously dozing, spitting, and begging—was to plunge into a fiery river, and swim for life to the nearest strip of ⟨shadow⟩ SHADE. So, with people lounging and lying wherever shade was, with but little hum of tongues or barking of dogs, with occasional jangling of discordant church bells, and rattling of vicious drums, Marseilles, a fact to be STRONGLY smelt and tasted, lay broiling in the sun one day.

Moreover, the reference in the manuscript to the lizard, 'passing like a swift shadow' was emended to 'passing swiftly', presumably because even the faintest hint of any word associated with shade at this point was considered to mar the climax of the third paragraph.[1]

Obviously, this method is most impressive when it is creating fragments of the world which impinge forcefully on the senses. Yet, for all its power, the vision in such cases may be of the simplest kind. Garis is right to point out the simplicity of Dickens's vision here since the reader, blinded by the sheer power of the vision, may remain unaware of its simplicity. Yet it is by such means that Dickens 'bounces us'— in E. M. Forster's phrase—into an immediate acceptance of the sheer substantiality of his world. Furthermore, Garis, who complains that the passage has little structural relevance, goes astray in choosing this passage as thoroughly representative of Dickens's narrative art. Although the passage has features common to some of Dickens's very best work, in other ways it is not typical. Very often, the sensational appeal in Dickens's narrative is complicated by other effects and the vision correspondingly more complex while, so far as structural relevance is concerned, these opening paragraphs of *Little Dorrit* do not give an accurate picture of Dickens's practice. Besides, Dickens is not always at his best in the opening of a novel. The openings of barely half his novels can be called really satisfactory, namely those of *David Copperfield, Bleak House, Hard Times, Great Expectations,*

[1] Victoria and Albert Museum, Forster Collection, 48. E. 1. Original MS. of *LD*, Vol. IA, Bk. I, Chap. I, pp. 1–2 (a late [and only surviving] proof reads 'burning' after 'lay' in first sentence, 'Hindoos, Russians', 'scorched' after 'dust was', and omits 'up in the scorched trees', while the First Edition reads 'passing swiftly over'); cf. *LD*. pp. 1–2.

Our Mutual Friend, and *Edwin Drood*. The opening of *A Tale of Two Cities* is dull and that of *Martin Chuzzlewit* a ghastly failure. It seems unfair that out of seven mature novels of Dickens, Garis should select the opening with the least structural relevance and put this alongside a successful opening to a novel of George Eliot's. Garis, for instance, might have chosen the opening of *Edwin Drood* which does have the subtle structural relevance which he recommends in the openings of George Eliot's *Middlemarch* and *The Mill on the Floss*:

An ancient English Cathedral Tower? How can the ancient English Cathedral tower be here! The well-known massive grey square tower of its old Cathedral? How can that be here! There is no spike of rusty iron in the air, between the eye and it, from any point of the real prospect. What is the spike that intervenes, and who has set it up? Maybe it is set up by the Sultan's orders for the impaling of a horde of Turkish robbers, one by one. It is so, for cymbals clash, and the Sultan goes by to his palace in long procession. Ten thousand scimitars flash in ths sunlight, and thrice ten thousand dancing-girls strew flowers. Then, follow white elephants caparisoned in countless gorgeous colours, and infinite in number and attendants. Still the Cathedral Tower rises in the background, where it cannot be, and still no writhing figure is on the grim spike. Stay! Is the spike so low a thing as the rusty spike on the top of a post of an old bedstead that has tumbled all awry?

This does not only record the delirious sensations of an opium addict, it presents the basic ironic situation of the novel, the cruel oriental fantasies brooding beneath the respectable surface of Cloisterham and a mind dangerously unable to keep the two worlds apart. It introduces the main character of the novel, the Thug lurking behind the mask of the Cathedral choir-master. It provides the germ for the development of the story, the contradiction between the upright Christian *persona* of John Jasper and the inner drives of sexual passion and sadistic malice which will culminate in jealousy, murder, and an execution.[1]

[1] Robert Garis, *The Dickens Theatre*, pp. 5–15, 10–12. E. M. Forster, *Aspects of the Novel*, p. 76. *ED*, Chap. I, p. 1; the novel's final scene was to take place in the condemned cell according to *F*, vol. iii, pp. 425–6. If the theory advanced in Felix Aylmer, *The Drood Case* (1964) is correct, it invalidates some, but by no means all, of my argument here.

Very often, Dickens uses the appeal to the senses as part of a larger structure and a more complex vision. Thus, in *David Copperfield*, the picture of the desolate schoolroom at Salem House is not painted for its own sake. It helps to build up the larger picture of David's mind, the refraction of a scene through the abandoned boy's mournful eyes, and it is also part of the wider vision of the book, the compassionate view of childhood which the reader comes to share. The revisions in the manuscript, in the paragraph immediately before the description of the schoolroom, show that Dickens wished to stress the pathos of a cruel separation from mother and home:

Salem House was a square brick building with wings; of a bare and unfurnished appearance. All about it was so very quiet, that I said to Mr. Mell I supposed the boys were out; but he seemed surprised at my not knowing that it was holiday-time. THAT ALL THE BOYS WERE AT THEIR SEVERAL HOMES. THAT MR. CREAKLE, THE PROPRIETOR, WAS DOWN BY THE SEA-SIDE WITH MRS. AND MISS CREAKLE; AND THAT I was sent in holiday-time as a punishment for my misdoing, all of which he explained to me as we went along.[1]

In *Little Dorrit*, the descriptions of the shabby beggarliness of the 'attendants on insolvency' at the Marshalsea gates and of the seedy house in which Fanny and Frederick Dorrit lodge help to focus so sharp a vision of poverty in Book I it can hardly fail to move the reader's compassion. In *Hard Times*, the effect of Louisa's tragic catastrophe is heightened by the wonderfully realistic description of the thunderstorm which immediately precedes it. In *Our Mutual Friend*, the account of the ragged school is more than a piece of graphic social reporting; its emotional bias prepares the reader for an antipathy against the two examples of the new educated poor, Charley Hexam and Bradley Headstone, who are to play villainous roles in the story.[2]

The description in *Dombey and Son* of Little Paul's christening on a bitterly cold day is a brilliant instance of an effect sustained at length through an appeal to the senses. The

[1] Original MS. of *DC*, Vol. IA, Chap. V, p. 23; cf. *DC*, p. 77.
[2] *LD*, Bk. I, Chap. IX, pp. 91, 93; *HT*, Bk. II, Chap. XII, pp. 212–14; *OMF*, Bk. II, Chap. I, pp. 214–16 (see Philip Collins, *Dickens and Education*, pp. 159–71).

effect is indicated in the notes to the novel: 'Icy christening—describe the ceremony' (memoranda for No. II); and a detailed study of the episode shows how thoroughly Dickens has organized his material to carry out this intention. Yet the purely sensational is only one element in a more complicated effect. The iciness also has an emotional and spiritual significance. Coldness lies at the heart of Mr. Dombey's personality. His cold pride, his freezing attitude towards his family and the world, provide the main source of tragedy in the novel, while the treatment of the christening as if it were a funeral ironically prepares for the cold nurture and premature death of Dombey's highly prized son.[1]

4. *Power and Feeling*

Dickens should be restored to the context of a traditional rhetoric which need not be cheap, unintelligent, or without high seriousness and purpose. Thus De Quincey, whose writings Dickens greatly admired, and Conrad both make the point that the higher literature can be communicated only through the medium of emotive effects. De Quincey writes that 'the function' of 'the literature of *power*' is 'to *move*' and argues that such a literature 'speaks ultimately, it may happen, to the higher understanding or reason, but always *through* affections of pleasure and sympathy'. Conrad makes a further link between the sensations and emotions: 'the artistic aim . . . must also make its appeal through the senses, if its high desire is to reach the secret spring of responsive emotions.'[2]

What Conrad means can be best understood from a scientific point of view. Experimental psychologists have pointed out that sensation and emotion are interrelated in the process of perception:

Primarily, therefore, sensation is *sense-perception, i.e.* perception transmitted *via* the sense organs and 'bodily senses' (kinaesthetic,

[1] Original MS. of *D & S*, Victoria and Albert Museum, Forster Collection, 47. A. 19 (Vol. IA); *D & S*, Chap. V, pp. 52–8, 60–1.
[2] Dickens was sufficiently interested in De Quincey to acquire his *Works*, Uniform Edition, 13 vols. (1858) (see *Catalogue of the Library of Charles Dickens*, p. 27, and Edgar Johnson, op. cit., vol. ii, p. 1131); Thomas De Quincey, 'Pope', *North British Review*, ix (1848), quoted in *De Quincey*, ed. Sidney Low, p. 154; Joseph Conrad, preface to *The Nigger of the Narcissus*.

vaso-motor sensation, etc.). On the one hand, it is an element of presentation, since it transmits to the presenting function the perceived image of the outer object; on the other hand, it is an element of feeling, because through the perception of bodily changes it lends the character of affect to feeling . . . Feeling-tone is connected in a particularly intimate way with organic sensations.[1]

If fiction, therefore, is to reflect the real world convincingly, it must also mirror the process by which that world is revealed to the reader. Thus, it must present the inter-relationship of sensation and emotion. Moreover, since emotion or feeling functions as a valuation of sensations, such a process affords us our primary, meaningful vision of the world:

Feeling . . . is an entirely *subjective* process, which may be in every respect independent of external stimuli, although chiming in with every sensation. Even an 'indifferent' sensation possesses a 'feeling tone', namely, that of indifference, which again expresses a certain valuation. Hence feeling is also a kind of *judging*, differing, however, from an intellectual judgment, in that it does not aim at establishing an intellectual connection but is solely concerned with the setting up of a subjective criterion of acceptance or rejection. The valuation by feeling extends to *every* content of consciousness, of whatever kind it may be.[2]

How Dickens manages the complicated relationship of sensation and feeling at its least intricate can be seen in this example from the manuscript of *Martin Chuzzlewit*:

Many and many a pleasant stroll they had in Covent Garden Market: snuffing up the perfume of the fruits and flowers, wondering at the MAGNIFICENCE OF THE PINE ⟨pine⟩ apples and melons; catching glimpses down side avenues, of rows and rows of old women, seated on inverted baskets shelling peas; looking unutterable things at the fat bundles of asparagus with which the dainty shops were fortified as with a breastwork; and, at the

---

[1] C. G. Jung, *Psychological Types*, p. 586; G. F. Stout, *A Manual of Psychology* (1929), p. 377. Despite their rather forbidding language, I have deliberately quoted from scientists, here and below, since they offer a dispassionate view of the mental processes involved; novelists other than Dickens (George Eliot is a good example) have, of course, shown that they understand these processes.

[2] Jung, *Types*, p. 544; cf. R. S. Woodworth, *Psychology* (1940), p. 407, Stout, op. cit., p. 388.

herbalists' doors, gratefully inhaling scenes as of veal-stuffing yet uncooked, dreamily mixed up with capsicums, brown-paper, seeds: even with hints of LUSTY snails and fine young curly leeches. Many and many a pleasant stroll they had among the poultry markets, where ducks and fowls, with necks unnaturally long, lay innocently stretched out in pairs, ready for cooking; where there were speckled eggs in ⟨baskets⟩ MOSSY BASKETS; white country sausages beyond impeachment by surviving cat or dog, or horse or donkey; new cheeses to any wild extent; live birds in coops and cages, looking much too big to be natural, in consequence of those receptacles being much too little; rabbits, alive and dead, innumerable. Many a pleasant stroll they had among the COOL REFRESHING SILVERY fish-stalls, with a kind of moonlight effect about their stock in trade, excepting always for the ruddy lobsters. Many a pleasant stroll among the waggon-loads of FRAGRANT hay, beneath which dogs and tired waggoners lay fast asleep, oblivious of the pieman and the public-house.[1]

This passage makes a strong appeal to the senses and the various sense-perceptions are selected and carefully organized so as to create a single pleasant or agreeable effect. How sensation and feeling work together in the passage can be seen in the revisions. By appealing further to the senses of sight, smell, or temperature which he has already been exciting in the rest of the passage, Dickens deliberately increases the immediacy of the experience. At the same time, the sense-impressions which he adds all have an agreeable tone and so intensify the pleasant effect of the passage. Dickens is working here with what we have seen called 'feeling tone' or 'affective tone of sensations' and he appreciates intuitively what can be set down as a scientific law:

We now turn to consider the special sensations of sight, sound, smell, taste, touch, and temperature. The affective tone of these sensations varies, first, with their intensity, secondly, with their duration, and thirdly, with their quality . . . We may formulate the general rule for the relation of intensity and affective tone as follows. A sensation must reach a certain minimum of intensity in order to have an appreciable feeling-tone. Further rise in

[1] Original MS. of *MC*, Victoria and Albert Museum, Forster Collection, 47. A. 17 (Vol. IIA), Chap. XL, pp. 23–4 (First Edition omits 'innocently'); cf. *MC*, pp. 621–2.

intensity of sensation is accompanied by a rise in intensity of feeling-tone.

Pleasantness-unpleasantness is the most universally recognized of Wundt's three dimensions of 'feeling-tone'. It involves a 'set' towards acceptance or rejection of an experience and so provides our valuation of the world in its most rudimentary form. This is vision at its simplest but most fundamental. Forster has noted the pleasant tone which pervades *David Copperfield*.[1] Such a tone provides a foundation for the general vision of affirmation, the 'yea-saying' towards life and experience, in much of Dickens's fiction.

Dickens may focus a more intricate vision through the interaction of sensation and feeling. The way he handles the start of the search for Lady Dedlock in the manuscript of *Bleak House* shows that he may do this with a deliberate art:

. . . there was a bill, on which I could discern the words, "Found Drowned"; and this, and an inscription about Drags, possessed me with the awful suspicion shadowed forth in our visit to that place. I had no need to remind myself that I was not there, by the indulgence of any feeling of mine, to increase the difficulties of the search, or to lessen its hopes, or enhance its delays and I remained quiet; but what I suffered in that dreadful spot, I never can forget. AND STILL IT WAS LIKE THE HORROR OF A DREAM. ⟨Nothing had been found not – ?–⟩ A man yet dark and muddy, in ⟨great⟩ LONG SWOLLEN sodden boots and a hat like them, was called out of a boat, and whispered with Mr. Bucket, who went away with him DOWN SOME SLIPPERY STEPS—as if to look at something secret that he had to show. They came back, wiping their hands upon their coats, after turning over something wet; ⟨my horror was so real that I hid my face⟩ but O thank God it was not what I feared! . . .

We appeared to retrace the way we had come. Not that I had taken note of any particular objects IN MY PERTURBED STATE OF MIND, but judging from the general character of the streets. We called at another office or station for a minute, and crossed the river again. During the whole of this time, and during the whole search, my companion, wrapped up on the box, never relaxed in his vigilance for a SINGLE moment; but, when we

[1] Stout, op. cit., pp. 381–2. Woodworth, *Psychology*, pp. 404–5; cf. the same author's standard work, *Experimental Psychology* (1950), pp. 235–6. *F*, vol. iii, p. 12.

crossed the bridge HE SEEMED, IF POSSIBLE, TO BE MORE
ON THE ALERT THAN BEFORE. HE stood up to look over
the parapet; he alighted, and went back after a shadowy FE-
MALE figure that flitted past us; and he gazed into the profound
black pit of water, with a face that made my heart die within me.
The river had a fearful look, so overcast and secret, creeping away
so fast between the low flat lines of shore: so heavy with indistinct
and awful shapes, both of substance and shadow: so deathlike
and mysterious. I have seen it many times since then, by sunlight
and by moonlight, but never free from the impressions of that
journey. In my memory, the lights upon the bridge are always
burning dim; the cutting wind is eddying round the homeless
woman whom we pass; the monotonous wheels are whirling on;
and the light of the carriage-lamps reflected back ⟨upon me⟩,
LOOKS PALELY IN UPON ME—a face, ⟨from⟩ RISING OUT
OF the dreaded water.[1]

Dickens's revisions not only give the sensations of Esther
Summerson a more powerful immediacy but also intensify the
effect of terror and horror. Esther's sense of disorientation,
her impression of a nightmarish experience registers the full
impact which horror and terror are making on her. The
substitution of 'long swollen sodden boots' for 'great sodden
boots' not only gives a sharper visual impression of the man
who has spent much of his time in water it also suggests the
effect of water on the corpse for which the man has been
dragging the river and so intensifies the terror and horror of
the situation. Similarly, Dickens intensifies Esther's feeling of
horrified expectancy by adding her impression of the Inspector's increased alertness as they cross the bridge and by making
it clear that the figure is a female. Again, the optical illusion,
which is realized with greater clarity and immediacy in the
revised version, also makes the horror of the situation and
Esther's terror more acute. Furthermore, suspense as well as
terror is increased by the revisions. So also is sympathy for
Esther and, through her, pity for her mother, Lady Dedlock.
The elements of pity and terror are important since Dickens is

[1] Original MS. of *BH*, Victoria and Albert Museum, Forster Collection,
47. A. 30 (Vol. IIB), Chap. LVII, pp. 2–3 (full stop added after 'delays' and
'and' deleted in proof which omits 'O' before 'thank God' and 'for' after
'vigilance', while 'Found Drowned' is in capitals in the original); cf. *BH*,
pp. 770–1.

working towards a tragic vision of Lady Dedlock. By intensifying the sensations in the passage, Dickens increases its
emotional power and this in turn focuses a vision of Lady
Dedlock which transcends her earlier satirical portrait and her
melodramatic postures.

Both De Quincey and Conrad single out sympathy from the
emotions which focus the higher vision. The artist, writes
Conrad, speaks

. . . to the subtle but invincible conviction of solidarity that knits
together the loneliness of innumerable hearts, to the solidarity in
dreams, in joy, in sorrow, in aspirations, in illusions, in hope, in
fear, which binds men to each other, which binds together all
humanity,—the dead to the living and the living to the unborn.

This account adequately describes Dickens's compassionate
vision at its best. Conrad's description also helps to explain
its timeless quality. Such a vision may include but also goes far
beyond the benevolence which was a contemporary reaction
to the cold philosophy of Benthamism and the heartless
economic doctrines of Malthus, Ricardo, and the Manchester
School.[1]

This vision has depth, extensiveness, and intensity. Though
by no means always simple, it cannot (compared with the
vision I shall speak of later) be called complex; its power, in
fact, derives from its homogeneous nature, its comprehensive
scope and its deep roots in fundamental human experience.
Such a power is revealed all the more forcefully through the
singleness of the vision and its comparative simplicity.
Consider, for example, how Dickens focuses as powerful a
sympathetic view of Boythorn as possible in the following
extract from the manuscript of *Bleak House*:

Presently we heard him in his bed-room thundering "Ha, ha,
ha!" and again "Ha, ha, ha!" until ⟨-?-⟩ THE FLATTEST echo
in the neighbourhood seemed to catch the contagion, and to laugh
as enjoyingly as he did, or as we did when we heard him laugh.

⟨He had such a round full⟩ WE ALL CONCEIVED A PRE-
POSSESSION IN HIS FAVOUR; for there was ⟨something in
the⟩ A STERLING QUALITY IN THIS LAUGH, AND IN HIS

[1] Joseph Conrad, preface to *The Nigger of the Narcissus*. Humphry House,
The Dickens World, pp. 36–105; for a full account of the relationship between
benevolence and philosophical and economic doctrines, see esp. pp. 68–70,
75–6.

⟨RICH⟩ VIGOROUS HEALTHY VOICE, AND IN THE round-
ness and fulness with which he uttered every word he spoke, and
in the very ⟨passion⟩ FURY of his superlatives, which seemed to
go off like blank cannons and hurt nothing. But we were hardly
prepared to have it so confirmed by his appearance, when Mr.
Jarndyce presented him. He was not only a very handsome old
gentleman—upright and stalwart as he had been described to us—
with ⟨–?–⟩ A MASSIVE GREY head, a lion face, a figure that
might have become corpulent but for his being so continuously in
earnest that he was never at rest, and a chin that might have subsided into a double chin but for the vehement emphasis in which it
was constantly required to assist; but he was such a true gentleman in his manner, so chivalrously polite, his face was lighted by
a smile of so much sweetness and tenderness, and it seemed so
plain that he had nothing to hide, but showed himself exactly as
he was—incapable (as Richard said) of anything on a limited
scale, and firing away with those blank great guns, because he
carried no small arms whatever—that really I could not help
looking at him with equal pleasure as he sat at dinner, whether he
smilingly conversed with Ada and me, or was led by Mr. Jarndyce into some great volley of superlatives, or threw up his head
like a bloodhound, and gave out that ⟨Ha, ha ha!⟩ TREMEN-
DOUS Ha, ha, ha!

The revisions here make us sympathize all the more with Boythorn's joy, appearance, vitality, and character. Moreover,
this effect was increased still further when Dickens altered
'a lion face' to 'a fine composure of face when silent' in proof.[1]

This sympathetic vision in Dickens's fiction has its reverse
side. As against the optimism, there is the gloom to which
Edmund Wilson has drawn attention.[2] There is rejection as
well as acceptance. Yet antipathy is managed by means of
the same technique as sympathy. Thus, the manuscript and
corrected proofs of *Little Dorrit* show how Dickens deliberately gives the gloomy Mrs. Clennam's portrait a distinctly
unpleasant tone:

Arthur followed him up the staircase, which was panelled off
into spaces like so many MOURNING tablets; and into a dim

---

[1] Original MS. of *BH*, Victoria and Albert Museum, Forster Collection,
47. A. 27 (Vol. IA), Chap. IX, pp. 17–18 ('gave it no' was substituted for 'was
never at' in proof); cf. *BH*, pp. 116–17. Corrected proofs of *BH*, Chap. IX, p. 83.
[2] Edmund Wilson, 'Dickens: The Two Scrooges', *The Wound and the Bow*
(1961), pp. 1–93.

bed-chamber, THE FLOOR OF WHICH HAD GRADUALLY
SO SUNK AND SETTLED, THAT THE FIREPLACE WAS
IN A DELL. On a ⟨grim⟩ black BIER-LIKE sofa ⟨like a bier⟩
IN THIS HOLLOW, propped up behind with ⟨an angular⟩ ONE
GREAT ANGULAR black bolster, like the block at a state
execution in the good old times, sat his mother in a widow's dress
SHE AND HIS FATHER HAD BEEN AT VARIANCE FROM
HIS EARLIEST REMEMBRANCE. TO SIT SPEECHLESS
HIMSELF IN THE MIDST OF RIGID SILENCE, GLANCING
IN DREAD FROM THE ONE AVERTED FACE TO THE
OTHER, HAD BEEN THE PEACEFULLEST OCCUPATION
OF HIS CHILDHOOD. She gave him one glassy kiss, and four
STIFF fingers MUFFLED IN WORSTED. THIS EMBRACE
CONCLUDED, HE ⟨He⟩ sat down on the opposite side of her little
table. There was a fire in the grate, as there had been night and day
for fifteen years. There was a kettle on the hob, as there had been
night and day for fifteen years. There was a ⟨–?–⟩ LITTLE
MOUND of damped ashes on the top of the fire, and another little
mound swept together under the grate, as there had been night and
day for fifteen years. There was a smell of black dye in the airless
room, which the fire had been drawing out of the ⟨sofa for fifteen
years and was now⟩ CRAPE AND STUFF OF THE WIDOW'S
DRESS FOR FIFTEEN MONTHS, AND OUT OF THE BIER-
LIKE SOFA for fifteen years.[1]

A further vision in Dickens's fiction neither accepts nor rejects
the world but surveys it with a critical detachment. This detached vision is focused largely through irony. The same
technique which was used to intensify the effect of sympathy
and of antipathy may also be used to increase the power of the
ironic vision. Consider, for example, the following satirical
view of Circumlocution from the manuscript of *Little Dorrit*:

This glorious establishment had been early in the field, when the
⟨?secret modern golden –?– modern art and mystery⟩ ONE
SUBLIME ⟨–?– SECRET INVOLVING⟩ PRINCIPLE INVOLV-
ING THE ⟨WHOLE ?SECRET⟩ DIFFICULT ⟨–?–⟩ ART of
governing a country, was first distinctly revealed to statesmen.
It had been foremost to study that bright revelation, and to carry

[1] Original MS. of *LD*, Vol. IA, Bk. I, Chap. III, p. 25, corrected proofs of
LD, Bk. I, Chap. III, p. 25 (before 'into a dim', MS. and proofs read 'and'
which First Edition omits, while 'She . . . childhood' is in late [and only
surviving] proof but not in MS.); cf. *LD*, p. 33.

its ⟨pervading⟩ SHINING influence through the whole of the official proceedings. Whatever was required to be done, the Circumlocution Office was beforehand with all the public departments in THE ART OF perceiving—How not to do it.

Through this ⟨?good/ ?great⟩ DELICATE perception, through the tact with which it invariably seized it, and through the genius with which it always acted on it, the Circumlocution Office had risen to overtop all the public departments; and the public condition had risen to be—what it was . . . All this is true, but the Circumlocution Office went beyond it.

Because the Circumlocution Office went on mechanically, every day, keeping this ⟨great ?art/ ?act⟩ WONDERFUL, ALL-SUFFICIENT WHEEL of statesmanship, How not to do it, in motion. Because the Circumlocution Office was down upon any ill-advised public servant who was going to do it, or who appeared to be by any surprising accident in remote danger of doing it, with a minute, and a memorandum, and a letter of instructions, that extinguished him. It was this ⟨great – ?–⟩ SPIRIT OF NATIONAL EFFICIENCY IN the Circumlocation Offlce that had gradually led to its having something to do with everything . . .

Sometimes, angry spirits attacked the Circumlocution Office. Sometimes, parliamentary questions were asked about it, and even parliamentary motions made or threatened about it, by demagogues so LOW AND ignorant as to hold that the real recipe of government was, How to do it.[1]

The conscious rhetoric, which consists in piling up words and expressions used in an ironic sense, intensifies the over-all effect. Moreover, the attack gains strength through being an indirect one; the position which is being undermined is ironically assumed by the author.

Paradoxically, Dickens's method can, on occasions, produce a greater degree of failure than would have been the case if it had not been used. Thus, the mawkishness of the scene in *David Copperfield* in which Martha Endell tries to drown herself is made even worse by Dickens's deliberate attempt to intensify his effect. This can be seen clearly in the manuscript:

I have never known what despair was, except in the tone of those words.

[1] Original MS. of *LD*, Vol. IA, Bk, I, Chap. X, pp. 11–12 ('How not to do it' at the end of the first paragraph is in capitals in the original); cf. *LD*, pp. 104–6.

"I can't keep away from it. I can't forget it. It haunts me DAY AND NIGHT. It's the only thing in all the world that I am fit for, or that's fit for me. Oh, the DREADFUL river!"

The thought passed through my mind that in the face of my companion, as he looked upon her without speech or motion, I might have read his niece's history, if I had known nothing of it. I never saw, IN ANY PAINTING OR REALITY, horror and compassion so impressively blended.[1]

The attempt to reassure the reader about the nature of the experience and its effect betrays Dickens's uneasiness. The passage should be contrasted with Esther Summerson's account of the dragging of the river for Lady Dedlock in which Dickens is confident enough to remove a similar direct statement to the reader about the intensity of the experience, 'My horror was so real that I hid my face'.

What happens when Dickens does not use this method of organizing his material with the thoroughness needed to unify and intensify effects efficiently may be illustrated from the manuscript of *Martin Chuzzlewit*. Immediately after the adequate picture of the pleasures of visiting Covent Garden Market, Dickens lapses into a half-hearted tinkering with an effect:

But never half so good a stroll, as down among the steam-boats on a bright morning.

There they lay, alongside of each other; hard and fast for ever, to all appearance, but designing to get out somehow, and quite confident of doing it; and in that faith shoals of passengers, and heaps of luggage, were proceeding HURRIEDLY on board. Little steamboats looking by comparison almost as small and BEING IN REALITY quite as brisk as the RESTLESS animalculae that live in the water dashed up and down the stream incessantly. TIERS UPON TIERS OF VESSELS, scores of masts, labyrinths of tackle, idle sails, splashing oars, gliding row-boats, lumbering barges; sunken piles, with ugly lodgings for the water-rat within their mud-discoloured nooks; church steeples, warehouses, house-roofs, arches, bridges, men and women, children, casks, cranes, boxes, horses, coaches, idlers, and hard-labourers: there they were, all jumbled up together, any summer morning, FAR beyond Tom's power of separation.

---

[1] Original MS. of *DC*, Victoria and Albert Museum, Forster Collection 47. A. 26 (Vol. IIB), Chap. XLVII, pp. 2–3; cf. *DC*, p. 681.

In the midst of all this turmoil, there was an incessant roar from every packet's funnel, which quite expressed and carried out the uppermost emotion of the scene. They all appeared to be perspiring and bothering themselves, exactly as their passengers did; they never left off fretting and chafing, in their own hoarse manner, once; but were always panting out, without any stops, "Come along do make haste I'M VERY NERVOUS come along oh good gracious we shall never get there how late you are do make haste I'm off directly come along!" Even when they had left off and had got safely out into the current, on the smallest provocation they began again: for the bravest packet of them all, being stopped by some entanglement in the river, would immediately begin to fume and pant afresh, "OH HERE'S A STOPPAGE WHAT'S THE MATTER DO GO ON THERE I'M IN A HURRY IT'S DONE ON PURPOSE DID YOU EVER OH MY GOODNESS DO GO ON THERE!" AND SO, IN a state of mind bordering on distraction, would be last seen going slowly through the mist into the summer light beyond, that made it red.

Tom's ship, however; or, at least, the packet-boat in which Tom and his sister took the greatest interest on one particular occasion; was not off yet, by any means; but was at the height of its disorder. The press of passengers was very great; another steam-boat lay on each side of her; the gangways were choked up; distracted women, obviously bound for Gravesend, but turning a deaf ear to all representations that this particular vessel was about to sail for Antwerp, persisted in secreting baskets of refreshments behind bulkheads and water-casks, and under seats; and very great confusion prevailed.[1]

The faulty rhetoric of this passage is worth scrutinizing. Dickens begins with the intention, plainly stated in his first sentence, of sustaining—if not increasing—the pleasant tone already created in the preceding picture of Covent Garden Market. In the second paragraph, however, he drops this intention in favour of the bustling and excited congestion which he now begins to sense the description of the dockside scene should centre on. All Dickens's revisions show that he was seeking to create this effect in the paragraph. 'Hurriedly' adds to the bustling excitement; 'Tiers upon tiers of vessels' and 'FAR beyond Tom's powers of separation' to the effect

[1] Original MS. of *MC*, Vol. IIA, Chap. XL, pp. 24–5 and reverse of p 25; cf. *MC*, pp. 622–3.

of congestion. The simile 'looking by comparison almost as small and being in reality quite as brisk as the RESTLESS animalculae that live in water', was later deleted[1] presumably because, although its reference to briskness contributes to the intended effect, the reference to size, which is exaggerated to the point of absurdity, distracts the reader's attention from the central theme. Unfortunately, other material which remains in the paragraph not only fails to contribute to the unity of idea and effect but actively contradicts it. In this category are 'idle sails', 'gliding row-boats', 'lumbering barges', 'sunken piles', 'idlers', all of which create either a static impression or one of slow movement. So uneasy is Dickens by this stage that he feels it necessary to state his effect boldly to the reader in the first sentence of the third paragraph: 'In the midst of all this turmoil, there was an incessant roar from every packet's funnel, *which quite expressed and carried out the uppermost emotion of the scene*' [my italics]. This sentence reads almost like a note of Dickens's intention not quite transmuted into its proper narrative form. The embarrassing monologue of the steamboat hardly realizes the intended effect but continues to state it in a barely disguised authorial voice. The phrase, 'going slowly', which also contradicts the central effect of bustling excitement was scarcely improved when it was altered later[2] to 'drifting slowly'. Only by the final paragraph has Dickens so worked himself into the proper feeling for his effect that he goes on to realize it in a confident and efficient manner. This passage is fascinating since it catches Dickens, as it were, in the very act of translating his idea for an effect into practice. As a result of his failure, he has left us this snapshot of an untidy workshop which tells us a good deal about his method.

To sum up then, Dickens sometimes fails in his use of this method in two ways. Either he does not use the method efficiently or he uses it correctly but with an inferior effect and vision. Yet when he is successful, the method can be seen to perform an important function in his narrative art. It focuses an intense, and sometimes a profound, vision which

---

[1] I infer this point from a comparison of MS. and First Edition; the few fragments of the proofs which have survived do not include this passage.

[2] I infer this. See previous note for explanation.

has both power and immediacy.[1] Though complexity of effect and vision is a further matter, it is built, as we shall see, out of these more simple forms.

5. *The Relationship between Simple and Complicated Effects*

A further question about the two passages from *Martin Chuzzlewit*, analysed separately in the previous section, is worth asking since it raises the intriguing problem of how simple and complicated effects are related in Dickens's narrative art. Why, then, does Dickens succeed in conveying an impression of the delights of Covent Garden Market and immediately afterwards fail to describe the bustling excitement and congestion of the dockside scene as effectively as he might have done?

The two passages must be considered in a wider context. The description of Covent Garden Market is preceded by the long idyllic account of Tom and Ruth's happy domestic life together which is *lyrical* in mood; into this happy idyll, the picture of their visits to Covent Garden Market with its pleasant tone fits quite naturally. The description of the dockside scene, however, is followed by the *dramatic* episode of Jonas Chuzzlewit's attempted flight to the Continent. These two larger sections of the novel, one lyrical, the other dramatic, exert an influence on the description of the dockside scene. Thus, Dickens begins by intending to treat the episode as a further instance of the idyllic life of the Pinches, thus sustaining the agreeable tone: 'But never half so good a stroll, as down among the steamboats on a bright morning.' As the passage continues, however, it catches fire in several places and ends in a steady blaze of dramatic excitement. Such a mood, tinged as it is with amusement, provides a fitting transition to the encounter with Mrs. Gamp and her

---

[1] Lest this account of the deliberate intensifying of effects be taken to confirm the question-begging charge that Dickens exaggerates, one technical fact should be pointed out. Since sensation and emotion in fiction can be aroused only through 'memory images', which scientists agree are normally only pale reflections of real experience, effects must be intensified if a convincing impression is to be made on the reader; cf. G. F. Stout, op. cit., pp. 136–40, R. S. Woodworth, *Psychology*, pp. 348–9.

sinister hints about murder on board the Antwerp packet, the discovery of Jonas Chuzzlewit on board the steamboat, and the dramatic impact which the mysterious letter from Nadgett makes upon him. Unfortunately, the more successful the description of the dockside scene is as a preparation of mood for what is to follow, the less suitable it is to sustain the preceding mood. Worse still, although the intention to sustain the first major effect is no sooner stated than dropped, a vague wish to link the two major effects still continues to haunt the passage and a fatal hesitation weakens the second effect.

The technical problem, here, is clearly a difficult one. Why did Dickens fail to solve it? What we know of his life at this time suggests that his failure resulted from haste and weariness. *Martin Chuzzlewit* was being written and serialized in monthly parts, each part appearing shortly after it had been written. The fifteenth monthly part, Chapters XXXIX, XL, and XLI, comprises the idyllic account of the Pinches' domestic life in London and the dramatic episode of Jonas's attempted flight. Now, since Dickens conceived and treated each monthly number to some extent as a unity[1], he would wish to dovetail the two major episodes of No. XV and their effects as neatly as possible. The fifteenth monthly number was published in April 1844, and was almost certainly written during the winter months, most probably in February or March.[2] From Forster, we know that Dickens found the writing of *Martin Chuzzlewit* an extremely anxious and exhausting task. There had been a drastic fall in circulation to twenty thousand, which increased by only three thousand when Dickens, on the strength of his success with *American Notes*, tried the effect of sending Martin to America. By November 1843 Dickens was complaining of 'a book taking so much out of one as Chuzzlewit', 'it is impossible to go on worknig the brain to that extent for ever', and his financial anxiety

---

[1] See the preface to the First Edition of *PP* (1837), and Dickens's letter to Mrs. Brookfield (20 Feb. 1866), *HD*, p. 599.

[2] Dickens could not have had much of *Chuzzlewit* in hand at this time. Up to the end of 1843, he was also engaged on *A Christmas Carol* and wrote in a letter to Professor Felton (2 Jan. 1844), *HD*, p. 102: 'To keep the Chuzzlewit going, and do this little book, the Carol, in the odd times between two parts of it, was, as you may suppose, pretty tight work.'

had reached such a pitch that he was seriously contemplating living abroad.[1]

Even when biographical pressures are absent, however, the joins in a story would seem to provide a difficult problem in terms of effect. On the one hand, unity of effect is to be preserved in a piece of description or a minor incident. On the other hand, such a description or incident is to join together two major sections of the story with very different, if not contradictory, effects. How is this problem to be solved? Some contradictory effects, particularly those of sympathy and irony, form a natural relationship and so bind together the heterogeneous material which they organize. Thus, in *Pickwick*, this kind of complex effect ensures a smooth transition from a cheerful to a gloomy mood. Chapter IV, which describes the adventures of the Pickwickians at the Field Day and the picnic with the Wardles, creates the mood of cheerfulness and vitality so often associated with this novel. Chapter V opens with two paragraphs that sustain this mood. Dickens describes the bright pleasant view which Mr. Pickwick contemplates from Rochester Bridge. This attractive reverie is suddenly interrupted by the ironic comment of 'the dismal man' which completely reinterprets the vision of Mr. Pickwick in a pessimistic manner: 'How common the saying ... "The morning's too fine to last." How well might it be applied to our every-day existence.' The dismal man goes on to review the prospect of suicide by drowning.

As Dickens matured, he showed increasing skill in building minor descriptions and incidents which create simple impressions into larger units and more complicated effects. He began by operating on a small scale. Thus, in *Oliver Twist*, the macabre description of Oliver's first night among the coffins at the undertaker's is carefully related from Oliver's viewpoint. His terror and the horror of the situation are calculated to arouse pity for him as the author makes clear when he comments: 'Nor were these the only dismal feelings which depressed Oliver. He was alone in a strange place; and we all know how chilled and desolate the best of us will

---

[1] Edgar Johnson, op. cit., vol. i, pp. 453–5; to John Forster (1, 2 Nov. 1843), *F*, vol. ii, pp. 45, 48, 47; for other sources of anxiety and weariness, see Johnson, op. cit., vol. i, pp. 491–505.

sometimes feel in such a situation. The boy had no friends to care for, or to care for him.' In *The Old Curiosity Shop*, a graphic picture of the bustling excitement of a festive town makes Nell's fear that she may be parted from her grandfather all the more real. A dilapidated summer-house provides an appropriate setting for Quilp's ironic humour and malice at Sampson Brass's expense.[1]

From the middle period of his career onwards, Dickens became increasingly more subtle and ambitious. In *Martin Chuzzlewit*, for example, the picture of an idyllic sunset in the peaceful countryside provides an ironic setting for Tigg's murder and an opportunity for a moment's regret in the victim which moves our pity for him. In *David Copperfield*, Dickens gives us two detailed views of Canterbury. In both, he insists on the calm agreeable antiquity of the place. Canterbury is associated with the change for the better in David's fortunes and the first picture sustains this pleasant mood. The second description, however, contrasts the present agitation of David at the prospect of Dora's death with the centuries of calm immutability that Canterbury represents. This contrast reflects the complex vision of the novel which is both compassionate and ironic. It does not shirk the poignancy of earlier experience yet refers it to the calmer and more critical context that time will provide:

Early in the morning, I sauntered through the dear old tranquil streets, and again mingled with the shadows of the venerable gateways and churches. The rooks were sailing about the cathedral towers; and the towers themselves, overlooking many a long unaltered mile of the rich country and its pleasant streams, were cutting the bright morning air, as if there were no such thing as change on earth. Yet the bells, when they sounded, told me sorrowfully of change in everything; told me of their own age, and my pretty Dora's youth; and of the many, never old, who had lived and loved and died, while the reverberations of the bells had hummed through the rusty armour of the Black Prince hanging up within, and, motes upon the deep of Time, had lost themselves in air, as circles do in water.

In *Great Expectations*, the dismal picture of Barnard's Inn

---

[1] *OT*, Chap. V, p. 29; *OCS*, Chap. XIX, XXI, pp. 148, 162 (cf. Chap. LI, pp. 381–2).

not only makes Pip's disappointment at his first lodgings in London more effective but it also foreshadows the frustration of Pip's great expectations: 'I had supposed that establishment to be an hotel kept by Mr. Barnard, to which the Blue Boar in our town was a mere public house . . . So imperfect was this realisation of the first of my great expectations, that I looked in dismay at Mr. Wemmick.' The qualification 'first' barely hints that there will be other disappointments, thus playing a tiny but effective part in the grand ironic structure of the novel. In *Our Mutual Friend*, the picture of the queer living-room of the Boffins has its own inherent impressiveness. It also provides an ironic burlesque on the *nouveau riche*. Unlike the simple sarcastic picture of the Veneerings' 'bran-new' residence, it sets the pretensions of such a class (represented by Mrs. Boffin's half of the room) alongside the more homely background (represented by Mr. Boffin's half) from which the *nouveau riche* have sprung. We have only to compare the view from the roof of Todgers's in *Martin Chuzzlewit* with the view from the dust heap in *Our Mutual Friend* to appreciate the skill and subtlety in using a piece of description that Dickens developed.[1]

The manuscript of *Bleak House* helps to show how Dickens learned to bind a book together into a more meaningful whole. It also confirms that, even as a conscious artist, Dickens could operate in the same novel on two different levels of achievement. Nevertheless, the difference here indicates all the more sharply the progress which Dickens was making in the art of the novel by this time.

Within the space of a single page, in the same chapter of *Bleak House*, Dickens describes two houses. One of these houses is Mr. Boythorn's:

⟨It was an old⟩ HE LIVED IN A PRETTY HOUSE, FOR-MERLY THE Parsonage-house, with a lawn in front, a BRIGHT flower-garden at the side, ⟨and a⟩ AND A WELL-STOCKED ORCHARD AND kitchen-garden in the rear, enclosed with ⟨an old⟩ A VENERABLE red wall that had of itself a ripened ruddy look. But, indeed, everything about the place wore an aspect of

[1] *MC*, Chap. XLVII, p. 724; *DC*, Chaps. XXXIX, LII, pp. 564, 742–3; *GE*, Chap. XXI, pp. 162–3; *OMF*, Bk. I, Chaps. II, V, pp. 6, 55–6; *MC*, Chap. IX, pp. 130–1, *OMF*; Bk. I, Chap. V, p. 57.

MATURITY AND abundance. The OLD LIME-TREE WALK
WAS LIKE A GREEN CLOISTER, THE VERY SHADOWS
OF THE cherry-trees and apple-trees were ⟨?loaded/?laden⟩
HEAVY with fruit, the gooseberry-bushes were so laden that
their branches arched and rested on the earth, the strawberries
and raspberries grew in like profusion, and the peaches basked
⟨upon⟩ BY THE HUNDRED ON the wall. Tumbled about among
the spread nets and the glass frames sparkling and winking in the
sun, there were such heaps of ⟨gourds and PODS AND⟩ DROOP-
ING PODS, AND marrows, and cucumbers, that every foot of
ground appeared a vegetable treasury, while the smell of sweet
herbs and all kinds of wholesome growth (TO SAY NOTHING
OF THE NEIGHBOURING MEADOWS WHERE THE HAY
WAS CARRYING) made the whole air a great nosegay. Such
stillness and composure reigned within the orderly precincts of
the OLD red wall, that even the feathers hung in garlands to
scare the birds hardly stirred; and the wall had such a ripening
influence that where, here and there high up, a disused nail and a
scrap of list still clung to it, it was easier to fancy that they had
mellowed with the changing seasons, than that they had rusted
and decayed according to the common fate.[1]

The other house is Chesney Wold, the country seat of Sir
Leicester and Lady Dedlock:

It was a picturesque old house, in a fine park richly wooded.
Among the trees, and not far from the residence, he pointed out
the spire of the little church of which he had spoken. O, the
solemn woods over which the light and shadow travelled swiftly,
as if Heavenly wings were sweeping on benignant errands, through
the summer air; the smooth green slopes, the glittering water, the
garden where the flowers were so symmetrically arranged in
clusters of the richest colours, how beautiful they looked! The
house, with gable and chimney, and tower, and turret, and dark
doorway, and broad terrace-walk, twining among the balustrades
of which, and lying heaped upon the vases, there was one great
flush of roses, seemed scarcely real in its light solidity, and in the
serene and peaceful hush that rested on all around it. To Ada and
to me, that, above all, appeared the pervading influence. On
everything, house, garden, terrace, green slopes, water, old oaks,
fern, moss, woods again, and far away across the openings in the

---

[1] Original MS. of *BH*, Vol. IB, Chap. XVIII, p. 15 ('red' after 'venerable', 'a'
before 'green cloister' and 'scrap' deleted and 's' added to 'cloister' in proof);
cf. *BH*, pp. 247–8.

prospect, to the distance lying wide before us with a purple bloom upon it, there seemed to be such undisturbed repose.

The manuscript is so badly scored and interlineated at this point that almost all the deletions are illegible. It is, however, just possible that 'light solidity' could be an addition since it appears to have been deleted above one of the original lines before being added for a second time.[1]

Both the previous descriptions might appear to be of the same order of achievement. Dickens has used the same method to describe each house. In each case, there is a simple unity of effect. Both houses are presented as attractive, Boythorn's home in its maturity and fruitfulness and Chesney Wold in its serene beauty. Both descriptions, that is, are deliberately organized to create a sympathetic view. All the revisions in the description of Boythorn's house and grounds intensify this effect and focus a more idealistic vision. In the case of each house, then, the vision is idealistic, some would even say sentimental.

Yet however harshly the description of Boythorn's home may be judged, that of Chesney Wold cannot finally be condemned on the grounds of idealization or sentimentality. Whatever is idealistic or sentimental, the very commonplaces, conventional responses, and clichés of feeling in this description are turned to great effect by Dickens later in the novel. For Esther Summerson comes to view Chesney Wold for a second time, in very different circumstances. The first time she had not known it was her mother's home. Then, nearly three hundred pages later, immediately following the painful scene in which Esther learns that she is the illegitimate daughter whom Lady Dedlock dare not acknowledge, this is how Dickens presents Chesney Wold through Esther's eyes:

The day waned into a gloomy evening, overcast and sad, and I still contended with the same feelings. I went out alone; and after walking a little in the park, watching the dark shades falling on the trees, and the fitful flight of the bats, that sometimes almost touched me, was attracted to the house for the first time.

[1] Ibid., p. 246; original MS. of *BH*, Vol. IB, Chap. XVIII, pp. 14–15 ('on' added after 'rested' in proof).

Perhaps I might not have gone near it, if I had been in a stronger frame of mind. As it was, I took the path that led close by it.

I did not dare to linger or to look up, but I passed before the terrace garden with its fragrant odours, and its broad walks, and its well-kept beds and smooth turf; and I saw how beautiful and grave it was, and how the old stone balustrades and parapets, and wide flights of shallow steps, were seamed by time and weather; and how the moss and ivy grew about them, AND AROUND THE OLD STONE PEDESTAL OF THE SUN-DIAL and were trained to keep the bounds; and I heard the fountain falling. Then the way went by long lines of DARK windows, diversified by turreted towers, and porches, of eccentric shapes, where old stone lions and grotesque monsters bristled outside dens of shadow, and snarled at the night over the FAMILY escutcheons they held in their grip. Thence the path wound underneath a gateway, and through a court-yard where the principal entrance ⟨seemed – ?–⟩ WAS (I HURRIED QUICKLY ON), and by the stables where none but deep voices seemed to be, whether in the ⟨– ?–⟩ MUR-MURING OF THE WIND THROUGH THE strong mass of ivy ⟨whispering to the wind⟩ holding to a HIGH red wall, or in the LOW COMPLAINING OF THE WEATHERCOCK, OR IN THE barking of the dogs, or in the slow striking of a clock. So, encountering presently a sweet smell of limes whose rustling I could hear, I turned with the turning of the path, to the south front; and there, above me, were the balustrades of the Ghost's Walk, and one lighted window that might be my mother's.

At the proof stage, 'feelings' was altered to 'distress' in the opening sentence, 'trained' was inserted before 'moss' in the first sentence of the second paragraph while 'and were trained to keep their bounds' was deleted; and 'night' in the following sentence was changed to 'gloom' in the first proof and in the second proof 'evening' was inserted before 'gloom' and 'family' deleted.[1]

The manuscript shows how Dickens deliberately intensifies the picture of a menacing, ghostly old mansion by adding such touches as 'DARK windows', 'I HURRIED QUICKLY ON', 'the MURMURING OF THE WIND THROUGH the strong mass of ivy', 'the LOW COMPLAINING OF THE WEATH-ERCOCK'. The *numinous* quality of this description is all the

[1] Original MS. of *BH*, Vol. IIA, Chap. XXXVI, pp. 9–10 ('which' after 'bats' substituted for 'that' in proof); cf. *BH*, pp. 514–15. Corrected proofs of *BH*, Chap. XXXVI, p. 361.

more important since it raises the story of Esther and her
mother from the level of the rather melodramatic conversation in the park to the heights of a genuine fate. The scandal
which threatens to, and eventually does, ruin the Dedlock
family is realized with particular effectiveness in the expression, 'where old stone lions and grotesque monsters
bristled outside dens of shadow, and snarled at the ⟨night⟩
EVENING GLOOM over the ⟨FAMILY⟩ escutcheons they
held in their grip'. Dickens's hesitation over 'family', which is
first inserted, then deleted, shows clearly what he meant to
imply figuratively by this piece of animism.[1] Fate is, in fact,
seen here and elsewhere in *Bleak House* not as a logical outcome of character[2] but as a terrible *presence* which is conjured up, like the Furies, by man's actions—in this case, by
Lady Dedlock's 'sin'.

At this point, it is interesting to note that immediately
before Dickens presents this new view of Chesney Wold he
directs our attention back to the earlier picture of the house:

I was alone; and, calm and quiet below me in the sun and shade,
lay the old house, with its terraces and turrets, on which there
had seemed to me to be such repose when I first saw it, but which
now looked like the obdurate and unpitying watcher of my mother's
misery.

Dickens now points out the irony in that former promise of
serenity and peace as Esther, shocked by her new knowledge,
glances back into the past. How deliberate Dickens's artistry
was here can be confirmed by the proofs in which he intensifies the irony still further by inserting 'complete' before
'repose'.[3] Furthermore, in that earlier view of Chesney Wold,
Dickens had carefully hinted, by his choice of the verbs,
'appeared' and 'seemed', instead of 'to be', and by that sly
description of the house as 'scarcely real in its light solidity'
that first appearances may be deceptive in the long run. Life
may seem promising yet teach us bitter disappointment

---

[1] Dickens had been deeply impressed when he read the MS. of Robert
Browning's *The Blot on the Scutcheon* in Nov. 1842; see Edgar Johnson, op.
cit., vol. i, p. 441.

[2] This is true even in the case of Richard Carstone; see below, pp. 351–2.

[3] Original MS. of *BH*, Vol. IIA, Chap. XXXVI, p. 8; cf. *BH*, p. 513.
Corrected proofs of *BH*, Chap. XXXVI, p. 360.

within the context of earlier brighter visions. Even the world of romantic possibilities, of the old superstitious legend and the conventional Gothic *frisson*, may find an unexpected and down-to-earth realization which seems all the more terrifying. Perhaps this is partly what Dickens means in his preface to the First Edition (1853) by 'the romantic side of familiar things'; he might also have referred, here, to 'the familiar realization of romantic things':

The way was paved here, like the terrace overhead, and ⟨all at once⟩ MY FOOTSTEPS from being noiseless made an echoing sound upon the flags. Stopping to look at nothing, but seeing all I did see as I went, I was passing quickly on, and in a few moments should have passed the lighted window, when my echoing footsteps brought it suddenly into my mind that there was a dreadful truth in the legend of the Ghost's Walk; that ⟨I was the phantom of the f–?– on the⟩ IT WAS I, WHO WAS TO BRING CALAMITY UPON THE STATELY HOUSE; AND THAT MY WARNING FEET WERE HAUNTING IT EVEN THEN. Seized with an augmented terror of myself which turned me cold, I ran from myself and everything, retraced the way by which I had come, and never paused until I had gained the lodge-gate, and the park lay sullen and black behind me.[1]

Dickens may be bringing out his novel in the much-maligned serial form yet skilful construction and a masterly control could hardly be better illustrated than the way he organizes these two contrasting views of Chesney Wold, hundreds of pages apart, into an ironic vision of the Dedlock scandal and the Dedlock fate. It would hardly be going too far to assert that, by means of this kind of structural organization which pervades *Bleak House*, Dickens is raising the mystery of Lady Dedlock and Esther's birth from the trite melodramatic material out of which it is wrought into something on a much higher plane altogether. Instead of the cheap thrills of a conventional and hackneyed intrigue acted out against some crudely daubed Gothic background, instead of the clumsily manipulated fortunes with which we are invited to involve ourselves on the lowest, most vicarious, level in, say, T. P. Prest's *Ela, the Outcast* (1838) or J. M. Rymer's *Ada the*

[1] Original MS. of *BH*, Vol. IIA, Chap. XXXVI, p. 10; cf. *BH*, p. 515.

Betrayed (1845),[1] we are given a detached vision which often approaches, if it does not always quite attain, a genuine tragic irony.

[1] Louis James, *Fiction for the Working Man*, pp. 106–10. Dickens's early novels were plagiarized by Prest.

IV

SYMPATHY AND IRONY

1. *Dickens and Bulwer-Lytton*

Poe's ideas about unity and effect led him to a curious concept of the novel that Dickens would never have accepted. For Poe, the long story, like the long poem, was 'simply a flat contradiction in terms':

> In almost all classes of composition, the unity of effect or impression is a point of the greatest importance. It is clear, moreover, that this unity cannot be thoroughly preserved in productions whose perusal cannot be completed at one sitting . . . The ordinary novel is objectionable, from its length, for reasons already stated in substance. As it cannot be read at one sitting, it deprives itself, of course, of the immense force deprivable from *totality*.[1]

Obviously Poe is unjust to the novel, though his bias towards the short story is understandable; it was where his own peculiar genius lay. Certainly, he anticipated much that the researches of experimental psychologists, particularly those of the *Gestalt* school, have since confirmed. Perception does seek to break down the chaos of experience into units which can be more readily assimilated. The mind will normally attend to a single stimulus for only a limited period. What Poe ignored about the process of perception, however, has also been confirmed by scientists, if not by common sense. The units of experience, when assimilated, are built into larger and more meaningful wholes. Attention may be sustained by varying the stimulus or even by discontinuing it for a period.[2] Poe seems to have remained blind to the possibility that simple effects might be built into an over-all unity of impression. The most obvious case is that of suspense which is

[1] E. A. Poe, 'The Poetic Principle', 'Twice-Told Tales', *Edgar Allan Poe*, ed. M. Alterton and H. Craig, pp. 378, 358–9.

[2] R. S. Woodworth, *Psychology*, pp. 447–51, 45–6, 320; cf. his *Experimental Psychology*, pp. 80, 624, and G. F. Stout, *A Manual of Psychology*, p. 133.

increased by breaks in reading rather than decreased. Clearly
enough, at one level, suspense gives *Edwin Drood*, say, or
much of *Great Expectations*, a unity of effect, the interest that
is aroused by a mystery.

True, a novel could be a mere succession of independent
effects. But such a novel would strike us as deficient. On the
other hand, how Dickens solves this problem of the fragmentation of effect involves much more than what may have so
far seemed only a cunning arrangement of interlocking
effects. It is here on the contrary that we meet structure,
effect, and vision in their most complex, integrated, and en-
riching form. (I do not refer simply to the craftsmanship
required of Dickens as a serial writer which is examined below
in Chapter VIII.)

One clue to this more complicated rhetoric of Dickens may
be found in the theories of Bulwer-Lytton, a close associate
of Dickens and a strong influence on him throughout his
career. Dickens and Bulwer first met in 1835; they greatly
admired each other's work, and their relationship became
extremely close after 1850. Dickens had a high opinion of
Bulwer's originality, skill, and power, and the story and
treatment in several of Bulwer's novels so strongly influenced
Dickens's invention and handling of similar plots, characters,
and themes as to be properly regarded as important source
material.[1]

The most striking example of Bulwer's enormous influence
on the literary judgement of Dickens occurs in the much-
misunderstood episode of the so-called happy ending to
Great Expectations. This example is all the more remarkable
when one considers that Dickens was at the height of his
fame, skill, and confidence.[2] Critics have generally assumed

[1] To Sir Edward Bulwer-Lytton (23 Jan., 12 May, 17 Sept. 1861) *HD*,
pp. 514, 517, 525; Jack Lindsay, *Charles Dickens*, pp. 167, 196–8, 234–5, 281,
364–9, 406–8, Earle Davis, *The Flint and the Flame*, pp. 106–8, 168, 240–1.

[2] That his hand in *GE* was a sure one may perhaps be confirmed by the
proofs, which, unlike those of earlier novels, seem to have been comparatively
lightly corrected. The proofs for *AYR* I have seen (corrected proofs of *GE*,
Victoria and Albert Museum, Forster Collection, 48. E. 24) are scarcely marked
except for corrected punctuation. Professor K. J. Fielding has drawn my
attention to another set in the Pierpont Morgan Library which he says might
be described as 'relatively slightly corrected, with main attention to punctuation and the precise choice of a word here and there'.

that Dickens agreed to change the ending of *Great Expectations*, on Bulwer's advice, for the worst possible reason.[1] One wonders whether some critics have properly compared the two endings, line by line. Thus, Edgar Johnson claims: 'He [Bulwer] urged Dickens to change it for one closing on a happier note. Could not Estella's heart be softened by sorrow and she and Pip brought together after all?'[2] Yet it is not completely true that the rejected ending is an unhappy one. Dickens suggests in the rejected ending that Estella is regenerated by suffering: 'for, in her face and in her voice, and in her touch, she gave me the assurance, that suffering had been stronger than Miss Havisham's teaching, and had given her a heart to understand what my heart used to be'. These words are incorporated in Estella's dialogue in the new ending: 'now, when suffering has been stronger than all other teaching, and has taught me to understand what your heart used to be'.[3] If the regeneration of Estella is improbable in the new ending, then it is improbable in the rejected ending too. If we accept the account of Estella's regeneration in the rejected ending, then we should also accept the reconciliation between Pip and Estella in the new ending, since this is only a logical development of that regeneration. The valid objection to the themes of regeneration and reconciliation is that they violate the tone of pessimistic irony which pervades and helps to unify the novel. But this objection may be levelled equally against both endings; perhaps critics do not object to the rejected ending because the break in tone is much weaker and therefore overlooked.

In a letter about the altered ending, Dickens explains: 'Bulwer, who has been, as I think you know, extraordinarily taken by the book, so strongly urged it upon me, after reading the proofs, and supported his view with such good reasons, that I have resolved to make the change.' Thus, Dickens does not indicate one but several reasons. With what we can learn of Bulwer's ideas about aesthetics and the art of fiction it seems very unlikely that all Bulwer's reasons were commercial

---

[1] For example, Lindsay, op. cit., pp. 345, 371.

[2] Edgar Johnson, *Charles Dickens: His Tragedy and Triumph*, vol. ii, p. 969; cf. Christopher Ricks, '*Great Expectations*', *Dickens and the Twentieth Century*, ed. John Gross and Gabriel Pearson (1966), p. 210.

[3] *GE*, Appendix: 'The Cancelled Conclusion', p. 461; Chap. LIX, p. 460.

or aimed at a cheap kind of popularity. A further letter adds
weight to this argument: 'Bulwer was so very anxious that
I should alter the end of *Great Expectations* . . . and stated his
reasons so well, that I have resumed the wheel and taken
another turn at it. Upon the whole, I think it is for the better.'[1]
It seems more probable that Bulwer would have urged on
Dickens something like the case presented above, that a
reconciliation between Pip and Estella was a natural development from Estella's regeneration which Dickens had already
made clear in his original ending. Moreover, even if Bulwer
did urge popular appeal as one of his reasons, it certainly
need not follow that he considered this kind of appeal alien to
the greatest literature.

Bulwer had studied the aesthetics of narrative art and its
popular appeal in some depth.[2] He closely associates together
two factors which help to explain the popular appeal of great
literature. These factors are the archetypal situation and the
universal experience of passions and character:

Goethe, treating of the drama, has said, that "to be theatrical
a piece must be symbolical; that is to say, every action must have
an importance of its own, and it must tend to one more important
still." It is still more important, for dramatic effect, that the
dramatis personae should embody attributes of passion, humour,
sentiment, character, with which large miscellaneous audiences
can establish sympathy; and sympathy can be only established
by such a recognition of a something familiar to our own natures,

[1] To John Forster (1 July 1861), *F*, vol. iii, pp. 335–6; to Wilkie Collins
(23 June 1861), *C*, p. 110. When Dickens suggested an unhappy ending to
A Strange Story, which ran in *AYR* immediately before *GE*, as the natural
tendency of the novel, Bulwer-Lytton rejected the advice; see Dickens's letter
to Bulwer-Lytton (20 May 1861), *HD*, p. 519. Professor K. J. Fielding points out
to me that the ending of *GE* we have is not entirely unambiguous and that the
ambiguity is deliberately increased both in proof and in the book as distinct
from the serial version.

[2] Edward Bulwer-Lytton, 'On Certain Principles of Art in Works of Imagination', 'Readers and Writers', 'The Sympathetic Temperament', *Miscellaneous
Prose Works* (1868), vol. iii, pp. 360, 497–8, 367–9, 361, 355, 365–6, 350, 194,
198–9, 368–9, 370; the essays were originally contributed in a series entitled
'Caxtoniana' to *Blackwood's* (1862–3) and first published as a complete collection
in 1863. 'On Art in Fiction' [1838], *Pamphlets and Sketches*, Knebworth
Edition, vol. xxxiv (1874), pp. 344–7, 323, 329, 331, 352. Bulwer uses the
term 'archetype', in the Jungian sense, in 'The Sympathetic Temperament',
Miscellaneous Prose, vol. iii, p. 195; cf. C. G. Jung, *Psychological Types*,
pp. 601–10.

or to our own conception of our natures, as will allure us to transport ourselves for the moment into the place of those who are passing through events which are not familiar to our actual experience.

From this, we can better appreciate the deep thinking which lay behind the following shrewd remark:

He who addresses the abstract reason, addresses an audience that must for ever be limited to the few; he who addresses the passions, the feelings, the humours, which we all have in common, addresses an audience that must for ever comprise the many. But either writer, in proportion to his ultimate renown, embodies some new truth, and new truths require new generations for cordial welcome. This much I would say meanwhile: Doubt the permanent fame of any work of science which makes immediate reputation with the ignorant multitude; doubt the permanent fame of any work of imagination which is at once applauded by a conventional clique that styles itself "the critical few."

Though Bulwer does distinguish between certain technical aspects of the drama and the novel, several of the laws which, he believes, govern dramatic art reappear as laws governing the art of fiction. In both drama and the novel, for example, he stresses that passions with which the reader can sympathize are essential in creating universal appeal:

It is always a living being in whom we sympathize. And the rarer and more unfamiliar the situation of life in which the poet places his imagined character, the more in that character itself we must recognise relations akin to our own flesh and blood, in order to feel interest in its fate. Thus, in the hands of great masters of fiction, whether dramatists or novelists, we become unconsciously reconciled, not only to unfamiliar, but to improbable, nay, to impossible situations, by recognising some marvellous truthfulness to human nature in the thoughts, feelings, and actions of the character represented, granting that such a character *could* be placed in such a situation.

He also insists that idealization is essential to all true art:

If we look to the greatest novel which Europe has yet produced ... we find the characters therein are vivid and substantial, capable of daily application to the life around us, in proportion as they are types and not portraits ... Those critics who, in modern times, have the most thoughtfully analysed the laws of aesthetic beauty, concur in maintaining that the real truthfulness of all works of imagination—sculpture, painting, written fiction—is so purely in the imagination, *that the artist never seeks to represent the positive truth, but the idealised image of a truth.* As Hegel well observes, "that which exists in nature is a something purely individual and particular. Art, on the contrary, is essentially destined to manifest the general."

Both these principles, the need for idealization and for sympathetic characters, play an important role in Dickens's narrative art.

Again, like Dickens, Bulwer regards communication as paramount, and rhetoric as the fundamental principle of narrative art. Yet, like Dickens, he is not advocating a crude appeal to the reader:

The first object of a novelist is to interest his reader; the next object is the quality of the interest. Interest in his story is essential, or he will not be read; but if the quality of the interest be not high, he will not be read a second time.

The ironic factor in Dickens's complex rhetoric helps to ensure that rereading will prove an interesting experience.

The ideas of complexity and rhetoric are linked in Bulwer's thought. Referring to the creative act of an original genius, he introduces the idea of complexity under the formula, 'life and intellect':

But the moment Art creates, it puts into its creations life and intellect; and it is only in proportion as the life thus bestowed endures beyond the life of man, and the intellect thus expressed exceeds that which millions of men can embody in one form, that we acknowledge a really great work of Art.

By 'life', Bulwer means the life of the passions. In 'On Art in Fiction', for example, he asserts that the primary concern of the great literary artist is not manners, not even character as such, but the passions. The same point is made in a later essay: 'And thus, as his domain is the passions, he must seek a plot which admits of situations for passion, and characters in harmony with such situations.' Moreover, the successful portrayal of the passions, as we have seen above, is partly a matter of rhetoric, for the appeal of the passions to the audience or reader must be made through sympathy. By sympathy, Bulwer means something very precise:

As Adam Smith has very well argued in his 'Theory of Moral Sentiments'—"Sympathy, though its meaning was, perhaps, originally the same as pity or compassion, is a word that may now without much impropriety be made use of to denote our fellow-feeling with any passion whatever." And the reader will have observed that it is in that sense that I employ the word. A person thus nervously impressionable may, from the very intensity of his regard for himself, easily transport his fancy to the situation of others, so long as he can picture himself in those situations, or so long as they appear to affect his comfort or safety.

It is through this kind of sympathy that the writer creates a convincing picture of the passions in his characters' lives:

Perpetually passing out of himself and his own positive circumstantial condition of being into other hearts and into other conditions, the poet obtains his knowledge of human life by transporting his own life into the lives of others. He who would create a character must, while creating, move and breathe in his own creation—he who would express a passion must, while expressing, feel his own heart beating in the type of man which the passion individualises and incarnates; thus sympathy is to the poet the indispensable element of his knowledge.

It is by the same means that the reader shares the lives and experience of the characters:

All delineations of passion involve the typical; because whoever paints a passion common to mankind presents us with a human type of that passion, varied, indeed, through the character of an individual and the situations in which he is placed; but still, in the expression of the passion itself, sufficiently germane to all in whom that passion exists, whether actively or latently, to permit the spectator to transfer himself into the place and person of him who represents it.

The artist elicits for his characters 'under all that is peculiar to their nature or their fates, the necessary degree of sympathy from emotions of which the generality of mankind are susceptible'. The rhetoric of sympathy, then, is a means whereby both writer and reader may pass through a similar experience.

Human psychology is such that the writer and the reader carry out their separate functions by enacting the same process and that process is sympathetic involvement in the lives and passions of characters.

Bulwer indicates that great literature is a combination of this process with a second factor which he calls 'intellect'. By intellect, here, Bulwer can hardly mean simply the intellect of his characters; it is rather the intellect of the artist. In terms of the intellect, an adequate parallel to the process of sympathetic involvement would be a series of judgements on the characters and their passions. In terms of rhetoric, this would not imply direct comment by the author so much as a system whereby judgement was directed within the reader. One remark by Bulwer in 'On Art in Fiction' deserves singling out:

We must let the heart be a student as well as the head. No man who is a passionless and cold spectator, will ever be an accurate analyst, of all the motives and springs of action. Perhaps if we were to search for the true secret of Creative Genius, we should find that secret in the intenseness of its Sympathies.

Although he is correcting, perhaps over-correcting, the fault of intellectualization, Bulwer insists on the dual character of the writer's attitude towards his creation, the antithesis between his intellect and his feelings and, paradoxically, the need for co-operation between them. In the matter of *Great Expectations*, Bulwer may well have pointed out that the harsh ironic fate of the hero needs to be balanced by a more compassionate ending, that too severe a judgement on Pip would leave the reader with a cynical vision of life, alienate his sympathy, and spoil the final effect of the book. Since Dickens had criticized the ending of a story on very similar grounds six years earlier,[1] he would have been all the more likely to appreciate the force of Bulwer's objection. Furthermore, as we can see from *Hard Times*, Dickens was also preoccupied with the antithesis between 'heart' and 'head' and their proper relationship.

Yet how far did Bulwer's ideas about fiction in general influence Dickens? Certainly, *Caxtoniana*, in which Bulwer

[1] To Miss Emily Jolly (17 July 1855), *HD*, p. 374.

finally clarified his ideas and from which many of the previous quotations have been taken, belongs to the period when Dickens was so strongly under Bulwer's influence as to modify the ending of *Great Expectations*. It is even possible that discussion with Dickens prompted this series of essays and that there was a genuine exchange of ideas. A discussion between them on coincidence in *A Tale of Two Cities*[1] suggests a general dialogue on narrative art which may well have been conducted on the same fairly high level. In his scattered comments on narrative art and more especially in his practice, Dickens shares many basic concepts with Bulwer which include the need for idealization, the importance of the rhetoric of sympathy, the great possibilities in fiction (as distinct from the drama) of the multiple catastrophe, the severe demands made by verisimilitude in the novel, the rich manner in which the sub-plots of fiction may fill out the picture of a whole society, the wide scope offered by the portrayal of evil and criminal characters and more especially by the analysis of the criminal's guilt, the importance of showing the influence of early environment on the criminal's character.[2] The traffic in ideas was not only one way, for Bulwer was prepared to master the special art of weekly serialization

---

[1] To Sir Edward Bulwer-Lytton (5 June 1860), *HD*, pp. 498–9.

[2] Bulwer-Lytton, 'On Art in Fiction', *Pamphlets and Sketches*, pp. 351, 346, 347, 326–8. For Dickens's conscious practice of these principles, see below, pp. 252–4, 232–5, Dickens's letters to Mrs. Brookfield (20 Feb. 1866), Miss Emily Jolly (30 May 1857), Mrs. Gaskell (3 May 1853), Miss King (24 Feb. 1855), *HD*, pp. 599–600, 427–8, 288, 360; to W. H. Wills (13 Apr. 1855), *W*, p. 161; and cf. the cases of Bill Sikes, Jonas Chuzzlewit, and Bradley Headstone, Dickens's remarks on Jonas's upbringing in his Preface to the First Cheap Edition of *MC*, (1849) and Uriah Heap's account of his own upbringing, *DC*, Chap. XXXIX, pp. 574–5. Yet again I am indebted to Professor K. J. Fielding who points out that John Forster was the link between Dickens and Bulwer-Lytton and kindly refers me to generous quotations from a collection of unpublished letters which passed between Forster and Bulwer (2 Feb. 1838–25 Dec. 1845); this collection, owned by Lady Hermione Cobbold of Knebworth, is now in the Hertfordshire County Record Office. These letters help to substantiate the contention that Bulwer was an influence on Dickens throughout his career. Professor Fielding adds that Bulwer taught Forster a good deal and that Forster's criticism of the novel in the *Examiner* shows him to have been steeped in a knowledge of how the novelist communicated with his readers. Forster, of course, acted as friend, adviser, and literary agent for both Dickens and Bulwer-Lytton. Since Bulwer's theories were also applied to drama, it may be relevant that he and Dickens collaborated closely over the work on *Not So Bad As We Seem*.

under Dickens's tuition[1] at the same time that Dickens was prepared to listen to his advice about the conclusion of *Great Expectations*. Furthermore, any influence of Bulwer on Dickens may have begun very early. He may have been familiar with Bulwer's 'On Art in Fiction', which was originally published in the *Monthly Chronicle* in 1838, or at least with its ideas through his early relationship with Bulwer. It is indisputable that many of the principles of narrative art in Bulwer's early essay were put into practice by Dickens from 1838 onwards with striking success.

Further insight into what a complex reaction in the reader may involve is given by a contemporary of Bulwer-Lytton and Dickens, Leslie Stephen, when he defines the critic's ideal relationship with the work he is reading as a paradox of involvement and detachment:

> To be an adequate critic is almost to be a contradiction in terms; to be susceptible to a force, and yet free from its influence; to be moving with the stream, and yet to be standing on the bank.

And when Stephen goes on to describe the critic's ideal attitude as 'to feel strongly, and yet to analyse coolly'[2], he is describing the kind of reaction I would expect the rhetoric of sympathy and irony to help to produce in the responsible reader. But before this complex effect can be understood, it is necessary to consider the rhetoric of sympathy and the rhetoric of irony separately.

2. *The Rhetoric of Sympathy*

Sympathy in Dickens's fiction is taken for granted and has never been properly analysed. As we have seen, Bulwer-Lytton was astute enough to distinguish between two kinds of sympathy, yet Dickens was conscious of four distinct kinds which critics and even professional writers on aesthetics confuse.[3] Linguistic and scientific authorities have confirmed

[1] To Sir Edward Bulwer-Lytton (12 May, 17 Sept. 1861), *HD*, pp. 517–19, 525–6; cf. letter to Wilkie Collins (12 July 1861), *C*, p. 112.

[2] Leslie Stephen, 'Hours in a Library'. No. XVII. 'Charlotte Bronte', *Cornhill Magazine*, xxxvi (1877), reprinted in *Hours in a Library* (1909), vol. iii, p. 2.

[3] See William McDougall, *An Introduction to Social Psychology* (1960), p. 78. E. F. Carritt, *An Introduction to Aesthetics* (1949), pp. 88–9, does not satisfactorily distinguish the various senses of 'sympathy'.

that there really are these distinctions to be made in examining sympathy. Thus, the *OED* subdivides the extant general meaning of the word into the four senses with which Dickens was familiar and on which a brief study by the social psychologist, William McDougall, throws some light.[1]

Because Dickens was aware of these four distinct kinds of sympathy, he was able to use them with great skill to enrich his work. For example, he was conscious of the kind of sympathy by means of which a writer can bring a living concrete experience to his readers. Thus, he describes the phenomenon as a form of sympathy: 'There was a clock in the room, which the stranger often turned to look at. Tom made frequent reference to it also: partly from a nervous sympathy with its taciturn companion.' He shows that he understands the mechanism involved: Wardle's excitement is said to have 'communicated itself to Mr. Pickwick also'. He describes the process as a kind of infection or contagion which spreads rapidly and cannot be resisted, an analogy also adopted by modern science: Noah Claypole is said to be 'infected' by the Jew's intense excitement and the joyful antics of Mark Tapley are described as 'contagious'. He sees the process as a kind of bodily possession by the emotions of another person: Jobling is said to have 'been so horribly frightened . . . that his terror seizes' Guppy.[2] He is also aware of the wide variety of emotions involved; even the few instances already cited range from joy and laughter to excitement, anxiety, and terror.

This is the type of sympathy which McDougall calls 'primitive passive sympathy' or the 'sympathetic induction of the emotions' and which he carefully distinguishes from 'active sympathy':

The fundamental and primitive form of sympathy is exactly what the word implies, a suffering with, the experiencing of any feeling or emotion when and because we observe in other persons or creatures the expression of that feeling or emotion . . . A merry face makes us feel brighter; a melancholy face may cast a gloom

---

[1] McDougall, op. cit., pp. 69, 77–82, 131–2, 144–9. McDougall's account of sympathy is so well established that it is cited without comment in James Drever, *A Dictionary of Psychology* (1952), p. 285.

[2] *MC*, Chap. V, p. 74; *PP*, Chap. IX, p. 114; *OT*, Chap. XLV, p. 345; *MC*, Chap. LIV, p. 832; *BH*, Chap. XXXII, p. 459.

over a cheerful company; when we witness the painful emotion of others, we experience sympathetic pain; when we see others terror-stricken or hear their scream of terror, we suffer a pang of fear though we know nothing of the cause of their emotion or are indifferent to it; anger provokes anger; the curious gaze of the passer-by stirs our curiosity; and a display of tender emotion touches, as we say, a tender chord in our hearts. In short, each of the great primary emotions . . . seems to be capable of being excited by way of this immediate sympathetic response.

This is very close to sense 3b in the *OED*: 'The quality or state of being affected by the condition of another with a feeling similar or corresponding to that of the other; the fact or capacity of entering into or sharing the feelings of another or others; fellow feeling. Also, a feeling or frame of mind evoked by and responsive to some external influence.' McDougall singles out laughter as the most familiar and infectious instance of the sympathetic induction of emotion: 'Laughter is notoriously infectious all through life, and this . . . affords the most familiar example of sympathetic induction of an affective state.' Dickens also understood this process: 'the flattest echo in the neighbourhood seemed to catch the contagion, and to laugh as enjoyingly as he did, or as we did when we heard him laugh'; 'there was something contagious in Kit's laugh, for his mother, who had looked grave before, first subsided into a smile, and then fell to joining in it heartily, which occasioned Kit to say that he knew it was natural, and to laugh the more.'[1]

Furthermore, Dickens extends the idea of the sympathetic induction of emotion to include inanimate objects: 'The dark servant . . . was quickly heard reascending the stairs in such a tremulous state, that the plates and dishes on the tray he carried, trembling sympathetically as he came, rattled again, all the way up.' This extension was the basis of his celebrated use of both animism and of pathetic fallacy: 'The panting of the horses communicated a tremulous motion to the coach,

---

[1] *BH*, Chap. IX, p. 117; *OCS*, Chap. XXII, p. 167. This capacity for empathy is not unrelated to Dickens's later career as a reader in which he acted the parts of many of the characters in his novels. Robert Garis argues that Dickens always wants to steal the show in his novels; it is arguable that, on the contrary, the novels reveal Dickens's enormous capacity for being many other, quite different, people.

as if it were in a state of agitation. The hearts of the passengers beat loud enough perhaps to be heard; but at any rate, the quiet pause was audibly expressive of people out of breath, and holding the breath, and having the pulses quickened by expectation.' Animism and pathetic fallacy in Dicken's fiction are rather more than conventional tricks taken over from a traditional element in poetry.[1] Through these devices, Dickens harnesses a vital primitive response which enriches the sense of life in his novels and focuses a genuine vision of a spiritual world pervading and encompassing the everyday scene. Dickens shows all things to be interlocked in a mutual bond of sympathy, a view which the growth of science may have reduced to the kind of quaint nonsense to be found in Burton's *Anatomy of Melancholy* but which still has a psychological and spiritual significance for which men may yearn in a world of stifling materialistic values. Dickens, in fact, restores to the vision of the artist in his own time that ancient view of the 'Great Chain of Being'[2] and of the 'Correspondences' which we find, say, in Sir John Davies's *Orchestra* or Sir Thomas Browne's *The Garden of Cyrus*. Thus, Dickens is able to view society in *Little Dorrit* as one great prison or the world of Victorian money-grubbing in *Our Mutual Friend* as a vast dunghill. This kind of vision is described by Carlyle, whose writings Dickens read and greatly admired:

Of this latter sort are all true Works of Art: in them (if thou know a Work of Art from a Daub of Artifice) wilt thou discern Eternity looking through Time; the Godlike rendered visible . . . Man thereby, though based, to all seeming, on the small Visible does nevertheless extend down into the infinite deeps of the Invisible, of which Invisible, indeed, his life is properly the bodying forth . . . the Universe is but one vast Symbol of God.

Carlyle's influence on Dickens's social and historical ideas has also been recognized but not his influence on Dickens's

---

[1] *D & S*, Chap. XX, p. 273; *TTC*, Bk. I. Chap. II, p. 6. By the nineteenth century, pathetic fallacy has very largely become a dead element in English poetry; cf. Arnold's use of the device as an embellishment in, say, *Sohrab and Rustum*, ll. 480–5, with Milton's genuine cosmic vision in *Paradise Lost*, Bk. IX, ll. 780–5.

[2] See Arthur O. Lovejoy, *The Great Chain of Being* (Cambridge, Mass., 1942).

spiritual beliefs.[1] Yet it is a similar authentic experience of a single spiritual life vibrating throughout the Dickens world which gives birth to the living symbol (as distinct from the dead cipher) in Dickens's fiction, a distinction with which the novelist was almost certainly familiar in Carlyle's work:

Of Symbols, however, I remark farther, that they have both an extrinsic and intrinsic value; oftenest the former only . . . But, on the whole, as Time adds much to the sacredness of Symbols, so likewise in his progress he at length defaces, or even desecrates them; and Symbols, like all terrestrial Garments, wax old . . . Alas, move whithersoever you may, are not the tatters and rags of superannuated worn-out Symbols (in this Ragfair of a World) dropping off everywhere . . . Those same Church-Clothes have gone sorrowfully out-at-elbows; nay, far worse, many of them have become mere hollow Shapes, or Masks, under which no living Figure or Spirit any longer dwells; but only spiders and unclean beetles in horrid accumulation, drive their trade; and the mask still glares on you with its glass-eyes; in ghastly affectation of Life.

The 'sympathetic induction of emotion' can be clearly seen at work in a particular rhetorical device which Dickens uses. The reader's response is embodied within the dramatic context of the story. A character, that is, takes over the reader's point of view and by registering his reaction helps to stimulate, direct, and strengthen it. Dickens was certainly aware of the nature of this device and its usefulness. When Mark Tapley, for example, appears for the first time in *Martin Chuzzlewit*, Dickens makes every effort to establish him at once as a sympathetic character. Thus, in the manuscript of the novel, Dickens deliberately adds Tom Pinch's immediate reaction which is favourable to Mark and so helps to induce a favourable reaction in the reader: ' "And how spruce you are, too!" said Mr. Pinch, SURVEYING HIM WITH GREAT PLEASURE. "Really I didn't think you were half such a tight-made fellow, Mark!" ' Again, in the manuscript of *Bleak House*, Dickens shapes the reader's response to

[1] Thomas Carlyle, *Sartor Resartus* [1833–4], People's Edition (1872), Bk. III, Chap. III, pp. 149–56; see also Mildred G. Christian, 'Carlyle's Influence upon the Social Theory of Dickens', *The Trollopian* [now *Nineteenth-Century Fiction*] (March, June 1947), 27–35, 11–26. For a similar view of 'symbols' and how they differ from 'signs', see C. G. Jung, *Psychological Types*, pp. 601–10.

Richard's tragic and ironic plight into an appropriate pity through a similar reaction in Esther Summerson; his first version of Esther's reaction, a rather egocentric state of shock, is carefully altered to a genuine concern: 'IT ⟨I had been shocked⟩ HAD GIVEN ME A PANG to hear him sob, and see the tears start out between his fingers; but that was infinitely less AFFECTING TO ME, than the hopeful animation with which he said these words.'[1] A further instance of this device occurs in the episode from *Hard Times* in which Sissy Jupe tells Louisa the story of her father's one outburst of anger.[2]

The 'Sympathetic induction of emotion' has a further importance. It is the basis of all other forms of sympathy which Dickens uses. Consider the form, sometimes called affinity, of which Dickens shows he was well aware when he comments on 'the child's unconscious sympathy with youth' and an 'old man's enthusiasm . . . felt in sympathy with the only creature to whom he was linked by ties of long association'. This form corresponds to sense 3a in the *OED* and is described by McDougall as follows:

Active sympathy . . . is of prime importance for the development of the sentiment of affection between equals . . . It involves a reciprocal relation between at least two persons; either party to the relation not only is apt to experience the emotions displayed by the other, but he desires also that the other shall share his own emotions; he actively seeks the sympathy of the other, and, when he has communicated his emotion to the other, he attains a peculiar satisfaction which greatly enhances his pleasure and his joy . . . the sharing of our emotion by another intensifies our own emotion by way of the fundamental reaction of primitive sympathy.

Many of the factors in what McDougall calls 'active sympathy' and the *OED* 'conformity of feelings, inclinations, or temperament, which makes persons agreeable to each other; community of feeling, harmony of disposition' can be seen in the following:

After this, whenever Sissy dropped a curtsey to Mr. Gradgrind in the presence of his family, and said in a faltering way, "I beg

---

[1] Original MS. of *MC*, Victoria and Albert Museum, Forster Collection, 47. A. 15 (Vol. IA), Chap. V, p. 31; cf. *MC*, p. 66. Original MS. of *BH*, Vol. IB, Chap. XXIII, p. 4; cf. *BH*, p. 323.　　　　[2] See below, pp. 125–6.

your pardon, Sir, for being troublesome—but—have you had any letter yet about me ?" Louisa would suspend the occupation of the moment, whatever it was, and look for the reply as earnestly as Sissy did. And when Mr. Gradgrind regularly answered, "No, Jupe, nothing of the sort," the trembling of Sissy's lip would be repeated in Louisa's face, and her eyes would follow Sissy with compassion to the door.[1]

Louisa is sharing Sissy's distress about her father, the reciprocal principle which McDougall stresses. We see 'the sympathetic induction of emotion' at work in 'the trembling of Sissy's lip repeated in Louisa's face'. The passage is of immense importance in the novel since it indicates Louisa's better nature. The rejection of this sympathetic bond with Sissy marks a special crisis of the book and leads to Louisa's catastrophe. The resumption of the sympathetic relationship with Sissy marks a further crisis and results in the dénouement. Without a full appreciation of the sympathetic link between Sissy and Louisa we cannot grasp either Louisa's character or the function of Sissy in the novel.

Again, the sympathetic induction of emotion is involved in another type of sympathy especially important in Dickens's case. This type of sympathy is the specific sense 3c in the definition of the *OED*: 'The quality or state of being thus affected by the suffering or sorrow of another; a feeling of compassion or commiseration.' McDougall explains:

Pity in its simplest form is tender emotion tinged with sympathetically induced pain. It differs from sorrow, which also is essentially a painful tender emotion, in the sympathetic character of the pain, and in that it does not imply the existence of any sentiment of affection or love, as sorrow does, and is therefore a more transient experience, and one with less tendency to look before and after . . . The pain of sorrow is, then, a self-regarding pain, whereas the pain of pity is not; hence pity is rightly regarded as the nobler emotion.

Consider, for example, the passage from *Hard Times* in which Sissy describes her father's failure and the beating of Merrylegs:

"Father, soon after they came home from performing, told Merrylegs to jump up on the backs of the two chairs and stand

---

[1] *OCS*, Chap. LIV, p. 408; *MC*, Chap. XI, p. 181; *HT*, Bk. I, Chap. IX, pp. 61–2.

across them—which is one of his tricks. He looked at father and didn't do it at once. Everything of father's had gone wrong that night, and he hadn't pleased the public at all. He cried out that the very dog knew he was failing, and had no compassion on him. Then he beat the dog, and I was frightened, and said, 'Father, father! Pray don't hurt the creature who is so fond of you! O Heaven forgive you, father, stop!' And he stopped, and the dog was bloody, and father lay down crying on the floor with the dog in his arms, and the dog licked his face."

Louisa saw that she was sobbing; and going to her, kissed her, took her hand, and sat down beside her.[1]

The effect on the reader is one of moderate compassion sharpening to acute pathos. Now that we are in a position to isolate the various elements which make up the effect we should appreciate the skilful way the effect has been engineered. The element of pain is sympathetically induced by a clever device. It is difficult for Dickens to represent an internal emotional state without an 'objective correlative' in the physical world. He therefore has Jupe displace the pain of his own humiliation on to the dog. Physical pain represents mental pain, the beaten dog symbolizes the humiliated clown, and we feel the humiliation of Jupe in the pain of the whipped dog. Again, tender emotion is conveyed in the protective consoling act of the dog when it licks the face of the clown. At the climax of the effect, both elements, that of pain ('the dog was bloody') and that of tender emotion ('the dog licked his face') are brought together. The sympathy of the reader is also channelled through the reaction of Sissy and Louisa to the episode. The element of pain is conveyed by Sissy's tears and that of tender emotion expressed by the protective gesture of Louisa.

That Dickens was conscious of sympathetically induced pain in the relationship between author, book, and reader whenever pity is evoked, of the dangers of its creating a ludicrous effect, and, indeed, of its comic possibilities, can be seen in the penultimate paragraph of a chapter in *Pickwick*. Dickens also shows he is aware of the mechanisms involved when he sets out to create a serious effect of pathos. In the

[1] *HT*, Bk. I, Chap. IX, p. 60.

manuscript of *Oliver Twist*, for example, occurs the following revised passage:

At length, a low cry of pain broke the stillness that prevailed; and uttering it, the boy awoke. His left arm ⟨hung heavy and useless at his⟩, RUDELY BANDAGED IN A SHAWL, hung heavy and useless at his side; and the bandage was saturated with blood. He was so weak, that he could scarcely raise himself into a sitting posture; and when he had done so, he looked feebly round for help, and groaned with pain. Trembling in every joint, from cold and exhaustion, he made an effort to stand upright; but, shuddering from head to foot, fell prostrate on the ground.

After a short return of the stupor in which he had been so long plunged, ⟨the boy again rose⟩ OLIVER: URGED BY A CREEPING ⟨–?– STILLNESS⟩ SICKNESS AT HIS HEART, WHICH SEEMED TO WARN HIM THAT IF HE LAY THERE, HE MUST SURELY DIE: GOT UPON HIS FEET, AND ESSAYED TO WALK. His head was dizzy; and he staggered to and fro like a drunken man; but he kept up, nevertheless, and, WITH HIS HEAD DROOPING LANGUIDLY ON HIS BREAST, went stumbling onward, he knew not whither.[1]

True, the first sentence produces an element of sympathetically induced pain, while the original version of the second sentence, with its stress on the helpless condition of the arm, appeals to the protective tender emotion. The revisions, however, sharpen the pathos of Oliver's plight. Thus, it looks as if Dickens may not have intended at first to refer to the bandaging of the arm with the shawl or to the blood, but, by adding these further reminders of suffering, he once more induces pain in the reader. Moreover, the two elements which make up the effect of pathos are brought closer together by being included in one sentence and by being concentrated on one object, the arm, and therefore invite a more intimate fusion. This fusion is helped considerably by the added phrase, 'rudely bandaged in a shawl', for while 'rudely' suggests a painful process 'bandaged' indicates some sort of protective care and 'shawl', perhaps, has faint maternal associations. Again, in the opening sentence of the second paragraph, Dickens had at first intended to stress only the helplessness

[1] *PP*, Chap. X, p. 131. Original MS. of *OT*, Victoria and Albert Museum, Forster Collection, 47. A. 2 (Vol. IB), Bk. II, Chap. VI, pp. 11–12; cf. *OT*, Chap. XXVIII, p. 206.

of Oliver but added an element of physical suffering with the phrase, 'a creeping sickness at the heart'. My argument that Dickens wished to stress suffering at this point is supported by a further revision of this phrase, for Dickens had at first written 'stillness' and then emended this to 'sickness'. In the final sentence, on the other hand, Dickens stresses the element of helplessness when he adds 'with his head drooping languidly on his breast'; physical suffering is already present in 'his head was dizzy'. Again we see the concentration on a single object, the head this time, which helps the separate elements in the effect to fuse.

How Dickens deliberately tries to control the drift towards staginess in his use of pathos can be seen in the climax of the episode in which Louisa deserts Bounderby to confront her father. Significantly enough, pain is coupled with a tender protective gesture: 'Her father's face was ashy white, and he held her in both his arms.' The manuscript shows that Dickens had originally intended to try for the effect here through a piece of particularly stagey dialogue: ' "You did not tell me, ⟨-?-⟩ unhappy daughter." '[1] Fortunately he erased this dialogue, which only makes a clumsy attempt to induce pain in the reader, and substituted a mime that is more eloquent than spoken words.

The fourth kind of sympathy which Dickens uses implies approval. The *OED* refers to this type under 3d as the 'weakened sense', its development is very late and the other three senses are much older. It is worth pointing out, therefore, that the word may be used as a critical term without implying the sense of approval and, furthermore, that the sense of approval need not be restricted to 'moral approval'. This is confirmed by McDougall as regards the sympathetic induction of emotion, 'This primitive sympathy implies none of the higher moral qualities', and he also points out that 'sympathy, then, whether in the active or the passive form, is not the root of altruism' though he adds that sympathy does play an auxiliary role in the formation of moral sentiments: 'But, although it is not in itself the root of altruism, it is a most valuable adjunct to the tender emotion in the formation of altruistic sentiments and in stimulating social cooperation.'

[1] *HT*, Bk. II, Chap. XII, p. 218; original MS. of *HT*, Chap. XXVIII, p. 31.

This helps to explain why Stephen Blackpool's indictment of the misery inflicted by contemporary industrialism wins our approval, whereas that of Slackbridge fails to do so. Stephen tells Rachel:

"I ha' fell into th'pit, my dear, as have cost wi'in the knowledge o' old fok now livin, hundreds and hundreds o' men's lives—fathers, sons, brothers, dear to thousands an' thousands, an' keeping 'em fro' want and hunger. I ha' fell into a pit that ha' been wi' th' Fire-damp crueller than battle. I ha' read on't in the public petition, as onny one may read, fro' the men that works in pits, in which they ha' pray'n and pray'n the lawmakers for Christ's sake not to let their work be murder to 'em, but to spare 'em for th' wives and children that they loves as well as gentlefok loves theirs. When it were in work, it killed wi'out need; when 'tis let alone, it kills wi'out need. See how we die an' no need, one way an' another—in a muddle—every day!"

Slackbridge addresses the workers of Coketown:

"Oh my friends, the down-trodden operatives of Coketown! Oh my friends and fellow-countrymen, the slaves of an iron-handed and a grinding despotism! Oh my friends and fellow-sufferers, and fellow-workmen, and fellow-men! I tell you that the hour is come, when we must rally round one another as One united power, and crumble into dust the oppressors that too long have battened upon the plunder of our families, upon the sweat of our brows, upon the labour of our hands, upon the strength of our sinews, upon the God-created glorious rights of Humanity, and upon the holy and eternal privileges of Brotherhood!"[1]

In Stephen's case there is a sympathetic bond with the reader while Slackbridge leaves us cold. Stephen is a living instance of the misery he condemns while, with his empty pompous clichés, Slackbridge fails to move our sympathy for the down-trodden operatives.

The four kinds of sympathy need not occur in isolation. A more complicated effect may be produced when they combine. In the account of the 'new relationship' between the child and Father of the Marshalsea, as indeed in so much of *Little Dorrit*, the sympathy of approval, affinity, and pathos are so

---

[1] *HT*, Bk. III, Chap. VI, p. 272; Bk. II, Chap. IV, p. 138.

closely interwoven that they appear to fuse together and focus a powerful and profound vision:

At first, such a baby could do little more than sit with him, deserting her livelier place by the high fender, and quietly watching him. But this made her so far necessary to him that he became accustomed to her, and began to be sensible of missing her when she was not there. Through this little gate, she passed out of childhood into the care-laden world . . .

With no earthly friend to help her, or so much as to see her, but the one so strangely assorted; with no knowledge even of the common daily tone and habits of the common members of the free community who are not shut up in prisons; born and bred, in a social condition, false even with a reference to the falsest condition outside the walls; drinking from infancy of a well whose waters had their own peculiar stain, their own unwholesome and un-natural taste; the Child of the Marshalsea began her womanly life.

No matter through what mistakes and discouragements, what ridicule (not unkindly meant, but deeply felt) of her youth and little figure, what humble consciousness of her own babyhood and want of strength, even in the matter of lifting and carrying; through how much weariness and hopelessness, and how many secret tears; she trudged on, until recognised as useful, even indispensable. That time came. She took the place of eldest of the three, in all things but precedence; was the head of the fallen family; and bore, in her own heart, its anxieties and shames.[1]

The satisfying richness of this compassionate vision is due in no small measure to the complexity of the emotional appeal. It is not simply that this appeal rapidly alternates between pathos and approval but that each interacts with and rein-forces the other. We pity Amy and her father in their im-prisonment and bereavement and we also admire Amy's struggle to take her dead mother's place. Yet the record of this struggle, in its turn, focuses an even more compassionate vision of the widower and of the small girl's painful strivings to shoulder the heavy burden of adulthood. While throughout all this the growing affinity between father and daughter seems all the more compelling because it reflects our approval and compassion.

As we saw earlier, a sound rhetoric may impose severe

[1] *LD*, Bk. I, Chap. VII, pp. 71–2 (instead of 'trudged', the MS., proofs, and First Edition read 'drudged' which makes better sense).

limitations on Dickens's narrative and vision. Some further limitations, as well as possibilities, are disclosed by a study of the *means* by which the rhetoric of sympathy is managed in Dickens's fiction.

Viewpoint, for example, opens up great possibilities. With the exception of *Bleak House*, Dickens fairly consistently adopts throughout one novel either the first person or omniscience. Both these conventions offer Dickens considerable scope for the manipulation of sympathy. Clearly, viewpoint affords a ready means of identification; it enables the sympathetic induction of emotion to operate more smoothly and powerfully. In this respect, omniscience is more flexible than first person narrative since it allows a shift to the viewpoint of any character in the story. On the other hand, first person narrative creates a more intense sympathy since the effect, here, is cumulative. Obviously, this partly explains the strong sympathy we feel for Pip or David Copperfield, though the case of Esther Summerson shows that care is needed in handling first person narrative. Since the primitive form of sympathy need not imply approval, we can readily identify with either a moral or an immoral character when we share his viewpoint. Thus, the occasional shift to the viewpoint of Oliver Twist, on the morning after the burglary for example, helps us to share his experience more directly and so intensifies our concern for him. The case of the villain, however, a comparatively new technique in English fiction, makes the point all the more forcefully. The shift to Fagin's viewpoint in court and the condemned cell or to Jonas Chuzzlewit's viewpoint during and after the murder of Montague Tigg ensures that we share the Jew's terror or Jonas's guilt and so experience a certain measure of concern for their plight. The shift to Sikes's viewpoint during Nancy's murder and his subsequent flight is very similar to the case of Jonas Chuzzlewit.[1]

---

[1] The alternation of viewpoints in *BH* between first person narrative and omniscience helps to focus both a vision which is primarily sympathetic and one which is primarily ironic. Thus, a complex effect is at work, here, through viewpoint. Compare *OT*, Chap. LII, pp. 404–8; *MC*, Chaps. XLVI, XLVII, pp. 717–19, 720–2, 725–9; *OT*, Chaps. XLVII, XLVIII, pp. 362–71. Cf. Wayne C. Booth, *The Rhetoric of Fiction*, pp. 243–66, esp. pp. 245–9. Fred W. Boege, 'Point of View in Dickens', *Publications of the Moder Language Association of America*, lxv (1950), 90–105, does not cover the ground covered here.

On the other hand, certain means by which sympathy is created may limit or even cramp the development of Dickens's narrative and vision. The wholly sympathetic character is a case in point. Dickens was familiar with the concept of such a character as certain remarks about Pickwick, for instance, 'The pleasure was mutual; for who could ever gaze on Mr. Pickwick's beaming face without experiencing the sensation ?', or Boythorn, 'We all conceived a prepossession in his favour', make plain. The ready bond between the reader and the sympathetic character may be established through the sympathetic induction of agreeable emotions but it usually includes a strong element of approval. As approval, it provides the basis for the hero and heroine convention in its crudest and its most refined forms. It may, or it may not, imply moral approval. It involves a mechanism which has been at work within us since early childhood and some idea of its power over us may be gained by reflecting that it is the foundation of our moral, social, and adult selves. I refer to that kind of identification in which we *introject* and make a part of our own personalities those qualities or traits in others which we admire, or which are socially or morally approved of. Thus, in a book as in real life, we readily tend to identify ourselves (we may, of course, consciously resist this natural tendency) with a character who possesses these worthy traits. Aristotle lists these traits as good qualities which are worthy of praise. He includes nobility, many good children, riches, glory, honour, health, beauty, strength, stature, good old age, many good friends, prosperity, virtue, pleasure, justice, valour, temperance, magnanimity, magnificence. To this list we should certainly add vitality, a quality which includes several of those enumerated. There is nothing, in fact, with which we so readily sympathize as the quality of life itself; the recognition and approval of life in others is a reaffirmation of our own vital being, an expression of our delight in being alive. McDougall also says of this type of sympathy: 'The sentiment of affection for an equal generally takes its rise, not in simple tender emotion, but in admiration, or gratitude, or pity, and is especially developed by active sympathy.' The list of admirable traits includes qualities which may be acquired through accident and not merit; nevertheless, we instinctively approve of these amoral qualities in others and they automatically predispose us to consider a character who possesses them favourably. The rhetoric of sympathy demands from a writer something wider than the exclusively moral vision since this ignores an essential part of the human condition.[1]

Dickens, then, cannot evade certain rhetorical consequences which follow from the qualities he chooses to give his characters. Reliance upon the sympathy of approval can prove costly. Thus, on the fourth page of *Hard Times*, the reader is encouraged to sympathize at once with Sissy Jupe, although she has only just been introduced into the story and he has hardly more to go on than:

> But, whereas the girl was so dark-eyed and dark-haired, that she seemed to receive a deeper and more lustrous colour from the sun, when it shone upon her, the boy was so light-eyed and light-haired that the self-same rays appeared to draw out of him what little colour he ever possessed . . . His skin was so unwholesomely deficient in the natural tinge, that he looked as though, if it were cut, he would bleed white.[2]

On the credit side, here, the contrast with Bitzer brings out Sissy's natural good health while the hint that she shares a sympathetic bond with the sun, source of life and heat, also suggests an inner emotional warmth. Good health, which we find in Aristotle's list, is an amoral trait though there are moral implications to be developed, later, as regards instinctive life. The novel has opened with an ironical assumption of the utilitarian position and, since Sissy introduces the great counter-principle of the book, which she embodies and which is eventually to undermine the utilitarian position, an immediate preparatory sympathy is desirable. On the other side, we must admit certain limitations in the vision here. The contrast between Sissy and Bitzer is presented in a rather stark manner, more appropriate to the allegory or fable than the novel. Moreover, one admirable quality, however vitally presented and however strongly and instinctively we respond to it, cannot successfully suggest a complete person even of the

---

[1] *PP*, Chap. XI, p. 132; *BH*, Chap. IX, p. 117; James Drever, op. cit., p. 142, gives a definition of 'introjection'; Aristotle, *The 'Art' of Rhetoric*, I, v. vi, 1–16, ix, 1–13, tr. J. H. Freese, pp. 47–63, 91–3.

[2] *HT*, Bk. I, Chap. II, pp. 4–5.

simplest kind. Rhetoric and the cramped limits within which
Dickens worked in *Hard Times* conspire here. While space and
the thesis restricts what Dickens shall say about Sissy, rhetoric draws attention to a quality rather than a person. The
result is certainly life but a life which seems at variance with
the narrow limits in which it finds itself.

The limitations imposed by this particular rhetoric may
well be crippling. The tendency towards a polarization of
good and evil in Dickens's characterization is strengthened
by the sympathy of approval. To such a rhetoric, for example,
we partly owe a long line of insipid heroines. In *Hard Times*,
the attempt to win our unqualified approval imposes severe
limits on many characters. Thus, Dickens carefully arranges
that Louisa shall be pretty, and kind at first to Sissy, and
self-sacrificing as regards her brother. He ordains that the
circus people shall be remarkably gentle with 'a special inap-
titude for any kind of sharp practice, and an untiring readi-
ness to help and pity one another'.[1] He gives Stephen
Blackpool a perfect integrity and Rachael a sweet, gentle
disposition, almost angelic.

On the other hand, the sympathy of approval may give
some complexity to less sympathetic characters. Thus,
Gradgrind develops from something monstrous into a human
being. His determination to apply his system, however fanatical, does earn some grudging respect from us while a touch of
kindness, here and there,[2] towards Sissy prepares for a reversal of attitude towards him later in the book when he is
involved in disaster.

Repeatedly, in his revisions of manuscripts and proofs,
Dickens shows how acutely aware he was that vitality is
nearly always desirable in characters.[3] Thus, even at the late
stage of the corrected proofs of *Bleak House*, Dickens can
scrutinize the passage in which he introduces that lively
parasite, Harold Skimpole, and add a touch of vitality to the
very first sentence in which Skimpole is described: 'He ⟨had⟩

---

[1] *HT*, Bk. 1, Chap. VI, p. 35.

[2] Ibid., Chaps. V, XIV, pp. 27, 91–92.

[3] Corrected proofs of *BH*, Chap. VI, p. 49, cf. *BH*, p. 68. Corrected proofs
of *DC*, Chap. XLI, pp. 421, 422, 424 (First Edition reads 'back' after second
'rustling'); cf. *DC*, pp. 596, 597, 600. Original MS. of *MC*, Vol. IA, Chaps. IX,
V, III, pp. 15, 30, 35; cf. *MC*, pp. 139, 66, 27.

WAS A LITTLE BRIGHT CREATURE, WITH A RATHER LARGE HEAD; BUT a ⟨refined⟩ delicate face, and a sweet voice, and there was a perfect charm in him.' In this respect, Dickens does not neglect even the most minor characters. Thus, the rather wooden figures of Dora's aunts in the manuscripts of *David Copperfield* are given more life by touches of vitality added at the proof stage. The whole of the following substantial passage was added within a page or so of the first appearance of Dora's aunts in the story:

They both had little bright round twinkling eyes, by the way, which were like birds' eyes. They were not unlike birds, altogether; having a sharp, brisk, sudden manner, and a little short, spruce way of adjusting themselves, like canaries.

Two other minor additions were made later: 'But Miss Clarissa giving me a look (JUST LIKE A SHARP CANARY), as requesting that I would not interrupt the oracle'; 'They reappeared with no less dignity than they had disappeared. THEY HAD GONE RUSTLING AWAY AS IF THEIR LITTLE DRESSES WERE MADE OF AUTUMN-LEAVES; AND THEY CAME RUSTLING IN, IN LIKE MANNER.' Again, the wonderful vitality of Pecksniff may seem marvellous but it is no miracle; Dickens works hard for the effect. In the manuscript of *Martin Chuzzlewit*, for instance, when Pecksniff is ejected in such a humiliating manner from the brass and copper founder's house, it is an afterthought of Dickens which gives him a superb touch of resilience: 'Mr. Pecksniff put on his hat, and walked with great deliberation and in profound silence to the fly, GAZING AT THE CLOUDS AS HE WENT, WITH GREAT INTEREST.' As with vitality, so other qualities which invoke the sympathy of approval are added or strengthened in Dickens's revisions. A touch of gaiety is added to the first description of Mark Tapley, 'he turned a whimsical face and VERY merry pair of BLUE eyes on Mr. Pinch', and a touch of buxom good health to the attractive portrait of Mrs. Lupin, 'and roses, WORTH THE GATHERING TOO, on her lips'. It is interesting to see that the same principle of rhetoric which liberates all the marvellous life of Pecksniff is also responsible for a certain limiting measure of idealization in the portraits of Mark Tapley and Mrs. Lupin.

A third means of arousing sympathy for a character concerns pity. Dickens was aware both of the mechanisms which produce this effect and the wide range which it covers. In the proofs of *Hard Times*, for example, we can see that Sleary's asthma was an afterthought; Dickens had already adequately portrayed the impediment in Sleary's speech when he decided in his very first description of this character to add asthma as the underlying cause: ' "Thquire!" said Mr Sleary, WHO WAS TROUBLED WITH ASTHMA, AND whose breath came far too thick and heavy for the letter s, "Your thervant!" '[1] Dickens's choice of expression 'troubled with', when he might have used the neutral verb 'had' (or other fairly weak expressions), is revealing. Though the effect of sympathy here could hardly be slighter, it is completely adequate.

We reserve the term 'pathos' for what are in fact only the more extreme degrees of pity. A comment by McDougall gives us some clue as to how this effect might be managed:

The element of pain in pity is sympathetically induced pain, and the element of sweetness is the pleasure that attends the satisfaction of the impulse of the tender emotion ... shown by the fact that pity may be wholly devoid of this element of sweetness without losing its essential character—namely, in the case of pity evoked by some terrible suffering that we are powerless to relieve; in this case the pain of the obstructed tender impulse is added to the sympathetic pain, and our pity is wholly painful.

Thus, the helplessness of the victim in a painful predicament arouses the effect of pathos. And the greater the degree of helplessness and the keener the suffering the more acute the pathos will be. The intensity of this reaction is understandable when we consider that the protective instinct and its accompanying tender emotion was evolved by nature to ensure succour for the helplessness of the child. Nor is it remarkable that so many scenes of pathos involve a child as victim.

A wish for strong effects of pathos certainly dictated the basic predicaments in which Dickens sets so many of his characters. Poverty, imprisonment, and persecution come

---

[1] Corrected proofs of *HT*, Victoria and Albert Museum, Forster Collection, 48. E. 27, Chap. VI, 155; cf. *HT*, Bk. I, Chap. VI, pp. 35–6.

immediately to mind. So does Dickens's fondness for childhood as a subject, and particularly for the orphan or abandoned child; the long line stretches from Oliver to the Landless twins. Even so hostile a critic as Q. D. Leavis has praised Dickens's genius as a chronicler of childhood and certainly in his vision of childhood Dickens has achieved some of his greatest triumphs, though here also may be found some of his feeblest efforts. The possibilities and limitations of the rhetoric of pathos may make for a David Copperfield or Little Dorrit on the one hand and an Oliver Twist or Little Nell on the other. Even in the briefest sketch, however, the mature Dickens may focus his compassionate vision of the child through a powerful and authentic pathos which he produces with a conscious skill. Thus, in the manuscript of *Little Dorrit*, a tiny but remarkable touch, which is added in revision and may well have been an afterthought, suddenly brings an entire little life before us in a single flash of intensely moving vision: ' "Baby had a twin sister who died when ⟨?Baby⟩ WE COULD JUST SEE HER EYES—EXACTLY LIKE BABY'S—ABOVE THE TABLE, AS SHE STOOD ON TIPTOE HOLDING BY IT" '.[1] It is the concreteness of the picture which moves us here, the direct manner in which the small and helpless condition of the child is so presented to our senses that we can no more deny our feelings than we would in real life.

Yet with adults, too, helplessness may be exploited as an essential factor in pathos. Here also the final result may vary. The effect may be somewhat stagey as when Louisa pleads in vain to her father for an answer to her problem or, worse still, when Lady Dedlock describes her secret agony to her illegitimate daughter or, worst of all, when Nancy explains the plight of the prostitute to Rose Maylie. On the other hand, the effect may be authentic and powerful as when the proud Sir Leicester Dedlock collapses or when Gradgrind appeals in vain to Bitzer for mercy on behalf of his son.[2]

---

[1] Q. D. Leavis, *Fiction and the Reading Public*, p. 158. Original MS. of *LD*, Vol. IA, Bk. I, Chap. II, p. 14; cf. *LD*, p. 19. (In the MS. Pet was originally called Baby.)

[2] *HT*. Bk. II, Chap. XII, pp. 215–19; *BH*, Chap. XXXVI, pp. 508–13; *OT*, Chap. XL, pp. 301–2, 304–7; *BH*, Chaps. LIV, LVI, pp. 743–4, 761 ff.; *HT*, Bk. III, Chap. VIII, pp. 287–9.

Pathos attains its most acute form when the forces, piling up against the helpless victim, reduce his case to utter hopelessness. This, at its most extreme, is the agony of Christ or of Lear on 'the rack of this tough world'. Yet the effect may be produced by the minor crucifixions of life and literature. Thus, Signor Jupe in the extract quoted earlier[1] is brought to realize that his case is hopeless. Significantly enough, he abases himself on the floor, accepting his fate, symbolized by the dog all bloody from the beating, which he now embraces. The hopelessness of his case is stressed by the gesture of the dog which now licks the face of the master who has beaten it, so desperate is his distress, his need for compassion.

Since death is the most powerful of all adversaries, potentially it is the source of the keenest pathos. Death may be not only the most dramatic climax of a life but the most pathetic also. It is no accident then that death plays a major part in so many scenes of pathos, that so many scenes of pathos are, in fact, death scenes. Here again, rhetoric dictates a frequent choice of subject to Dickens. Furthermore, if death and childhood separately may produce acute pathos, then what may they do together? So, in Dickens's fiction, we find the death of the child repeated over and over again.[2]

What is the *function* of sympathy in Dickens's narrative art? Is it to create an effect for its own sake, as Q. D. Leavis and others have assumed, or is there a more creditable purpose? Not only Dickens but other novelists, from Bulwer-Lytton to Conrad, have stressed that sympathy is a vital factor in narrative art. Trollope, for example, writes: 'No novel is anything, for the purposes either of comedy or tragedy, unless the reader can sympathize with the characters whose names he finds upon the page. Let an author so tell his tale as to touch his reader's heart and draw his tears, and he has, so far, done his work well.' 'How I did not go mad,' Dostoyevsky comments on his efforts with the plot and characters of *The Idiot*, 'I don't understand', and the important role sympathy played here can be gauged from the following notes: 'Must make it all very polished, sympathetic (brief and to the point) and entertaining'; 'If Don Quixote and

---

[1] See above, p. 125–6.
[2] For a discussion of Dicken's death-bed scenes, see below, pp. 284–9.

Pickwick, as positive characters, are sympathetic to the reader and come off, it is because they are funny. If the hero of my novel, the prince, is not funny, he possesses another sympathetic characteristic, namely, he is innocent!'; 'The main problem is the character of the idiot . . . To make the hero's character as charming as possible, one has to invent a sphere of action for him'.[1] What then is there in the function of sympathy that great novelists have found indispensable?

In all four types of sympathy there is one common factor. All the illustrations from Dickens's fiction, quoted above, exhibit it most strikingly. This factor is the identification of the sympathizer with the person or object to whom the sympathy is directed. The basis of this identity lies in the sympathetic induction of emotion, which is the foundation of all other types of sympathy. The function of all types of sympathy will therefore be found in the identification, 'feeling into' (*einfuhlung*) or empathy which induction of emotion makes possible. Dickens understood the principle of empathy well enough. In *Oliver Twist*, for example, he depicts, and turns to comic advantage, the dramatic effects of Giles's fearful tale on his audience of fellow servants. Dickens also grasped that sympathy in the process of 'feeling into' was a kind of imaginative identification: ' "I never saw such a melting thing in all my life!" said Richards, who naturally substituted for this child one of her own, inquiring for herself in like circumstances.' He seems to have recognized that a strong emotional identification between two persons, Tattycoram, say, and Miss Wade, might be an almost bodily possession: ' "Oh, Tatty!" murmured her mistress, "take your hands away. I feel as if some one else was touching me!" ' Finally, Dickens consciously acknowledged that sympathy was a form of identification for when Mr Wopsle reads 'the affecting tragedy of George Barnwell' at Pip, Dickens not only describes the process accurately but he actually uses one of the terms: 'What stung me, was the identification of the whole affair with my unoffending self. When Barnwell began to go wrong, I declare I felt positively apologetic, Pumblechook's indignant stare so taxed me with it.' Indeed, Dickens's chief interest in

---

[1] Anthony Trollope, *An Autobiography* [1883] (1946), p. 206. Fyodor Dostoyevsky, *The Idiot*, tr. David Magarshack (1958), pp. 18, 21.

the theatre seems to have been with the interaction between actor and audience. Thus, he admiringly describes the art with which the French actor Lemaitre in Paris 'did the finest things' so that 'two or three times a great cry of horror went all round the house' and from the writing of *Oliver Twist* to his own performances of 'Sikes and Nancy' on the stage, Dickens saw his art as one which depended on identification with his characters.[1]

3. *The Rhetoric of Irony*

F. R. Leavis writes of an 'ironic method' which Dickens uses in *Hard Times* but, although he gives illustrations of Dickens's irony, he does not explain what this method is. As in the case of sympathy, however, there are several kinds of irony at work in Dickens's fiction, several methods in fact. Their variety accounts for some of the richness of ironic tone in Dickens's novels and it is because Dickens is aware of these various kinds of irony that he can use them so skilfully and effectively.

The existence of these distinct types of irony can be corroborated outside Dickens's work. In an admirable little study, the only useful account of types of irony, Sedgewick distinguishes almost all the types of irony which Dickens uses so deliberately.[2] Moreover, the factor which this scholar insists on as common to all these forms of irony is 'a clash between appearance and reality', an idea especially helpful in appreciating Dickens's vision of life as an ironic tragi-comedy of deception.

Thus, Dickens shows he is well aware of the most familiar type of irony, irony as a figure of speech. When, for example, Mr. Spottletoe, on the absence of old Martin Chuzzlewit, echoes sarcastically,

"Gone while we are sitting here. Gone. Nobody knows where

---

[1] *OT*, Chap. XXVIII, pp. 208–9; *D & S*, Chap. III, p. 23; *LD*, Bk. 1, Chap. XVI, p. 196; *GE*, Chap. XV, p. 110; *F*, Vol. iii, pp. 100–2.

[2] F. R. Leavis, '*Hard Times*. An Analytic Note', *The Great Tradition* (1962), pp. 250, 252–3; G. G. Sedgewick, *Of Irony: Especially in Drama* (Toronto, 1948), pp. 5–6, 7, 9, 13, 33, 49. Other works on irony in the drama include Alan R. Thompson, *The Dry Mock: A Study of Irony in Drama* (Berkeley, 1948), J. A. K. Thompson, *Irony: An Historical Introduction* (1926). There is no general study of irony in the novel, though Wayne C. Booth, *The Rhetoric of Fiction*, deals in some detail with the topic from a special point of view.

he's gone. Oh, of course not! Nobody knew he was going. Oh, of course not! The landlady thought up to the very last moment that they were merely going for a ride; she had no other suspicion. Oh, of course not! She's not this fellow's creature. Oh, of course not!",

we are told that he added 'to these exclamations a kind of ironical howl' and that 'It was in vain for Mr. Pecksniff to assure them that this new and opportune evasion of the family was at least as great a shock and surprise to him as to anybody else'.

At first sight, Sedgewick's definition appears to cover this instance quite adequately:

> In essence it is a pretence . . . the purpose of which is mockery or deception of one sort or another; and its force derives from one of the keenest and oldest and least transient pleasures of the reflective human mind—the pleasure in contrasting Appearance with Reality. The proper signification of the words constitutes the appearance; the designated meaning is the reality.

Yet is Dicken's use of the figure here a mere flash of surface wit in the general comedy of the Chuzzlewit family quarrel or can it be related to the vision of the book, an instance of the self-defeating paranoid delusions which accompany the selfish pursuit of wealth?[1] Spottletoe tries to use irony as a weapon against Pecksniff but a more subtle irony is thereby directed against himself.

A more striking example occurs in *Hard Times*: 'Book the First—Sowing'; 'Book the Second—Reaping'; 'Book the Third—Garnering'. At first sight, this may seem a piece of conventional wit, almost a cliché, in which the pleasant appearance of seeding and harvesting with all its gay and joyful associations of hope and fulfilment is contrasted with the cruel reality of the Gradgrind fate. But there is more to it than that. The very choice of a natural image, itself the archetype of growth and fruition, is contrasted with the harsh wasteland which the Gradgrinds make of their lives and the Gradgrind philosophy makes of Coketown. Moreover, the industrial period of the novel is thus set within the wider

[1] *MC*, Chap. IV, p. 62; cf. the case of Chevy Slyme, ibid., Chap. VII, pp. 106–9.

context of man's history which has been largely an agricultural one; the complacent view of Gradgrind is set against a cosmic vision of man, a vision which is also realized in the ironical idea of Time the Manufacturer who will have the last word on the products of the Gradgrind educational factory. The irony here, therefore, does not simply play wittily on the surface of the novel. It is at one with the theme—it *is* the theme, in a nutshell. Moreover, Dickens's notes make it clear that he was working with a deliberate artistry here. At the bottom of the list of memoranda for No. II, the following note is added: 'Republish in 3 books? 1. Sowing, 2. Reaping, 3. Garnering'. The serial version of *Hard Times* was not divided into books and the idea of a division into three books was therefore an afterthought. Since this improvement was not made in the serial version, it seems likely the idea occurred to Dickens only when the first weekly number at least had been published; yet since the note occurs so early in the number plans, the ironic idea it expresses may well have helped to shape the precise pattern the story was to follow.[1] Similarly, 'Book the First, Chapter I. The One Thing Needful' and 'Book the Third, Chapter I. Another Thing Needful', are not cases of verbal play alone. The careful symmetry in the placing betrays a piece of architecture, a building outwards from the very structure of the novel which leads the attention inwards again to an awareness of that structure.

The definition of irony as a figure of speech in Sedgewick's book hardly does justice to the rich manner in which Dickens may exploit this verbal type of irony. The argument is even more conclusive in the case of a title like 'Great Expectations'. The use of the figure here is so skilful as to concentrate within the two words of the title the ironic plot of the novel in miniature. Dickens's ironic art, in fact, has towards the end of his career reached such a peak of development that he can confidently advertise appearance and reality, boldly practise concealment and revelation (in terms of irony) and mystery and solution (in terms of plot) at the head of every page of a novel.

[1] *HT*, Bk. I, Chap. XIV, pp. 90–5. Original MS. of *HT*; see below, pp. 218–25, for confirmation of my view that titles played some part in Dickens's plotting.

Nevertheless, irony as a figure can prove extremely limiting. In the manuscript of *Oliver Twist*, for example, Dickens deliberately attempts to increase the irony in this crude and heavy-handed manner:

"And mind you don't poison it," said Mr Sikes, laying his hat upon the table.
This was said in jest; but if the ⟨robber⟩ SPEAKER could have seen the evil ⟨smile⟩ LEER with which the Jew bit his pale lip as he turned round to the cupboard, he might have thought the caution not wholly unnecessary, or the wish (at all events) to improve upon the distiller's ingenuity not very far from the old gentleman's MERRY heart.[1]

The irony, here, seems almost tacked on to the context. The ironic concept of Fagin as a merry old gentleman should have been kept exclusively to suggest Oliver's naïve view of him. In general, when the figure is absorbed into a wider context, it appears less obtrusive and more natural.

The normal place for irony as a figure of speech seems to be in satirical passages where it brings out the critical attitude of the book towards the subject:

Sir Leicester has no objection to ⟨a long⟩ AN INTERMIN-ABLE Chancery suit. It is ⟨an⟩ A SLOW, expensive, British, constitutional kind of thing. To be sure, he has not a vital interest in the suit in question, her part in which was the only property my Lady brought him; and he has a shadowy impression that for his name—the name of Dedlock—to be in a cause, and not in the title of that cause, is a ridiculous accident, But he regards the Court of Chancery, even if it should involve an occasional delay of justice and a trifling amount of confusion, as a something, devised in conjunction with a variety of other somethings, by the per-fection of human wisdom, ⟨to settle⟩ for the ⟨eternal⟩ ⟨FINAL⟩ ETERNAL settlement (HUMANLY SPEAKING) of everything. And he is upon the whole of a fixed opinion, that to give the sanction of his countenance to any complaints respecting it, would be to encourage some person in the lower classes to rise up somewhere—like Wat Tyler.[2]

[1] Original MS. of *OT*, Vol. IA, Bk. I, Chap. XIII, p. 32; cf. *OT*, Chap. XIII, p. 87.
[2] Original MS. of *BH*, Vol. IA, Chap. II, p. D ('most' inserted before 'ridiculous' in proof); cf. *BH*, p. 13.

The irony, here, is made all the sharper and more effective by the revisions in the manuscript. Sir Leicester's attitude to Chancery is mockingly echoed in the author's voice. The substitution of 'interminable' for 'long' and the insertion of 'slow' make the truth about Chancery and, therefore, about Sir Leicester's character absolutely clear while the use of irony as a figure, which culminates in 'the perfection of human wisdom, for the eternal settlement (humanly speaking) of everything', accurately represents the attitude of Sir Leicester and at the same time distinguishes it from the critical vision of Chancery and Sir Leicester. There is a further subtlety in the rhetoric and the vision here. Sir Leicester is ironically attacked through his championing the cause of Chancery and Chancery through its being championed by Sir Leicester.

Irony as a figure may also be effectively used in dialogue wherever the author's tone of voice and that of a character naturally coincide. Thus, in the following sarcastic interchange, Mr. Bounderby and Mrs. Sparsit are skilfully led on to judge each other, much to the reader's delight:

"Mrs. Sparsit, ma'am, I rather think you are cramped here, do you know? It appears to me, that, under my humble roof, there's hardly opening enough for a lady of your genius in other people's affairs."

Mrs. Sparsit gave him a look of the darkest scorn, and said with great politeness, "Really, Sir?"

"I have been thinking it over, you see, since the late affairs have happened, ma'am" said Bounderby, "and it appears to my poor judgment—"

"Oh! Pray, Sir," Mrs. Sparsit interposed, with sprightly cheerfulness, "don't disparage your judgment. Everybody know show unerring Mr. Bounderby's judgment is. Everybody has had proofs of it. It must be the theme of general conversation. Disparage anything in yourself but your judgment, Sir," said Mrs. Sparsit, laughing.

Mr. Bounderby, very red and uncomfortable, resumed:

"It appears to me, ma'am, I say, that a different sort of estabshment altogether would bring out a lady of *your* powers."[1]

Dickens was consciously aware of the principle of the contrary or opposite in irony, and he also seems to have been

---

[1] *HT*, Bk. III, Chap. IX, pp. 295-6.

conscious of the role of shock in irony, as a revision in the manuscript of *Martin Chuzzlewit* makes clear:

He advanced with outstretched arms to take the old man's hand. But he had not seen how the hand clasped and clutched the stick within its grasp. As he came smiling on, and got within his reach, old Martin, with his burning indignation crowded into one vehement burst, and flashing out of every line and wrinkle in his face, rose up, and struck him down upon the ground.

With such a well-directed nervous blow, that down he went, as heavily and true as if the charge of a Life-Guardsman had tumbled him out of a saddle. And whether he was stunned BY THE SHOCK, or only confused by the wonder and novelty of this warm reception, he did not offer to get up again.[1]

Like the mechanism of 'distancing', that of shock can be observed in all forms of irony. By assuming the contrary, the ironist so 'distances' the victim from the real situation that he momentarily disarms him or weakens the defences of his position. But no sooner is the truth behind the appearance revealed or understood than it falls upon the victim with increased force, while the principle of the opposite ensures maximum shock in rousing the temporarily lulled mind to reality.

Dickens knows how to use the irony of understatement, as in the following example from *Hard Times*, and the assumed restraint which he accords to the inspectors is worthy of the Socratic method which Sedgewick defines as 'understatement expanded into the principle of a whole life', as 'a war upon Appearance waged by a man who knows Reality': 'The millers of Coketown . . . were ruined, when such inspectors considered it doubtful whether they were quite justified in chopping people up with their machinery.' We might even apply to Dickens's attitude here Sedgewick's remark that 'with the sympathy of a teacher who feels himself perfectly articulate he [Socrates] depressed his own wisdom, and coming down in playful earnest to their level of ignorance, he would teach them [his opponents and pupils] to express their real meanings'. Certainly this indirect method of exposing one of the worst horrors of the industrial revolution, the

[1] *LD*, Bk. I, Chap. III, p. 37. Original MS. of *MC*, Vol. IIB, Chap. LII, p. 30; cf. *MC*, p. 803.

appalling dangers of unfenced machinery which the agitation
for factory legislation was bringing to light, is far more
devastating than the specific instance which appears in the
proofs but not in the printed text:

"Thou'st spoken o' thy little sisther There agen! Wi' her child
arm tore off afore thy face!"
    She turned her head aside, and put her hand to her eyes.
    "Where dost thou ever hear or read o' *us*—the like o' *us*—as
being otherwise than onreasonable and cause o' trouble? Yet think
o' that Government gentleman comes down and mak's report.
Fend off the dangerous machinery, box it off, save life and limb,
don't rend and tear human creaturs to bits in a Chris'en country!
What follers? Owners sets up their throats, cries out, 'Onreasonable! Inconvenient! Troublesome!' Gets to Secretaries o' States wi'
deputations, and nothing's done. When do *we* get there wi' *our*
deputations, God help us! We are too much int'rested and nat'rally
too far wrong t'have a right judgment. Haply we are; but what
are they then? I' th' name o' th' muddle in which we are born and
live and die, what are they then!"
    "Let such things be, Stephen. They only lead to hurt; let them
be!"
    "I will, since thou tell'st me so. I will. I pass my promise."[1]

Whereas Socratic Irony uses understatement, Dickens's
more usual method of undermining a position makes extensive use of irony as a figure of speech. Like Socratic Irony, the
device consists in a prolonged assumption of the position
which is being attacked. This type of irony employs the
principle of the innocent mask and that of shock in their most
deadly form. The victim or his point of view is allowed to
take over completely and his own words, tone, attitudes
condemn him. The method is often allied to a kind of *reductio
ad absurdum* in which the victim's extremism is allowed to
run riot. One thinks of Honeythunder in *Edwin Drood* or
Grandgrind's idealized image of himself or the Gradgrind
view of the working people of Coketown:

In short, it was the only clear thing in the case—that these
same people were a bad lot altogether, gentlemen; that do what

---

[1] *HT*, Bk. II, Chap. I, p. 110. Corrected proofs of *HT*, Chap. XIII, 190,
191; cf. *HT*, Bk. I, Chap. XIII, p. 88 (the deleted passage was originally
between 'muddle cleared awa' ' and 'Thou'rt an Angel'); see also R. B. Wood-
ings, 'A Cancelled Passage in *Hard Times*', *The Dickensian*, 1x (1964), 42–3.

you would for them they were never thankful for it, gentlemen;
that they were restless, gentlemen; that they never knew what
they wanted; and that they lived upon the best, and bought
fresh butter; and insisted on Mocha coffee, and rejected all but
prime parts of meat, and yet were eternally dissatisfied and un-
manageable.[1]

Again when we examine Dickens's use of the irony of
understatement in the following, 'You are, we will say in
round numbers, twenty years of age; Mr. Bounderby is, we
will say in round numbers, fifty. There is some disparity in
your respective years, but in your means and positions there
is none; on the contrary, there is a great suitability',[2] we
might consider Sedgewick's definition of this type as appropriate: 'Such understatement is really "saying one and
gyving to understande the contrarye". For the thing as
stated, the Appearance, falls so far short of the thing itself,
the Reality, as to be for all practical purposes a different
entity.' Yet we would not be justified in dismissing the irony
here, in Sedgewick's phrase, as 'language mocking itself'.
This is an irony which is woven into the texture of a situation.
With all the consequences of that disparity in age to come,
it is an irony aimed with double force against the speaker,
Gradgrind.

The influence of the theatre on Dickens's fiction can be seen
in many fine instances of dramatic irony as well as some
stagey examples. Of this type of irony, Sedgewick writes:
'Dramatic irony . . . is the sense of contradiction felt by
spectators of a drama who see a character acting in ignorance of his condition.'
And Dickens was fully aware of this concept:

"Oh, ask your friend to come here, sir", said Mrs. Bardell. "Pray,
ask your friend here, sir."
"Why, thankee, I'd rather not," said Mr Jackson, with some
embarrassment of manner. "He's not much used to ladies' society,
and it makes him bashful. If you'll order the waiter to deliver him
anything short, he won't drink it off at once, won't he!—only try
him!" Mr. Jackson's fingers wandered playfully round his nose, at

---

[1] *ED*, Chap. VI, pp. 57–9; *HT*, Bk. I, Chap. II, p. 3, Chap. V, p. 24.
[2] Ibid., Bk. I, Chap. XV, p. 98.

this portion of his discourse, to warn his hearers that he was speaking ironically.[1]

All the distinctive features of dramatic irony are consciously stressed here: the audience, the unsuspecting victim (so unsuspecting in fact that she preens herself among her friends at Jackson's presence), and the inside information enjoyed by the audience at the victim's expense. Finally, through his description of Jackson's gesture, Dickens shows he is fully aware the situation is an ironical one.

Again, Dickens's manuscripts indicate that he used dramatic irony quite consciously. When William Dorrit, the ex-Marshalsea prisoner, asks one of the monks if he does not find the secluded life in the Great Saint Bernard convent 'dreary' and 'monotonous', the space 'so small', 'so very limited', 'so very contracted', there is a certain pointedness in his remarks. An insertion, however, which looks like an after-thought, turns the effect into one of keen dramatic irony. The monk unwittingly touches Dorrit on a sore spot when he suggests that the Englishman can hardly appreciate what it means to be shut up, and Dickens carefully puts a word which suggests imprisonment into his mouth: ' "Monsieur ⟨was ?an the English traveller surrounded by all appliances⟩ WAS NOT USED TO CONFINEMENT." ' Again, when Henry Gowan is painting Blandois, who is really the murderer Rigaud, Dickens cannot resist exploiting the situation to the full:

"There he stands, you see. A bravo waiting for his prey, a distinguished noble waiting to save his country, the common enemy waiting to do somebody a bad turn, AN ANGELIC MES-SENGER WAITING TO DO SOMEBODY A GOOD ONE— whatever you think he looks most like!"

"Say, Professore Mio, a poor gentleman waiting to do homage to fashion and beauty," remarked Blandois with his ominous smile.

"Or say, Cattivo Soggetto Mio," returned Gowan, touching the painted face with his brush in the part where the real face had moved, "a murderer after the fact."[2]

[1] *PP*, Chap. XLVI, p. 653.
[2] Original MS. of *LD*, Vol. IIA, Bk. II, Chap. I, p. 8, Chap. VI, p. 14 (proofs read 'turn' after 'good' and 'elegance' after 'homage to' and omit 'with his ominous smile"); cf. *LD*, pp. 441, 493.

True, Dickens sometimes uses dramatic irony in the very worst kind of theatrical manner, when the situation contains melodramatic elements and is acted out by melodramatic characters. Perhaps the most flagrant example is the kind of brief aside which Dickens appears to borrow straight from the stage melodrama, as when Carker sneers in a sinister and threatening manner behind Dombey's back. In the earlier novels, situations which are potentially rich in dramatic irony may take the cruder kind of melodramatic turn. In such scenes, for example, as that in which Noah Claypole overhears the conversation between Nancy and Mr. Brownlow which is to lead to Nancy's murder or the episode in which Mr. Dombey secretly observes Mrs. Brown extort from Rob the Grinder Edith and Carker's place of refuge, interest seems to centre on the melodrama of the situation rather than on its ironical implications. The effect is more sensational than ironic.[1]

Yet even situations in which a villainous character gloats over the prospect of a victim in his power may be free from an objectionable theatricality. This seems to occur when the character is not melodramatically conceived and irony gets the upper hand, as in the scene in which Mrs. Sparsit eavesdrops on Louisa and Harthouse in the wood, or in the following:

> For Silas Wegg felt it to be quite out of the question that he could lay his head upon his pillow in peace, without first hovering over Mr. Boffin's house in the superior character of its Evil Genius. Power (unless it be the power of intellect or virtue) has ever the greatest attraction for the lowest natures; and the mere defiance of the unconscious house-front, with his power to strip the roof off the inhabiting family like the roof of a house of cards, was a treat which had a charm for Silas Wegg.
>
> As he hovered on the opposite side of the street, exulting, the carriage drove up.
>
> "There'll shortly be an end of *you*," said Wegg, threatening it with the hat-box. "*Your* varnish is fading".
>
> Mrs. Boffin descended and went in.
>
> "Look out for a fall, my Lady Dustwomen," said Wegg.
>
> Bella lightly descended and ran in after her.
>
> "How brisk we are!" said Wegg. "You won't run so gaily to your old shabby home, my girl. You'll have to go there, though."

[1] *D & S*, Chap. XXVI, p. 365; *OT*, Chap. XLVI, pp. 347–55; *D & S*, Chap. LII, pp. 726–37.

A little while, and the Secretary came out.

"I was passed over for you," said Wegg. "But you had better provide yourself with another situation, young man."

Mr. Boffin's shadow passed upon the blinds of three large windows as he trotted down the room, and passed again as he went back.

"Yoop!" cried Wegg. "You're there, are you? where's the bottle? You would give your bottle for my box, Dustman!"

Having now composed his mind for slumber, he turned homeward. Such was the greed of the fellow, that his mind had shot beyond halves, two-thirds, three-fourths, and gone straight to spoliation of the whole. "Though that wouldn't quite do," he considered, growing cooler as he got away. "That's what would happen to him if he didn't buy us up. We should get nothing by that."

We so judge others by ourselves, that it had never come into his head before, that he might not buy us up, and might prove honest, and prefer to be poor. It caused him a slight tremor as it passed; but a very slight one, for the idle thought was gone directly.

"He's grown too fond of money for that," said Wegg; "he's grown too fond of money." The burden fell into a strain or tune as he stumped along the pavements. All the way home he stumped it out of the rattling streets, *piano* with his own foot, and *forte* with his wooden leg, "He's GROWN too FOND of MONEY for THAT, he's GROWN too FOND of MONEY." [*Dickens's Capitals*][1]

The irony is complex and subtle, here, since it is neatly turned against Silas Wegg; he projects his own obsessive money-grubbing on to Boffin. There is, therefore, a kind of double dramatic irony, an outer frame of awareness of which the character, for all his relish in his knowledge and power, remains ignorant. Moreover, it is through his own greed and, like Mrs. Sparsit, though his own machinations to produce the downfall of others that Silas Wegg is preparing his own ruin. That Dickens was aware of the important role played by 'distancing' in ironic vision can be seen in his reference to Wegg's 'power to strip the roof off the inhabiting family like the roof of a house of cards'.

In the early novels of Dickens too, whenever characters enjoy a genuine comic life which raises them above the level

[1] *HT*, Bk. II, Chap. XI, pp. 211, 212; *OMF*, Bk. III, Chap. VII, pp. 501–2.

of melodrama, a dramatic irony may be achieved which can vie with the best in seventeenth- and eighteenth-century comedy. In such a class are several of those eavesdropping escapades of Quilp, the scene for example in which the dwarf witnesses his supposed widow and mother-in-law disparaging his person when they think him dead and then pounces on them.[1]

A fourth type of irony is of very great importance in any discussion of Dickens's narrative art. This type, which I propose to call *Structural Irony* or the *Cumulative Irony of Events*, is rather neglected by Sedgewick. Thus, he does not couple the idea of 'the irony of fate or circumstance' with his own concept, the 'general irony of drama'.

Structural irony may extend throughout a considerable part of a novel and may even be, as in *Hard Times* and *Great Expectations*, the very soul of the plot. It may account for some of Dickens's most effective scenes, the discovery by Pip, for example, that the convict, Magwitch, is his secret benefactor or that Biddy and Joe are married. But since it imposes a fairly rigid pattern on plot, structure, and form, structural irony may also be responsible for drastic limitations on Dickens's narrative art, on both his invention and his vision.

The pattern expresses itself in a series of crises, consisting of ironical hints (the device of foreshadowing) and culminating in a climax. This climax is the discovery or the peripety of which Aristotle writes so instructively:

A revolution [peripety] is a change . . . into the reverse of what is expected from the circumstances of the action; and that produced, as we have said, by probable or necessary consequence . . . a discovery—as, indeed, the word implies—is a change from unknown to known, happening between those characters whose happiness or unhappiness forms the catastrophe of the drama, and terminating in friendship or enmity. The best sort of discovery is that which is accompanied by a revolution as in the *Oedipus*.

When Dickens realizes the complete pattern of structural irony, including the links between catastrophe and character which Aristotle called *hamartia* and *hubris*, it is tempting to

[1] *OCS*, Chap. XLIX, pp. 365–9.

see in his art no more than an awareness of the homely truth that blindness and pride go before a fall:

> The birds, who, happily for their own peace of mind and personal comfort, were in blissful ignorance of the preparations which had been making to astonish them, on the first of September, hailed it no doubt, as one of the pleasantest mornings they had seen that season. Many a young partridge . . . strutted complacently among the stubble, with all the finicking coxcombry of youth.

Yet it is worth bearing in mind that Aristotle's terminology was being used to describe the structure of the novel in Dickens's lifetime, in particular by Dickens's close associate, Bulwer-Lytton, who had studied Aristotle's *Poetics* and that Dickens was aware of this terminology and uses the terms, 'reverse of fortune' and 'catastrophe' in contexts which involve a pattern of structural irony. When the Lammles, for example, are ruined at the climax of their own financial machinations by those of their fellow conspirator, Fledgeby, Mrs. Lammle refers to the ironic catastrophe as 'a reverse of fortune'. Again, when Dickens plans the careful ironical structure which is to culminate in the crushing of Rigaud, he refers to it in his notes as the 'Rigaud catastrophe'. Moreover, Dickens repeatedly shows he is conscious of a mental or spiritual blindness which often takes on a wilful or defiant form and is very close to the classical notion of the 'error of judgement' which grows into 'overweening pride' and so tempts providence and invites correction by fate.[1]

The example from *Pickwick* was jocular but a serious instance can be seen in the following passage which describes how the neglect of slums, like Tom-all-Alone's, so recoils on Society that its most exclusive and disdainful rulers are involved with the slums in the most intimate and humiliating manner:

> But he has his revenge. Even the winds are his messengers, and

---

[1] Aristotle, *Poetics*, xi. 1, 4–5, tr. Thomas Twining, second edition (1812), reprinted in Everyman Library (1941), pp. 22–3. The second edition of Twining's translation was the standard translation throughout the first half of the nineteenth century and the one most likely to have been read, if at all, by Bulwer-Lytton or Dickens; see also Edward Bulwer-Lytton, 'On Art in Fiction', *Pamphlets and Sketches*, pp. 326, 348, and below, pp. 304–5. *PP*, Chap. XIX, p. 247; *OMF*, Bk. III, Chap. XVII, p. 620; original MS. of *LD*, Vol. IA; Humphry House, *Aristotle's Poetics* (1961), p. 93–5.

they serve him in these hours of darkness. There is not a drop of Tom's corrupted blood but propagates infection and contagion somewhere. It shall pollute, this very night, the choice stream (in which chemists on analysis would find the genuine nobility) of a Norman house, and his Grace shall not be able to say Nay to the infamous alliance. There is not an atom of Tom's slime, not a cubic inch of any pestilential gas in which he lives, not one obscenity or degradation about him, not an ignorance, not a wickedness, not a brutality of his committing, but shall work its retribution, through every order of society, up to the proudest of the proud, and to the highest of the high. Verily, what with tainting, plundering, and spoiling, Tom has his revenge.

In one panoramic sweep, we are offered a meaningful vision of the organic world of *Bleak House* which the structure of the novel serves to stress. True, this vision is, in part, a scathing view of a contemporary social problem and much contemporary evidence lies behind it. The story of the crusade for sanitary reform, and the part Dickens played in it, is possibly too well known to repeat here, except to note that in 1848, the same year as the earlier cholera epidemic spread to England, 6,903 people died from smallpox, the disease specifically referred to in *Bleak House*, and that in 1851, the same year Dickens began to serialize the novel, he claimed at a meeting of the Metropolitan Sanitary Association that sanitation was the most urgent problem facing the nation. Unlike his support for penal reform, Dickens's advocacy of sanitary reform remained unequivocal; articles in *Household Words*, and before that in John Forster's *Examiner*, amount to a full-scale propaganda campaign. Yet the problem is not presented simply as propaganda in *Bleak House*. It is used imaginatively to lay bare the anatomy of a whole society. To show that society is one and will be one—in sickness, if health is denied. So that the very hierarchy of classes which try to frustrate and deny the indivisibility of a community only succeed in proving its essential unity in the fearful communion of disease, deformity, and death. Obviously, this view goes much further than the laying of drains, however commendable. Dickens is not simply suggesting a solution here; his vision is rather the apocalyptic, cosmic vision of Carlyle, who also saw the ironic link between neglect and retribution in a passage which records an incident similar to that in *Bleak House* and may even have been one of Dickens's sources:

A poor Irish Widow, her husband having died in one of the Lanes of Edinburgh, went forth with her three children, bare of all resource, to solicit help from the Charitable Establishments of that City. At this Charitable Establishment and then at that she was refused; referred from one to the other, helped by none;—till she had exhausted them all; till her strength and heart failed her: she sank down in typhus-fever; died, and infected her Lane with fever, so that 'seventeen other persons' died of fever there in consequence. The humane Physician asks thereupon, as with a heart too full for speaking, Would it not have been *economy* to help this poor Widow? She took typhus-fever, and killed seventeen of you!—Very curious. The forlorn Irish Widow applies to her fellow-creatures, as if saying, "Behold I am sinking, bare of help: ye must help me! I am your sister, bone of your bone; one God made us: ye must help me!" They answer, "No, impossible; thou art no sister of ours." But she proves her sisterhood; her typhus-fever kills *them*: they actually were her brothers, though denying it! Had human creature ever to go lower for a proof?

Dickens's voice too is much more that of the warning prophet than the reformer. His vision has ranged far above the social and political spheres to an almost religious view of human destiny, has become the authentic witness of a fate, of a terrible moral order at work in the universe, scarcely Christian in any New Testament sense. The rhetoric of irony, like that of sympathy, may therefore give evidence of the supernatural world which pervades and orders our mundane existence.[1]

Though Dickens does not use the terms, many revisions in the manuscripts and corrected proofs draw attention to, or

[1] *BH*, Chap. XLVI, pp. 627–8. For the social background, see John Butt and Kathleen Tillotson, *Dickens at Work*, pp. 177–200; Trevor Blount, 'The Graveyard Satire of *Bleak House* in the Context of 1850', *Review of English Studies*, NS., xiv (1963), 370–8; John W. Dodds, *The Age of Paradox* (1953), p. 337; *Speeches*, p. 129; Philip Collins, *Dickens and Crime, passim*; Humphry House, *The Dickens World*, pp. 195, 199–201; K. J. Fielding and Alec W. Brice, 'Charles Dickens on "The Exclusion of Evidence" ', *The Dickensian*, lxiv (1968), 131–40, lxv (1969), 35–41, 'Dickens and the Tooting Disaster', *Victorian Studies*, xii (1968), 227–44. Thomas Carlyle, *Past and Present* [1834], People's Edition (1872), Bk. III, Chap. II, p. 128; cf. *Speeches*, p. 128: 'the air from Gin Lane will be carried, when the wind is Easterly, into May Fair, and . . . if you once have a vigorous pestilence raging furiously in Saint Giles's, no mortal list of Lady Patronesses can keep it out of Almack's'.

clarify, or create instances of *hamartia* or *hubris*.[1] Thus, in *Bleak House*, a few lines before the grisly discovery of Krook's dreadful fate, Dickens inserted in proof a passage which culminates in the following hubristic preparation for the catastrophe:

"Look!" whispers the lodger, pointing his friend's attention to these objects with a trembling finger. "I told you so. When I saw him last, he took his cap off, took out the little bundle of old letters, hung his cap on the back of the chair—his coat was there already, for he had pulled that off, before he went to put the shutters up—and I left him turning the letters over in his hand, standing just where that crumbled black thing is upon the floor."

Is he hanging somewhere? They look up. No.

"See!" whispers Tony. "At the foot of the same chair, there lies a dirty bit of thin red cord that they tie up pens with. That went round the letters. He undid it slowly, leering and laughing at me, before he began to turn them over, and threw it there. I saw it fall."

"What's the matter with the cat?" says Mr. Guppy. "Look at her!"

"Mad, I think. And no wonder, in this evil place."

An even more striking case occurs in the manuscript and corrected proofs of *Martin Chuzzlewit*. Here, we can watch young Martin's smugness about his professional future gradually taking shape. Dickens first adds an attempt at *hubris* as an afterthought in the manuscript:

"If I should turn out a great architect, Tom," said the new pupil one day, AS HE STOOD AT A LITTLE DISTANCE FROM HIS DRAWING, AND EYED IT WITH HUGE SATISFACTION, "I'll tell you what should be one of the things I'd build."

The idea is then sharply clarified in proof when Dickens alters 'huge satisfaction' to 'much complacency'. The ironical outcome of Martin's prospects as an architect is to be his dismissal by Pecksniff, the fiasco of his Eden enterprise, and his galling discovery that the school designed by himself is being acclaimed as a triumph of Pecksniff's. *Hubris* may

[1] Corrected proofs of *BH*, Chap. XXXII, p. 320; cf. *BH*, p. 455. Original MS. of *MC*, Vol. IA, Chap. XII, p. 24; cf. *MC*, p. 191. Corrected proofs of *MC*, Victoria and Albert Museum, Forster Collection, 48. E. 24, Chap. XII, p. 145. Original MS. of *BH*, Vol. IA, Chap. V. p. 10; cf. *BH*, p. 58. Corrected proofs of *BH*, Chap. LI, p. 492; cf. *BH*, p. 695.

sometimes be a kind of *hamartia*, an over-confident blindness to
what fate may bring which seems arrogant only in retrospect.
Such is the complacency of young Martin, which leaves him
vulnerable to the blows of fate, or Richard Carstone's earliest
reaction to the fatal influence of Chancery, which is given
a sharper irony by revisions in the manuscript of *Bleak
House*:

"At all events, Ada, ⟨it shall never make enemies of⟩ CHAN-
CERY WILL WORK NONE OF ITS BAD INFLUENCE ON
us. We have happily been brought together, thanks to our good
kinsman, and it ⟨should only make⟩ CAN'T DIVIDE us ⟨friends⟩
NOW!"

Yet mental blindness may grow into something wilful as when
Richard, for all his warnings and disappointments, sets himself recklessly against fate in persisting with the Chancery suit.
Thus, a characteristic boast of Richard is revised in proof so as
to bring out the irony even more strongly: ' "We are doing
very well," pursued Richard. "Vholes will tell you so. We
are REALLY spinning along" '.

The pattern of structural irony occurs very frequently in
Dickens's novels. One further example is much more subtle
and complex than might at first appear:

Thomas Gradgrind took no heed of these trivialities of course,
but passed on as a practical man ought to pass on, either brushing
the noisy insects from his thoughts, or consigning them to the
House of Correction. But, the turning of the road took him by the
back of the booth, and at the back of the booth a number of children were congregated in a number of stealthy attitudes, striving
to peep in at the hidden glories of the place.
This brought him to a stop. "Now, to think of these vagabonds,"
said he, "attracting the young rabble from a model school."
A space of stunted grass and dry rubbish being between him
and the young rabble, he took his eyeglass out of his waistcoat
to look for any child he knew by name, and might order off.
Phenomenon almost incredible though distinctly seen, what did he
then behold but his own metallurgical Louisa, peeping with all her
might through a hole in a deal board, and his own mathematical
Thomas abasing himself on the ground to catch but a hoof of the
graceful equestrian Tyrolean flower-act!

The ground for the little catastrophe is carefully prepared by

Gradgrind's arrogant dismissal of the circus in the first paragraph; his rejection of the imaginative and affective side of human nature sets in motion against him the machinery of the natural law. The ensuing catastrophe is the kind that Aristotle recommends. It contains both a discovery and a peripety and possesses the proper qualities of surprise and probability. Surprise is not only registered through 'phenomenon almost incredible' but the specific reference to 'his own metallurgical Louisa' and 'his own mathematical Thomas' brings out all the irony in the neat reversal of Gradgrind's expectations as father and educationist. Yet the probability of the incident has been carefully prepared; earlier in the chapter, the education of the Gradgrind children has been described in an ironic tone which culminates in the slight but pregnant hint: '. . . everything that heart could desire. Everything? Well, I suppose so'.[1] The passage, however, is more subtle than this. The basic movement of the novel originates in the spiritual blindness of Gradgrind, which is the blindness of a whole philosophy, of a society, of an age. Again, the spiritual myopia of Gradgrind is suggested by the business of the eyeglass which he needs to make out what his children are up to under his very nose; thus the physical action of the passage expresses and underlines the wider spiritual message. Moreover the incident is related organically to the rest of the novel both in form and in content. It foreshadows the major double catastrophe in which daughter and son show so alarmingly the unexpected yet quite inevitable effects of the Gradgrind system of education on their adult lives. The passage is, in fact, the major catastrophe of the novel in miniature. It is more. Since the incident provides an ominous warning, which Gradgrind is to ignore at his peril, it is the act of wilful defiance which will trigger off that major catastrophe. Thus, the passage is a tiny model of the whole ironic structure of the novel. As such it is vision as well as structure—a prophetic picture, that is, of the way that an outraged natural law brings about a nemesis in the fullness of time.

Any investigation into the *function* of irony must begin, I believe, with the principle of 'distancing'. This principle is

[1] *HT*, Bk. I, Chap. III, pp. 11–12, 10.

clear in the examples of the different types of irony quoted earlier. 'Distance' is most obvious in dramatic irony since the exclusive possession of information at once sets a character, audience, or reader apart from the victim who remains ignorant. Indeed, the sense of distance which this kind of superior knowledge creates may amount almost to the viewpoint of a god, as it does with Silas Wegg, inducing fantasies of ominscience and omnipotence; the remark about tearing off the roof is particularly significant here. In structural irony, too, the perception that a pattern is shaping or has shaped a human life together with the prophetic sense that one can see more clearly than the character involved isolates the observer or reader. This effect may even be managed through the viewpoint of a character like David Copperfield or Pip who looks back over the gulf of time aware of the ironic pattern in his own life or the lives of others. Again, in structural as in dramatic irony, the sense of distance at its most extreme may give the impression of the godlike glance, transcending time and space and sweeping panoramically over the range of human destiny, an effect powerfully induced by certain omniscient passages of *Bleak House*. In the two verbal forms of irony, distance is present in the gap which opens up between the deceptive appearance, presented by an ironical statement, and the true interpretation, which the reader is invited to share.

In 1912 Bullough noted the important role played by distance in the aesthetic experience:

One of the best-known examples is to be found in our attitude towards the events and characters of the drama: they appeal to us like persons and incidents of normal experience, except that that side of their appeal, which would usually affect us in a directly personal manner, is held in abeyance . . . The jealous spectator of *Othello* will indeed appreciate and enter into the play the more keenly, the greater the resemblance with his own experience—*provided* that he succeeds in keeping the Distance between the action of the play and his personal feelings . . . The same qualification applies to the artist. He will prove artistically most effective in the formulation of an intensely *personal* experience, but he can formulate it artistically only on condition of a detachment from the experience *qua personal*. Hence the statement of so many artists that artistic formulation was to them a kind of catharsis, a

means of ridding themselves of feelings and ideas the acuteness
of which they felt almost as a kind of obsession.[1]

Though he hints at the doctrine of alienation in the drama
long before Brecht and his disciples had given it this special
name, and instances other methods of achieving and controlling distance, Bullough does not mention irony. Neither does
Brecht.

The idea of aesthetic distance may seem comparatively
modern, yet it was known in Dickens's time:

I may remark that there is a certain refining effect frequently
produced by keeping the original cause of a feeling at a distance,
and viewing it thus through a medium. Thus the sensation of
healthy functions is one of our principle enjoyments; the hue and
fulness that are the outward aspect of health are pleasurable by
association, and according to Alison are beautiful; the one degree
of remove from direct consciousness converts a sensual pleasure
into a sentimental one. Waving corn-fields, heavy and ripe, are
agreeable objects by association with the supply of our bodily
wants, and the delight is refined upon by keeping at some distance
the actual and ultimate sensations that give all the force to the
appearance. A feeling that in the reality would be called by
comparison gross and sensual, becomes sentimental when the
mind has some intervening object to rest upon.

Dickens was certainly conscious of distance as a special
factor in the viewpoint of the spectator and fully aware that
it modified the effect of experience: 'the animal . . . displayed
various peculiarities, highly interesting to a bystander, but
by no means equally amusing to any one seated behind him'.
He further suggests that an element of criticism may enter
when spectators are detached from the emotions of partici-
pants: 'The actors in the mimic life of the theatre, are blind
to violent transitions and abrupt impulses of passion or
feeling, which, presented before the eyes of mere spectators,
are at once condemned as outrageous and preposterous.'
Dickens seems also to have been aware that distance or
detachment plays an important part in ironic situations, as

[1] Edward Bullough, "Psychical Distance" as a Factor in Art and an Aesthetic Principle', *The British Journal of Psychology*, **V. 2.** (1912), reprinted in
E. Bullough, *Aesthetics* (1957), pp. 97, 99–100.

the following passage from the manuscript of *Little Dorrit* shows:

> Before parting, at Physician's door, they both looked up at the sunny morning sky, into which the smoke of a few early fires and the breath and voices of a few early stirrers were peacefully rising, and then looked round upon the immense city, and said, If all those hundreds and thousands of beggared people WHO WERE YET ASLEEP, could only know, as they two spoke, ⟨what was impending over them⟩ THE RUIN THAT IMPENDED OVER THEM, what a FEARFUL cry AGAINST ONE MISERABLE SOUL would go up TO HEAVEN![1]

Here Dickens stresses the sense of detachment created by exclusive knowledge about the fate of others. Physician and Bar, who can foresee the terrible financial crash which will follow the suicide of Merdle, survey the metropolis as one vast panorama of unsuspecting victims. This panoramic view sets the pair (and the reader who shares their viewpoint) at some distance from the prospect they contemplate. The addition of 'who were yet asleep' further isolates the pair who are awake and watchful from the thousands of victims who remain in the most blissful of all states of ignorance. This ignorance, which is not only stressed but perhaps even symbolized by the idea of sleep, is set sharply against the idea of 'ruin', which particularizes the fate hanging over the victims and is also added as a second thought. In their foreknowledge of human fate on the grand scale, Physician and Bar share almost a godlike viewpoint and the sense of cosmic distance is reinforced by the idea of a cry for vengeance which will go up 'to Heaven'. This idea, which might well in another context have been something of a cliché, was again inserted as an afterthought.

More recently than Bullough and Brecht, there has been some recognition that irony is a method of distancing[2] but no theoretical discussion of this point. In my view, irony comprises a sense of 'grim amusement' and a sense of detached judgement. The function of irony is, I believe, to make

---

[1] Alexander Bain, *The Senses and the Intellect* (1855), p. 401. *PP*, Chap. V, p. 61; *OT*, Chap. XVII, p. 118. Original MS. of *LD*, Victoria and Albert Museum, Forster Collection, 47. A. 35 (Vol. IIB), Bk. II, Chap. XXV, p. 21; cf. *LD*, p. 708.   [2] See esp. Wayne C. Booth, op. cit., pp. 243–4, 316–21.

possible a cool, objective, and satisfying view of experience through distancing. By distancing us from anxiety or other emotions (except amusement), by freeing us from identification, irony releases our critical faculty. This element of release corresponds to the old concepts of Romantic Irony and the Irony of Detachment or Spiritual Freedom.

The function of irony can be further illustrated by comparing two views of the same scene.[1] In the manuscript of *Hard Times*, Dickens revises his first description of Coketown as follows:

Coketown, to which Messrs. Bounderby and Gradgrind now walked, was a triumph of fact ⟨and figures⟩; it had no greater taint of fancy in it than Mrs. Gradgrind herself. Let us strike the key-note, Coketown, before pursuing our tune.

It was a town of red brick or of brick that would have been red if the smoke AND ASHES had allowed it; but, as matters stood it was a town of UNNATURAL red and black like the ⟨face of⟩ PAINTED FACE OF an ugly savage. It was a town of machinery and tall chimneys, out of which interminable serpents of smoke trailed themselves sluggishly for ever and ever, and never got uncoiled. It had a black canal in it, and a river that ran purple with ill-smelling dye, and vast piles of building full of windows where there was a rattling and a trembling all day long, and where the piston of the steam-engine worked monotonously up and down, like the head of an elephant in a state of melancholy madness. It contained several large streets all very like one another, and many small streets still more like one another, inhabited by people equally like one another, who ALL went in and out at the same hours, WITH THE SAME SOUND UPON THE PAVEMENT, to do the same work, and to whom every day was the same as yesterday and to-morrow, and every year the counterpart of the last and the next.

[1] Original MS. of *HT*, Chap. V. pp. 12–13 ('n ugly' and 'sluggishly' were deleted and 'pavement' altered to 'same pavements' in proof), Chap. X, p. 6; cf. *HT*, Bk. I, Chaps. V, X, pp. 22, 63. Corrected proofs of *HT*, Chap. V, 147 [I conjecture that the phrase was added in proofs which have not survived since, although MS. and surviving proofs omit this phrase, it occurs in *HW*, ix (8 Apr. 1854), 168]; cf. *HT*, Bk. I, Chap. V, p. 23, and see Thomas Carlyle, *Chartism* [1839], *Critical and Miscellaneous Essays*, People's Edition (1872), vol. vi, p. 150, 'O reader, to what shifts is poor Society reduced, struggling to give still some account of herself, in epochs when Cash Payment has become the sole nexus of man to man!', *Signs of the Times* [1829], *Critical and Miscellaneous Essays*, vol. ii, p. 247, 'Thus religion too is Profit, a working for wages; not Reverence, but vulgar Hope or Fear'.

These attributes of Coketown were in the main inseparable from
the work by which it was sustained; against them were to be set
off, comforts of life which found their way all over the world,
AND ELEGANCIES OF LIFE WHICH MADE WE WILL NOT
ASK HOW MUCH OF THE FINE LADY, WHO COULD
SCARCELY BEAR TO HEAR THE PLACE MENTIONED.

Five chapters later in the manuscript, Dickens presents a
second description of Coketown which has also been revised:

In the hardest working part of Coketown; ⟨where⟩ IN THE
INNERMOST FORTIFICATIONS OF THAT UGLY CITADEL,
WHERE Nature was as strongly bricked out as killing airs and
gases were bricked in: at the heart of the labyrinth of narrow courts
upon courts, and close streets upon streets, which had come into
existence piecemeal, every piece in a violent hurry for some one
man's purpose, and the whole an unnatural family, shouldering,
and ⟨jostling⟩ TRAMPLING, and pressing one another to death;
in the last close nook of this great exhausted receiver, where the
chimneys, for want of air to make a draught, were BUILT IN AN
IMMENSE VARIETY OF stunted and crooked shapes, as though
every house put out a sign of the kind of people who might be
expected to be born in it; among the multitude of Coketown,
generically called "the Hands,"—a race who would have found
more favour with some people, if Providence had seen fit to make
them only hands, or, like the lower creatures of the seashore, only
hands and stomachs—lived a certain Stephen Blackpool.

The second description of Coketown is organized around a
single theme which gives it a unity of feeling-tone. A pure, that
is an uncomplicated, antipathy is created in the reader towards the unnatural industrial horror of Coketown which
stifles and cripples its inhabitants. The conscious artistry here
can be seen in the revisions through which Dickens intensifies
the effect of antipathy. He increases the repelling claustro-
phobic atmosphere of Coketown by the insertion of 'in the
innermost fortifications of that ugly citadel'. By emending
'jostling' to 'trampling', he not only avoids the repetition of a
similar idea and makes a smoother transition from 'shouldering' to the climax, 'pressing one another to death', he also
emphasizes still further the cramping and stifling results of
industrial haste and anarchy. Finally, he adds to the horror of
a crippling environment by calling attention to 'an immense

variety' of deformed shapes. There are, however, two basic
weaknesses in this passage. First, there is an unsuccessful
kind of 'distancing'—if we can properly call it that. To
represent the stifled and crippled people of Coketown symbolically through their cramped and misshapen houses is
imaginative and it is certainly an instance of that vision of
'correspondence' and oneness in the Dickens world referred
to earlier. But, unfortunately, while Dickens consciously
strives to intensify the horror of industrialization and while
the ultimate horror is rightly seen to be the stunting of
human beings, the indirect manner of realizing this ultimate
horror, its whimsical displacement from people on to things,
weakens the final impression. Secondly, without a successful
kind of distancing, any intensification of effect only focuses
a simple vision more sharply. So that the very rhetoric of the
passage defeats its own ends.

The earlier description of Coketown also creates a strong
antipathy towards the ugly and unnatural nightmare of
Coketown. At first sight, the conscious artistry might seem
similar to that in the second description. Thus, antipathy is
increased by the addition of 'and ashes', 'unnatural', and
'painted' and by the strengthening of the theme of monotony
in the second paragraph. It is only when we compare the
second paragraph with the first that we see a very different
method in operation; the effect of antipathy, here, is complicated by irony. There is a contrast between the position,
ironically assumed in the first paragraph with 'triumph of
fact', 'no greater taint of fancy', and the ugly reality, smoke-
bound, evil-smelling, and monotonous, that follows. Dickens's
deliberate rhetoric, which can be seen in his revisions in
the second paragraph, does not therefore simply increase
the effect of antipathy, but, by doing so, by drawing attention more sharply to the ugly reality behind Gradgrind and
Bounderby's delusions, this conscious artistry strengthens the
contrast with the first paragraph and so intensifies the ironic
effect. The whole passage continues to be shot through with
irony. There is irony in the imagery. The unnatural apparatus
of industry is described through images drawn from the
natural world of animals and savages; an ironic contrast is
obviously implied in the comparison, here, but a further

irony is suggested, I think, in the paradoxical, jungle-like character of industrial civilization. Again, the subtle irony here is stressed through Dickens's revisions. The insertion of 'unnatural' and 'painted' helps to draw attention to the antithesis between natural and unnatural and to the appearance of civilization behind which the ugly reality of a savagery worse than the natural kind is concealing itself. There is a further ironical contrast between the town's ugly and uncongenial character and the comforts and elegance it produces through its manufactured goods, an irony which is realized more fully through a revision in the third paragraph. Through adding the ironic idea of a society which is glad to adorn itself with the products of a place which it is too snobbish to name, Dickens intensifies the power of his satirical vision. Irony is sustained in three further paragraphs (which I have not quoted). Structural irony and the irony of understatement combine in an omniscient comment which stresses the theme and hints at possible developments in the story: 'A town so sacred to fact, and so triumphant in its assertion, of course got on well? Why no, not quite well.' There is an irony in the town's very architecture in which even the pretensions to spirituality embody themselves in the forms of the materialistic world whose values dominate the life of Coketown. Ironically enough, too, society, which has changed work into a religion and the outward forms of religion into those of work, is indignantly surprised to discover that the working people turn their backs on religion proper. Once more Dickens can be seen, here, deliberately clarifying his vision, making it into a sharper and more specific indictment of the acquisitive values of society:

everything was fact between the lying-in hospital and the cemetery, and what you couldn't state in figures, OR SHOW TO BE PURCHASABLE IN THE CHEAPEST MARKET AND SAL-ABLE IN THE DEAREST, was not, and never should be, world without end, Amen.

In proof, Dickens inserts into his parody of the doxology from the Prayer Book the phrase, 'or show to be purchasable in the cheapest market and salable in the dearest', thus bringing into collision the most profane of all the economic formulas of *laissez-faire* and the most sacred text in the affirmation of Christian faith; the result is to imply ironically that the eternal faith and the gospel according to wealth and work are one, thus exposing more than a social evil—revealing a shocking blasphemy against the Holy Spirit.

Both Dickens's descriptions of Coketown do, in fact focus an adverse vision of the ravages made by industrial society through an antipathy created in the reader. But the second view is one of simple rejection only. The first view is more complex, more subtle and more effective in its criticism. There is still a strong adverse feeling—one which utterly rejects the world of Coketown but because we are also carefully distanced, through the ironical presentation, from our own immediate emotional reaction to Coketown, our final judgement is more detached, more objective. Our intellect is freed from the cruder form of emotional rejection to share in a more sophisticated vision.

V

THE COMPLEX EFFECT

1. *The Rhetoric of Sympathy and Irony*

Do sympathy and irony invariably coexist as separate rhetorics in Dickens's narrative art or may there be an interplay between them? A comparison between the very different functions of sympathy and irony suggests the possibility of such an interplay. It is noteworthy that these functions are diametrically opposite in purpose. The rhetoric of sympathy aims at an *identification* between the reader and the living experience of the novel; the rhetoric of irony aims at *distancing* the reader from such experience. The rhetoric of sympathy seeks to establish an emotional bond between the reader and the characters, an emotional *involvement* in their lives and fortunes; the rhetoric of irony tries to set up a standpoint of *detachment*. The vision focused through the rhetoric of sympathy is one of *acceptance* and benevolence, of compassion and approval; the vision focused through the rhetoric of irony is cool, objective and *critical*. True, sympathy may be the instrument of a crude and naïve vision or of one which is calm, wise, and moral whereas irony may be used in the interests of a biased or even hysterical judgement. In general, however, sympathy tends towards an emotive view of experience while irony tends to be the point at which a critical intellect enters into the vision. Repeatedly in his work, Dickens represents the intellect and the emotions as an antithesis between 'head' and 'heart'. Yet the interaction between these two, their contradiction, conflict and synthesis, also plays a vital role in Dickens's view of human psychology, in his *Weltanschauung*, and in the concept of rhetoric and vision that he seeks to realize in his narrative art.

Dickens's general view of human psychology may seem a simple, if not superficial, version of the modern view. In the context of its time, his view appears more complex, much bolder, and more advanced than the utilitarian theory which was the prevalent intellectual fashion. Much of the work of John Stuart Mill, for instance, was vitiated by the ludicrously over-simplified conception of human psychology which he inherited from his father: 'the formation of all human character by circumstances, through the universal Principle of Association, and the consequent unlimited possibility of improving the moral and intellectual condition of mankind by education'. James Mill's *Analysis of the Phenomena of the Human Mind* (1829) was published four years before Dickens's first story. Yet it was 1861 before John Stuart Mill recognized the need to extend the idea of utility to include the pleasures of the higher emotions and the imagination and it was only in 1869, while editing his father's work with Alexander Bain, that he finally acknowledged the serious limitations of the associationalist psychology advanced in *Analysis of the Phenomena of the Human Mind*. Dickens was not unaware of the association of ideas, as the dialogue of Flora Finching and Jingle shows. Barely nine years, however, after the first edition of James Mill's *Analysis*, and at a time when utilitarianism appeared to have survived the earlier onslaught of Coleridge and to be going from strength to strength, Dickens attacked the philosophy at its weakest point, its basic assumption about human motivation. In *Oliver Twist*, Dickens ridicules the belief that self-interest was the sure foundation of human behaviour on which a philosophy (that consisted of a theory of ethics, legislation, and political economy) might be raised. Again, in *Hard Times*, Dickens embodies the idea of self-interest with a satirical emphasis in Tom Gradgrind and Bitzer.[1]

In *Hard Times*, Dickens fully acknowledges the tragic extent to which intellect and affections may clash. He thus returns, in part, to a position abandoned by many leading intellectuals of the period. The painful conflict between

---

[1] J. S. Mill, *Autobiography* [1873], World's Classics (1924), p. 91; J. S. Mill, *Utilitarianism* [*Frazer's*, 1861] (1863); Jeremy Bentham, *Deontology* (1834), pp. 125 ff. *OT*, Chap. X, p. 66; it is interesting to compare the date this episode was published in *Bentley's Miscellany* (July 1837) with that of the *Deontology*. *HT*, Bk. III, Chaps. VII, VIII, pp. 284–5, 287–9; cf. Dickens's notes in the Original MS. of *HT*: 'Carry on Tom—selfish—calculations all go to No. I' (memoranda for No. II), 'Bitzer true to his bringing up' (Chap. XXXV).

reason and emotion had been insisted upon throughout a long Christian tradition, culminating during the seventeenth century in that tragic view of self-division so powerfully expressed by Fulke Greville. Eighteenth-century rationalism seriously underestimated the affective side in this conflict and the utilitarianism of the early nineteenth century retreated even further into unreality. The fantasy of 'economic man' is a prime instance of this retreat. Utilitarianism is partly a development of eighteenth-century rationalism and partly a reaction against the romanticism which came to dominate the first decades of the nineteenth century and which stressed the importance of instincts, feelings, and imagination, of all that was spontaneous, natural, and creative, in the life of man. James Mill, in particular, set his face against the feelings, believing that the rational in man might solve all his problems; both he and Bentham committed themselves to a narrow, rigid, and determinist theory of the association of ideas as the sole explanation of human psychology. Dickens, therefore, in upholding the case for affections and imagination in man, is also sharing the general romantic viewpoint. The label 'sentimental radical' as distinct from 'philosophical radical' is, perhaps, not so objectionable as it might at first appear.[1]

The link between Dickens and romanticism in this respect was almost certainly Carlyle. No really close attention has been paid to the possibility that Carlyle strongly influenced Dickens's view of human psychology.[2] Yet, apart from *The French Revolution* and *Latter-Day Pamphlets*, Dickens had in his possession a copy of the second edition of Carlyle's *Critical and Miscellaneous Essays* (1840). In *Signs of the Times* (1819), Carlyle attacks Bentham and the notion that self-interest provides an adequate account of man's motivation. In *Characteristics* (1831), he attacks the utilitarians by name, opposes

---

[1] The label is applied by Bagehot; see Humphry House, *The Dickens World*, p. 170.

[2] Not even by Louis Cazamian, *Le roman social en Angleterre 1830–1850*, Second Edition (Paris, 1934), vol. i, pp. 111–259, vol. ii, pp. 1–46, though he acknowledges Carlyle's influence on Dickens in a general way. Moreover, although Cazamian recognizes the importance and the impact of the psychological element in Dickens's fiction, ibid., vol. ii, pp. 44–5, he does not discern its complex nature, considering it only as an idealistic reaction.

their mechanistic view of life, and puts forward the view that the healthy organism whether human or social, functions as a totality whereas disease springs from one-sideness and self-division:

> The healthy know not of their health, but only the sick: this is the Physician's Aphorism; and applicable in a far wider sense than he gives it. We may say, it holds no less in moral, intellectual, political, poetical, than in merely corporeal therapeutics . . . In the Body, for example, as all doctors are agreed, the first condition of complete health is, that each organ perform its function unconsciously, unheeded; let but any organ announce its separate existence, were it even boastfully, and for pleasure, not for pain, then already has one of those unfortunate 'false centres of sensibility' established itself, already is derangement there. The perfection of bodily wellbeing is, that the collective bodily activities seem one; and be manifested, moreover, not in themselves, but in the action the yaccomplish. . . In fact unity, agreement is always silent, or soft-voiced; it is only discord that loudly proclaims itself. So long as the several elements of Life, all fitly adjusted, can pour forth their movement like harmonious tuned strings, it is a melody and unison; Life, from its mysterious fountains, flows out as in celestial music and diapason. . . Thus too, in some languages, is the state of health well denoted by a term expressing unity; when we feel ourselves as we wish to be, we say that we are *whole*.

Again, Carlyle sees the grave psychological and spiritual danger in the intellectual approach to life, 'The beginning of Inquiry is Disease: all Science, if we consider well, as it must have originated in the feeling of something being wrong, so it is and continues to be but Division, Dismemberment, and partial healing of the wrong', and this danger is exacerbated when intellectual life is restricted to the purely logical.

Dickens's dedication of *Hard Times* to Carlyle may, therefore, be much more widely significant than has been acknowledged. But, although Carlyle stresses the importance of the Unconscious, sometimes appearing to give the concept an almost modern psychological meaning, sometimes equating it with the time-old mystical notion of the-ground-of-all-being, although he accords a vital role to the imagination and intuition, and comes very close to formulating the idea of repression, it is Dickens rather than Carlyle who expresses this idea clearly:

> Mr Dombey undergoes no violent internal change, either in this book, or in life. A sense of his injustice is within him all along. The more he represses it, the more unjust he necessarily is. Internal shame and external circumstances may bring the contest to the surface in a week, or a day; but it has been a contest for years, and is only fought out then.

The phrase 'to the surface', which was altered to 'to a close' in the later preface, is especially revealing and the metaphor used here anticipates the graphic picture of the mind adopted in much twentieth-century psychology.[1]

The idea of repression, boldly worked out in terms of a human life, is presented in its most complete and convincing form in *Hard Times*, which contains the fullest exposition of Dickens's general view of human psychology. Here, he tries to show that the conflict between the reason, on the one hand, and the instincts, affections, and imagination, on the other, may be agonizingly real. Such a conflict may be resolved by the conscious acceptance of both 'head' and 'heart' or it may be driven underground through faulty education and result in the stunting of personality, mental breakdown, and even crime. The result of repressing affections, instincts, and imagination in favour of a one-sided rational development is the impoverishment of Bitzer's personality, the nervous collapse of Louisa with its sexual undertones, and the degeneration of Tom Gradgrind into selfishness and thieving. The autobiography of John Stuart Mill was published in 1874. Dickens can hardly have had direct knowledge about this, but it is possible that he could have learnt about it from Carlyle; part of his novel is a remarkable forecast of Mill's own story, an astonishingly accurate prediction of the psychological consequences of a given philosophical attitude rigorously carried through into an educational system. To

---

[1] *Catalogue of the Library of Charles Dickens*, p. 18; Thomas Carlyle, *Critical and Miscellaneous Essays*, People's Edition, vol. ii, pp. 239–40, vol. iv, pp. 36–7, 1–6, 9, 14, 20–22. Preface to the First Cheap Edition of *D & S* (1858); the later Preface to the Charles Dickens Edition (1867) also substitutes 'after a long balance of victory' for 'then'. The slight variations in the two prefaces were noted by Kathleen Tillotson, *Novels of the Eighteen-Forties*, p. 166, footnote (2).

any one ignorant of Mill's upbringing, Gradgrind's education
of his children may appear a gross and incredible caricature;
Mill's early chapters show that it is hardly an exaggeration
at all. What is more, Mill experienced a neurotic breakdown in
his adolescence and was eventually compelled to acknowledge
the claims of the emotions both in his own life and in his
philosophical ideas.[1] He gradually modified and softened the
harsh and rigid utilitarianism of Bentham and his father.

It is perhaps surprising that *Hard Times* appeared the year
before Spencer's *Principles of Psychology* and Bain's *The
Senses and the Intellect* which mark the beginning of a biologi-
cally and physiologically orientated psychology that was to
lead in turn to the new psychology of our century. As against
G. H. Lewes's picture of him as a man with no interest in
general cultural thought, Dickens does in fact seem to have
been receptive to biological ideas throughout his life. It has
been pointed out recently that his reaction to Lyell's *The
Antiquity of Man* (1863) was a calm and sympathetic one and
that an article in *All the Year Round* treated Darwin's *On the
Origin of Species* (1859) lucidly and respectfully. What has
escaped notice, however, is that sixteen years before Darwin's
book and a year before the storm broke over the appearance
of Robert Chambers's *Vestiges of the Natural History of
Creation* (1844), Dickens in the first number of *Martin
Chuzzlewit* (January 1843) shows a familiarity with the
theory of the higher species evolving from the lower; he cites
two versions of a theory of evolution which he attributes in a
satirical passage to Monboddo and Blumenbach who look at
first sight like typical Dickensian coinages but were a Scottish
judge of the eighteenth century whose ideas even anticipated
those of Lamarck and a German who is now acknowledged as
the father of anthropology. Yet the stress on the theory of
evolution distracts attention from the development during the
nineteenth century of other important concepts in biology and
physiology. Dickens numbered several distinguished medical

---

[1] Unlike Edgar Johnson, *Charles Dickens*, vol. ii, p. 809, and F. R. Leavis,
The Great Tradition, pp. 250–1, K. J. Fielding, 'Milland Gradgrind', *Nineteenth-
Century Fiction*, xi (1956), 148–51, argues that Gradgrind cannot be strictly
identified with James Mill but concedes, 149, that Mill's educational system
'made no appeal whatsoever to the imagination'. See J. S. Mill, *Autobiography*,
pp. 92 ff., for his own comment on his upbringing; ibid., pp. 113–25.

men among his friends and in his library he had works on medicine and physiology, including Dr. J. Elliotson's *Human Physiology*, which incorporates part of Blumenbach's *Institutiones Physiologicae* (1840), Sir Charles Bell's *Anatomy and Philosophy of Expression* (1847), Dr. R. Hooper's *Medical Dictionary* (1848), and J. B. Harrison's *Medical Aspects of Death* (1852). The physiological counterpart to the psychological notions of self-division and integration is that the organism, in its healthy natural state, functions as a totality when it responds to the environment, an idea expressed for example in Spencer's *Psychology*:

The impossibility of dissociating the psychical states which we class as intellectual from those which we class as emotional, may be clearly discerned . . . the state of consciousness produced by a single beautiful tone, presents cognition and emotion fused into one . . . all cognition implies emotion, and all emotion implies cognition . . . there can be no conscious adjustment of an inner to an outer relation without all these [Memory, Reason, Feeling, and Will] being involved.

Such a concept is anticipated in *Hard Times*. In the state of health, 'head' and 'heart', the rational and the affective sides of man, co-operate as complementary functions.[1]

This idea of a co-operation between reason and emotion in a fully conscious and responsible view of life can be traced back to Dickens's early career. Pickwick's ultimate awareness of all that the Fleet Prison means, for example, is presented as a total response, an agony which arouses his intellect at the same time that it inflames his feelings: ' "My head aches with these scenes, and my heart too." '[2] Already then, Dickens sees perception as a dual process in the observer which has a dual effect on him; Dickens is thus beginning to formulate a view of both rhetoric and vision as a complex activity that accords with his notions of human psychology.

Co-operation between 'heart' and 'head', between the emotions and the critical intellect, implies a co-operation between the rhetorics of sympathy and irony in Dickens's

---

[1] Johnson, op. cit., vol. ii, p. 1132; *MC*, Chap. I, p. 6; *Catalogue of the Library of Charles Dickens*, pp. 42, 11, 62, 55, 48; Herbert Spencer, *The Principles of Psychology* (1855), pp. 585–6, 613.

[2] *PP*. Chap. XLV, p. 645.

narrative art. Such a co-operation, which might be described
as *the rhetoric of sympathy and irony*, does in fact function as
follows. Through the identification which sympathy makes
possible, the reader becomes as intimately involved in the
experience of the novel as if he were living within its world
while, through irony, he remains detached and able to make
an objective and critical assessment of the experience he is
living through. In this way, both intellect and emotion are
invited to respond to the vision of the novel and what may
seem contradictory attitudes in author and reader are united
in the paradox of a complex art. The limitations imposed on
vision by the rhetorics of sympathy and irony separately may
now be transcended, for a complex rhetoric makes a complex
vision possible. Such a rhetorical art has acknowledged
boldly and made use of the fact that man has a dual nature,
that he may even be self-divided, but that in the final synthesis he is one and entire. Such an art aims at an act of healing
within man, a making whole, rather than at simply bringing
about the reform of man's institutions through propaganda.

How deliberately does Dickens operate this complex rhetoric and how successful is he in doing so ? That Dickens was
thinking consciously in terms of the rhetoric of sympathy and
irony at the major stages of his planning and writing can be
corroborated by examining his notes and manuscripts
closely. In his plans for *Bleak House*, for example, Dickens
warns himself that he must treat Turveydrop Senior, the
Model of Deportment, with a certain pathos: 'old Turveydrop—Pathetic too—blesses people—My Son! etc' (memoranda for No. V). The pathetic effect is, therefore, an addition
to another effect Dickens has in mind. The only other note on
Turveydrop Senior which indicates an effect makes absolutely
plain that this other effect was irony: 'Mr. Turveydrop— "My
children you shall always live with me'—meaning, I will
always live with you' (Chap. XXIII). The text of the novel confirms how far the portrait of Turveydrop Senior is presented
through a satirical irony. The Model of Deportment might so
easily have provided a pasteboard target for Dickens's satirical wit. Yet through a complex rhetoric, here, Dickens communicates to the reader a more complex vision of even a
minor character. The touch of the pathetic in the finished

portrait of this relic of Beau Brummell's England involves the
reader in his story and so prevents his being dismissed merely
as an absurd figure of fun; it gives him a spark of life beyond
his satirical function. Dickens's comic vision is therefore not
necessarily simple. Even the comic world, the author seems
to be saying, cannot be dismissed as a mere joke.

As in the planning, so in the writing and revision of *Bleak
House*, Dickens can be shown to have had the rhetoric of
sympathy and irony very much in mind.[1] Certain emenda-
tions in the manuscript of this novel, for instance, indicate
that the co-operation between 'heart' and 'head', which we
saw at work in the passage from *Pickwick*, is the basis of a
deliberate rhetoric and can be equated with the complex
effect I have described:

"⟨Strange indeed⟩ AH COUSIN," said Richard. "⟨You heard
what that old man said in explanation of I am afraid for Mr.
Krook elegantly said (I am afraid – ?– an older and duller – ?– than
yours, Think This CHANCELLOR-LIKE THEY RACK OR
GRUB ON IN A MUDDLE⟩ STRANGE, INDEED! ALL THIS
WASTEFUL ⟨– ?–⟩ WANTON CHESS-PLAYING *IS* VERY
STRANGE. TO SEE THAT COMPOSED court yesterday JOG-
GING ON SO SERENELY, ⟨– ?–⟩ and to think of the ⟨– ?–⟩
WRETCHEDNESS OF THE PIECES ON THE BOARD,
GAVE ME the headache and the heartache both together. ⟨– ?–⟩
MY HEAD ACHED WITH WONDERING HOW IT HAP-
PENED, IF men ⟨be⟩ WERE NEITHER fools, ⟨or ill⟩ NOR
rascals; ⟨it and don't want them to be either⟩ AND MY HEART
ACHED TO THINK THAT they COULD POSSIBLY be either."

In this heavily revised passage, the image of the chess-board
which lends the vision of Chancery such ironic distance seems
to have been a second thought. The ironic reference to the
'composed' court 'jogging on so serenely' which is sharply set
against the misery it causes is also an afterthought. The
insertion of the phrase, 'wretchedness of the pieces on the
board', which was arrived at only after much rethinking,
shows how the complex effect is drawing together both the
pathetic element ('wretchedness') and the element of ironic
distance and detachment ('of the pieces on the board') into a

---

[1] Original MS. of *BH*, Vol. IA ('pathetic' = 'ludicrous' is twentieth-century
usage), Chap. V, p. 10, Vol. IB, Chap. XXIII, p. 3 *BH*, pp. 58, 320–1.

closer unity. Finally, the gloss on Richard's vision of Chancery as both a 'headache' and a 'heartache' is added as an after-thought. This gloss stresses that what rouses the intellect into a painful awareness is the ironic prospect of deception or self-deception to which men may be falling prey ('My head ached with wondering how it happened, if men were neither fools nor rascals') and what causes emotional concern is the tragedy of such a prospect ('my heart ached to think that they could possibly be either'). The passage has a further structural irony for it is immediately followed by Richard's hubristic claim that Chancery will never work its bad in-fluence on Ada and himself, an idea which was also clarified by the revisions examined earlier.

A further striking instance of Dickens's deliberate use of the complex effect occurs later in the manuscript of *Bleak House*. Once again Dickens is consciously using this complex rhetoric to focus the same tragi-ironic vision of Chancery. If anything, the effect is even more complex and used with increased subtlety:

He was as vivacious as ever, and told us he was very industrious; but I was not easy in my mind about him. It appeared to me that his industry was all misdirected. I could not find that it led to anything, but the formation of delusive hopes in connection with the suit already the pernicious cause of so much sorrow and ruin. He had got at the core of that mystery now, he told us; and noth-ing could be plainer than that the will under which he and Ada were to take, I don't know how many thousands of pounds, must be finally established, if there were any sense or justice in the Court of Chancery—but O what a great *if* that sounded in my ears—and that this happy conclusion could not be much longer delayed. He proved this to himself by all the weary arguments on that side he had read, and every one of them sunk him deeper in the infatuation. He had even begun to haunt the Court. He told us how he saw Miss Flite there daily; how they talked together, and he did her little kindnesses; and how, WHILE HE LAUGHED AT HER, HE PITIED HER FROM HIS HEART ⟨he pitied her WITH ALL HIS SOUL from his heart⟩. But he never thought—NEVER, ⟨Richard⟩ my POOR, dear, SANGUINE Richard, capable of so much happiness then, and with such better things before him!—what a fatal link was riveting between his fresh youth and her faded age; between his free hopes and her caged birds, and her hungry garret, and her wandering mind!

It is highly significant, here, that Dickens was not satisfied with his first version of Richard's view of Miss Flite as a compassionate one alone but that, after some fumbling, he added the idea of Richard's laughing at the victim of Chancery *at the same time* as he pities her. By using the conjunction 'while', Dickens stresses that both of Richard's reactions to Miss Flite, though contradictory in themselves, are paradoxically brought together in some complementary manner. A kind of critical distance is added to Richard's view of Miss Flite through his finding her ridiculous, though the degree to which Richard's view is detached and critical, the quality of his view that is, must be questioned. Indeed, this is one of the more complex and powerful ironies of the passage. The overall vision is a view by a third person of Richard's view of Miss Flite. This second overall vision is deliberately focused through a second complex effect since Dickens carefully draws attention, by two insertions made in the same phrase, to both the pity ('poor') and the irony ('sanguine') in Esther's view of Richard. Once again the very close juxtaposition of sympathy and irony brings the separate elements in the complex effect into a more intimate unity. The result of refracting the vision of Chancery, here, first through Richard's view of Miss Flite's fate and then through Esther's view of Richard, as a second victim, is of course to double the force of the irony. Yet it does more than this. It sets up a second kind of distance outside the first and, paradoxically, by channelling the reader's reaction through the concern of a second character for the approaching tragedy of a second victim, it involves the reader even more intensely in the tragic experience of Chancery. It is through this complex rhetoric that Dickens presents a vision of Chancery which is far more deadly in its aim and impact than a mere satirical attack. The reader is not simply invited to laugh grimly at Chancery, he is led into experiencing the pathetic result of Chancery on its victims. Through the tragic irony of the vision, the reader is set both within the world of *Bleak House*, amid all its suffering, and yet at a distance. Though such a distance affords a certain detachment and objectivity, it cannot be described as safe and remains an uncomfortable, if critical, vantage point.

2. *The Transmutation of Fact*

Although much scholarship, including a whole book by Edwin Pugh, has been devoted to the task of identifying the Dickens 'originals', the critical study of how Dickens treats his 'originals' has been rather neglected. Yet such a study promises to throw some light on Dickens's methods of composition and his craftsmanship.

A good illustration is provided by the material Dickens used in creating Miss Havisham of *Great Expectations* (1860–1). This material shows that three separate ideas went to the making of the character.[1] Thus, the idea of the upper-class female recluse is to be found in a letter of 1856 from Dickens to Forster:

The murder over the way (the third or fourth event of that nature in the Champs Elysées since we have been here) seems to disclose the strangest state of things. The Duchess who is murdered lived alone in a great house which was always shut up, and passed her time entirely in the dark. In a little lodge outside lived a coachman (the murderer), and there had been a long succession of coachmen who had been unable to stay there, and upon whom, whenever they asked for their wages, she plunged out with an immense knife, by way of an immediate settlement. The coachman never had anything to do, for the coach hadn't been driven out for years; neither would she ever allow the horses to be taken out for exercise. Between the lodge and the house, is a miserable bit of garden, all overgrown with long rank grass, weeds, and nettles; and in this, the horses used to be taken out to swim—in a dead green vegetable sea, up to their haunches. On the day of the murder, there was a great crowd, of course; and in the midst of it up comes the Duke her husband (from whom she was separated), and rings at the gate. The police open the gate. "C'est vrai donc," says the Duke, "que Madame la Duchesse n'est plus?"—"C'est trop vrai, Monseigneur."—"Tant mieux," says the Duke, and walks off deliberately, to the great satisfaction of the assemblage.

---

[1] *F*, vol. iii, pp. 127–9; 'Where We Stopped Growing', *HW*, vi (1 Jan. 1853), reprinted in *MP*, pp. 362–3; in an interesting article, Martin Meisel, 'Miss Havisham Brought to Book', *Publications of the Modern Language Association of America* lxxxi (1966), 278–85, indicates further 'originals' but overlooks the hint for the motivation of Miss Havisham in Forster's *Life*; see also William Allingham, 'The Dirty Old Man', *HW*, vi (8 Jan. 1853), 396–7. For some further interesting comments, see K. J. Fielding, 'Dickens and the Past: The Novelist of Memory', *Experience in the Novel*, ed. Roy Harvey Pearce (New York and London, 1968), pp. 114–16.

As Dickens himself says, what interested him about this episode were the odd facts of human behaviour it revealed. He does succeed in communicating this interest and the stress tends to remain upon facts. Few words are used emotively. Although he is describing a murder, there is not the slightest attempt to record, speculate on, work up, any effect of horror; the only reference to violence is to the violence of the victim. All that Dickens does find of a sensational nature in the episode are certain scandalous tit-bits of information: the eccentric behaviour of the recluse, her refusal to pay her coachmen, her assaults on them, her separation from her husband, the reaction of her husband to the murder which is both amusing and shocking. This is the kind of information the local gossip would have relished and it is hardly surprising that Dickens would have found it interesting for, as he makes clear, he was himself a neighbour of the Duchess. As for effect, there is no attempt to involve the reader emotionally with any of the characters. Even the victim is not allowed one jot of sympathy; on the contrary, both alive and dead she appears slightly funny. There is a certain grim humour about her manner of settling accounts with her coachmen and about her husband's satisfaction with the news that she is well and truly disposed of. Yet it is not quite true to say the whole incident is passed off as a black joke. Although it is surprising to find that, for all his fascination with murder, Dickens does not mention any details of the crime, yet he cannot resist dwelling on one or two bizarre details connected with the affair: that touch, for example, about the Duchess's spending all her time in the dark or his description of the horses appearing to swim up to the haunches in the dead green sea of overgrown grass and weeds. Far from there being any effort to unify the impression created by the passage, the effect is allowed to wander back and forth between the curiosity evoked by odd behaviour, the relish excited by scandal, the amusing and the bizarre. This is as it should be here. It gives an impression of life recorded directly—unedited and disorderly.

In a second anecdote sent by Dickens to Forster some time during the spring of 1856, there is a hint for the motivation of Miss Havisham. Since this anecdote is cited by Forster immediately after the account of the Duchess's murder and is used to illustrate the same general point, both anecdotes may have been taken from the same letter; if so, they would have been closely associated in Dickens's mind. The relevant part of the second anecdote is as follows:

The Squire had married a woman of the town from whom he was now separated, but by whom he had a daughter. The mother, to spite the father, had bred the daughter in every conceivable vice. Daughter, then 13, came from school once a month. Intensely coarse in talk, and always drunk. As they drove about the country in two open carriages, the drunken mistress would be perpetually tumbling out of one, and the drunken daughter perpetually tumbling out of the other. At last the drunken mistress drank her stomach away, and began to die on the sofa. Got worse and worse, and was always raving about Somebody's where she had once been a lodger, and perpetually shrieking that she would cut somebody else's heart out. At last she died on the sofa.

Forster claims that Dickens would have regarded this material as too improbable for treatment as fiction. Certainly, Dickens is once more giving a factual illustration of the oddness of human behaviour. Again the effect shifts in an incongruous manner, this time from interest in a curious case of human motivation to farce and then to the horror of an alcoholic's death.

Along with the themes of the eccentric upper-class female recluse and the sexually frustrated woman who seeks revenge through a perversely educated child, a third idea went to the making of Miss Havisham. The source of this idea, that of the jilted bride for ever fixed in her traumatic wedding pose, can be found in an article Dickens contributed during 1853 to *Household Words*:

Another very different person who stopped our growth, we associate with Berners Street, Oxford Street; whether she was constantly on parade in that street only, or was ever to be seen elsewhere, we are unable to say. The White Woman is her name. She is dressed entirely in white, with a ghastly white plating round her head and face, inside her white bonnet. She even carries (we hope) a white umbrella. With white boots, we know she picks her way through the winter dirt. She is a conceited old creature, cold and formal in manner, and evidently went

simpering mad on personal grounds alone—no doubt because a
wealthy Quaker wouldn't marry her. This is her bridal dress. She
is always walking up here, on her way to church to marry the false
Quaker. We observe in her mincing step and fishy eye that she
intends to lead him a sharp life. We stopped growing when we got
at the conclusion that the Quaker had had a happy escape of the
White Woman.

As in so many of his portraits in the novels, Dickens
repeats an epithet. But the repetition of 'white', here, creates
no other effect than curiosity at the eccentric behaviour of the
woman and suggests monomania which is then explained.
Not a trace of sympathy for the mad jilted creature is encouraged. On the contrary, her disagreeable features are stressed
and she is dismissed as a ridiculous figure. It is almost suggested that she got what she would have deserved had she
finally captured her man and made his life a misery. Although
there is a comic touch to the portrait, the comedy scarcely
achieves the stature of Charity Pecksniff's desertion by
Moddle at the altar; it remains on the cruder level of music-
hall jokes about the jilted bride and the henpecked husband.
The material does not create a unified impression but a
succession of separate effects. It begins as a picture of eccen-
tricity which whets the reader's curiosity about human behaviour, shifts to a catalogue of disagreeable traits, and ends
in a jocular vein. Again, there is the untidiness we might
expect to find in a record of real life.

The main interest of all three 'originals' then, lies in the
information about human oddity which they convey. The
stress is upon facts rather than effects, as we would wish in a
good report. Wherever there are effects they remain mild and
simple, and the major appeal is to the reader's curiosity. The
Duchess, the deserted wife, and the jilted bride are victims
yet we are not encouraged to feel the faintest pity for them.
Occasional touches of humour in the pictures of the Duchess
and the White Woman are slight and disagreeable features in
the latter are not insisted on very strongly. We are not
provoked into reacting with horror or disgust at the murder
of the Duchess, at the depravity of the wife's motivation, or
at the White Woman's madness. Apart from an occasional
instance of little weight, the possibilities of irony in the

three situations are not exploited. In no case is there an attempt to present a strong unity of effect through a rigorous selection of subject matter. Such effects as there may be are even permitted to clash and weaken each other. What is absent from the material, in fact, is rhetoric (as I have defined it), a structure determined by effect and vision.

The 'originals' should be compared with the study of Miss Havisham[1] into which Dickens finally combined and transmuted them. The following description is Pip's (and the reader's) earliest impression of her:

Whether I should have made out this object so soon, if there had been no fine lady sitting at it, I cannot say. In an arm-chair, with an elbow resting on the table and her head leaning on that hand, sat the strangest lady I have ever seen, or shall ever see.

She was dressed in rich materials—satins, and lace, and silks— all of white. Her shoes were white. And she had a long white veil dependent from her hair, and she had bridal flowers in her hair, but her hair was white. Some jewels sparkled on her neck and on her hands, and some other jewels lay sparkling on the table. Dresses, less splendid than the dress she wore, and half-packed trunks, were scattered about. She had not quite finished dressing, for she had but one shoe on—the other was on the table near her hand—her veil was but half arranged, her watch and chain were not put on, and some lace for her bosom lay with those trinkets, and with her handkerchief, and gloves, and some flowers, and a Prayer-book, all confusedly heaped about the looking-glass.

At first, Miss Havisham is described as if she were any normal well-to-do bride, making the final preparations for her wedding. Only a faint hint that anything is amiss is betrayed by Pip's reference to her strangeness and her white hair. Unlike the White Woman, there is nothing repelling about Miss Havisham so far. Nor is she ridiculous. On the contrary, she is a rather grand lady preparing for a most important public appearance. The richness and splendour of her dress, the brightness of her many jewels, appear to lend her dignity,

[1] GE, Chap. VIII, pp. 52, 53, 55; Chap. XXII, pp. 169–72 (cf. Chap. XLII, pp. 330–4). Original MS. of GE, Wisbech and Fenland Museum, Townshend Collection, Chap. VII, p. 6 [AYR, iv (29 Dec. 1860), 268, omits 'curious']; cf. GE, Chap. VIII, p. 56. Ibid., Chaps. XXXVIII, XLIV, XLIX, pp. 289–93, 346, 374–82; Chap. LIX, p. 458 (cf. 'The Cancelled Conclusion', 'Appendix', p. 461).

even a kind of brilliance, which is ironical in view of what is to follow in the next paragraph:

It was not in the first few moments that I saw all these things, though I saw more of them in the first moments than might be supposed. But, I saw that everything within my view which ought to be white, had been white long ago, and had lost its lustre, and was faded and yellow. I saw that the bride within the bridal dress had withered like the dress, and like the flowers, and had no brightness left but the brightness of her sunken eyes. I saw that the dress had been put upon the rounded figure of a young woman, and that the figure upon which it now hung loose, had shrunk to skin and bone.

All the great expectations of wholesome fulfilment we normally entertain for a bride are suddenly shattered. All the sensuous prospects of young married life and fruition that we associate with her wedding day are skilfully reversed into their opposites. Miss Havisham's pose as a bride turns out to be a bitter ironical burlesque. Behind the appearance is the mocking reality of withered age, sterility, and decay. Dickens uses form with considerable subtlety here. The powerful ironic effect is produced by a reversal which is both a discovery and a peripety. Through the discovery of the truth we are led by Dickens into experiencing the same pattern which Miss Havisham's catastrophe followed. At once, we divine roughly what has happened to her. We relive, in some measure, therefore, through that earlier ironic shock, the discovery by Miss Havisham that her great expectations were to come only to dust and decay. Furthermore, the appalling visual signs of her catastrophe begin to waken our pity. The normal ravages of time in the human face and body might have been expected to arouse a certain pity. But there is much more than this here. These are ravages of time set in the perspective of earlier hopes. This is old age seen as defeat, the mocking, humiliating defeat of all the dearest promises that life holds out to the greater part of womankind. Our pity is redoubled. Finally, there is, towards the close of the paragraph, still one more effect, which Dickens proceeds to intensify:

Once, I had been taken to see some ghastly waxwork at the Fair, representing I know not what impossible personage lying in state. Once, I had been taken to one of our old marsh churches to see a skeleton in the ashes of a rich dress, that had been dug out of a vault under the church pavement. Now, waxwork and skeleton seemed to have dark eyes that moved and looked at me. I should have cried out, if I could.

Dickens is not piling on the horror here for its own sake. It is part of a larger effect. The spectacle which provokes this horror, the living corpse in its bridal shroud, 'Without this arrest of everything, this standing still of all the pale decayed objects, not even the withered bridal dress on the collapsed form could have looked so like grave-clothes, or the long veil so like a shroud', also arouses pity and irony through the defeat which it represents. An image of tragic defeat is, in fact, the final visual impression that Pip carries away with him from this scene:

Miss Havisham's face . . . had dropped into a watchful AND BROODING expression—most likely when all the things about her had become transfixed—and it looked as if nothing could EVER lift it up again. Her chest had dropped, so that she stooped; and her voice had dropped, so that she spoke low, and with a curious dead lull upon her; ALTOGETHER, she had the appearance of having dropped, ⟨altogether⟩ BODY AND SOUL, WITHIN AND WITHOUT, under the weight of a ⟨blow⟩ CRUSHING BLOW.

Revisions in the manuscript, which stress the overwhelming defeat registered by Miss Havisham's posture, the utter helplessness to which the traumatic shock has reduced her, deliberately aim at winning the reader's sympathy. Yet, even here, the effect is no simple one. The situation which evokes pity is skilfully set in an ironic frame, for the immediate context of this description of defeat is a kind of victory. Immediately before the description, Miss Havisham notes with satisfaction that her plan to involve Pip with Estella and eventually to break his heart is beginning to succeed; he admits to Miss Havisham that he is both smitten with Estella and wounded by her treatment of him. Immediately after the description, Estella beats Pip in a game of cards; significantly, perhaps, the game is 'beggar my neighbour'. In this incident are to be found the roots of a tragic and ironic

growth which will spread throughout the novel. Love has
become a power game to Miss Havisham and Estella. Love
was the cause of proud Miss Havisham's great defeat in life.
Through love, she will avenge this defeat. Estella will defeat
Pip in this sinister game also. But through her apparent victory, Miss Havisham will sustain a second defeat with its own
pathos, irony, and horror. And Estella will only lose in the
end.

A comparison between the study of Miss Havisham and the
'originals' at once brings out three striking points of difference.
First, the picture of Miss Havisham is much more complex.
This complexity does not result simply from combining material from three 'originals'. It is a matter not of addition but
of coalescence and transmutation, of a compound not a mixture. The Duchess's neglect of her house simply resulted from
her idiosyncrasy as a recluse. But the neglect and decay of
Satis House is a parallel to the physical decay of its mistress while both forms of disintegration are outward manifestations of her emotional decay. Furthermore, by establishing a living correspondence between inward and outward
decay, Dickens is presenting his vision of a world which is
spiritually one, insisting that the spiritual truth about things
is what really matters. The ultimate statement of the truth
in *Great Expectations* is to be found in the ironic, pathetic, and
horrifying symbol of the wedding-cake which has gone rotten.
Putrefaction appears to spawn a lower parasitical life which,
in its turn, feeds on decay. As a form of the archetypal Life-
in-death, Miss Havisham also signifies that, when love dies,
something is born quite as active, furtive, and repulsively
malevolent as the parasites which feed on the rotting cake.
Indeed, the effect created by Dickens's description of the
putrefaction and parasitical life is deliberately intensified
through revisions in the manuscript:

Every discernible thing in it ⟨looked as if it was⟩ WAS COVER-
ED WITH DUST AND MOULD, AND dropping to pieces . . . I
saw ⟨spiders⟩ SPECKLED-LEGGED SPIDERS WITH
BLOTCHY BODIES running home to it, and running out from
it.[1]

[1] Original MS. of *GE*, Chap. X, p. 19; cf. *GE*, Chap. XI, pp. 78–9, and see
also Chap. XLIX, pp. 380–1.

The promise of love has putrefied into hatred, malice, and revenge.

Again, Dickens develops and transforms the idea of the Duchess's living in the dark. Instead of an addiction to total darkness, Miss Havisham is given an aversion to daylight which she shuts out of her rooms in favour of candlelight. Watches and clocks are stopped at the precise time when she learned that her bridegroom had deserted her. She refuses to acknowledge the days of the week. In turning her back on time and the light of the sun, Miss Havisham is rejecting life and nature. By refusing to accept the goodness of growth, she allows ascendancy to the nightmarish evil of decay. The horror, pathos, and irony aroused by the spectacle of such a condition are clear marks of the tragedy it represents.

Similarly, when Dickens transforms the motivation of the deserted wife into Miss Havisham's master-motive, he complicates his presentation of it. The motivation and the form it takes do remain roughly the same. A woman who has been rejected by a man seeks revenge by corrupting a young girl. She then uses the girl as a weapon against the male who is vulnerable through his love for the girl. In the case of *Great Expectations*, Dickens substitutes the sexual relationships of the girl for the original relationship between the girl and her father and he directs Miss Havisham's spite against the male sex in general instead of the man who had deserted her. These changes make the general design much neater and offer greater possibilities as regards the plotting of the story. But the really important difference is that Miss Havisham's motive, unlike that of the deserted wife, is made to create an effect. We view her plan through a thin veil of irony. Since the viewpoint throughout the novel is Pip's, only an ironic reading can penetrate his earlier naïvety and obtuseness. At first, Miss Havisham's plan is passed off as a kind of sport, a competitive game; there is only the faintest hint of something sinister. But when Dickens finally comes out into the open about it he deliberately draws attention to the irony of hatred masquerading as love:

"Hear me, Pip! I adopted her to be loved. I bred her and educated her, to be loved. I developed her into what she is, that she might be loved. Love her!"

She said that word often enough, and there could be no doubt that she meant to say it; but if the often repeated word had been hate instead of love—despair—revenge—dire death—it could not have sounded from her lips more like a curse.

Certainly, the irony distances what might otherwise have appeared melodramatic. The handling of Miss Havisham's motivation in this respect need only be contrasted with the stark treatment of Orlick's motivation[1] to make this point clear. Even more important, however, the irony is dove-tailed into the larger effect and vision of the novel since it also draws critical attention to the naïvety, obtuseness, and self-deception out of which Pip's own ironic tragedy grows. In addition, Miss Havisham's motivation is made part of a further pattern of irony for, like the plan of the deserted wife, that of Miss Havisham is made to recoil on her.

A second striking point of comparison is the way in which the heterogeneous material of the 'originals' with its weak and contradictory effects is wrought into an effective unity in the finished portrait. This is by no means the simple kind of unity we saw Dickens working for in the picture of another recluse, Mrs. Clennam. In the manuscript of *Little Dorrit*, we could watch Dickens deliberately increasing the simple effect of gloom. But here the effect is a complex one.

Thirdly, unity and complexity help to explain the extre-mely powerful effect and vision which the figure of Miss Havisham contributes to *Great Expectations*. What is the nature of this vision, how do the effects help to focus it, and how is it related to the over-all effect and vision of the novel? As a victim of her own self-deception, first about Compeyson and later about life and love, so neatly summed up in her false bridal pose, Miss Havisham is viewed as both an ironic and tragic figure. In her wilful deception of Pip, she in her turn sows the seeds of further ironic tragedy. Dickens's view of Miss Havisham, therefore, belongs to his general vision of life as an ironic tragi-comedy of deception. Such a vision is complex to the point of paradox since it demands that man should enter into the suffering of life's victims even while he stands back and criticizes their folly. Irony, therefore, ensures

[1] *GE*, Chap. XXIX, pp. 226–7; Chap. LIII, pp. 402–6.

a proper critical distance from Miss Havisham's delusions and deceptions but pity binds us to her fate, the long agony which will culminate in her remorse, redemption, and the final ordeal of her death by fire. The vision of an ironic tragi-comedy of deception is at the very core of *Great Expectations* and thus explains Miss Havisham's central importance in the book. The frustration of her own great expectations as regards love foreshadows and incites her to engineer the shattering disappointment of Pip's hopes of love. Pip's longing for wealth and status is shown to be motivated by his desire for Estella. True, his burning sense of social inferiority and in-justice, which are inflamed by Estella's conduct at their first meeting, are factors in his motivation. The sense of inferiority may partly explain both the submissive role he adopts towards Estella and his compensatory drive towards status. But the fundamental point is that both Pip's sexual and life goals are distorted through his relationship with Estella.[1] That this relationship is the starting-point of his later development is made absolutely clear at their first meeting. The ironic tragedies of Miss Havisham and Pip illustrate the corrupting power of unsatisfied love. The early deprivation of maternal love and the unloving attitude of his sister are important factors in Pip's development. Like Miss Havisham, Pip is the victim of the false values which a perverse attitude to love has bred in him, and, if we censure Pip's snobbishness, his social climbing, his pursuit of idleness and unearned wealth, we also pity him when the ironic blows of fate tear away one delusion after another from his eyes. For, like Miss Havisham, Pip also suffers the traumatic shocks that flesh may be heir to. And, parallel to the almost physical blow which appears to crush Miss Havisham at their first interview, we find that inward bleeding wound which

[1] Alfred Adler, *Understanding Human Nature* (New York, 1949), pp. 65–75, 149–56; Lewis Way, *Alfred Adler: An Introduction to His Psychology* (1956), p. 167; *GE*, Chap. VIII, *passim*, but esp. pp. 57–8; in my view, a close analysis does not confirm the argument of J. Hillis Miller, *Charles Dickens: The World of His Novels*, pp. 268, 252–3, that snobbishness or guilt springing from alien-ation are the prime-movers in Pip's development. *GE*, Chap. II, pp. 6–7; cf. Chap. VIII, pp. 57–8. Ibid., Chap. XLIV, p. 345; here Dickens uses the meta-phor from which the psychological term, *trauma*, was derived and the aptness of the image may be attributed to its accuracy as a description of Pip's mental state.

Pip feels he has received on learning that Estella will marry
Bentley Drummle; finally, the kind of horror which complicates the vision of Miss Havisham marks the tragedy as
belonging to a special type. There is a very dark side indeed
to the world of *Great Expectations*, a side not only represented
by the sadistic malice of Mrs. Joe Gargery, Miss Havisham,
and Estella or by the murderous assaults of Orlick but also
by the cruel, organized, social violence of the public whippings
and hangings, the mass sentencings to death, and the bestial
savagery of the convict prisons and hulks. Even Pip is not
without some responsibility, since his perverse submissiveness
to Estella arouses and inflames her sexual cruelty towards
him.[1] This dark vision can, I think, be summed up as the
negation and inversion of love, with all the horrors that this
may imply. The corruption which Miss Havisham embodies
is more than her own personal inward state. It is the dark
shadow of spiritual corruption which touches Pip and almost
the entire world of *Great Expectations*. This is the full meaning
of the horror which the rotting wedding breakfast spawns.
This is the final ironic tragedy which it represents.

So much for the kind of use Dickens made of other people's
lives in his fiction, but what use did he make of his own life?
Clearly, fiction and autobiography are different forms with
different aims[2] and there may be special problems where a
novelist is dealing with material with which he is personally
involved. There may be less detachment than when he is
dealing with other material than the circumstances of his own
life. Obsession may replace calmness and objectivity. Self-
justification may oust self-criticism. There is the danger of
self-pity. Moreover, no personal experience is likely to be less
detached, more obsessive, and more liable to encourage self-
justification and self-pity than the traumatic experience.
Now, since Dickens successfully transformed into fiction the
two most deeply wounding experiences of his life, the incident
of the blacking factory and the love affair with Maria Beadnell,
it is worth while inquiring how he managed to do this.

---

[1] Julian Moynahan, 'The Hero's Guilt: The Case of *Great Expectations*',
Essays in Criticism, x (1960), 60–79, argues that much of the violence in the
book can be seen as a projection of Pip's repressed feelings.

[2] Cf. René Wellek and Austin Warren, *Theory of Literature*, p. 78.

The incident of the blacking factory provided the source for the episode of Murdstone and Grinby's in Chapter XI of *David Copperfield*. Since Dickens recorded this incident in a fragment of autobiography, which Forster has preserved,[1] Dickens's treatment of the episode in fragment and novel can be compared. In both accounts, the boy's dominant attitude is a self-pity which betrays wounded pride and snobbishness. Young David and Charles are shown as special cases, which deserve special treatment, much more than as victims of a common neglect of children, like Oliver Twist or Jo. There is grief and indignation that David or Charles, of all people, should be deprived of an education and sink into the proletariat, an unconcealed aversion to rubbing shoulders with working-class boys like Mealy Potatoes, and a smug satisfaction that the other boys treat him as a little gentleman in spite of all. We can accept Dickens's self-pity since it tells us part of the truth about the man but in fiction, in which sympathy is needed to bind us to the fortunes of a hero, self-pity is liable to antagonize us. What is extraordinary is that we can accept David's self-pity too. We hardly experience more than a moment's uneasiness. Yet, surprisingly, Dickens incorporated the fragment of autobiography in the novel with hardly any verbal changes. What he has done with it, however, is to break it up into several sections and interweave it with other matter. This other matter concerns Micawber who makes his first appearance in this chapter. Micawber is the reason why we can tolerate David's self-pity.

Even so perceptive a critic as Cockshut finds himself baffled by Micawber.[2] This is because he considers Micawber only as an eccentric character, independent of structure and theme, and so ignores his function in the novel. What is interesting about the characters of David and Micawber at this stage in the story is a striking point of similarity between them. Shabby gentility is a trait they have in common. David has genteel pretensions in spite of his socially depressed circumstances. So has Micawber—in fact, this together with his manic-depressive type of optimism is the whole point about

---

[1] *F*, vol. i, pp. 27–50. The MS. of *DC* is so fluent at this point that it confirms Dickens is copying from the fragment of autobiography.

[2] A. O. J. Cockshut. *The Imagination of Charles Dickens*, pp. 114–15.

him. But whereas David's case is treated as near-tragedy and a subject for pity, the case of Micawber is presented as comedy. This is true even of his periods of suicidal despair. Micawber may therefore be regarded as a comic projection of David in this respect. But he is much more than comic relief and contrast. He provides a burlesque on David's own genteel pretensions.

Micawber supplies a kind of ironic 'chorus' or comment on a serious attitude in the work and so sets the reader at a critical distance from it. In this respect, Micawber's function is vital. Dickens's preoccupation with the pathos of his own earlier predicament is so intense, so uncritical, that he can only transfer the record of his experience without significant changes to the novel. Yet his deep-seated ironic sense, his critical vision of life, excluded as it is from an immediate view of his own predicament, is projected as the vision of another character in the novel and Wilkins Micawber is born. It is impossible to say how far Dickens's rhetoric is instinctive here and how far deliberate. But that this view of Micawber's function is substantially correct can be confirmed by noting the precise points in the narrative at which he appears. These are, in fact, the points at which David's despair becomes most unbearable and his self-pity most insufferable.[1]

The enduring pain of that second great traumatic experience of Dickens, which concerned Maria Beadnell, is well attested in a letter of 1855:

And so I suffered, and so worked, and so beat and hammered away at the maddest romances that ever got into any boy's head and stayed there, that to see the mere cause of it all, now, loosens my hold upon myself. Without for a moment sincerely believing that it would have been better if we had never got separated, I cannot see the occasion of so much emotion as I should see any one else. No one can imagine in the most distant degree what pain the recollection gave me in *Copperfield*. And, just as I can never open that book as I open any other book, I cannot see the face (even at four-and-forty), or hear the voice, without going wandering away over the ashes of all that youth and hope in the wildest manner.

---

[1] *DC*, Chaps. XI, XII, pp. 155 ff., 162 ff., 167 ff., 170 ff., 173 ff.

This letter was written after Dickens had heard from Maria again for the first time since their boy and girl affair. Forster goes on to indicate that Dickens found plenty to laugh at when he met Maria, now Mrs. Winter.[1] That the scene in *Little Dorrit*, however, in which Arthur Clennam meets Flora Finching, is by no means a simple record of Dickens's ridiculous and embarrassing interview with his boyhood sweetheart may be confirmed by considering two important pieces of evidence. First, there is the matter of Dickens's earlier treatment of the affair with Maria Beadnell in *David Copperfield*. Secondly, there is the deliberate artistry in the handling of this autobiographical material which the manuscript and corrected proofs of *David Copperfield* and *Little Dorrit* reveal.

A scrutiny of the way Dickens presents this affair in *David Copperfield* shows that he had already started to adjust himself to this early traumatic experience. That he transmuted the original suffering by adding an ironic dimension to his vision of it can be seen in his deliberate use of the complex effect in the manuscript and corrected proofs. Thus, in a passage which was cancelled at the proof stage, Dickens had originally summed up the affair with Dora as follows:

> For all this I know that I was in my heart so innocent and pure, so earnest, so impassioned and so true that while I laugh, I mourn a little and while I think of the discretion I have gained since then, I remember with a touch of sorrow, what I have lost.

This passage was presumably cancelled because the idea was repeated in the closing lines of the chapter and Dickens felt that so neat a summing-up was more appropriate there:

> Of all the times of mine that Time has in his grip, there is none ⟨-?-⟩ that **IN ONE RETROSPECTION I CAN SMILE** ⟨can laugh⟩ at half so much, and think of half so tenderly.[2]

In this passage from the manuscript, the effects of irony and tender pathos are again stressed so as to focus a more critical

[1] *F*, vol. i, pp. 72–4.
[2] Original MS. of *DC*, Victoria and Albert Museum, Forster Collection, 47. A. 25 (Vol. IIA), Chap. XXXIII, pp. 20–1, 23½, corrected proofs of *DC*, Chap. XXXIII, pp. 343–4; cf. *DC*, pp. 487, 490 (the deleted passage was originally between 'five wits by love' and 'Of course when I awoke').

and sympathetic vision while Dickens adds the phrase 'in one retrospection', thus indicating that the two effects and the two views are meant to coalesce and form a complex unity.

A deliberate artistry of a similar kind can be seen in the later handling of the Maria Beadnell/Mrs. Winter affair in the manuscript and corrected proofs of *Little Dorrit*:[1]

The return of Mr Casby, with his daughter Flora, put an end to these meditations. Clennam's eyes NO SOONER fell upon THE OBJECT OF his old passion, ⟨Clennam felt for the first time in his life, how much he must have changed⟩ THAN IT SHIVERED AND BROKE TO PIECES.

Most men will be found sufficiently true to themselves to be true to an old idea. It is no proof of an inconstant mind, but exactly the opposite, when the idea will not bear close comparison with the reality, and the contrast is a fatal shock to it. Such was Clennam's case. In his youth he had ⟨truly⟩ ARDENTLY loved this woman, and had heaped upon her all the locked-up wealth of his affection and imagination. That wealth had been, in his desert home, like Robinson Crusoe's money: ⟨useless,⟩ exchangeable with no one, lying idle in the dark to rust, until he poured it out for her. Ever since that MEMORABLE time, though he had, until the night of his arrival, AS COMPLETELY dismissed her from any association with his Present or Future as if she had been dead (which she might EASILY have been for anything he knew), he had kept the old fancy of the Past unchanged, in its old sacred place. And now, after all, the last of the Patriarchs coolly walked into the parlour, saying in effect, "Be good enough to throw it down and ⟨trample on⟩ DANCE UPON it. This is Flora."

Flora, always tall, had grown to be very ⟨fat⟩ BROAD TOO, and short of breath; but that was not much. Flora, whom he had left a lily, had become a peony; but that was not much. Flora who had ⟨been enchanting⟩ SEEMED ENCHANTING IN ALL SHE SAID AND THOUGHT, was DIFFUSE AND silly. That was ⟨a good deal⟩ MUCH. Flora, ⟨who had been artless⟩ WHO HAD BEEN SPOILED AND ARTLESS LONG AGO, was determined to be ⟨artless⟩ SPOILED AND ARTLESS ⟨still⟩ NOW. That was a ⟨knock-down⟩ FATAL blow.

This is Flora!

[1] Original MS. of *LD*, Vol. IA, Bk. I, Chap. XIII, pp. 10–11, 13–14 corrected proofs of *LD*, Bk. I, Chap. XIII, p. 108; cf. *LD*, pp. 150, 155.

"I am sure," giggled Flora, tossing her head with ⟨an exaggera-tion⟩ A CARICATURE of her ⟨old⟩ girlish manner, such as a mummer might have presented at her own funeral, if she had lived and died in classical antiquity, "I am ashamed to see Mr. Clennam, I am a mere fright, I know he'll find me fearfully changed, I am actually an old woman, it's shocking ⟨?now⟩ TO BE SO FOUND OUT, IT'S (It's) really shocking!"

At the proof stage, 'dance' was substituted for 'trample', 'fatal' for 'knock-down', and 'too' inserted after 'broad'.

These revisions in the manuscript and proofs confirm that Dickens was consciously transmuting this experience from his own life into the substance of a work of art by means of a complex rhetoric. True, life may have stepped in and justified the process of transformation which was already beginning in *David Copperfield*. But the fact is that the ironic possi-bilities in the material are fully exploited with an artist's care. Thus, his earlier version of the first paragraph recorded only that Arthur felt himself greatly changed at the sight of Flora; the revised version not only records Arthur's extreme state of shock but stresses that the shock was an ironic one, the sudden and unexpected revelation of a reality which completely shatters the old delusive image. The actual form here is that of an ironic discovery, a complete reversal of a former belief; it is also a peripety since it involves the catas-trophe of the love affair. The ironic contrast between former appearance and present reality is also stressed by the revi-sions made in the third paragraph while criticism of Flora's silliness and Arthur's blindness appears in the careful sub-stitution of 'had seemed' for 'had been' and the frank ad-mission that Flora had been 'spoiled' as well as 'artless' in the past. This note of criticism is sustained in the final paragraph. By a kind of caricature, Flora now exposes her own earlier girlish silliness. Her final naïve remark draws attention un-wittingly to Arthur's shocking discovery and her apt use of the expression, 'to be so found out', carefully added as a second thought, implies a further criticism of her own character and Arthur's blindness. This remark, of course, carries a double load of irony for she means it coquettishly and is hardly aware how true it is; her use of the debased sense of the word 'shocking' bears a particularly subtle ironical meaning. By establishing an ironic frame of reference, Dickens feels free to recall more forcefully all that Flora (and Maria) had meant to Arthur (and him). Thus 'ardently' is substituted for 'truly' and 'memorable' is inserted before 'time'. The substitution of 'dance' for 'trample' not only marks a shift to an ironic image from one of pain but also shows how closely pathos and irony are interwoven in Dickens's rhetorical thinking, how much he is struggling to master a painful experience through an ironic transmutation, and indeed how accurately Dickens's tragi-comic vision may be said to find expression through the balance and fusion of opposing elements in a complex rhetoric.

Dickens's conscious seeking for an equilibrium between sympathy and ironic comedy, between involvement with suffering and a critical and amused detachment, can be seen in a later summing-up of Arthur's mature attitude to Flora:

> She left about half of herself at eighteen years of age behind, and grafted the rest on to the relict of the late Mr. F; thus making a moral mermaid of herself, which her once boy-lover contemplated with feelings wherein his sense of the sorrowful and his sense of the ⟨ridiculous⟩ COMICAL were ⟨strangely⟩ CURIOUSLY blended ⟨though not fully for the sorrowful had the upper hand⟩.

The examples of Flora's ridiculous romantic delusions, which are exposed by Arthur in the following paragraph, make absolutely clear that 'the sense of the comical' referred to by Arthur is of the ironic type. The careful deletion of 'though not fully for the sorrowful had the upper hand' shows how Dickens feels it necessary to control the painful experience in Clennam, in himself, and in the reader, by striking an exact balance between involvement in and distance from the earlier experience. It is interesting to see that he first acknowledges how overwhelmingly painful the experience had been and that he stresses the idea of a 'blend' between contradictory feelings; this notion of coalescence, here, should be compared with the phrase, 'in one retrospection', which was added as a second thought in David Copperfield's final mature vision of his courtship of Dora Spenlow.

The sense of balance, control, and personal release is reflected in two letters written a few months after the fourth number in which Clennam meets Flora. One of these letters contains this remark: 'There are some things in Flora in number seven that seem to me to be extraordinarily droll, with something serious at the bottom of them after all. Ah, well! was there *not* something very serious in it once?'

In the second letter, Dickens indicates that the particular experience has been so controlled and distanced it now conveys the universality which is the true stamp of art: 'I am so glad you like Flora. It came into my head one day that we have all had our Floras, and that it was a half-serious, half-ridiculous truth which had never been told. It is a wonderful gratification to me to find that everybody knows her. Indeed, some people seem to think I have done them a personal injury, and that their individual Floras (God knows where they are, or who!) are each and all Little Dorrits!'[1]

This sense of balance, control, and release is, I think, partly what we mean by the aesthetic experience and certainly what I mean by the function of the complex effect. It is worth stressing that the use of the complex effect results in both control and freedom. For the control which distance exercises over painful material leaves Dickens free to increase the power of his effects and the depth and sharpness of his vision.

3. *Balance and Control: Cynicism and Sentimentality*

Occasionally, the balance between sympathy and irony, the control which each effect exerts on the other, may be undesirable. A good example, which also shows that Dickens was conscious of the problem involved, occurs in his notes for *Little Dorrit*.[2] In his plan for No. XI, Dickens added to the outline for Chapter II the instruction, 'Transpose this and the following chapter' and to the outline for Chapter III the instruction, 'Transpose this, and the preceding chapter'. This decision to reverse the order of the second and third chapters can only be understood, I think, in terms of effect. No advantage in clarity or contrast is gained by the transposition nor is a question of chronology involved. The original Chapter II, 'On the Road', was intended to build up a strong

---

[1] *F*, vol. iii, p. 137; to the Duke of Devonshire (5 July 1856), *HD*, p. 404.
[2] Original MS. of *LD*, Vol. IIA.

effect of pity for Little Dorrit in her new circumstances: 'Bring out Little Dorrit's new position—removed from her old cares about her father—quite displaced' (II, Chap. II). This effect of pathos was to be continued in Chapter IV: 'A Letter from Little Dorrit'; 'Always think of your poor child Little D' (II, Chap. IV). The original Chapter III, 'Mrs General', was satirical and ironical: 'Her character—history and varnishing properties' (II, Chap. III). Dickens evidently decided that the satirical account of Mrs. General would weaken the effect building up in Chapter II and reaching a climax in Chapter IV. No more striking tribute to the power of irony and pathos to disturb each other could be paid than this transposition of chapters. Dickens is not aiming at complexity here but at intensity. He wishes to focus a highly satirical vision of Mrs. General, on the one hand, and, on the other, a deeply moving vision of Little Dorrit's poignant alienation. As Dickens presents these two visions, they are quite separate. They are not juxtaposed, contrasted, interwoven, or related in any way. Indeed, the power of these two visions depends upon their very simplicity. What Dickens's determination to keep the two effects and visions separate does show, therefore, is the ready relationship which sympathy and irony will establish if brought into proximity.

The absence of this relationship, however, may encourage tendencies towards sentimentality and cynicism in Dickens's narrative art. For example, when Dickens tries to arouse an extreme degree of sympathy while his effect and vision remain simple, the result may well be the demand for a naïve identification, a crude and total involvement which is sure to be resisted by the sophisticated reader. Thus, the reader is expected to join in the universal grieving for Rose Maylie during her illness: 'Morning came; and the little cottage was lonely and still. People spoke in whispers; anxious faces appeared at the gate, from time to time; women and children went away in tears.' On the other hand, whenever a mordant irony becomes divorced from a charitable context it may degenerate into flippant and facetious forms in which a cruel, even a sadistic relish, makes its appearance:

Let it not be supposed by the enemies of "the system," that, during the period of his solitary incarceration, Oliver was denied the benefit of exercise, the pleasure of society, or the advantages of religious consolation. As for exercise, it was nice cold weather, and he was allowed to perform his ablutions, every morning under the pump, in a stone yard, in the presence of Mr Bumble, who prevented his catching cold, and caused a tingling sensation to pervade his frame, by repeated applications of the cane. As for society, he was carried every other day into the hall where the boys dined, and there sociably flogged as a public warning and example. And so far from being denied the advantages of religious consolation, he was kicked into the same apartment every evening at prayer time, and there permitted to listen to, and console his mind with, a general supplication of the boys, containing a special clause, therein inserted by authority of the board, in which they entreated to be made good, virtuous, contented, and obedient, and to be guarded from the sins and vices of Oliver Twist.[1]

Detachment may be pushed beyond flippancy, facetiousness, and cruelty to the stage of cold heartless superiority which marks the most extreme degree of irony. It is this cynicism and the reader's total lack of sympathy with the wearisome phantasms of the early Chuzzlewits which ruins the first chapter of *Martin Chuzzlewit*:

Firstly, that it may be safely asserted, and yet without implying any direct participation in the Monboddo doctrine touching the probability of the human race having once been monkeys, that men do play very strange and extraordinary tricks. Secondly, and yet without trenching on the Blumenbach theory as to the descendants of Adam having a vast number of qualities which belong more particularly to swine than to any other class of animals in the creation, that some men certainly are remarkable for taking uncommon good care of themselves.[2]

4. *Power and Complexity*

Paradoxically, the control or balance which the complex effect exercises in Dickens's narrative art also results in increased power. As we saw earlier, the simple effect can produce intensity but by magnifying a simple vision it may show up defects like sentimentality and naïvety all the more sharply. The complex effect, however, preserves the advantage yet

[1] *OT*, Chap. XXXIII, p. 246, Chap. III, pp. 14–15 (cf. Chap. IV, p. 22).
[2] *MC*, Chap. I, p. 6.

transcends the limitation of the simple effect. In essence, the complex effect sets together two simple effects which then interact. As a result, what were originally simple effects may now be intensified within the new whole without risk. Furthermore, interaction may even mean that an increase in the intensity of one effect produces an increase in the intensity of the other. When Dickens uses the simple effect alone, he gains power at the expense of complexity. When he uses the complex effect, he combines complexity and power. Thus, whereas the simple effect sometimes gives the impression that Dickens is imprisoned within his rhetoric, the complex effect conveys a feeling of artistic liberation.

Many instances in the manuscripts and corrected proofs of the novels show how Dickens uses this complex rhetoric quite consciously to increase the power and complexity of many of his scenes. He does not, however, always use this rhetoric with complete efficiency. The following scene, in which David Copperfield discovers that Agnes Wickfield loves him, is a case in point. Few critics would, I think, deny that the scene gains from the considerable amount of material which has been added in revisions:

"You have a secret," said I. "Let me share it, Agnes."
She ⟨sat quite still and⟩ cast down her eyes, and trembled.

"I could hardly fail to know, even if I had not heard—but from other lips than yours, Agnes, which seems strange—that there is some one upon whom you have bestowed the treasure of your love. Do not shut me out of what concerns your happiness so nearly! If you can trust me, as you say you can, and as I know you may, let me be your friend, your brother, in this matter, of all others!"

With an appealing, almost a reproachful, glance, she rose from the window; and hurrying across the room as if without knowing where, put her hands before her face, and burst into such tears as smote me to the heart.
AND YET THEY AWAKENED SOMETHING IN ME, BRINGING PROMISE TO MY HEART. WITHOUT MY KNOWING WHY, ⟨HER⟩ THESE TEARS ALLIED THEM-SELVES WITH THE QUIETLY SAD SMILE WHICH WAS SO FIXED IN MY REMEMBRANCE ⟨. WHAT WAS THIS THAT SO SHOOK ME WITH HOPE AND FEAR!⟩, AND SHOOK ME MORE WITH HOPE THAN FEAR OR SORROW.

"Agnes! Sister! Dearest! what have I done!"

"Let me go away, Trotwood. I am not well. I am not myself. I will speak to you by and by—another time. I will write to you. Don't speak to me now. Don't! don't!"

I SOUGHT TO ⟨RECALL⟩ RECOLLECT WHAT SHE HAD SAID, WHEN I HAD SPOKEN TO HER ON THAT FORMER NIGHT, OF HER AFFECTION NEEDING NO RETURN. IT SEEMED A VERY WORLD THAT I MUST SEARCH THROUGH IN A MOMENT.

"Agnes, I cannot bear to see you so, and think that I have been the cause. My dearest girl, dearer to me than anything in life, if you are unhappy, let me share your unhappiness. If you are in need of help or counsel, let me try to give it to you. If you have indeed a burden on your heart, let me try to lighten it. For whom do I live now, Agnes, it if is not for you!"

"Oh, spare me! I am not myself! Another time!" was all I could distinguish.

WAS IT A SELFISH ERROR THAT WAS LEADING ME AWAY? OR, HAVING ONCE A CLUE TO HOPE, WAS THERE SOMETHING OPENING TO ME THAT I HAD NEVER DARED TO THINK OF?

"I must say more. I cannot let you leave me so! For Heaven's sake, Agnes, ⟨do not wrong me⟩ LET US NOT MISTAKE EACH OTHER after all these years, and all that has come and gone with them! I must speak plainly. If you have any lingering thought that I could envy the happiness you will confer; that I could not resign you to a dearer protector, of your own choosing; that I could not, from my removed place, be a contented witness of your joy; dismiss it, for I don't deserve it! I have not suffered quite in vain. You have not taught me quite in vain. There is no alloy of self in what I feel for you."

She was quiet now. In a little time, she turned her pale face towards me, and said in a low voice, broken here and there, but very clear:

"I owe it to your pure friendship for me, Trotwood—which, indeed, I do not doubt—to tell you, you are mistaken. I can do no more. If I have sometimes, IN THE COURSE OF YEARS, wanted help and counsel, they have come to me. If I have some-times been unhappy, the feeling has passed away. If I have ever had a burden on my heart, it has been lightened for me. If I have any secret, it is ⟨not⟩—NO NEW ONE; AND IS—NOT what you suppose. I cannot REVEAL IT, OR divide it. It has long been mine, and must remain mine."

"Agnes! Stay! A moment!"

She was going away, but I detained her. I clasped my arm about her waist. ⟨I drew her to a seat.⟩ "In the course of years!" "It is not a new one!" New thoughts and hopes were whirling through my mind, and all the colours of my life were changing.[1]

Much remains wrong with this scene. The use of repetition, for example, makes some of the dialogue seem false. Yet what is wrong can be traced to the original version rather than to what has been added. In both manuscript and proofs, interpolations consist of material with an ironic reference. That is, Dickens adds the bulk of an effect in rethinking. Through David's dawning consciousness, the reader's attention is directed towards the dramatic irony of the situation. If the episode is read without the interpolated material, Agnes's tearful distress, David's almost brutal blundering, and the sentimental awkwardness of his platonic utterances appear embarrassingly pronounced. Yet, when irony is interwoven throughout, so as to balance these embarrassing and painful intimacies, the scene bears reading. Since the novel exposes David's blindness in matters of the heart and encourages us to view the painful follies of a young man's loves both compassionately and critically, Dickens's insistence on an ironic dimension in this scene helps to make our vision of David a complex one. Nevertheless, the revision here is careless. Dickens seems so loath to adjust his original material that it sometimes contradicts what he adds. Thus, the gradual dawning of the truth on David, which almost reaches its climax in the third interpolated paragraph, contradicts the attitude of renunciation that he takes up in the next paragraph.

Dickens is usually much more successful in using the complex effect to achieve both power and a complex vision. In such cases, he does not hastily improvise a loose and clumsy association between the rhetorics of sympathy and irony. On the contrary, both rhetorics may be closely and adroitly interlocked in the original version. When such an intimate relationship already exists, revisions which increase the power

---

[1] Original MS. of *DC*, Vol. IIB, Chap. LXII, pp. 33–4 (the three additional paragraphs are interpolated from the reverse of p. 33), corrected proofs of *DC*, Chap. LXII, pp. 611–12 (MS. reads 'never dared', proofs read 'not dared'); cf. *DC*, pp. 860–1.

of one effect will noticeably increase the power of the other.
Dickens's account of the night of Ham's engagement to
Little Em'ly provides a good illustration.[1]

As David approaches the house-boat with Steerforth,
Dickens indicates the ominous, ironic frame within which the
entire scene is to be set:

He maintained all his delightful qualities to the last, until we
started forth, at eight o'clock, for Mr. Peggotty's boat. Indeed,
they were more and more brightly exhibited as the hours went
on; for I thought even then, and I have no doubt now, that the
consciousness of success IN HIS DETERMINATION TO PLEASE,
inspired him with a new DELICACY OF perception, and made it,
subtle as it was, more easy to him. If any one had told me, then,
that all this was a brilliant game, played for the excitement of the
moment, for the employment of high spirits, in the ⟨HOLLOW⟩
<u>THOUGHTLESS</u> love of superiority, in a mere wasteful careless
course of winning what was worthless to him, and next minute
thrown away—I say, if any one had told me such a lie that night,
I wonder in what manner of receiving it my indignation would
have found a vent!
Probably only in an increase, had that been possible, of the
ROMANTIC feelings of fidelity and friendship with which I
walked beside him, over the dark wintry sands, towards the old
boat; the wind sighing around us ⟨as it⟩ EVEN MORE MOURN-
FULLY, THAN IT had sighed and moaned upon the night when
I first darkened Mr. Peggotty's door.

By adding 'in his determination to please' and 'DELICACY
OF perception', Dickens insists still further upon Steerforth's
attractive qualities, to which David and the Peggoty family
are sympathetically drawn, but the insertion of 'hollow'
(which is modified to 'thoughtless' in proof) hints more ominously at a very different side to Steerforth's character. Thus,
the very charm of Steerforth is also presented as one source of
the forthcoming disaster and any increase in that charm will
make disaster appear all the more certain. An increase, therefore, in the sympathetic effects through which Steerforth's

[1] Original MS. of *DC*, Vol. IB, Chap. XXI, pp. 22–5, 27, corrected proofs
of *DC*, Chap. XXI, pp. 219, 224 and 'overmatter to Copperfield—November
Number' (proofs read 'honest joys', First Edition reads 'honest joy'); cf.
DC, pp. 310–13, 315, 317–18.

attractiveness is being conveyed to the reader increases
the impact of the ironic hints which follow. The process
might be likened to a stereoscopic view. At first, the impression seems flat, then suddenly gains depth, in this case
an ominous reality. The sympathetic view of Steerforth is
never denied, only reinterpreted; otherwise, he would be a
completely melodramatic figure. Again, by inserting 'romantic', Dickens suggests that David's feelings are not to be
relied upon and draws further attention to his blindness.
Yet David's naïve trust is also not without its appeal. Thus,
sympathy with the romantic sentiments of youth, runs
alongside an ironic hint that a reappraisal is inevitable in the
fullness of time. Here, we can see the subtle and complex
moral vision which Dickens is beginning to focus through his
rhetoric for, if the romantic faith of youth has its attractive
nobility and goodness, nevertheless it may not stand the test
of experience. Once again, the rhetorics of irony and sympathy
are interlocked. The more the reader's attention is directed to
David's attractive but naïve trust in Steerforth, the more
striking is the irony in David's situation.

Just before David and Steerforth enter the house, Dickens
adds the idea of the wind's sighing and moaning 'even more
mournfully than' on an earlier visit, thus giving a renewed
life to what might otherwise have been mere dead metaphor.
The use of pathetic fallacy is almost classical, yet authentic,
not a decorative borrowing. Some terrible catastrophe is
foreshadowed.

To this ominously ironic frame a further effect of sympathy
may now be related. We are given a picture of Mr. Peggoty's
happiness at his niece's engagement to Ham:

Mr. Peggotty, his face lighted up with uncommon satisfaction,
⟨and⟩ AND LAUGHING WITH ALL HIS MIGHT, HELD his
rough arms wide open, as if for little Em'ly to run into them;
Ham, with a mixed expression in his face of admiration, exultation,
and a lumbering sort of bashfulness that sat upon him very well,
held little Em'ly by the hand, as if he were presenting her to Mr.
Peggotty; little Em'ly herself, blushing and shy, but delighted
with Mr. Peggotty's delight, as her joyous eyes expressed, was
stopped by our entrance (for she saw us first) in the very act of
springing from Ham to nestle in Mr. Peggotty's embrace . . .

The little picture was so instantaneously dissolved by our
going in, that one might have doubted whether it had ever been ...
Mr. Peggotty was so proud and overjoyed to see us, that he did not
know what to say or do, but kept over and over again shaking
hands with me, and then with Steerforth, and then with me, and
then ruffling his shaggy hair all over his head, and laughing
WITH SUCH GLEE AND triumph⟨antly⟩, that it was a treat to
see him.

"Why, that you two gent'lmen—gent'lmen growed—should
come to this here roof to-night, of all nights in my life," said Mr.
Peggotty, "is such a thing as never happened afore, I do rightly
believe! Em'ly my darling, come here! Come here, my little witch!
There's Mas'r Davy's friend, my dear! There's the gentl'man as
you've heerd on, Em'ly. He comes to see you, along with Mas'r
Davy, on the brightest night of your uncle's life as ever was or will
be, Gorm the t'other one, and horroar for it! "

After delivering this speech all in a breath, and with extraordinary animation and pleasure, Mr. Peggotty put one of his
large hands RAPTUROUSLY on each side of his niece's face,
and kissing it a dozen times, laid it with a gentle pride and love
upon his broad chest, and patted it as if his hand had been a
lady's ...

"If you two gent'lmen, gent'lmen growed," said Mr. Peggotty,
"don't ex-cuse me for being in a state of mind, when you understand matters, I'll arks your pardon. Em'ly, my dear!—She
knows I'm a going to tell," HERE HIS DELIGHT BROKE
OUT AGAIN, "and has made off."

Mr. Peggotty's joy at the happy occasion is sympathetically
induced in the reader throughout this passage and all the
insertions which Dickens makes deliberately intensify this
effect.

Yet the more Dickens strengthens the impression of Mr.
Peggotty's happiness, the sharper becomes the ironic effect
of what threatens it. So closely interwoven are the contagion
of Mr. Peggotty's joy and the ominous irony which over-
shadows it that the two effects blend as Peggotty explains all
that Em'ly means, and will continue to mean, to him:

"She ain't my child; I never had one; but I couldn't love her
more. You understand! I couldn't do it!"
"I quite understand," said Steerforth.
"I know you do, sir," returned Mr. Peggotty, "and thank'ee

again. Mas'r Davy, he can remember what she was; you may judge for your own self what she is; but neither of you can't FULLY know what she has ⟨been and⟩ BEEN, is, AND WILL BE, to my loving 'art."

Dickens's revisions not only increase the value of Peggotty's delight in Em'ly, they also give the prospect of its destruction a keener edge. Indeed, as Mr. Peggotty's joy mounts to a crescendo, his happiness becomes so total an experience, so exclusive of the faintest possibility of danger or the slightest need for caution, that it betrays him into a prediction which will turn out to be hubristically ironic:

"Here's the man that'll marry her, the ⟨day⟩ MINUTE she's out of her time."

Ham staggered, as well he might, under the blow Mr. Peggotty dealt him in his unbounded joy, as a mark of confidence and friendship.

Dickens deliberately increases the over-confidence and irony of this statement by the substitution of 'minute' for 'day'.

The happy domestic idyll, a frequent subject in Dickens's fiction, may often be criticized as sentimental or naïve. Certainly the pains Dickens takes to make such episodes attractive through the rhetoric of sympathy often results in a greater degree of idealization. Yet we have only to compare the pictures of Dingley Dell or the Cratchit household, the home life of the Maylies and little Oliver or Kit at the Garlands, or the domestic rhapsody of Tom and Ruth Pinch to appreciate that the case of this episode from *David Copperfield* is quite different.[1] Here, the very naïvety of the happiness, the simplicity of the vision which the rhetoric focuses, is related to a wider, more sophisticated, and critical context. The sheer intensity of the idyll makes the question which is being raised all the more appropriate. A conversation between David and Steerforth, which closes the chapter, dramatizes the dialogue that Dickens is carrying on with the reader:

"A most engaging little beauty!" said Steerforth, taking my arm. "Well! It's a quaint place, and they are quaint company, and it's quite a new sensation to mix with them."

[1] *PP*, Chap. XXVIII, pp. 374–95; 'A Christmas Carol', *CB*, pp. 43–9; *OT*, Chap. XXXII, pp. 237–9; *OCS*, Chap. XXII, pp. 168–70; *MC*, Chap. XXXIX, pp. 599–601.

"How fortunate we are too," I returned, to have arrived to witness their happiness in that intended marriage! I never saw people so happy. How delightful to see it, and to be made the sharers in ⟨it THEIR FEELINGS⟩ THEIR HONEST ⟨FEEL-INGS⟩ JOYS, as we have been!"

"That's rather a chuckle-headed fellow for the girl; isn't he?" said Steerforth.

He had been so hearty with him, and with them all, that I felt a shock in this ⟨reply⟩ UNEXPECTED AND COLD REPLY. But turning quickly upon him, and seeing a laugh in his eyes, I answered, much relieved:

"Ah, Steerforth! It's well for you to joke about the poor! You may skirmish with Miss Dartle, or try to hide your sympathies in jest from me, but I know better. When I see how perfectly you understand them, ⟨and⟩ HOW EXQUISITELY YOU can enter into ⟨joy⟩ HAPPINESS like this ⟨good⟩ PLAIN fisherman's, or humour a love like my old nurse's, I know that there is not a joy or sorrow, not an emotion, of such people, that can be indifferent to you. And I admire and love you for it, Steerforth, twenty times the more!"

He stopped, and, looking in my face, said, "Daisy, I believe you are in earnest, and are good. I wish we all were!"

Dickens juxtaposes a naïve faith in happiness and goodness and a critical questioning here. His revisions intensify the clash between the two attitudes. The fact that the questioning comes through Steerforth should not put us off.

Throughout the scene, Dickens is insisting on a moral vision which is complex, subtle, and mature. He is not only suggesting that simple natural goodness may fail to be a match for evil but also implying that the simpler or purer the goodness the more surely it may invite the assault of evil.[1] The complex rhetoric, with its interacting effects of sympathy and irony, draws attention to this interdependence of good and evil. Again, Dickens warns us that blindness may not be without blame since it assists in the triumph of evil. The very goodness and innocence of man may be the mainspring of tragedy since it may provoke disaster. Such a view

[1] This is a state of affairs much commented on by mystics and philosophers. It provides the central theme of De Sade's *Justine* (1787) and Richardson's *Clarissa* (1748). Cf. Jacob Boehme, *Six Theosophic Points and Other Writings*, tr. J. R. Earle (Michigan, 1958), p. 79.

of human fate extends beyond a code of right and wrong to a greater spiritual awareness and responsibility. Beyond the conflict of good and evil to that warfare between illusion and illumination which mystics, from Lao Tzu and the Buddha to St. John of the Cross and Jacob Boehme, all agree is the ultimate spiritual struggle.[1]

The particular narrative art which Dickens shows in his handling of the night of Ham's engagement is repeated in a later chapter of *David Copperfield*. In the scene which immediately precedes the discovery that Em'ly has eloped with Steerforth, the same vision is focused by means of the same rhetoric and a close examination of the manuscript will confirm that this rhetoric is also a conscious one.[2] A similar kind of vision, which is focused even more skilfully through the complex rhetoric of sympathy and irony, may be studied in the manuscript of *Bleak House*.[3] In Chapter III, when Esther Summerson meets Ada and Richard for the first time, Dickens carefully and consciously builds up an impression of cheerfulness. Through the rhetoric of sympathy, he presents an attractive picture of youthful gaiety, warmth, and hope, involving us wholeheartedly in the fortunes of three young people on the threshold of their careers, and at every possible point he deliberately intensifies the cheerful effect as the revisions in the manuscript clearly show:

So Mr. Kenge gave me his arm, and we went round the corner, under a colonnade, and in at a side door. And so we came, along a passage, into a comfortable sort of room, where a young lady and

[1] Lao Tzu, *Tao Te Ching*, i, ll. 1–2; Kaiten Nukariya, *The Religion of The Samurai* (1913), p. 123, enlightenment in Zen Buddhism is an 'emancipation of mind from illusion concerning self'; St. John of the Cross, *The Dark Night of the Soul*, tr. Kurt F. Reinhardt (New York, 1957), pp. 17–19, 'desires make the soul blind'; Jacob Boehme, op. cit., pp. 67–79, 89, 93–4, 99–101, 102–4. Cf. *The Bible of the World*, ed. R. O. Ballou (New York, 1939), p. 1351: 'The world about us, according to much Buddhist doctrine, is delusion, the ego is not genuine, not a true reality but only a degrading composite of temporary obstructive delusions.'

[2] Original MS. of *DC*, Vol. IIA, Chap. XXXI, pp. 24–5; cf. *DC*, Chap. XXXI, pp. 448–50.

[3] Original MS. of *BH*, Vol. IA, Chap. III, pp. 20 ('nineteen' substituted for 'seventeen' in proof, and I conjecture that 'heartily', which occurs in the MS. but is omitted in the surviving proofs, was deleted in an earlier proof since there is much evidence that there was more than one set of proofs), 21–2 (proofs omit 'together' after 'out'), 22; cf. *BH*, pp. 29–30, 32–3.

a young gentleman were standing near a great, LOUD-ROARING fire. A screen was interposed between them and it, and they were leaning on the screen, talking.

They both looked up when I came in, and I saw in the young lady, with the fire shining upon her, ⟨the most⟩ SUCH A beautiful ⟨face –?– face imaginable⟩ GIRL! WITH SUCH rich golden hair, ⟨and⟩ SUCH soft blue eyes, and ⟨?a⟩ SUCH A bright, ⟨–?–⟩ INNOCENT, trusting face!

"Miss Ada," said Mr. Kenge, "this is Miss Summerson."

She came to meet me with a smile of welcome and her hand extended, but seemed to change her mind in a moment, and heartily kissed me. In short, she had such a NATURAL, CAPTI-VATING, winning manner, that in a few minutes we were sitting in the window-seat, WITH THE LIGHT OF THE FIRE UPON US, TALKING TOGETHER, as ⟨happy⟩ FREE AND HAPPY as could be.

What a load off my mind! It was so delightful to know that she could confide in me, and like me! it was so good of her, and so encouraging to me!

The young gentleman was her distant cousin, she told me, and his name Richard Carstone. He was a handsome youth, with an ingenuous face, and a ⟨most engaging⟩ MOST ENGAGING ⟨LIGHT-HEARTED⟩ laugh; and after she had called him up to where we sat, he stood by us, in the light of the fire too, talking gaily, LIKE A LIGHT-HEARTED BOY. He was very young; not more than seventeen then, if quite so much, but nearly two years older than she was. They were both orphans, and (what was very unexpected and curious to me) had never met before that day. Our all three coming together for the first time, in such an unusual place, was a thing to talk about; and we talked about it; and the fire, which had left off roaring, winked its RED EYES at us—as Richard said—like ⟨an⟩ A DROWSY old Chancery lion.

Additions at the beginning and end of the passage stress the comfortable warmth of the setting with its bright cheerful fire. Various insertions in the description of Ada are calcu-lated to make her appear even more winsome. Yet intensifi-cation is not pursued to the point of grossness; the deletion of 'heartily' in proof suggests that Dickens considered this adverb too strong to depict even the warmest salutation of a stranger by a refined young lady. That the brightness of the fire is intended to assist in creating a general mood of warmth and cheerfulness can be seen in the careful addition of the

words, 'with the light of the fire upon us, talking together', to
the picture of Ada and Esther's happy affinity. As in Ada's
case, Richard's warmth and attractiveness are insisted upon
and the light-hearted gaiety of youth is added to his sympathetic traits.

The warm cheerful mood is sustained throughout the
interview with the Lord Chancellor which follows. Even this
figure, that had presided over the cruel and diabolical farce
of chancery in the opening chapter of the novel, crowned with
an almost satanic 'halo' of fog, now appears momentarily as a
human being with attractive qualities:

Presently he rose courteously, and released her, and then he
spoke for a minute or two with Richard Carstone; not seated, but
standing, and altogether with more ease and less ceremony—as if
he STILL knew, though he *was* Lord Chancellor, how to go
straight to the candour of a boy.

"Very well!" said his lordship aloud. "I shall make the order.
Mr. Jarndyce of Bleak House has chosen, so far as I may judge,"
and this was when he looked at me, "a very good companion for
the young lady, and the arrangement altogether seems the best
of which the circumstances admit."

He dismissed us pleasantly, and we all went out together, very
much obliged to him for being so affable and polite; by which he
had certainly lost no dignity, but seemed to us to have gained some.

The subtle restrained irony in this pleasant picture of the
Lord Chancellor's courtesy is all the more deadly in view of
what is to follow.

Yet even when Miss Flite, who is to play the role of an
ominous 'chorus', accosts the young people the cheerful mood
is at first skilfully maintained. It is only as the scene progresses that the cheerful effect is twisted into an ironic
reference:

We looked at one another, half laughing at our being like the
children in the wood, when a curious little old woman in a squeezed
bonnet, and carrying a reticule, came curtseying ⟨up⟩ AND
SMILING UP TO US, with an air of great ceremony.

"O!" said she. "The wards in Jarndyce! Ve-ry happy, I am
sure, to have the honour! It is a good omen for youth, and hope,
and beauty, when they find themselves in this place, and don't
know what's to come of it".

"Mad!" whispered Richard, not thinking she could hear him.

"Right! Mad, young gentleman," she returned so quickly that he was quite abashed. "I was a ward myself. I was not mad at that time," curtseying ⟨?low at/?between each⟩ LOW, AND SMILING BETWEEN EVERY LITTLE sentence. "I had youth, and hope. I believe, beauty. It matters very little now. Neither of the three served, or saved me. I have the honour to attend Court regularly. With my documents. I expect a judgment. Shortly. On the Day of Judgment. I have discovered that the sixth seal mentioned in the Revelations is the Great Seal. It has been open a long time! Pray accept my blessing."

As Ada was a little frightened, I said, to humour the POOR old lady, that we were much obliged to her.

"Ye-es!" she said, mincingly. "I imagine so. And here is Conversation Kenge. With *his* documents! How does your honourable worship do?"

"Quite well, quite well! Now don't be troublesome, that's a good soul!" said Mr. Kenge, leading the way back.

"By no means," said the poor old lady, keeping up with Ada and me. "Anything but troublesome. I shall confer estates on both,— which is not being troublesome, I trust? I expect a judgment. Shortly. On the Day of Judgment. This is a good omen FOR YOU. Accept my blessing!"

It is fascinating, here, to observe in the manuscript the conscious skill with which Dickens works. By inserting the two references to Miss Flite's smiling, he draws attention to the cheerful impression which she at first makes. It is only with the second reference that an ominous irony is beginning to creep in and suggest a very different interpretation of her remark about 'a good omen'; whether she fully realizes it or not, Miss Flite's smile is an ironic one. A tragic note is sounded by the addition of 'poor' to Esther's view of the old lady; this tragic note has its own sinister undertones when we consider the final fate of Ada and Richard. But the irony attains its keenest edge when Dickens adds the phrase, 'for you', to Miss Flite's second remark about 'a good omen'; as a result, the omen no longer aims itself generally, like the first, against 'youth', 'hope', and 'beauty', but specifically in a most sinister manner against the two wards present.

Like the warning of some Shakespearean soothsayer or apparition, Miss Flite's ominous 'chorus' is intended as a shock and, as such, is highly successful. By being placed at the close of the chapter and thus providing its 'curtain', her second entrance into the story gains in effectiveness. Yet the effectiveness of her sinister warning derives much more from its sharp ironic contrast with the cheerful impression which has preceded it. It is not enough to say generally, as Earle Davis does, that Dickens's use of contrast is one of his most outstanding skills as a narrative artist. The skill he displays, here, is of a different, and altogether higher, order than the simpler kinds of contrast cited by Davis[1] or the contrast, say, between heat and cold in the opening pages of *Little Dorrit*. In Chapter III of *Bleak House*, we experience something much more complex and subtle, an ironic contrast which demands a reinterpretation of all that precedes.

The bright vision of youth on the threshold of life, with all its gaiety and hopes, is not denied. On the contrary, it is affirmed through the rhetoric of sympathy as a living experience in which the reader can participate. The sudden ironic reinterpretation of this vision in the light of a cruel and evil fate, the sinister challenge to the most optimistic promise of youth, makes the foreshadowed tragedy all the more pathetic and terrible. Again, we are warned that the natural goodness of youth is no shield against destiny. This, indeed, is the heart of the dreadful mystery of pain. True, Dickens sometimes shows us the simple melodramatic face of evil. Yet, in depicting virtue and innocence overwhelmed by suffering, he poses the complex problem which lies at the core of a genuine tragic vision of man.

---

[1] Earle Davis, *The Flint and the Flame*, p. 133, and Chap. VIII, *passim*.

VI

STRUCTURE

1. *Genesis and Structure*

As the medium through which effect focuses vision, structure in Dickens's narrative does not exist as an end in itself but serves rhetorical, aesthetic, and moral purposes. From the outset, the development of an entire plot or a complete incident may be determined by an original 'germ' and the effect which this 'germ' has excited in Dickens's mind. Structure may thus be seen as a natural and organic growth from the original idea and its effect.

During the last sixteen years of his life, many of Dickens's original ideas for use in future stories or novels were written down in the notebook of memoranda (now known as the Berg notebook) which he kept between 1855 and 1870. The ideas include character traits, the 'germs' of plots and incidents, scraps of dialogue and occasional settings for a story. Almost invariably each idea recorded in the notebook already creates a strong effect. Significantly, most of the ideas create either an ironic or a sympathetic effect (or both effects together).[1]

Thus, the barest outline of a story will often indicate an ironic structure: 'The man who marries his cook at last, after being so desperately knowing about the sex'. Very frequently an idea in the form of an ironic reversal of fortune or an ironic discovery, or both together, excites Dickens. A woman, for instance, who has poisoned her father for his wealth discovers he is not rich. The really dangerous enemy turns out to be the one who is despised. A man is astonished to find out that unconsciously he has been making the most apt sarcastic remarks. On the other hand, the slightest sketch for a story may evoke pathos: 'The girl separating herself from the lover

---

[1] *F*, vol. iii, pp. 246–8, 253–9, 261; cf. Mrs. J. Comyns Carr, *Reminiscences* (1926), pp. 283, 286–92, 294.

who has shewn himself unworthy—loving him still—living single for his sake—but never more renewing their old relations. Coming to him when they are both grown old, and nursing him in his last illness'; 'The two people in the Incurable Hospital.—The poor incurable girl lying on a water-bed, and the incurable man who has a strange flirtation with her; comes and makes confidences to her; snips and arranges her plants; and rehearses to her the comic songs (!) by writing which he materially helps out his living'. Occasionally, the pathos evoked by an idea already borders on sentimentality: 'The little baby-like married woman—so strange in her new dignity, and talking with tears in her eyes, of her sisters "and all of them" at home. Never from home before, and never going back again'. As against this, Dickens can present sentimentality objectively by setting it within an ironic frame of reference. A woman, who strongly recalls Flora Finching, for example, deludes herself with the notion that a certain man who detests her is her Fate.

No less than five of eight ideas for *Little Dorrit* recorded in the notebook create an effect of either sympathy or irony. A thumbnail sketch of the Barnacles' house already incorporates the basic satirical idea which is later exploited at greater length in the novel; the impressive address is ironically revealed to have been purchased at the expense of dark cramped living quarters and a perpetual bad smell. The basic idea for Henry Gowan exposes the irony in the pose of the honest modest man of the world behind which the cynic reduces all values to his own perverse standards, subtly depreciating the good and elevating the bad.[1] The whole novel was originally conceived as an ironic idea: 'The people who lay all their sins negligences and ignorances, on Providence'. That this idea was later expanded into the first plan for the novel seems certain from a remark of Forster's: 'The book took its origin from the notion he had of a leading man for a story who should bring about all the mischief in it, lay it all on Providence, and say at every fresh calamity, "Well it's a mercy, however, nobody was to blame you know!" '
This brief plan already suggests a series of crises which repeat

---

[1] Cf. *LD*, Bk. I, Chaps. X, XXVII, pp. 109–11, 324–5; Bk. II, Chap. VI, pp. 488–90.

an ironic pattern. It is clear from the memoranda and number plans that Dickens was still intending to use this idea while planning at least the first four numbers. Indeed, this particular ironic structure figured so prominently in his thinking about the general shape and theme of the novel that the original title, 'Nobody's Fault', was only abandoned after planning the first three numbers. Dickens probably came to see that the idea of one man's responsibility for all the ills in the story conflicted with his awareness that an entire social, economic, and political group of people, which ranged from obstructionist bureaucrats like the Barnacles and their allies in Parliament to plain parasites like the Gowans, from bloodsucking landlords like Casby to swindlers like Merdle, were in fact responsible for the condition of England. Nevertheless, the ironic idea of 'nobody's fault' survives in the novel as a sharp satirical analysis of the irresponsibility of the governing and administrative class which *laissez-faire* encouraged.[1]

An idea for an effective piece of structure which is fully developed in the novel is recorded in the notebook as follows: 'His falling into difficulty, and himself imprisoned in the Marshalsea. Then she, out of all her wealth and changed station, comes back in her old dress, and devotes herself in the old way'. Forster describes this idea as 'the first notion of Clennam's reverse of fortune'. The pathos which it suggests is amply exploited, though complicated by irony, in the novel.[2]

Finally, the 'germ' for perhaps the greatest scene in *Little Dorrit* is recorded in the notebook: 'First sign of the father failing and breaking down. Cancels long interval. Begins to

---

[1] *F*, vol. iii, pp. 131-2. Original MS. of *LD*, Vol. IA. Dickens's analysis of the role played by the Barnacles and their allies is confirmed by that of Thomas Carlyle in 'Downing Street' [1850], *Latter-Day Pamphlets*, People's Edition (1872), pp. 74-107; Carlyle also makes scathing attacks on the idle class of dilettantes which unearned wealth produces, see esp. *Past and Present* [1843], People's Edition (1872), Bk. III, Chaps. III, VIII, XI, XII, pp. 129-32, 150-6, 168-72, 172-9; in a letter to Forster (?Apr. 1856), *F*, vol. iii, p. 136, Dickens identifies Merdle with the notorious John Sadleir who committed suicide in 1856, though the fall of George Hudson, the 'Railway King', (1847-8) was no doubt still fresh in the public memory. See also *LD*. Bk. I, Chap. XII, pp. 142-3; the ironic idea of 'nobody' is also used amusingly in Dickens's description of Arthur Clennam's reactions to his repressed love for Pet Meagles.

[2] *LD*, Bk. II, Chap. XXIX, pp. 754-61.

talk about the turnkey who first called him the Father of the Marshalsea—as if he were still living. "Tell Bob I want to speak to him. See if he is on the Lock, my dear" '. It is worth tracing Dickens's development of this idea from its first brief origin, through its treatment in the author's detailed plan for the novel to its final handling in the manuscript. In the notebook entry, the possibilities for irony and pathos, though implicit in the material, are barely realized; the situation might conceivably have been exploited for either an ironic effect or for one of pathos. But by the time Dickens came to sketch an outline of the episode in the number plans he was clearly aiming at a complex effect: 'So Mr. Dorrit returns to Rome, building, building, building the castle, that is to come down Crash! in the next chapter' (II, Chap. XVIII); 'Pave on to Mrs. Merdle's great dinner "My dear, will you go and see if Bob is on the lock. Ladies and gentlemen, ⟨–?–⟩ welcome to the Marshalsea. I am the Father of the Marshalsea. This is my child. Born here" HIS WATCH, and *clothes* Imaginary Pawnbroker's Dies. Uncle steals down to him in the night and dies kissing his hand' (II, Chap. XIX). Even so, Dickens realizes the full power of the complex effect only through a conscious and carefully sustained rhetoric as he writes up the scene.[1] The revisions in the manuscript and proofs confirm how deliberately and consistently he was working to increase both the effects of irony and pathos:

She was at his side, and touching him, but he still perversely supposed her to be in her seat, and called out, still leaning over the table, "Amy, Amy. I don't feel quite myself. Ha. I don't know what's the matter with me. I particularly wish to see Bob. Ha. Of all the turnkeys, he's as much my friend as yours. See if Bob is in the lodge, and beg him to come to me."

All the guests were now in consternation, and everybody rose.

"Dear father, I am not there; I am here, by you."

"Oh! You are here, Amy! Good. Hum. Good. Ha. Call Bob. If he has been relieved, and is not on the lock, tell Mrs. Bangham to go and fetch him."

---

[1] Original MS. of *LD*, Vol. IIA. Ibid., Vol. IIB, Bk. II, Chap. XIX, pp. 8–10 ('occasionally' before 'shedding' deleted in proof, while MS. reads 'the' before 'admission', proofs read 'that'), corrected proofs of *LD*, Bk. II, Chap. XIX, pp. 489–90; cf. *LD*, pp. 647–9.

She was gently trying to get him away; but he resisted, and would not go.

"I tell you child," he said petulantly, "I can't be got up THE NARROW stairs without Bob. Ha. Send for Bob. Hum. Send for Bob—best of all the turnkeys—send for Bob."

He looked confusedly about him, and, becoming conscious of the number of faces by which he was surrounded, addressed them:

"Ladies and gentlemen, the duty—ha—devolves upon me of—hum—welcoming you to the Marshalsea. Welcome to the Marshalsea! The space is—ha—limited—limited—the parade might be wider; but you will find it apparently grow larger after a time—a time, ladies and gentlemen—and the air is, all things considered, very good. It blows over the—ha—Surrey hills. Blows over the Surrey hills. This is the Snuggery. Hum. Supported by a small subscription of the—ha—Collegiate body. In return for which—hot water ⟨always ready⟩—general kitchen—and little domestic advantages. Those who are habituated to the—ha—Marshalsea, are pleased to call me its Father. I am accustomed to be complimented by strangers as the—ha—Father of the Marshalsea. Certainly, if years of residence may establish a claim to so—ha—honourable a title, I may accept the—hum—conferred distinction. My child, ladies and gentlemen. My daughter. Born here!"

She was not ashamed of it, or ashamed of him. She was pale and frightened; but she had no other care than to soothe him and get him away, for his own dear sake. She was between him and the wondering faces, turned round upon his breast with her own face raised to his. He held her clasped in his left arm, and between whiles her low voice was heard TENDERLY imploring him to go away with her.

"Born here," he repeated, ⟨OCCASIONALLY⟩ SHEDDING TEARS. "Bred here. Ladies and gentlemen, my daughter. Child of an unfortunate father, but—ha—always a gentleman. Poor, no doubt, but—hum—proud. Always proud, It has become a—hum—NOT INFREQUENT custom for my—ha—personal admirers—personal admirers solely—to be pleased to express their desire to acknowledge my semi-official position here, by offering—ha—little tributes, which usually take the form of—ha—Testimonials—pecuniary Testimonials. In the acceptance of those—ha—voluntary recognitions of my humble endeavours to—hum—to uphold a Tone here—a Tone—I beg it to be understood that I do not consider myself compromised. Ha. Not compromised. Ha. Not a beggar. No; I repudiate the title! At the same time far be it from me to—hum—to put upon the fine feelings by which my partial friends are actuated, the slight of scrupling to admit that those offerings are—hum—highly acceptable. On the contrary, they are most acceptable. In my child's name, if not in my own, I make the admission in the fullest manner, at the same time reserving—ha—shall I say my personal dignity? Ladies and gentlemen, God bless you <u>ALL</u>!''

By this time, the ⟨agony of⟩ <u>EXCEEDING</u> mortification under- gone by the Bosom had occasioned the withdrawal of the greater part of the company into other rooms . . .

The broad stairs of his Roman palace were ⟨reduced⟩ <u>CON- TRACTED</u> in his failing sight to the narrow stairs of his London prison; and he would suffer no one but her to touch him, his brother excepted. They got him up to his room without help, and laid him down on his bed. And from that hour his <u>POOR MAIMED</u> spirit, only ⟨mindful of⟩ <u>REMEMBERING</u> the place where it had broken its wings, cancelled the dream through which it had since groped, and knew of nothing beyond the Marshalsea. When he heard footsteps in the street, he took them for the <u>OLD WEARY</u> tread in the yards. When the hour came for locking up, he sup- posed all strangers to be excluded for the night. When the time for opening came again, he was so anxious to see Bob that they were fain to patch up a narrative how that Bob—many a year dead then, gentle turnkey—had taken cold, but hoped to be out to- morrow, or the next day, or the next at furthest.

He fell away into a weakness so extreme that he could not raise his hand. But, he still protected his brother according to his long usage; and would say <u>WITH SOME COMPLACENCY</u>, fifty times a day, when he saw him standing by his bed, ''My good Frederick, sit down. You are very feeble indeed.''

The impressive tragi-comedy of William Dorrit's collapse well illustrates the complex and powerful vision which Dickens may focus by fully exploiting sympathetic and ironic possi- bilities in an original idea.

The entire plot of *Great Expectations* was conceived and worked out in terms of a complex effect.[1] Dickens makes it clear that the whole plot was to turn on Pip's discovery that Magwitch was his benefactor:

'such a very fine, new, and grotesque idea has opened upon me, that I begin to doubt whether I had not better cancel the little

[1] *F*, vol. iii, pp. 327–9.

paper, and reserve the notion for a new book . . . it so opens out before *me* that I can see the whole of a serial revolving on it, in a most singular and comic manner.' This was the germ of Pip and Magwitch.

The remarkable impression of unity achieved by the extremely complex structure of *Great Expectations* derives from Dickens's first happy inspiration and the disciplined manner in which he carried it out. That a rigorous unity was his intention can be seen by his remarks about the whole story 'revolving' on the original idea. Nevertheless, unity is not the only triumph of *Great Expectations*. The plot powerfully realizes the theme of false expectations and false values. But the novel ultimately makes on the reader an impression not only of power but of complexity. *Great Expectations* may be an ironic satire on snobbishness, social climbing, and the values of the parasite and dilettante in an acquisitive society but it is also a record of personal tragedy. That this complex vision is to be focused by a complex rhetoric Dickens also makes clear:

I have made the opening, I hope, in its general effect exceedingly droll. I have put a child and a good-natured foolish man, in relations that seem to me very funny. Of course I have got in the pivot on which the story will turn too—and which indeed, as you remember, was the grotesque tragi-comic conception that first encouraged me.

Since 'conception' refers to the discovery that Pip's great expectations of wealth and social status have been engineered by a convict, a strong tinge of irony is implied in 'grotesque'. Dickens's words, here, show how intimately inter-connected effect, structure, and vision are in his method of composition. He is inspired in the first instance not merely by an idea but by an idea which excites a strong effect ('grotesque idea'). The whole structure of the novel is to turn on this idea and is already being built up, in the first few pages, with the encounter between Pip and Magwitch. The discovery that Pip's benefactor is the convict will depend for its full impact on all that has gone before and will reinterpret it. Thus, a structural irony pervades the novel and is already at work in the title. Finally, the idea for the novel, the structure which expresses it, and the effect which it creates are seen by Dickens as vision, for they are dignified by the description, 'a grotesque tragi-comic conception'. It is impossible to say in what state of development the original idea for *Great Expectations* leaped from the brain of Dickens. What is certain is the logical interdependence of the parts of this idea, once the vital role played by effect has been acknowledged. If Dickens had begun only with the idea of a boy whose great expectations turned out to be engineered by a convict, an effect of maximum irony would require the boy to develop into a snobbish status seeker. If, on the other hand, Dickens had begun with the idea of a snobbish status seeker with great expectations of social advancement then an effect of maximum irony would demand that his secret benefactor turn out to be the most objectionable social outcast, a transported convict. Whether we begin from plot, that is, or from character, the ironic effect is the determining factor. It is effect which links plot and character and dominates structure. And it is from an ironic effect and from its complication by a tragic sympathy that the ultimate vision of *Great Expectations* is developed.

The link between effect, structure, and vision can also be seen in the genesis of *Hard Times*. The full significance of the list of alternative titles for this novel has passed unnoticed. Dickens is involved here, I believe, in no less important a task than in clarifying the vision of his book.

True, some evidence suggests Dickens had decided on the theme of *Hard Times* before 20 January 1854, the date which heads the list of titles. On 23 January 1854, for example, he reminded Miss Coutts: 'The main idea of it is one on which you and I and Miss Brown have often spoken.' Seven months earlier, he wrote to his sub-editor:

I have thought of another article to be called "Frauds upon the Fairies," *a propos* of George Cruikshank's editing. Half playfully and half seriously, I mean to protest most strongly against alteration, for any purpose, of the beautiful little stories which are so tenderly and humanly useful to us in these times, when the world is too much with us early and late; and then to re-write "Cinderella" according to Total Abstinence, Peace Society, and Bloomer principles, and expressly for their propagation.

This article anticipates the ideas contained in 'Hard Heads and Soft Hearts' and 'Heads and Tales', two of the titles considered for *Hard Times*,[1] Indeed, the idea behind 'Frauds upon the Fairies' goes back seven years to *Dombey and Son*:

It being a part of Mrs. Pipchin's system not to encourage a child's mind to develop and expand itself like a young flower, but to open it by force like an oyster, the moral of these lessons was usually of a violent and stunning character: the hero—a naughty boy—seldom, in the mildest catastrophe, being finished off by anything less than a lion, or a bear.

Hard Times, like an episode in *The Mudfog Papers* fifteen years earlier, only takes the conflict between imagination and moral utility one stage further by eliminating fancy altogether from the process of education:

Not that they knew, by name or nature, anything about an Ogre. Fact forbid! . . .
No little Gradgrind had ever seen a face in the moon; it was up in the moon before it could speak distinctly. No little Gradgrind had ever learnt the silly jingle, Twinkle, twinkle, little star; how I wonder what you are! No little Gradgrind had ever known wonder on the subject, each little Gradgrind having at five years old dissected the Great Bear like a Professor Owen, and driven Charles's Wain like a locomotive engine-driver. No little Gradgrind had ever associated a cow in a field with that famous cow with the crumpled horn who tossed the dog who worried the cat who killed the rat who ate the malt, or with that yet more famous cow who swallowed Tom Thumb: it had never heard of those celebrities, and had only been introduced to a cow as a graminivorous ruminating quadruped with several stomachs.

Moreover, the championing of fancy against fact of the utilitarian brand had been established as the policy of *Household Words* four years before *Hard Times*:

No mere utilitarian spirit, no iron binding of the mind to grim realities, will give a harsh tone to our Household Words. In the bosoms of the young and old, of the well-to-do and of the poor, we would tenderly cherish that light of Fancy which is inherent in the human breast . . . To show to all, that in all familiar things,

---

[1] To Miss Coutts (23 Jan. 1854), *N*, vol. ii, p. 537; to W. H. Wills (27 July 1853), *HD*, p. 291. The article, 'Frauds on the Fairies', appeared in *HW*, viii (1 Oct. 1853) and is reprinted in *MP*, pp. 406–12; I am indebted to Professor George H. Ford for drawing my attention to this article.

even in those which are repellant on the surface, there is Romance enough, if we will find it out.[1]

I am not, therefore, suggesting that Dickens was formulating the theme of *Hard Times*, while he considered the alternative titles, but that he was working out this theme in terms of structure, effect, and vision.

Neither Forster in his *Life* nor Butt and Tillotson in *Dickens at Work* supply a full list of the titles in the manuscript or indicate their correct sequence, though a complete transcript has recently been published in the Norton Critical Edition of *Hard Times*, ed. George H. Ford and Sylvère Monod (New York, 1966). Dickens, in fact, drew up two lists of titles for this novel, one dated 20 January 1854, and now bound in with the rest of the author's notes in the manuscript, the other in a letter of the same date which Forster quotes:

'I wish you would look' (20th of January 1854) 'at the enclosed titles for the *H.W.* story, between this and two o'clock or so, when I will call. It is my usual day, you observe, on which I have jotted them down—Friday! It seems to me that there are three very good ones among them. I should like to know whether you hit upon the same.' On the paper enclosed was written: 1. According to Cocker. 2. Prove it. 3. Stubborn Things. 4. Mr. Gradgrind's Facts. 5. The Grindstone. 6. Hard Times. 7. Two and Two are Four. 8. Something Tangible. 9. Our Hard-headed Friend. 10. Rust and Dust. 11. Simple Arithmetic. 12. A Matter of Calculation. 13. A Mere Question of Figures. 14. The Gradgrind Philosophy. The three selected by me were 2, 6, and 11; the three that were his own favourites were 6, 13, and 14; and as 6 had been chosen by both, that title was taken.

Then, in a footnote to the passage, he adds what are in fact several titles from the manuscript:

To show the pains he took in such matters I will give other titles also thought of for this tale. 1. Fact; 2. Hard-headed Gradgrind; 3. Hard Heads and Soft Hearts; 4. Heads and Tales; 5. Black and White.

---

[1] *D & S*, Chap. VIII, p. 102. The third serial part containing this chapter appeared in Dec. 1846. Cautionary tales in verse, against truancy and sulkiness for instance, were included in at least one collection of traditional nursery rhymes printed at Seven Dials in the early forties; see 'The Royal Book of Nursery Rhymes', reprinted in Charles Hindley, *The History of the Catnach Press* (1887), pp. 197–8. *SB*, pp. 640–1; *HT*, Bk. I, Chap. III, p. 9; 'A Preliminary Word', *HW*, i (30 Mar. 1850), 1, reprinted in *MP*, p. 167.

The selection process and the final choice of 'Hard Times' were not, however, as random as Forster seems to imply. Unlike Forster, Butt and Tillotson show considerable insight into what Dickens was about:

These rejected titles and those in the manuscript . . . remain of interest, since they seem to indicate the limits within which the book would move. The irony implicit in *Something Tangible, A Matter of Calculation*, and *A Mere Question of Figures* suggests that the novel will open up areas of experience beyond the reach of Mr. Gradgrind's philosophy, and the importance of feelings, disregarded by the political economists, is represented in *Hard Heads and Soft Hearts*, while *Heads and Tales* seems to forecast the opposition of fact and fancy so prominent in the scenes at Sleary's Circus troupe.

Nevertheless, only the full sequence of titles makes a complete investigation possible.[1] The original list of titles appears to be that in the manuscript. It is more than twice as long as the list in the letter; it is subdivided into two sections by a double line and, if we ignore the deletions, the second section very nearly corresponds to the list in the letter which reads almost like a fair copy. The only title which appears in the letter but not in the manuscript is 'The Gradgrind Philosophy' which comes last and may have been added as an afterthought; this title is important in filling out the scheme Dickens had in mind.

What was this scheme? How is it presented through the proliferation of titles in the manuscript? Proliferation there certainly is, one title suggesting another, and if, as Butt and Tillotson suggest, we do not see Dickens here in the initial stage of gestation yet it may still show another important stage in the creative process, that at which the original idea is clarified and crystallized in terms of vision, effect, and structure. Indeed, this attempt to be both comprehensive and precise accounts for the protean forms which his title takes on while these forms, in their turn, indicate the richness of the material he is handling. The process of clarification is not a mechanical association of ideas, not even a free association in the Freudian sense but something much nearer that controlled

[1] Original MS. of *HT*; see below, p. 358. *F*, vol. iii, pp. 44–5; John Butt and Kathleen Tillotson, *Dickens at Work*, p. 202.

association which Jung describes as the genuine creative process.[1] There is a constant return to certain basic ideas which are amplified and enriched by the associations that have taken place. Consequently, Dickens's vision becomes not less but more complex as he strives to formulate a comprehensive view.

Dickens starts off from the idea of inflexibility as a feature of the Gradgrind system: 'Stubborn Things'. At intervals, he returns to this idea with the image of the grindstone which also adds the further ideas of harshness and abrasion: 'The Grindstone', 'Mr. Gradgrind's grindstone', '⟨The Family Grindstone⟩', 'The ⟨universal⟩ general grindstone'. The abrasive quality suggests not only the rough process of putting an edge on or sharpening to a fine point but also of wearing away, so that both the intention of the Gradgrind system and a hint of its frustration by its own destructive power are set side by side. Similarly, the idea of something mechanical, as the antithesis of the natural, is present in the image of the grindstone alongside the hint of a more sinister 'machinery'.[2] As in every true symbol, both a positive and a negative potential are present, doubly important here, since catastrophe will develop organically from an over-positive assertion. Already, that is, the broad lines of structure and plot, together with the ironical effect they will make, are either present or are forming themselves in Dickens's mind. Inflexibility and harshness are also combined in 'Hard Times'. The very name 'Gradgrind' suggests all three ideas of inflexibility, harshness, and abrasion.

The inflexibility in his first title, 'Stubborn Things', immediately suggests Dickens's second title, 'Fact', a further key idea in his concept of the Gradgrind system. Inflexi-

[1] Butt and Tillotson, op. cit., p. 201; C. G. Jung, *Psychological Types*, pp. 574, 580.

[2] *The Grindstone* appears again twice. It was considered by Dickens as a possible title for the book which became *A Tale of Two Cities*; see Mrs. Comyns Carr, op. cit., pp. 282–3, for a transcript of the relevant passage in Dickens's notebook and a comment on Forster's unreliability here. Even more significantly, *The Grindstone* appears as the title of *TTC*, Bk. III, Chap. II; in this chapter, a grindstone becomes an instrument of retribution during the September Massacres, one among many punitive episodes in the French Revolution which Dickens has represented throughout his novel as an ironic fate or nemesis working itself out in the fullness of time.

bility and an obsession with factual knowledge based upon statistics go naturally together in Dickens's thinking. In Book II, Chapter II of *Hard Times*, we find him referring to the utilitarian political economists as 'The hard Fact fellows'. In a letter, he explains the satire of *Hard Times*:

My satire is against those who see figures and averages, and nothing else—the representatives of the wickedest and most enormous vice of this time—the men who, through long years to come, will do more to damage the real truths of political economy than I could do (if I tried) in my whole life.[1]

That Dickens is not attacking contemporary industrialism in the figure of Gradgrind but the utilitarian political economy which affected to explain and direct it[2] can be seen in the title, 'Mr. Gradgrind's Philosophy', and the note in which Gradgrind is given additional sons, named after two celebrated political economists: 'Any little Gradgrinds?   Say 3 Adam Smith Malthus Jane   No parts to play' (memoranda for No. I). The obsession with an inflexible system of facts is stressed elsewhere in the author's notes for *Hard Times*: 'Mr. Gradgrind. Facts and Figures. "Teach these children nothing but facts. Nothing but facts" ' (memoranda for No. I). And Dickens returns to this key idea several times in his list of titles: 'Thomas/⟨George⟩/John Gradgrind's facts'. A deletion later shows that Dickens identifies facts with the image of the grindstone, that is, with the ideas of inflexibility, harshness, and abrasion: 'Mr. Gradgrind's ⟨grindstone⟩ Facts'. A title, cancelled towards the end of the list, suggests again that catastrophe will develop ironically out of the Gradgrind reliance on facts: '⟨Damaging Facts⟩'.

Inflexibility and harshness now combine with the kind of intellect which deals in facts and figures, 'Hard-headed Gradgrind', an idea returned to in 'Our hard-headed friend'. With the theme beginning to embody itself in character, the harsh inflexible intellect suggests its antitheses, in feeling, 'Hard heads and soft hearts', and in imagination, 'Heads and Tales'. As a result, the basic dramatic conflict of the novel appears and perhaps the character of Sissy and the tragedy of Louisa Gradgrind are born. All this in its turn suggests

[1] To Mr. Charles Knight (30 Jan. 1854), *HD*, p. 329.
[2] Cf. Raymond Williams, *Culture and Society 1780-1950* (1963), p. 105.

further structure. The basic dramatic conflict of the novel, 'Black and White', is to be resolved: '⟨Extremes meet⟩'. This title, however, gives away too much and is cancelled.

A series of titles which follows shows Dickens trying to realize the theme in terms of structure and effect. One of these titles, also cancelled, suggests something may have been overlooked by the Gradgrind system and expresses what is lacking, ironically enough, in mathematical terms: '⟨Unknown quantities⟩'. The other titles, two of which have also been cancelled, all ironically state the extreme Gradgrind position: 'Two and Two are Four', 'Prove it', 'According to Cocker', 'Prove it!', 'Something tangible', '⟨No such thing Sir⟩', '⟨There's no such thing Sir⟩', 'Simple arithmetic', 'A ⟨mere⟩ matter of calculation', 'A mere question of figures'. Obviously, these titles hint at *hubris* and peripety, possibly at discovery also, worked into a pattern of structural irony and poetic justice.

A further sequence of associations, which leads to the final selection of a title and adds an important dimension to the vision of the novel, begins with the grindstone image. My suggestion that the grindstone image conjures up the idea of a 'machinery' of ironic fate at work is not fanciful when we consider that the title, 'The Grindstone', clearly suggests 'The Time Grinder', which is stressed by underscoring, as the next entry but one. 'The Grindstone' has grown out of 'Hard-headed Gradgrind' and after the antithesis, 'Hard heads and soft hearts', which follows immediately, 'The Time Grinder' suggests itself. Through this final image, Time enters into Dickens's vision as an inflexible and relentless agency of fate which will wear away the cocksure hardness of the Gradgrind system. This idea is returned to in the curious title, 'Rust and dust'.

In his notes, Dickens consciously elaborates the idea of time as the machine of an ironic fate. Time will really decide the development of character and the final destiny of the Gradgrind children. This cosmic view is ironically contrasted with Gradgrind's puny sense of time (which, as 'a matter of calculation' or 'the deadly statistical clock' finds its neatly ordered place within his system) when he deceives himself into thinking that he is settling his daughter's future on the opportune occasion of Bounderby's proposal: 'Children grow up. Time, a manufacturer. Passes them through his mill. Time for Mr. Gradgrind "to talk to" Louisa' (Chap. XIV). That Dickens saw time as the agency of an ironic and punitive fate in *Hard Times* is confirmed in the concluding paragraph of Chapter XIV by a classical reference which was deleted in proof:

She tried to discover what kind of woof Old Time, that greatest and longest-established Spinner of all, ⟨—one of the few I have heard of who is not at once a Crœsus and a Victim—⟩ would weave from the threads he had already spun into a woman. But, his factory is a secret place, his work is noiseless, and his Hands are mutes.[1]

Crœsus was the classical type of over-confident prosperity, warned by an ironically ambiguous oracle and punished by nemesis in the fullness of time.

Significantly, 'Hard Times' first appears almost immediately after 'The Time Grinder' and while Dickens is alternating between 'Mr. Gradgrind's grindstone' and 'The ⟨universal⟩ general grindstone', between the Gradgrind and the cosmic views of the system. The title is at first rejected, then confirmed twice. 'Hard Times' thus compresses the ideas of inflexibility, harshness, and abrasion together with the concepts of time as industrial setting, as historical period, and as the medium of fate.

2. *The Influence of Drama: Multiple Catastrophe*

The influence of drama on the structure of Dickens's novels has not, I think, been sufficiently recognized or properly evaluated. R. C. Churchill, for example, restricts the influence of the drama on Dickens's comedy to a matter of dialogue, dismissing the topic of structure with the usual critical clichés, vague references to 'improbabilities' and 'coincidences in the plot'. True, among the very earliest influences on Dickens's work seem to have been those of farce, burlesque, and melodrama, though it is worth noting that farce requires a skilful structure of a certain kind, which is vitally related to audience reaction. This apart, the

[1] Corrected proofs of *HT* Chap. XIV, 194; cf. *HT*, Bk. I, Chap. XIV, p. 95.

influence of the drama on Dickens's narrative art should be considered against the background of his growing conscious preoccupation with structure and form.[1]

It would be surprising if Dickens had not considered the relationship between form and effect in the masterpieces of dramatic literature, particularly those of Shakespeare and Ben Jonson, with which he certainly became familiar.[2] Thus, William Dorrit's hallucination at Mrs. Merdle's banquet, when the ghost of his past rises to haunt him and causes such consternation among her guests, owes much to the banquet scene in *Macbeth*; significantly, Dickens refers in the following monthly number to Banquo's ghost in connection with another dinner party which Mrs. Merdle attends. Since Dickens both produced and acted in Ben Jonson's plays, he surely considered them from the standpoint of audience reaction and certainly there are similarities between the structure and ironic tone of *Martin Chuzzlewit* and several of Jonson's plays, particularly *Volpone*. The attempt to organize the structure round the various manifestations of a central vice, a self-seeking which may be avaricious, hypocritical, irresponsible, or even criminal, is less successful in *Martin Chuzzlewit* than in *Volpone* yet in a novel of over eight hundred pages it remains a considerable achievement. The ironic structure, by means of which the hypocritical deceiver is himself deceived and unmasked, provides a powerful discovery and catastrophe in *Volpone* and is marred in *Martin Chuzzlewit* only by the improbable motivation of Old Martin and his melodramatic moral posturing.[3]

[1] R. C. Churchill, 'Dickens, Drama, and Tradition', *Scrutiny*, x (1942), reprinted in *The Importance of Scrutiny*, ed. Eric Bentley (New York, 1948), pp. 188–9; cf. Evelyn M. Simpson, 'Jonson and Dickens: A Study in the Comic Genius of London', *Essays and Studies*, xxix (1943), 82–92. Marvin Rosenberg, 'The Dramatist in Dickens', *Journal of English and Germanic Philology*, lix (1960), 1–12. An interesting study of the popular Victorian theatre's influence on Dickens's style and vision is William F. Axton's *Circle of Fire* (Lexington, 1966); see also *F*, vol. i, p. 14, and S. J. Adair Fitz-Gerald, *Dickens and the Drama* (1910), pp. 8, 66–7. Prefaces to *PP* (1837) and *MC*, (1844); cf. Kathleen Tillotson, *Novels of the Eighteen-Forties*, pp. 157–63.

[2] *F*, vol. ii, pp. 178, 182–3. Edgar Johnson, *Charles Dickens*, vol. i, p. 568, vol. ii, pp. 623, 1131; Fitz-Gerald, op. cit., pp. 17–21; Dickens had Ben Jonson's *Dramatic and Other Works* (1838) in his possession, *Catalogue of the Library of Charles Dickens*, p. 66.

[3] *LD*, Bk. II, Chap. XIX [monthly No. XVI], Chap. XXV [monthly No.

Dickens appears to have been very deliberate about the intrigue in *Martin Chuzzlewit*. One of the two very brief plans for this novel which Dickens committed to paper included: 'CHAPTER X Old Martin's Plot to degrade and punish Pecksniff in the end'.[1] One immediately thinks of the conspiring of Volpone and Mosca, of Brainworm, and of Face. That Dickens was conscious of structure and form and even of its classical terminology can be confirmed. Not only does he use the terms 'reverse of fortune' and 'catastrophe' but he had also met with a brief exposition of classical form, together with its terminology and a reference to Aristotle, in his reading. Dickens was so familiar with the work of Sterne that he boasted about his knowledge of *A Sentimental Journey* while *Tristram Shandy* was enough of a favourite to be taken to Switzerland with him and to come easily to hand. He is, therefore, hardly likely to have been unaware of the following passage:

Haste we now towards the catastrophe of my tale,—I say catastrophe (cries Slawkenbergius) inasmuch as a tale, with parts rightly disposed, not only rejoiceth (*gaudet*) in the *Catastrophe* and *Peripeitia* [*sic*] of a DRAMA, but rejoiceth moreover in all the essential and integrant parts of it;—it has its *Protasis, Epitasis, Catastasis*, its *Catastrophe* or *Peripeitia*, growing one out of the other in it, in the order *Aristotle* first planted them,—without which a tale had better never be told at all, says Slawkenbergius, but be kept to a man's self.

Moreover, Sterne immediately offers a gloss on three of these terms; if anything, his irony invites a thoughtful examination of the information he is conveying. Dickens also possessed a copy of *Greek Tragic Theatre* (1809), five volumes of plays by Aeschylus, Sophocles, and Euripides together with a dissertation on 'Antient Tragedy' by Francklin.[2]

XVII]. See Edwin B. Benjamin, 'The Structure of *Martin Chuzzlewit*', *Philological Quarterly*, xxxiv (1955), 39–47; Barbara Hardy, '*Martin Chuzzlewit*', *Dickens and the Twentieth Century*, pp. 107–20, argues against the view of Benjamin and others that *MC* is a well-constructed novel. The truth, I think, lies between these two views; the attempt at an overall structure related to theme marks a decided advance and meets with some success but is not wholly successful. See also Johnson, op. cit., vol. i, pp. 479–80.

[1] Original MS. of *MC*, Vol. IA [monthly No. IV].

[2] 'The Holly-Tree Inn' (1855), Chap. I, *CS*; cf. 'Where We Stopped Growing', *HW* (1 Jan. 1853), reprinted in *MP*, p. 360. *F*, vol. ii, p. 215. The copy of

Q

Admittedly, the influence of the drama on the structure of Dickens's novels is sometimes a crippling one. The grand finale, which concludes the earlier novels, is a borrowing from the theatre that seems especially artificial in the novel. Dickens mildly protested against the convention of the final round-up of characters as early as *Pickwick*.[1] By *David Copperfield*, however, he had learned to dispose of his characters in a much more natural and effective way.

It is possible to exaggerate the influence of the theatre on Dickens. He took what he wanted and gradually learned to transmute it into a proper narrative medium. What interested him about the technique of the dramatist was the way in which structure produced effect. Thus, the success of the conspiracy or intrigue in Ben Jonson's plays depends upon the sympathetic and ironic effects it creates. The vitality and resourcefulness of the conspirators or intriguers binds us to what we would otherwise find wholly disgusting antics, while the irony in the situations enables Jonson to expose and casti-gate foibles and vice—the hypocrisy, abuses of office, and greed of the *Volpone* world, for example. Significantly, hypocrisy, avarice, and the abuse of power are the main targets of Dickens's irony both in *Martin Chuzzlewit* and generally. It is also worth noting that the scene in which Pecksniff is exposed fails wherever it becomes a cataloguing of misdeeds and machinations and a series of moral postures; it succeeds wherever Dickens exploits either the irony in Pecksniff's catastrophe or the sympathy which Pecksniff's resilience, with all its irrepressible vitality in the face of disaster, evokes. The result is a complex vision which does equal justice to both the wickedness of hypocrisy and its lively resourcefulness.

On the other hand, a succession of discoveries, reversals of fortune, and catastrophes, which are handled without a

Sterne was probably his *Works* (1815), listed in *Catalogue of the Library of Charles Dickens*, p. 105; see ibid., p. 52, for the reference to *Greek Tragic Theatre*. Lawrence Sterne, *The Life and Opinions of Tristram Shandy, Gentle-man, The Works of Lawrence Sterne* (1815), vol. i, p. 284.

[1] We do not get anything like this grand finale type of conclusion in nove-lists who influenced Dickens's early development, Fielding, Smollett, Pierce Egan (*Life in London*) or Surtees (*Jorrocks's Jaunts and Jollities*), though we do sometimes find the final round-up of characters with brief biographies; *PP*, Chap. LVII, p. 800.

complex rhetoric in *Oliver Twist* and *The Old Curiosity Shop*, seems dull, sentimental, or mechanical. Rose Maylie falls sick, little Dick is discovered to have died, Oliver turns out to be well connected, Mr. Brownlow to be his father's best friend, Rose his aunt, and Monks his wicked half-brother. Nell and Grandfather are dispossessed by Quilp, Grandfather falls into the hands of card-sharpers and loses his money, Quilp discovers Brass has betrayed him, Nell and then Grandfather die. There is sometimes an unsuccessful attempt at pathos in these scenes but no irony. There may even be a dull moment in *Pickwick* when a catastrophe is handled without irony or pathos. The unsuccessful appeal to Winkle Senior is a case in point.[1]

In sharp contrast are scenes of discovery, reversal of fortune, or catastrophe in which a powerful irony and pathos are at work. Pickwick encounters the wretched and totally destitute Jingle or young Martin Chuzzlewit makes his painful discovery that the Eden on which he has staked all his hopes for a career as an architect is a miserable shanty town in a fever-infested swamp. Through the sheer impact which form and effect make on the reader in these instances, Dickens conveys a penetrating vision of the vanity of human wishes in all its pathos and irony. The brisk shabby genteel trickster's financial scheming comes to its end on the poor side of a debtor's prison. The young ambitious architect's self-centred optimism is an easy prey to the wily American land swindlers. This is true tragi-comedy. When form produces irony only, as in the Lammles' discovery on their honeymoon that they are both penniless fortune-hunters, the vision is much narrower, though suitable here for a satire on a certain aspect of the acquisitive society.[2]

It is increasingly difficult to find the weaker forms of discovery, reversal of fortune, and catastrophe in Dickens's later novels, though there are lapses. Perhaps even worse than the discovery that Chevy Slyme is in charge of the police who arrest Jonas Chuzzlewit is the sudden convenient appearance of the reformed Tattycoram at the Marshalsea with the vital

[1] *OT*, Chaps. XXXIII, XLIX, LI; *OCS*, Chaps. XI, XLII, LXIII, LXVII, LXXI, LXXII; *PP*, Chap. L.
[2] Ibid., Chap. XLII; *MC*, Chap. XXIII; *OMF*, Bk. I, Chap. X.

box of family secrets which Miss Wade has refused to surrender. Against such lapses must be set many triumphs in the
organization of form and effect. The young David Copperfield returns happily from his idyllic seaside holiday to discover that his mother has married the feared and detested
Murdstone. The ironic and pathetic shock here powerfully
focuses a complex vision of the naïvety and helplessness which
makes the child so vulnerable in an adult world with its own
aims and interests. Indeed, the whole story of David's childhood depends in no small measure for its effectiveness on the
skilfully organized rising and falling action as David's fortunes fluctuate and his traumatic experiences accumulate.
A deeply moving pathos, tinged with irony, arises from the
successive reversals of fortune, from David's failure to recognize the signs of approaching disaster and the cruel frustration
of his expectations of happiness. Thus, the initial idyll of
mother and home is threatened by Murdstone's appearance;
the happy holiday at Yarmouth is punctuated by the discovery of his mother's marriage. David falls into disgrace, is
whipped, bites his stepfather, and is sent away to school.
During the school holidays, David recaptures one unexpected
afternoon of the old domestic bliss with his mother only to
find it vanish again on the abrupt return of the Murdstones.
Then follows the death of David's mother and his abandon-
ment in the bottling factory. That Dickens was well aware of
the form here can be seen by his outline in the number plans
which stresses the reversals of fortune, thus: 'CHAPTER IV
I FALL INTO DISGRACE Progress of his mother's weakness
under the Murdstones. MISS MURDSTONE Beats him   Bites
Shut up and dismissed CHAPTER V—AND AM SENT AWAY
FROM HOME'; the division into serial parts also stresses the
rising and falling action. Many indeed of the episodes carefully organized in terms of form and effect are memorable
scenes in the novels, and arouse sympathy and irony as when
Inspector Bucket exercises 'dutiful friendship' while arresting
Mr. George for murder or when the Chancery suit is finally
settled at the expense of the entire estate and Richard
Carstone's death.[1]

---

[1] *MC*, Chap. LI; *LD*, Bk. II, Chap. XXXIII; *DC*, Chap. III. Original MS. of
DC, Vol. IA; see Butt and Tillotson, op. cit., p. 121. *BH*, Chaps. XLIX, LXV.

An important sign of Dickens's growing maturity is the gradual waning of the facetious kind of verbal irony which disfigured his earlier work. Dickens came to rely for his ironic effects much less on verbal forms and much more on structure. Irony in his work, therefore, becomes less obtrusive and seems more natural. As layers of ironic structure increasingly overlap and become interconnected, the irony appears richer, more subtle and searching. The first few chapters of *Great Expectations* are a case in point. Pip's theft of food for the starving convict begins a whole movement of the novel which centres on Pip's guilt. A steady structural irony builds up around Pip's fear that the theft will be discovered and this culminates at the end of Chapter IV in a double ironic reversal of fortune and an ironic discovery, the arrival of the Sergeant with the handcuffs which Pip mistakenly supposes are intended for himself. Chapter V begins with the discovery that the handcuffs have been brought to Joe's forge for repair and Pip is preserved from catastrophe. But this movement of the novel is also enriched by dramatic irony at every possible stage. Pip naïvely believes the convict's threats that the young man will devour his liver unless he does as he is told. His attempts to conceal his bread are taken as instances of bolting and he is dosed accordingly. When Pip's sister predicts a life of crime for him on account of his many questions about convicts and hulks, she unwittingly comments on his intended robbery and there is also irony in the way Pip literally applies his sister's words to his immediate predicament. There is also dramatic irony in the moral reflections made on Pip's character at the Christmas dinner. Dramatic irony fuses with structural irony when Pip's fears that the robbery in the pantry will be discovered culminate in his sister's discovery that the savoury pie is missing and the Sergeant's entrance with the handcuffs. The irony is complex. It is not confined to the naïvety of the child's viewpoint, though the searching evocation of childhood guilt and terror alone is remarkable. The irony extends to a certain naïvety in adults which the child sees through. The child's secret activities are misrepresented in accordance with the adult concept of the child as an object to be fed, dosed, punished, and so forth. Wopsle and Pumblechook's moralizing at the child's expense is exposed for what it is, a projection of adult gluttony on to the ill-fed Pip. Here we are dealing with an increase both in power and in the complexity of effect and vision.

Dickens's use of the multiple catastrophe provides a further instance of his growing skill in handling structure so as to achieve complex and powerful effects. It also illustrates how he passed beyond the influence of the theatre into a fuller exploitation of a narrative medium. A theory of the multiple catastrophe had been formulated by Bulwer-Lytton as early as 1838:

> The drama will bear but one catastrophe; the novel will admit of more . . . So also there is often a moral catastrophe, as well as a physical one, sometimes identified each with the other, sometimes distinct. If you have been desirous to work out some conception of a principle or a truth, the design may not be completed till after the more violent effects which form the physical catastrophe.[1]

It seems unlikely that Bulwer and Dickens did not discuss the theory during their literary conversations, especially since Dickens develops and puts something like this theory into practice on an impressive scale. There is one vital difference, however, between Bulwer's and Dickens's treatment of the multiple catastrophe. Dickens's practice of mixing comedy with other kinds of narrative made it possible for him to alternate a comic element with other elements in his multiple catastrophes.

The elements of multiple catastrophe can be seen emerging in Dickens's work as early as *Pickwick*. Pickwick's descent into the inferno of the Fleet Prison is followed fairly closely by Jingle's tragi-comic catastrophe, the comedy of Mrs. Bardell's fall, and a little later by Stiggins's ejection from the Marquis of Granby which is largely satirical in tone. In *Oliver Twist*, however, form tends to be lost in a crowd of incidents. Nancy's horrifying murder and Sikes's flight is followed by Monks's melodramatic exposure and that in its

---

[1] Edward Bulwer-Lytton, 'On Art in Fiction', *Pamphlets and Sketches*, pp. 350–1. Since the essay first appeared in the *Monthly Chronicle* during 1838, Dickens might well have become acquainted with Bulwer's theory very early in his career. The text in the earlier version is identical with the later except for minor changes in punctuation.

turn by the ironic terror of Sikes's end. The following chapter
provides a further melodramatic instalment of Monks's
defeat and the Bumbles' final catastrophe which is handled in
a comic manner. Immediately after this, we get the terror of
Fagin's condemnation and last night alive. In *The Old Curiosity Shop*, Kit's unjust condemnation, Dick Swiveller's illness,
Sampson Brass's arrest, the irony and horror of Quilp's
drowning, and Nell's sentimental death draw out the catastrophe too long. *Martin Chuzzlewit*, however, shows the device
beginning to assume the pattern which Dickens held to
fairly constantly in the later novels. Jonas Chuzzlewit's
exposure, arrest for murder, and suicide are immediately
succeeded by Pecksniff's exposure. Both scenes are ambitious-
ly conceived but unfortunately marred by melodramatic
posturing and the irony is often swamped by tedious moralizing. Unfortunately also, Jonas's exposure, arrest, and suicide are less impressive than Tigg's murder and the account
of Jonas's guilt, and so seem an anticlimax. Furthermore, the
desertion of Charity on her wedding morning loses something
by being postponed until the effect of the multiple catastrophe has evaporated. In *Dombey and Son*, Carker's death
is much more successful than Jonas's, since the inner experience of guilt is sustained throughout and made the cause
of death, but Dombey's financial ruin is postponed for several
chapters and though impressive is interrupted by Alice
Marwood's sentimental end. The spectacle of Captain Bunsby's
being taken in tow by Mrs. MacStinger, which follows, is
magnificent comedy but no true parallel to Dombey's fall
since it concerns the fortunes of subsidiary characters;
Captain Cuttle is only indirectly involved. *David Copperfield*,
however, shows a truly mature handling of parallel catastrophes. By bringing closely together the deaths of Dora,
Ham, and Steerforth and the departure of the Micawbers and
the Peggottys for Australia, Dickens deepens the impression
of David's final traumatic experience and moral crisis. Thus,
the difficult and important turning-point in a life which,
childhood apart, has largely been conveyed as a series of
relationships with other characters is managed skilfully and
David is given a weight in the novel which he has not had
since the early chapters. In the later novels, Dickens usually

adopts the device of two (sometimes three) parallel catastrophes, one comic, the others tragic or melodramatic, which
gain in effect by being concentrated in one serial part, usually
the concluding double number. Thus, the ironic comedy of
Guppy's final 'magnanimous' but unsuccessful proposal is
immediately followed by the ironic and pathetic tragedy of
Richard's final disappointment, collapse, and death. The
ironic comedy of Bounderby's exposure in *Hard Times* is at
once succeeded by the tragic pathos of Stephen's death. In
Little Dorrit, the ironic and satirical exposure of Casby, the
hypocritical and bloodsucking landlord, before his duped
victims, follows immediately on the ironic melodrama of
Rigaud's death in the collapsing house, while both catastrophes are played out against the general catastrophe of
Arthur Clennam's incarceration in the Marshalsea, which
with its irony and pathos dominates the final double number.
True, Dickens does not necessarily bring all his important
catastrophes together at the conclusion of his story. Thus,
in *Bleak House*, Lady Dedlock's tragic end occurs in the
eighteenth monthly number, in *Hard Times*, the ironic and
pathetic tragedy of Louisa's catastrophe and the failure of
the Gradgrind system in the sixteenth weekly number, and in
Little Dorrit, the tragic irony and pathos of William Dorrit's
collapse and the satirical irony and horror of Merdle's ruin
and suicide in the sixteenth and seventeenth monthly parts
respectively. But Dickens was too skilful an artist by this
time to carry the practice of the multiple catastrophe too far.
Had it even been possible to work these episodes into the
multiple catastrophes, such a conglomeration of effects would
have proved too much and such an extreme degree of manipulation would have seemed unnatural, if not stagey. In the final
weekly number of *Great Expectations*, the final tragi-comic blow
which Pip receives, his ironic discovery on deciding to propose
to Biddy that she has just married Joe, is immediately preceded by the comic interlude with Pumblechook who puts on
an aggrieved air at the disappointment of *his* great expectations of Pip. These episodes follow the tragic horror and
pathos of Magwitch's trial and death and Pip's illness in the
previous two weekly numbers. Finally, in the concluding
double number of *Our Mutual Friend*, the ironic comedy of

Silas Wegg's defeat is immediately followed by the ironic melo-drama of Bradley Headstone's and Rogue Riderhood's deaths.[1]

The multiple catastrophe lends Dickens's narrative art considerable power and complexity at one of its most strategic points, the conclusion of a story. It affords him an opportunity to create the most intense kinds of pathos and irony through the use of overlapping and interwoven structural patterns. In some measure, it enables him to overcome his greatest artistic handicap, his habit of fragmenting experience and vision into comic and pathetic, tragic and melodramatic, sensational and satirical elements. By the juxtaposition of parallel episodes in a common form, though with a different and even a contrasting effect and vision, Dickens suggests that life, for all its diverse appearances, has an underlying structure and plan. His ultimate vision thereby gains the unity, the force, and the complexity it has earlier foregone.

3. *Structure and the Moral Vision*

Structural patterns help to articulate moral implications in Dickens's vision. Unfortunately, misconceptions about coincidence and poetic justice in Dickens's narrative art may prevent a proper appreciation of his moral vision.

Most critics seem confused about coincidence. The realist, Gissing, for example, objects on the ground that coincidence is artificial, though a complaint that it offends against organic structure and smacks of too much artistic and imaginative licence creeps into his argument. Dickens has answered the charge that coincidence is unrealistic:

On the coincidences, resemblances, and surprises of life, Dickens liked especially to dwell, and few things moved his fancy so pleasantly. The world, he would say, was so much smaller than we thought it; we were all so connected by fate without knowing it; people supposed to be far apart were so constantly elbowing each other; and to-morrow bore so close a resemblance to nothing half so much as to yesterday.

[1] *PP*, Chaps. XL, XLI, XLII, XLVI, LII; *OT*, Chaps. XLVII, XLVIII, XLIX, L. LI, LII; *OCS*, Chaps. LXIII, LXIV, LXVI, LXVII, LXXI; *MC*, Chaps. LI, LII; *D & S*, Chaps. LV, LVIII, LIX, LX; *DC*, Chaps. LIII, LV, LVII, LVIII; *BH*, Chaps. LXIV, LXV [Final Double No.]; *HT*, Bk. III, Chaps. V, VI; *LD*, Bk. II, Chaps. XXXI, XXXII; *GE*, Chap. LVIII; *OMF*, Bk. IV, Chaps. XIV, XV.

Forster cites many instances.[1] The appeal to real life is an ultimate argument neither for nor against coincidence in fiction. The case must be settled elsewhere.

Certainly, there is something valid in the objection to coincidence. But the confusion of critics about what precisely this is arises out of their failure to distinguish between different uses of coincidence, all of which require a separate assessment. Lumping together all forms of coincidence, they condemn all indiscriminately. This is true, for example, of W. C. Phillips, who follows Gissing closely, or of W. J. Harvey, a more recent instance. Even T. S. Eliot who considers there might be a case for coincidence in the fiction of Dickens and Wilkie Collins does not distinguish between the various uses of coincidence.[2]

Farce, for example, depends very much on coincidence for its effect:

With a violent effort, Mr. Weller disengaged himself from the grasp of the agonised Pickwickian, and, in so doing, administered a considerable impetus to the unhappy Mr. Winkle. With an accuracy which no degree of dexterity or practice could have insured, that unfortunate gentleman bore swiftly down into the centre of the reel, at the very moment when Mr. Bob Sawyer was performing a flourish of unparalleled beauty. Mr. Winkle struck wildly against him, and with a loud crash they both fell heavily down.[3]

Coincidence, however, in novels with an intricate or organic structure draws attention to the manipulation of plot since it breaks the causal unity of the structure and mars the impression of natural growth which the action conveys. Gissing might well have cited many other instances in this category. Edwin Leeford's only sister happens to die on the morning she was to have married Mr. Brownlow. Back in London, young Martin and Mark Tapley bump into their friendly

[1] George Gissing, *Charles Dickens: A Critical Study*, pp. 62–3; *F*, vol. i pp. 91, 65, 353, vol. ii, p. 196, vol. iii, pp. 151, 178, 484–5. A study of the daily press will reveal a host of coincidences in real life far more remarkable than anything in fiction.

[2] W. C. Phillips, *Dickens, Reade, and Collins: Sensation Novelists*, pp. 134, 189–91; W. J. Harvey, '*Bleak House*', *Dickens and the Twentieth Century*, pp. 153–7; T. S. Eliot, 'Wilkie Collins and Dickens' [1927], reprinted in *Selected Essays*, (1945) pp. 427–9.

[3] *PP*. Chap. XXX, p. 412.

neighbours from Eden who have almost miraculously survived. Major Bagstock happens to know the father of Master Blitherstone and so can use the child as a means of making the acquaintance of Mr. Dombey. The first person Arthur Clennam meets outside the Marshalsea gates turns out to be Amy Dorrit's uncle, someone who can get him inside. Arthur happens to see Tattycoram and Rigaud in the street.[1]

In episodic structure, however, coincidence seems less objectionable. When Sam Weller discovers that Pickwick is the name of the proprietor of the coach in which Mr. Pickwick is travelling to Bath or when Micawber turns up in Canterbury outside the house in which David is having tea with the Heeps, the reader is not so offended.[2] In some respects, the episodic form may seem close to life with its apparent lack of plan and its chance meetings and perhaps, in this one instance, coincidence may be justified by an appeal to life.

The most important and extensive use of coincidence in Dickens's fiction is so acceptable that it usually passes unnoticed. Coincidence, in this case, is used to create an ironic effect. It is not objected to because, behind the appearance of chance, it implies design. In the final analysis, therefore, it does not break the aesthetic law of organic unity and it indicates an order at work in the universe. That Dickens was fully aware of the idea of coincidence as fate or design is clear in the following,

"It's a curious fact, sir, that he should have come and lived here, and been one of my writers, and then that you should come and live here, and be one of my writers, too . . .

"It's a curious coincidence, as you say," answers Weevle, once more glancing up and down the court.

"Seems a Fate in it, don't there?" suggests the stationer,

and in many other places.[3]

An awareness of the distinction between the ironic and the non-ironic uses of coincidence helps to settle the old argument between Dickens and Bulwer-Lytton about Madame Defarge's death and it helps us to appreciate Dickens's defence more fully:

[1] OT, Chap. XLIX, p. 373; MC, Chap. LIV, pp. 831–2; D & S, Chap. X, pp. 124–7; LD, Bk. I, Chap. VIII, pp. 79–80, Bk. II, Chap. IX, p. 530.
[2] PP, Chap. XXXV, p. 493; DC, Chap. XVI, p. 256.
[3] BH, Chap. XXXII, p. 446. Cf. ibid., Chaps. XIII, XVI, pp. 171, 219; MC, Chaps. XXXVIII, XLVI, pp. 589–90, 717; GE, Chap. XXVIII, p. 217.

I am not clear, and I never have been clear, respecting that canon of fiction which forbids the interposition of accident in such a case as Madame Defarge's death. Where the accident is inseparable from the passion and emotion of the character, where it is strictly consistent with the whole design, and arises out of some culminating proceeding on the part of the character which the whole story has led up to, it seems to me to become, as it were, an act of divine justice. And when I use Miss Pross (though this is quite another question) to bring about that catastrophe, I have the positive intention of making that half-comic intervention a part of the desperate woman's failure, and of opposing that mean death—instead of a desperate one in the streets, which she wouldn't have minded—to the dignity of Carton's wrong or right; this *was* the design, and seemed to be in the fitness of things.

That Dickens was not offering excuses or rationalizing after the event can be seen in at least one revision in the manuscript:

"Bad Fortune!" cries The Vengeance, stamping her foot in the chair, "and here are the tumbrils! And Evrémonde will be despatched in a wink, and she not here! See her knitting in my hand, and her EMPTY chair ready for her. I cry with vexation and disappointment!"

His careful addition of the epithet 'empty' graphically brings home the irony of Madame Defarge's absence. Dickens's use of the phrase 'divine justice' in his letter must not be interpreted as the cruder kind of poetic justice which deals out rewards and punishments without irony or preparation; it is a matter of an ironic fate. Carton's act of Christian self-sacrifice has outwitted the revolutionary demand for vengeance, while Madame Defarge is denied the one final spectacle for which she had yearned. Moreover, as Dickens correctly points out, her catastrophe springs from her own action. It is her lust for vengeance, in seeking to destroy the whole Evrémonde family, which proves her downfall. Miss Pross's success in the struggle is not altogether a lucky accident; her great physical strength has been demonstrated as early in the novel as the fourth chapter.[1]

[1] To Sir Edward Bulwer-Lytton (5 June 1860), *HD*, pp. 498–9. Original MS. of *TTC*, Victoria and Albert Museum, Forster Collection, 47. A. 37 (Vol. B), Bk. III, Chap. XV, p. 44; cf. *TTC*, p. 355. Ibid., Bk. I, Chap. IV, pp. 25–6.

Other instances of the role played by the ironic type of coincidence in the catastrophes and reversals of fortune in Dickens's novels have escaped notice because such episodes rank among Dickens's most effective scenes. In these cases, too, a supernatural machinery may be glimpsed behind the appearance of chance. As in the case of Madame Defarge's end, it is a matter of an ironic fate; the ironic design is invariably indicated. Thus, Sikes uses the noose as a means of escape; it is the vision of Nancy's eyes which causes him to slip and hang himself. Carker's death is no simple railway accident. He is irresistibly drawn to the monster which destroys him at a moment when he is completely possessed by guilt and terror. It is not simply chance that the pointing Roman on Tulkinghorn's ceiling finally points to the corpse of the murdered lawyer. Occasionally, Dickens's idea of fate appears to embrace both external and internal possibilities. Whether the spectre which haunts Sikes is an hallucination conjured up by his own inner drive towards punishment or whether it is an authentic vision sent by divine intervention or whether one form of retribution is an expression of the other remains ambiguous. This ambiguity is a source of richness since it takes in the many-sided nature of the question. Certainly, Dickens's appreciation that a deliberate design may lie behind apparent accidents accords with modern psychological insight.[1]

Sometimes, Dickens's fiction presents the crude moral vision which has brought the term 'poetic justice' into such opprobrium. Heroes and heroines, like John Westlock and Ruth Pinch or Charles Darnay and Lucie Manette, are granted their heart's delight; they hardly earn it. Villains, like Monks or Compeyson, come to a bad end. Probability may even be outraged to ensure the system of rewards and punishments. Pip finally secures the hand of a repentant Estella. Pecksniff and the Brasses are dismissed to an unlikely limbo, pale unconvincing shadows of their former vitality and enterprise.[2] Yet the notion of justice in Dickens's

---

[1] *OT*, Chap. L, pp. 388–91; *D & S*, Chap. LV, pp. 776–9; *BH*, Chap. XLVIII, pp. 664–5; see Sigmund Freud, *Totem and Taboo*, tr. James Strachey (1960), pp. 85–7, 154.

[2] *MC*, Chaps. XX, XIX, XLV, LIII; *TTC*, *passim*; *OT*, Chap. LIII,

fiction is rarely so crude and in several places Dickens shows
he was aware of the problem; he censures the narrow moral
vision which such a notion produces in fiction and in one
place claims he is deliberately avoiding the crude type of
poetic justice.[1] Repeatedly in his novels, Dickens probes an
area of complex moral issues. The rewards of life do not
necessarily go to those who merit them. Thus, the undeserving
young Martin Chuzzlewit may get the girl at the expense of
the virtuous Tom Pinch or Doyce's genius may go unrecog-
nized in his own land. Suffering may be imposed without
much alleviation upon the innocent. Jo dies while Sir Leicester
Dedlock lives on. Persons responsible for much social evil or
great personal wrong may survive and even flourish. The
Veneerings enjoy a fairly comfortable exile in Calais. The
Barnacles are not overthrown and are even permitted to
gloat over their victims and their own corrupt régime. The
strict demands of justice may well be sacrificed to probability.
Uriah Heep's final exit from the story, unlike that of Pecksniff and the Brasses, is consistent with his earlier enterprise
and vitality, a triumph of hypocrisy in fact. Punishment may
be inflicted out of all proportion to weakness or to crime. An
obstinate heroism proves fatal to Gridley. The ultimate
penalty *is* carried out on Magwitch by providence, however
much Dickens may deplore the cruel sentence of a human
court.[2] Such a vision of unmerited pain and disproportionate
suffering extends far beyond the limited range of conventional
poetic justice and takes in something close to the complex
moral view of genuine tragic experience.

We cannot always attribute to Dickens's work the simple
and inflexible moral vision of contemporary popular fiction

We have ever found, in our intercourse with our readers, that
those fictions in which the innocent—although environed by
snares, and nearly brought to destruction by the wicked and

p. 412; *GE*, Chaps. LIV, LIX, pp. 421–3, 460; *MC*, Chap. LIV, p. 837; *OCS*
Chapter the Last, pp. 548–9.

[1] Preface to the First Cheap Edition of *MC* (1849); *OMF*, Bk. II, Chap. I
pp. 214–15; *MC*, Chap. L, p. 767.

[2] *MC*, Chap. L, pp. 763–8; *LD*, Bk. II, Chap. XXVIII, p. 737, cf. Bk. II
Chap. XXII, p. 672; *BH*, Chap. LXV, p. 870, cf. Chap. LX, p. 824; ibid.
Chaps. XLVII, LXVI, pp. 649, 872; *OMF*, Bk. IV, Chapter the Last, p. 849;
LD, Bk. II, Chap. XXVIII, pp. 735–9; *DC*, Chap. LXI, pp. 851–5; *BH*, Chap
XXXV, XXIV, LV, pp. 498–9, 350–3, 758–9; *GE*, Chap. LVI, pp. 432–6

designing, ultimately triumphed, and proved the goodness of right over might, were welcomed and read with delight. Can there be a more convincing proof of the ennobling power of Romance, if it be directed in the proper channel? . . . Hence we punish and confound the vicious—hence we defend, applaud, and bring off victorious, the innocent, dealing a poetical, and in our innermost heart believe, a practical justice upon evil doers.

Neither can Trollope's satirical remarks on Nemesis, in *The Three Clerks* (1858), be applied indiscriminately to Dickens's fiction. There are vital differences between Dickens's handling of Nemesis and its treatment in the popular Victorian novel and in Trollope's burlesques. In the first of Trollope's examples, Nemesis is presented as something merely appended to the story. There is no suggestion of an organic structure, of an ironic fate at work, of the revelation of design:

'Then there are the retainers; they all come to grief, some one way and some another. I do that for the sake of the Nemesis.'
'I would not have condescended to notice them, I think,' said Norman.
'Oh! I must; there must be a Nemesis. The editor specially insists on a Nemesis.'

In Trollope's second example, there is an appropriate structure but the occasion is without dignity or high seriousness. Providence is represented as stooping to intervene in the most trivial of human affairs. Naturally, it appears ridiculous:

'Now, that's what my editor would call a Nemesis,' said Charley.
'Oh, that's a Nemesis, is it?'
'Johnson was cheated into doing my work, and getting me my supper; and then you scolded me, and took away my appetite, so that I couldn't eat it; that's a Nemesis. Johnson is avenged, only, unluckily, he doesn't know it, and wickedness is punished.'[1]

In the popular Victorian novel, there may well be no organic and ironic structure which builds towards retribution.

---

[1] James Rymer's preface to *Lloyds Penny Atlas and Weekly Register of Novel Entertainment*, i, (1842), cited in John W. Dodds, *The Age of Paradox*, p. 124; Dodds is doubtful about the moral claim here but Louis James, *Fiction and the Working Man*, pp. 78–9, argues that fiction of this type had a rigid moral structure which was not feigned but essential. Anthony Trollope, *The Three Clerks* [1858] (1925), Chap. XIX, p. 219, Chap. XXVI, p. 322.

Thus, in Mary Elizabeth Braddon's *Lady Audley's Secret* (1861), sheer good luck on the part of a character playing the role of detective brings about retribution. On the other hand, there may be an organic structure of a kind. Some sort of an ironic providence may be shown at work but the machinery may be assembled with a ridiculous haste. The effect is like watching a serious film speeded up into a jerky parody of the original. The catastrophe of *Love and Crime; or, the Mystery of the Convent* (1841) is a good instance:

'Vile wretch!' said the horror-struck Agnes, 'think you that the Omnipotent will permit you to do such an act, and not instantly blast your detested form? Hark you not how the thunder roars?'
. . . one side of the mansion, no longer able to resist the combined forces of the outrageous elements, fell with a hideous roar on the sands; and the monk, who, appalled at the tremendous peals, had started away from Agnes, was precipitated on the ruins below.[1]

Dickens, however, frequently presents an organic and ironic structure which is developed at a natural pace. The pattern is similar to that in *Love and Crime*. There is a warning which is ignored and providence finally intervenes. But in Dickens's work a true feeling for both irony and for fate demands a full and convincing expression of authentic experience. The distinction is almost that between superstitious explanation and the revelation of a genuine faith. The plot is not simply a mechanism working out a moral syllogism, it conveys an impression of life evolving in a meaningful pattern. Thus, the ironic episode of Rigaud's death when Mrs. Clennam's house collapses might reasonably be compared with the catastrophe of *Love and Crime*. In *Little Dorrit*, however, the catastrophe is prepared with a care and delicacy which runs through many hundreds of pages. Moreover, unlike the author of *Love and Crime*, Dickens does not clumsily point out the existence of his machinery. Certainly, justice requires that a warning be issued. But true ironic structure demands that ultimate reality be concealed behind an appearance. The proper compromise is the barest of hints. The catastrophe in *Little Dorrit* has the appropriate qualities of surprise and inevitability. Elsewhere, Dickens shows himself conscious of the need

[1] Quoted by Louis James, op. cit., p. 78.

to foreshadow without giving too much away.[1] In the corrected proofs of *David Copperfield*, a blatant hint during the storm scene at Yarmouth that David would not have been surprised to have met a figure from his childhood is deleted: 'I should not have been surprised, I think, to encounter ⟨, unchanged,⟩ some ⟨acquaintance of my childhood or some⟩ one who I knew must /then/be/ in London'. Again, in *Bleak House*, too strong a suggestion that Esther is Lady Dedlock's daughter is toned down in proof: 'Raising my eyes as he went out, I once more saw him looking at me after he had passed the door ⟨and in a manner that reminded me, I well remembered afterwards, of a person studying a likeness in a picture⟩'; Guppy had previously wondered how he came to recognize something familiar about Lady Dedlock's portrait.

In his very early novels, Dickens tends to exploit ironic structure and pattern for the sake of a simple but powerful effect. Thus, the structure of the episode in which Mrs. Bardell is tricked into entering the Fleet Prison increases the power of the comedy. Despite ominous warnings, Mrs Bardell makes an ironic mistake about the intentions of her lawyers, Dodson and Fogg. This feeds her vanity in front of her friends. Yet there is no searching study of the complexities of human behaviour here and the satirical comment on the deviousness of legal sharks and the gullibility of their clients is a simple one.[2]

In the later novels, an ironic error may determine the shape of a whole life or a crucial section of a life. David Copperfield makes grave misjudgements in both love and friendship. Richard Carstone comes to believe that the settlement of 'Jarndyce and Jarndyce' will make his fortune. Gradgrind's mistaken view of education ruins his son and daughter. Arthur Clennam persuades himself that love is not for him. Pip assumes that his secret benefactor is Miss Havisham who intends that he shall become a gentleman and marry Estella. Bella Wilfer thinks she detests Rokesmith and is interested only in wealth.[3] Naturally and organically, the ironic error

---

[1] Corrected proofs of *DC* (second set), Chap. LV, p. 560; cf. *DC*. p. 789. Corrected proofs of *BH*, Chap. IX, p. 89; cf. *BH*, p. 126, and see also Chap. VII, pp. 87–8.

[2] *PP*, Chap. XLV, *passim*.

[3] *DC*, Chap. LVIII, p. 813; *BH*, Chap. XXIII, pp. 320–1; *HT*, Bk. I,

develops into an inflated wilful form and the irony becomes
all the sharper when a hubristic stance is taken up. David
ignores Agnes's advice about Steerforth and his aunt's
advice about Dora. Richard first declares that he will never
be seduced by Chancery and then announces he will die
rather than abandon the suit. Gradgrind seeks to measure the
universe with a pair of compasses. Arthur Clennam says he
will never fall in love again. Pip's mistake about his great
expectations becomes a snobbish delusion in which he readily
sacrifices old homespun relationships. Bella Wilfer declares
she will never marry Rokesmith.[1] All these characters are
warned and ignore the warning. David is cautioned not only
by Agnes and Miss Trotwood but by the example of Annie
Strong and the cryptic call of the blind beggar, Richard by
Mr. Jarndyce, Esther, and Miss Flite. Gradgrind fails to
profit from an early shock outside Sleary's circus while Mrs.
Gradgrind suggests on her death-bed that something is lacking in her daughter's education. Arthur Clennam cannot take
in the evidence of his own eyes. Pip is as good as told by Miss
Havisham that she is not his secret benefactor. Bella Wilfer
feels uneasy about her mercenary attitude.[2] The vision which
this ironic structure helps to realize is moral in the classical
or religious sense. It does not investigate conduct as such but
presents the relationship between conduct and fate. It asserts
what happens when conduct sets in motion the mysterious
machinery of a spiritual universe. *Hamartia* in this type of
character is conceived, in the strict Aristotelian sense, as an
error of judgement committed in some kind of ignorance.
Such a character is too blind or obsessed to exercise a dramatic moral choice. Fate is the real protagonist of the Dickens
world and character is its victim. Revelation and release are

Chap. I, p. 1; *LD*, Bk. I, Chap. XXXII, p. 381; *GE*, Chaps. XVII, XVIII,
XXIX, pp. 125, 130, 219; *OMF*, Bk. I, Chap. IV, pp. 40–1.

[1] *DC*, Chaps. XXV, XXXV, pp. 367–8, 503–4; *BH*, Chaps. V, LI, pp. 58,
695, cf. Chap. XXXVII, p. 530; *HT*, Bk. III, Chap. I, p. 222; *LD*, Bk. I, Chap.
XXXII, p. 381; *GE* Chap. XIX, pp. 139, 150–1; *OMF*, Bk. II, Chap. XIII,
pp. 376–8.

[2] *DC*, Chaps. XLVI, XXXV, pp. 664, 519; *BH*, Chaps, XXXVII, XXIII,
III, pp. 524–5, 324, 32–3; *HT*, Bk. I, Chap. III, pp. 11–13, Bk. II, Chap. IX,
p. 199; *LD*, Bk. I, Chap. XXXII, p. 382; *GE*, Chaps. XIII, XV, pp. 96, 103, 108;
OMF, Bk. III, Chaps. IV, V, pp. 460, 465–6.

[3] See Humphry House, *Aristotle's Poetics*, p. 94.

a kind of grace which comes from above. Catastrophe is also exploited for sympathetic effects, so that a compassionate dimension complicates the final vision.

The deliberate care with which Dickens worked to express this ironic and moral pattern and the compassionate vision which accompanies it may be seen in many places in the manuscripts of the later novels. Thus, in the following scene from *Little Dorrit*, the manuscript shows that Dickens consciously strives to exploit to the full the pathos in the situation while, at the same time, he seeks to impose on his material, in the most complete and effective way, the pattern of an ironic and moral order:

"Let me confess then, that, forgetting how grave I was, and how old I was, and how the time for such things had gone by me with the many years of monotony and little happiness that made up my long life far away, without marking it—that, forgetting all this, I fancied I loved some one."

"Do I know her, sir?" asked Little Dorrit.

"No, my dear child."

"It is not the lady who has been kind to me for your sake?"

"Flora. No, no. Did you think—"

"I never quite thought so," said Little Dorrit, more to herself than him. "I did wonder at it a little."

"Well!" said Clennam, ABIDING BY THE FEELING THAT HAD FALLEN ON HIM IN THE AVENUE ON THE NIGHT OF THE ROSES, THE FEELING THAT HE WAS AN OLDER MAN, WHO HAD DONE WITH THAT TENDER PART OF LIFE, "I found out my mistake, and I thought about it a little—in short, a good deal—and got wiser. BEING WISER, I counted up my years, and considered what I am, and looked back, and looked forward, and found that I should soon be grey. I found that I had climbed the hill, and passed the level ground upon the top, and was descending quickly."

If he had known the sharpness of the pain he caused the patient heart, in speaking thus! While doing it, too, with the purpose of easing and serving her.

"I found that the day when any such thing would have been graceful in me, or good in me, or hopeful or happy for me, or any one IN CONNEXION WITH ME, was gone, and would never shine again."

O! If he had known, if he had known! If he could have seen the dagger in his hand, and the cruel wounds it ⟨made in the⟩ STRUCK

IN THE faithful ⟨?faithful⟩ BLEEDING breast of his Little
Dorrit!

"Well! All that is over, and I have turned my face from it. Why
do I speak of this to Little Dorrit? Why do I show you, my child,
the space of years that there is between us, and recall to you that
I have passed, by the amount of your whole life, the time that is
present to you?"

"Because you trust me, I hope. Because you know that nothing
can touch you, without touching me; that nothing can make you
happy or unhappy, but it must make me, who am so grateful to
you, the same."

⟨He looked at⟩ HE HEARD the THRILL IN HER VOICE,
HE SAW HER earnest face, he saw her clear true eyes, he saw the
quickened bosom that would have joyfully thrown itself before
him to receive a MORTAL wound directed at his breast, with the
dying cry, "I love him!" and the ⟨lightest⟩ REMOTEST suspicion of the truth ⟨was as far away from his mind⟩ NEVER
DAWNED UPON HIS MIND. No. He saw the devoted little
creature with her worn shoes, in her common dress, in her jail-
home; a slender child in body, a strong heroine in soul; and the
light of her domestic story made all else dark to him . . .

"Little Dorrit," he said, taking her hand again, and speaking
lower than he had spoken yet . . . "Always think of me as quite an
old man. I know that all your devotion centres in this room, and
that nothing to the last will ever tempt you away from the duties
you discharge here. If I were not sure of it, I should, before now,
have implored you, and implored your father, to let me make some
provision for you in a more suitable place. But you may have an
interest—I will not say, now, though even that might be—may
have, at another time, an interest in some one else; an interest not
incompatible with your affection here."

She was very, very pale, and slightly shook her head.

"It may be, dear Little Dorrit."

"No. No. No." She shook her head, after each SLOW repe-
tition of the word, with an air of ⟨quiet ?long⟩ QUIET DESOLA-
TION that he remembered long afterwards; ⟨remembered WELL
long⟩ THE TIME CAME WHEN HE REMEMBERED IT WELL,
LONG afterwards within those prison walls; within that ⟨prison⟩
VERY room.

By intensifying the blind and wilful attitude which Clennam
takes up towards life and love as fate, Dickens not only
sharpens the irony but also increases the grievousness of the
wounds which Little Dorrit receives. And, in doing this,

Dickens not only increases the pathos of her situation but also makes all the more apt the fate which will overtake Clennam when he discovers too late, as he believes, that Amy and he love each other.[1] The close interaction between the rhetorics of sympathy and irony, here, and the careful balance between detachment and compassion achieve a power and complexity of vision which is directed beyond the immediate occasion. The scene is more successful than its prototype in *David Copperfield*. The love scene between David and Agnes, though illustrating the central theme, seems only one dramatically effective episode in a life but the scene between Arthur and Amy is an integral part of a whole fate which extends into the future and will reach back into the past. It is a scene viewed not from the auditorium of a theatre but from the vantage point of a loving, though just, god.

It should not be inferred that Dickens's moral vision is, in general, a wholly Christian or even a consistent one. On the contrary, it has decided pagan, if not primitive, elements. The precise form of the punishments meted out in Dickens's catastrophes, with its apt irony, does not express a rational kind of justice but the ancient law of talion. Philip Collins has recently drawn attention to the complexity and ambivalence in Dickens's thinking about crime and punishment and has indicated its reactionary side.[2] The important role played by the *lex talionis* in the novels, however, also requires examination. The law of talion operates very extensively in Dickens's fiction and it appears to contradict the element of benevolence, a vague but sincere form of Christian charity, together with its compassionate vision. Nevertheless, the distinctive feature of the *lex talionis* is not its harshness but its rigid insistence on *exact* retaliation. The sharpness of the ironic effect derives from this exactness in retribution since no reversal could be more complete than when a character brings upon himself the very fate (or elements in that fate)

[1] Original MS. of *LD*, Vol. IB, Bk. I, Chap. XXXII, pp. 22–4 ('sameness' substituted for 'monotony' in proof, 'is it' before 'not' and 'Well!' before 'All' deleted in proof, while MS and proofs read 'my dear child', First Edition omits 'dear'); cf. *LD*, pp. 381–4, and see also Bk. II, Chaps. XXVII, XXIX, pp. 730–3, 760.

[2] Philip Collins, *Dickens and Crime*, *passim*, see esp. pp. 22–6.

which he had either tried to avoid or sought to bring upon others. The manner of punishment sharply recalls precise features of the offence.

Thus, Jingle's crimes were activated by desire for financial gain. His punishment takes the most extreme financial form— destitution on the poor side of a debtors' prison. Sikes tries to escape what must surely be a public execution for murder. He dies in a noose of his own making before a large crowd. Quilp describes how he would drown Brass if he had him in his power. Quilp himself is drowned. Mercy Pecksniff rushes thoughtlessly into marriage, believing she will lead her husband a dance. It is Jonas who makes her life a misery instead. Pecksniff thinks he is deceiving Old Martin who turns out to be deceiving Pecksniff. The proud Mr. Dombey marries a wife whose pride he cannot subdue. Steerforth uses his interest in sailing as a mask behind which to seduce Em'ly and he carries her away across the sea. He dies in a shipwreck at Yarmouth. Richard Carstone squanders his health and promise in legal proceedings in Chancery. He discovers that the costs of legal proceedings in Chancery have squandered the great fortune he hoped to secure. Gradgrind will not allow fairy stories into his children's nursery. His last sight of his disgraced son is in the costume of a circus performer playing in a dramatized version of Jack the Giant Killer. William Dorrit tries to live out his fantasy that the poor Marshalsea prisoner is a gentleman. When the fantasy becomes a reality, an hallucination that he is the poor prisoner once again exposes his shameful past to genteel society. Pip tries to repudiate his shabby past in favour of genteel aspirations but his future turns out to be quite as shabby as the past. The convict, a social outcast, is his benefactor. Bella Wilfer rejects him for mercenary reasons. In love with Rokesmith at last, she hears her former mercenary attitude in rejecting him ironically commended by Mr. Boffin. Gaffer Hexam preys upon drowned corpses in the Thames by taking them in tow. He is drowned by the very rope he has intended for his prey and takes the place of the corpse, drawn in tow behind his own boat.[1]

[1] *PP*, Chaps. X, XLII, pp. 128–31, 595–8; *OT*, Chap. L, pp. 388–91; *OCS*, Chap. LXVII, pp. 506, 510; *MC*, Chaps. XXIV, XXVIII, XXVIII,

These examples show that Dickens does not express the *lex talionis* in any stereotyped manner. On the contrary, his fresh and imaginative forms of expression show that he is in touch with genuine living experience, with the authentic lower levels of primitive feeling in modern man. What is brooding below the surface of benevolence and charity may be betrayed in fantasies like this:

"I was thinking," she returned, coming out of a deep study, "what I would do to Him, if he should turn out a drunkard . . . When he was asleep, I'd make a spoon red hot, and I'd have some boiling liquor bubbling in a saucepan, and I'd take it out hissing, and I'd open his mouth with the other hand—or perhaps he'd sleep with his mouth ready open—and I'd pour it down his throat, and blister it and choke him."

"I am sure you would do no such horrible thing," said Lizzie.

"Shouldn't I? Well; perhaps I shouldn't. But I should like to!"[1]

Dickens's moral vision gains rather than loses from the lack of a wholly consistent theological point of view. By encompassing a wide range of moral experience, albeit sometimes in a fragmentary way, it does not ignore the complexity of such experience in modern man.

XXX, LII, pp. 398, 456, 584, 478–9, 803; *D & S*, Chap. XXXVI, p. 520; *DC*, Chaps. XXII, XXXI, XL, XLVI, LV, pp. 324–5, 454, 583, 667, 794–5; *BH*, Chap. LXV, pp. 865–8; *HT*, Bk. I, Chap. III, p. 9, Bk. III, Chap. VII, pp. 282–3; *LD*, Bk. I, Chap. VII, pp. 73–4, Bk. II, Chap. XIX, pp. 647–50; *GE*, Chaps. XXVII, XXXIX, pp. 206, 304–5, 307–8; *OMF*, Bk. III, Chap. XV, pp. 589–97, Bk. I, Chaps. I, XIV, pp. 1–5, 172–5.

[1] *OMF*, Bk. II, Chap. II, p. 243.

VII

CHARACTERIZATION

1. *Character as Rhetoric*

UNLIKE their modern critics, many Victorian novelists saw the technique of creating successful characters as a distinct element in their narrative art with its own problems. This is true of novelists as different as Dickens, Trollope, and Wilkie Collins.[1] Any study of Dickens as a conscious artist should, therefore, consider his methods of characterization.

The psychological and social realism of Dickens's characters, their evolution from 'originals', their relationship to the structure of the novels in which they appear have been touched on in the present study and elsewhere. But character may not only be related to structure, it is itself structure and may be related to effect and vision. The role which character plays as rhetoric in Dickens's narrative art still requires to be fully examined.

2. *Simple Rhetoric in Characterization*

The case of characterization shows once again that in Dickens's fiction a simple effect and a simple vision are related. Consider, for example, the following passage:

The uncle and nephew looked at each other for some seconds without speaking. The face of the old man was stern, hard-featured, and forbidding; that of the young one, open, handsome, and ingenuous. The old man's eye was keen with the twinklings of avarice and cunning; the young man's, bright with the light of

---

[1] See, for instance, Dickens's letters to J. A. Overs (27 Sept. 1839), *P*, vol. i, pp. 587–8, (12 Apr. 1840), *N*, vol. i, p. 255; Anthony Trollope, *Autobiography*, pp. 205–6, 209–10; Wilkie Collins, preface to *The Woman in White* (1861). Cf. Richard Stang, *The Theory of the Novel in England 1850–1870*, pp. 127–32; Kenneth Graham, *English Criticism of the Novel 1865–1900* (Oxford, 1965), pp. 97–102.

intelligence and spirit. His figure was somewhat slight, but manly and well-formed; and, apart from all the grace of youth and comeliness, there was an emanation from the warm young heart in his look and bearing which kept the old man down. . . . It galled Ralph to the heart's core, and he hated Nicholas from that hour.[1]

The vision here could hardly be simpler. These characters are the handsome young hero and the wicked uncle of fairy-tale; they do not have the dignity and depth which genuine myth with its fully developed archetypal figures, like Siegfried and Hagen, possesses. Nevertheless, a debased form of the old magic is present. Dickens tries to show how the genius of vice is rebuked by the mystical power of virtue but the result is somewhat unconvincing. An analysis of the effects through which the vision is focused shows that essentially primitive appeals are being made. Dickens aims exclusively at the sympathy and antipathy of approval and disapproval. Furthermore, the rhetoric is working at such archaic levels of feeling that ethical and aesthetic qualities remain undifferentiated in a single judgement of acceptance or rejection. Thus, while the over-all vision purports to be a moral one it is in fact focused through an indiscriminate mixture of traits with an ethical appeal or repulsion, such as 'open', 'ingenuous', 'spirit', 'warm young heart', 'avarice', 'cunning', 'stern', and traits which move admiration or disapproval of the non-moral kind, such as 'handsome', 'all the graces of youth and comeliness', 'intelligence', 'hard-featured', 'forbidding'. That is, Dickens, consciously or unconsciously, takes advantage of a certain ambiguity in the rhetoric of sympathy. The ready confusion between moral and amoral kinds of approval can be seen particularly in the remark, 'His figure was somewhat slight, but manly and well-formed.'

Sometimes Dickens's vision is so primitive that characters may first be presented with only those amoral qualities which readers instinctively admire. Thus, heroines, like Dolly Varden, are liable to claim immediate approval merely because they are physically desirable:

A roguish face met his; a face lighted up by the loveliest pair of sparkling eyes that ever locksmith looked upon; the face of a

[1] *NN*, Chap. III, p. 24.

pretty, laughing, girl; dimpled and fresh, and healthful—the very impersonation of good-humour and blooming beauty.

On the other hand, the reader may be invited to disapprove at once of a character like Mrs. Brown, solely because she is ugly or has disagreeable personal habits:

> She was a very ugly old woman, with red rims round her eyes, and a mouth that mumbled and chattered of itself when she was not speaking. She was miserably dressed, and carried some skins over her arm. She seemed to have followed Florence some little way at all events, for she had lost her breath; and this made her uglier still, as she stood trying to regain it: working her shrivelled yellow face and throat into all sorts of contortions.

Sometimes, there is no moral ambiguity. Characters like the Bachelor or Betty Higden make their appeal for sympathy on the grounds of a plain goodness or strength of character. Characters like Monseigneur or Compeyson are calculated to repel with an equally plain variety of evil.[1]

Other forms of the rhetoric of sympathy may be used to focus a naïve vision. Almost all Dickens's characters have some kind of life. Some have little more than vitality:

> Sir Matthew Pupker especially, who had a little round head with a flaxen wig on the top of it, fell into such a paroxysm of bows, that the wig threatened to be jerked off every instant.[2]

Other characters, like Smike, Sloppy, or Oliver's chum, Dick, are scarcely more than objects of pity.

It cannot be argued that Dickens invariably slips into a simple rhetoric and vision whenever his skill or thinking deserts him. Like Bulwer-Lytton, Dickens argued for a certain idealization as part of his aesthetic faith and pursued it as a deliberate policy. In this matter, Dickens's vision becomes the close prisoner of his rhetoric. Idealization is focused through the rhetoric of sympathy and the process provides a classic instance of the simple effect intensified to an extreme degree in order to increase the power and clarity of

[1] *BR*, Chap. IV, p. 32; *D & S*, Chap. VI, p. 69; *OCS*, Chap. LII, p. 390; *OMF*, Bk. I, Chap. XVI, pp. 197–8; *TTC*, Bk. II, Chap. VII, pp. 102–3; *GE*, Chap. XXII, pp. 170–1.

[2] *NN*, Chap. II, p. 12.

vision. An example is Dickens's revision of his earliest description of Little Nell:

> I was arrested by an inquiry, the purport of which did not reach me, but which seemed to be addressed to myself, and was preferred in a ⟨?woman's⟩ SOFT SWEET voice THAT STRUCK ME VERY PLEASANTLY. I turned HASTILY round ⟨in a kind of surprise⟩ and ⟨the –?– question was repeated it –?– ⟩ found at my elbow a ⟨young female ?appreciably/ ?apparently in some agitation⟩ PRETTY LITTLE GIRL, who begged to be directed to a certain street.[1]

The more intently the effect is worked for, here, the more naïve the vision of the character becomes.

As Dickens matured, he did not entirely give up the practice of idealization but his treatment of it changed in two important respects. He came to recognize its limits, first perceiving uneasily that he might be pushing it too far. Thus, even in his characterization of Agnes, we find him deliberately toning down one piece of extreme eulogy. The manuscript shows that idealization is at first consciously increased:

> I cannot call to mind where or when, in my childhood, I had seen a stained glass window in a church. NOR DO I RECOLLECT ITS SUBJECT, THOUGH I THINK THERE WAS AN ANGEL IN IT. But I know that when I saw her turn round, in the grave light of the old staircase, and wait for us, above, I thought of that window; and that I associated something of its tranquil brightness with her ever afterwards.

The surviving proofs and the First Edition omit the clause, 'though I think there was an angel in it', and I conjecture it was deleted in an earlier set of proofs since at least two sets existed. A much more mature Dickens came to understand that, though idealization presented an authentic vision of the world, yet it was a vision restricted to certain kinds of character and to certain special circumstances. When Rosa Bud, for example, sees her world through a romantic haze after meeting

---

[1] Original MS. of *OCS*, Victoria and Albert Museum, Forster Collection, 47. A. 5 (Vol. IA), Chap. I, p. 3; cf. *OCS*, p. 2.

Tartar, we find her idealization of experience highly acceptable as a limited view set within the larger vision of life.[1]

Need a simple moral vision inevitably offend the sophisticated reader? The trouble with the absolutely moral character in Dickens's fiction may very well not be simple goodness in itself, which, as hagiology shows, may be both convincing and moving. Whenever the picture of simple goodness fails in Dickens's fiction, it is because it remains a statement rather than a demonstration. We are asked to accept the goodness of characters like Nell and Oliver, for the most part on trust, and we refuse to do so. Contrary to what House has argued, Oliver is not unreal because he triumphs over his environment. There are people who do, however rare. Dickens, in fact, acknowledges that the same family background may produce both vice and virtue[2] and, although he often asserts that environment is fate, he obviously intends Oliver to demonstrate the freedom of the will. It is Oliver's failure to do this, in any truly positive manner, which accounts for his lack of reality. Morality appears convincing only when it is genuinely put to the test. Oliver is a casualty of Dickens's rhetoric. Dickens was addicted to the choice of character as victim because of the opportunity this offered for sympathy and pathos. An inevitable result is his many passive characters. In the special circumstances, a passive hero in *Oliver Twist* was bound to prove a disaster.

The rhetoric of irony, like that of sympathy, may focus a simple view of character. Here belong those savagely scourged but extremely meagre satirical figures that Dickens creates when his indignation alone is aroused:

The individual who sat clipping and slicing as aforesaid at the Rowdy Journals, was a small young gentleman of very juvenile appearance, and unwholesomely pale in the face; partly, perhaps, from intense thought, but partly, there is no doubt, from the excessive use of tobacco, which he was at that moment chewing vigorously. He wore his shirt-collar turned down over a black

---

[1] Original MS. of *DC*, Vol. IA, Chap. XV, p. 27 (proofs read 'Agnes Wickfield' before 'ever'); cf. *DC*, p. 223. *ED*, Chaps. XXI, XXII, pp. 241, 242–3, 253–4.

[2] Humphry House, *The Dickens World*, pp. 220–1; *NN*, Chap. I, pp. 2–3; for environment as fate, see for example the preface to the First Cheap Edition of *MC* (1849), *D & S*, Chap. XLVII, pp. 647–8.

ribbon; and his lank hair, a fragile crop, was not only smoothed and parted back from his brow, that none of the Poetry of his aspect might be lost, but had, here and there, been grubbed up by the roots: which accounted for his loftiest developments being somewhat pimply. He had that order of nose on which the envy of mankind has bestowed the appellation "snub," and it was very much turned up at the end, as with a lofty scorn. Upon the upper lip of this young gentleman were tokens of a sandy down: so very, very smooth and scant, that, though encouraged to the utmost, it looked more like a recent trace of gingerbread than the fair promise of a moustache; and this conjecture his apparently tender age went far to strengthen . . .

Martin was not long in determining within himself that this must be Colonel Diver's son; the hope of the family, and future mainspring of the Rowdy Journal. Indeed he had begun to say that he presumed this was the colonel's little boy, and that it was very pleasant to see him playing at Editor in all the guilelessness of childhood, when the colonel proudly interposed and said:

"My War Correspondent, sir. Mr. Jefferson Brick!"[1]

More convincing are those characters who offer a working segment of authentic personality. Certain psychological mechanisms, Dickens saw, could be exploited for ironic effect. True, this led to a more complex view of human nature, but the view often remains extremely simple. In such cases, the mechanism is isolated from the rest of the personality and used for a momentary effect. The irony which might have searched through a human being is restricted to the investigation and exploitation of a mere quirk. When Jingle, for example, projects his own mercenary motives on to Tupman, it is not even clear whether he is unwittingly betraying himself or simply enjoying an outrageous joke at Rachael Wardle's expense. Dickens seems satisfied with the ironic joke between the reader and himself. When an intoxicated Stiggins warns Sam Weller against the temptation of the Demon Drink, there is an ironic comment on his hypocrisy but the situation and character are too crude to be convincing. Dickens certainly goes straight to the core of Fang, when he shows the magistrate projecting his own insolence and bullying malice on to Mr. Brownlow, yet Fang remains no more than a brief satirical sketch. An eavesdropping Tigg, who accuses Peck-

[1] *MC*, Chap. XVI, p. 261.

sniff of eavesdropping, forms part of nothing more searching
than a slapstick episode in which two heads have collided
before the same keyhole. We do not penetrate very far into
Fledgeby's character when he projects his own meanness on
to Riah; it is a satirical means by which Dickens draws
attention to the usury which lurks in Mayfair. Introjection
(or identification), displacement, and rationalization may be
treated by Dickens in the same fragmentary way. Thus, the
spectacle of Winkle's knees knocking together at the prospect
of a duel, while he rationalizes his terror as a humane con-
sideration for Dowler's widow-to-be, is hardly more than a
quickly evaporating joke. When Montague Tigg attempts to
enlarge his shabby genteel presence by referring to a famous
father, it only makes him more delightfully amusing; we
cannot even be certain whether it is another of his confidence
tricks or not. Unpleasantness apart, Mrs. Pipchin's displacement of her annoyance with Little Paul on to Master Blitherstone does not fit in with anything we have already learned
about her; rather the reverse—she seems unlikely to have let
any child have the last word.[1]

By contrast, when Pumblechook displaces his annoyance
at his reception at Satis House on to Pip, he illustrates his
excessive deference to social superiors and his bullying
attitude towards inferiors. Further instances show Dickens
using his insight into psychological mechanisms and taking
advantage of their inherent irony to explore character consistently and critically in some detail. Thus, the haunted
Sikes reads his own accusing thoughts into the ignorant faces
of people in Hendon. The drunken Chevy Slyme blames his
failure in life on a conspiracy against him and weakly identifies himself with what his rich relatives can do. William
Dorrit projects his own feebleness on to his brother and old
Nandy while his social insecurity is such that he develops a
paranoid suspicion of his own valet and Mr. Merdle's butler.
The case of Miss Wade provides a study of paranoia which has
the thoroughness and accuracy we find in a textbook of
psychiatry. Quilp's accusation that others are conspiring

---

[1] *PP*, Chaps, X, XLV, pp. 105, 636–7; *OT*, Chap. XI, pp. 71–5, esp. p. 72;
MC, Chap. IV, pp. 43–5; *OMF*, Bk. III, Chap. I, p. 422; *PP*, Chap. XXXVIII,
p. 530; *MC*, Chap. IV, p. 47; *D & S*, Chap. XI, p. 137.

against him and Pecksniff's projection of his own hypocritical scheming on to young Martin are part of the general comedy but the paranoid element in Uriah Heep's character is carefully analysed as an integral part of his personality. When Carker reads his own resentment and malice into the office staff's attitude towards Dombey, the relationship between projection and inferiority is traced. Dombey's identification with the family business, which swells his pride, is more than an odd quirk; it is the central fact of his life and the source of his tragedy. Projection may be part of a character's mental and spiritual blindness. Ironically, Skimpole in his autobiography accuses John Jarndyce of selfishness while Pip comes to recognize that he has projected his own ineptitude on to Herbert Pocket.[1]

One of Dickens's most fertile discoveries was the ironic relationship between the *persona* and the inner man. Though the contrast between the two has been laid down as a law by Jung, he has not indicated its irony. Yet as early as *Pickwick*, Dickens was aware of the ironic discrepancy between the mask and the face, though he still saw it at this stage as a fairly crude contrast between the dissembler's 'mask of friendship' and 'the grin of cunning' beneath it. As Dickens matured, he realized that the *persona* was no mere set expression put on and removed as readily as a papier mâché affair but a living part of the human personality with a delicately adjusted relationship to the rest of the psyche. He saw how a man might identify himself with his social attitude or role, how particularly true this was of professional people, the dry old solicitor, Grewgious, say, or the hardened criminal lawyer, Jaggers. Dickens appreciated that the inscrutable mask of a Tulkinghorn or the studied deportment of a Turveydrop Senior might come to express a whole attitude to life. Frequently, the novelist probes the man behind the mask with a sensitive irony. He shows how Inspector Bucket works with a ruthless dedication and efficiency behind a deceptively affable demeanour towards his intended prisoner. Again, Dickens

---

[1] *GE*, Chap. VIII, pp. 50–1; *OT*, Chap. XLVIII, p. 364; *MC*, Chap. VII, pp. 106–8; *LD*, Bk. II, Chap. XIX, pp. 641–4, Bk. I, Chap. XXXI, pp. 373–4, Bk. II, Chaps. XV, XVI, XXI, pp. 601–2, 619, 663–71; *OCS*, Chap. XI, p. 89; *MC*, Chap. XLIII, p. 670; *DC*, Chap. LIV, p. 778; *D & S*, Chap. XLVI, pp. 643–4, Chap. I, pp. 1–2; *BH*, Chap. LXI, p. 831; *GE*, Chap. LVIII, p. 456.

seeks out occasions when the mask slips a little. He catches Jaggers at an unguarded moment, revealing that the lawyer protects himself with a shell of callousness against his deep compassion for the wretched victims of the legal system. In this example, the compensatory relationship between the *persona* and the inner psyche, which Jung has stressed, is particularly clear, as it is also in the contrast between Boythorn's gentle nature and his blustering posture. More drastically, Dickens may engineer the total exposure of the man behind the mask. When Bumble's imposing uniform, with which he has completely identified his authority, is taken away, he is reduced to a henpecked nonentity. The inflation of personality through costume and appearance is critically examined in Casby's case while the fancy dress at Mrs. Leo Hunter's public breakfast betrays the absurd delusions of grandeur which some of the characters harbour. The living nature of the *persona* is attested by the almost physical deflation which Pecksniff appears to undergo when Mary rebuffs him. Dickens frequently demonstrates the rigidity of the *persona*. Mrs. Jellyby, for example, is so obsessed with her role of 'telescopic philanthropist', she remains oblivious to total domestic disaster. On recovering from her stroke, Mrs. Skewton's very first act is to order rose curtains; weak as she is, this ageing coquette's immediate concern is for her complexion. Dickens also makes use of a process similar to that which Jung calls 'the regressive restoration of the *persona*'. The novelist understands that, even when the social mask has been torn away, the most usual course is for it to be replaced with even greater firmness. At first, this process is described crudely. Florence Dombey, for example, discovers that Edith's composure is only 'a handsome mask' yet Edith, after a few tears, continues to preserve that mask. Later, the process is depicted with wonderful skill. Jagger's moment of weakness is more than made up for when he abuses a criminal client. The process partly explains Uriah Heep's brilliant reappearance as a penitent prisoner, posing triumphantly once again as an 'umble person although the ruthless ambition behind his earlier hypocritical posture has been completely exposed. Through his ironic studies of the *persona*, Dickens presents a view of society as a tissue of unreal attitudes and relationships founded on deceit rather than the substantial intercourse of genuine persons. A great deal of education in such a society is shown to be devoted to producing conformist *personae* rather than fostering true individuality.[1]

Projection, introjection, displacement, rationalization, and the *persona* are useful concepts in grasping and representing the structure of a type of character to be found in deceivers and self-deceivers of all kinds. The rich ironic possibilities offered by these mechanisms and segments of personality, together with the profound human truth which they express, help to explain why the Dickens world comes to be peopled by a race of such deceivers: hypocrites like Stiggins and Pecksniff, Heep and Casby, fortune hunters like Jingle and the Lammles, swindlers like Merdle and confidence men like Tigg, and scheming villains in the political and business worlds like Gashford and Carker, legal sharks like Dodson and Fogg, Sampson Brass and Vholes, fraudulently pious windbags like Chadband, and smooth parasites like Skimpole, old women like Mrs. Skewton who feign youth, and young men like Chick Smallweed and Jefferson Brick who feign age and experience, people striving to conceal their shady past like Lady Dedlock or William Dorrit, secret murderers or would-be murderers like Jonas Chuzzlewit and Hortense, John Jasper and Bradley Headstone, shabby genteel persons trying to keep up appearances like the Father of the Marshalsea and Micawber, *nouveaux riches* like the Veneerings claiming vast social connections, toadies like Pumblechook, Mrs. Camilla, and Sarah Pocket, people working a small racket like Squeers and

---

[1] C. G. Jung, *Psychological Types*, pp. 592–5, *Two Essays on Analytical Psychology*, pp. 161–6; *PP*, Chap. XI, p. 133 (the crudeness hardly matters here since Tupman is a burlesque on the lover and his sentiments); *ED*, Chap. IX, pp. 84–5; *GE*, Chaps. XX, XXIV, pp. 156–8, 187, 191; *BH*, Chaps. XIV, XI, XII, pp. 190, 140, 162–3, Chap. XLIX, pp. 672–9; *GE*, Chap. LI, pp. 391–3; *BH*, Chap. IX, pp. 116–18; *OT*, Chap. XXXVII, pp. 267–72, esp. p. 267; *LD*, Bk. I, Chap. XIII, pp. 144–6; *PP*, Chap. XV, esp. pp. 199–200; *MC*, Chap. XXX, pp. 484–5; *BH*, Chaps. XXIII, XXX, pp. 330, 332, 416–23; *D & S*, Chap. XXXVII, pp. 528–9; *D & S*, Chap. XXXVI, p. 507; *GE*, Chap. LI, pp. 393–4; *DC*, Chap. LXI, pp. 851–5 (Dickens also wished to attack Benjamin Rotch, one of the Middlesex Magistrates, 'pet prisoners', and the separate system in Pentonville, see Philip Collins, *Dickens and Crime*, pp. 162–3; *BH*, Chap. II, pp. 8, 12; *TTC*, Bk. II, Chap. VII, pp. 100–2; *LD*, Bk. II, Chap. V, pp. 475, 477.

Sowerberry, Mrs. Gamp and Betsey Prig, people plotting on the side of the angels like Old Martin and Boffin, and a host of self-deceivers ranging from Tappertit to Mr. Dombey, Young Martin to Richard Carstone, David Copperfield to Magwitch, Arthur Clennam to Pip, and Gradgrind to Bella Wilfer. A further reason for the large part played in the Dickens world by the deceiver is to be found in one aspect of Dickens's ultimate vision. He sees life as an arena of ironic deception. Whether we approach the Dickens world through vision or through character, we encounter irony as an essentially related factor.

3. *Complex Rhetoric in Characterization*

How Dickens achieves a strong initial impression of character is worth examining closely:

The man who growled out these words, was a STOUTLY-BUILT fellow of about five-and-forty, in a black velveteen coat, ⟨drab⟩ VERY SOILED DRAB breeches, lace-up half boots, and grey cotton stockings, which enclosed a very ⟨burly⟩ BULKY pair of legs, with large swelling calves;—the kind of legs, which in such costume, always look in an unfinished and incomplete state without a set of fetters to garnish them. He had a brown hat on his head, and a dirty Belcher handkerchief round his neck: with the long ⟨ragged⟩ FRAYED ends of which he ⟨wiped⟩ SMEARED the beer from his face as he spoke; disclosing, when he had done so, a broad heavy ⟨face⟩ COUNTENANCE with a beard of three days' growth, and two scowling eyes; one of which displayed various parti-coloured symptoms of having been recently damaged by a blow.[1]

Here, Dickens organizes most of his material so that it will create a unity of impression. His revisions strengthen an antipathy against the character by emphasizing all the more Sikes's dirty unkempt appearance and the suggestion that he is capable of violence. Dickens handles the suggestion of violence with particular skill. The reader is allowed to reach the conclusion that Sikes is a violent type indirectly and his

---

[1] Original MS. of *OT*, Vol. IA, Bk. I, Chap. XIII, pp. 28–9 (from the First Edition onwards the text reads 'five-and-thirty'); cf. *OT*, Chap. XIII, p. 86.

imagination is therefore engaged by the material. This technical principle was recommended by Mangin in the book on literary art which Dickens had in his library:

It may often have a much greater effect not to circumscribe the reader's imagination by painting to him every feature, but rather to give hints from which he may figure the object or the scene to himself: for the imagination when sufficiently roused is capable of conceiving them far more awful, sublime, beautiful, or affecting, than it is possible for words to describe, or for the pencil to delineate.[1]

Sikes's portrait may be profitably compared with the description of a similar character in one of Reynolds's novels:

Well, indeed, might the lady's-maid have described this formidable visitor as "an ill-looking man;"—for, although it was Sunday, he had not bestowed the slightest pains upon his toilette. His garments were coarse, shabby, and negligent as usual: his coal-black hair was as rough, and his whiskers were as bushy and fierce as ever;—and his eyes gleamed with a sinister expression that was habitual to them, from beneath the coarse, shaggy, overhanging brows. He kept his hat upon his head as he entered the room; and he carried in his hand a huge stick, or rather club, by means of which his powerful arm might have felled an ox at one blow.[2]

Compared with Sikes's dirty unkempt appearance, the vague references to the Magsman's shabbiness and untidiness seem very weak. The possibility that he may be a violent person is not suggested in any subtle indirect manner but clumsily forced on the reader with epithets like 'fierce', 'powerful', and 'sinister'. What he might have done with his club seems much less convincing than Sikes's black eye, plain proof he has been involved in violence. In the Magsman's case, untidiness and the suggestion of violence are not wrought into an effective unity through a strong effect of antipathy. The colour and roughness of the Magsman's hair, the coarseness and shagginess of his eyebrow do not arouse the powerful antipathy produced by Sikes's three days' growth of beard and his beer-smeared face and, while the Magsman has all that make-

[1] Edward Mangin, *Essays on the Sources of the Pleasures Received from Literary Compositions*, p. 38.
[2] G. W. M. Reynolds, *The Mysteries of the Court of London* (*1849–56*), vol. i (1850), p. 128.

up and props can do to make him a formidable ruffian, Sikes
has an authentic burliness to back up the threat of his violence. The Magsman's portrait, unlike that of Sikes, is without
genuine power.

Dickens's view of Sikes, however, and its effect on the
reader are not quite so simple as they appear. Paradoxically,
there is a kind of sympathy at work, here, as well as antipathy. For if the hints of potential violence add to our moral
revulsion against Sikes, they also infuse the character with the
promise of vitality. Any increase in the suggestion of violence,
therefore, not only strengthens the antipathy but also re-
inforces the impression of vitality to which the reader is instinctively attracted.

Vitality is invariably found side by side with a strong
antipathy in the characterization of all Dickens's successful
villains. Like so many of Dickens's other characters, these
villains are bursting with life. Vitality is particularly important in their case since, the question of ambivalence apart,
liveliness seems to provide the only immediate claim which
an immoral or disagreeable character may exert on the
reader's sympathies.[1] Thus, the sprightliness of Dickens's
villains ranges from the jaunty air of Jingle to the genteel
swagger of Rigaud. That Dickens was conscious of this aspect
of his characterization can be seen in a note for *Little Dorrit*
in which he indicates Rigaud's conduct with the single
reference: 'Swagger, swagger' (II, Chap. X). Often the
vitality centres on one or two distinctive features which add
an individual touch of life to the character. Thus, we get
Lord John Gordon's restless eyes, the blustering native-
beating Major Bagstock with his eyes starting out of his head,
Carker's cat-like smile, the Marquis St. Evrémonde's cruel
dilating nostrils, Madame Defarge's perpetual knitting,
Orlick's eternal slouching, John Jasper's lustrous black hair
and deep voice.[2] Even the pompous Bumble expresses his

---

[1] A certain pity for a villain enduring some terrible calamity, such as the
guilt-smitten Sikes, Jonas Chuzzlewit, or Bradley Headstone may be gradually worked up. This possibility is discussed in Mangin, op. cit., pp. 171-2.

[2] *PP*, Chap. II, pp. 9–10; *LD*, Bk. I, Chap. I, pp. 8–10; original MS. of *LD*,
Vol. IIA; *BR*, Chap. XXXV, pp. 266–7; *D & S*, Chaps. VII, XIII, pp. 83,
171; *TTC*, Bk. II, Chap. VII, pp. 102–3, Bk. I, Chap. V, pp. 32–3, Bk. II,
Chaps. XV, XVI, *passim*; *GE*, Chap. XV, p. 105; *ED*, Chap. II, p. 8.

elation at the prospect of acquiring Mrs. Corney's property
with a ridiculously solemn dance:

> Mr. Bumble's conduct on being left to himself, was rather
> inexplicable. He opened the closet, counted the teaspoons, weighed
> the sugar-tongs, closely inspected a silver milk-pot to ascertain
> that it was of the genuine metal; and, having satisfied his curiosity
> on these points, put on his cocked-hat ⟨edgeways⟩ CORNER-
> WISE, and danced WITH MUCH GRAVITY four distinct times
> round the table. Having gone through this very extraordinary
> performance, he took off the cocked-hat again; and, spreading
> himself before the fire with his back towards it, seemed to be
> mentally engaged in taking an EXACT inventory of the furniture.

The insertion of 'with much gravity' shows how careful
Dickens is to interpret such a display of high spirits strictly
in terms of Bumble's predominant trait, thus preserving
consistency of character while increasing the effect. That
Dickens was conscious of the vitality which he gave to
Bumble throughout the previous scene with Mrs. Corney can
be seen a page or two earlier in the manuscript when an
extra touch of liveliness is added as an afterthought:

> "It's no use disguising facts, ma'am," said Mr. Bumble, ⟨FLOU-
> RISH⟩ SLOWLY FLOURISHING THE TEASPOON with a
> kind of amorous dignity that made him doubly impressive.[1]

Again, care is taken to integrate the increased animation and
the beadle's slow dignified movements.

Quilp's vitality is as pronounced as his sadism. In fact, his
sadism often shows considerable liveliness, He makes faces at
a chambermaid and then wants to kiss her. At the risk of his
life, he hangs upside down from the roof of a coach to terrify
Mrs. Nubbles.[2] That Dickens was consciously infusing Quilp
with vitality can be seen in the manuscript.[3] From the outset,
Dickens deliberately makes Quilp very repulsive:

> The child was closely followed by an elderly man of remarkably

---

[1] Original MS. of *OT*, Vol. IA, Bk. II, Chap. I, pp. 18, 13 (from the 1846
edition onwards the text reads 'of no' and 'which made'); cf. *OT*, Chap. XXIII,
pp. 171, 169.   [2] *OCS*, Chap. XLVIII, pp. 356, 361.
[3] Original MS. of *OCS*, Vol. IA, Chap. III, p. 1, Chap. V, pp. 16, 15, Vol.
IB, Chap. XX, p. 10, Chap. XXII, p. 10, Vol. IA, Chap. IX, pp. 6–7; cf. *OCS*,
pp. 22, 40, 39, 163 [Chap. XXI], 177 [Chap. XXIII], 72.

hard features and forbidding aspect, and so low in stature as to be quite a dwarf, though his head and face were large enough for the body of a giant. His black eyes were restless, SLY, and cunning; his mouth and chin, bristly with the stubble of a coarse hard beard; and his complexion was one of that kind which never looks clean or wholesome. But what added most to the grotesque expression of his face, was a ghastly smile, which, appearing to be the mere result of habit and to have no connection with any MIRTHFUL OR COMPLACENT feeling, constantly revealed the few discoloured ⟨?teeth which⟩ FANGS THAT were yet scattered in his mouth, and gave him the aspect of a panting dog.

The novelist can afford to do this because he is already beginning to breathe life into Quilp with references to 'restless' eyes, 'bristly' chin and mouth, and 'the aspect of a panting dog'. As the tale proceeds, Quilp's repulsiveness increases yet so does his vitality. Indeed, the sheer incredibility of his monstrous habits is successfully contradicted by the indisputable life in the dwarf:

> The same glance at the mirror conveyed to her the reflection of a horribly grotesque and distorted face WITH THE TONGUE LOLLING OUT; AND ⟨?and⟩ the next instant the dwarf, turning about with a perfectly bland and placid look, inquired in a tone of great affection,
> "How are you now, my dear old darling?"
> Slight and ridiculous as the incident was, it made him appear such a little fiend, and withal such a keen and knowing one, that the old woman felt too much afraid of him to utter a single word, and suffered herself to be led with extraordinary politeness to the breakfast-table. Here he by no means diminished the impression he had just produced, for he ate hard eggs, shell and all, devoured gigantic prawns with the heads AND TAILS on, chewed tobacco and water-cresses at the same time and with extraordinary greediness, drank boiling tea without winking, bit his fork and spoon till they bent again, and in short performed so many horrifying and uncommon acts that the women were nearly frightened out of their wits, and began to doubt if he were really a human creature.

Revolting behaviour and animation have become one and the same activity. So much so that Dickens can dwell on very unpleasant personal habits with perfect freedom. Thus, in the manuscript, Quilp had taken a shower-bath. This was changed to very grubby ablutions with a towel, presumably in proof:

> Mr. Quilp withdrew to the adjoining room and turning back his coat-collar, proceeded to smear his countenance with a damp towel of very unwholesome appearance, which made his complexion rather more cloudy than it was before.[1]

Other revisions show that Dickens deliberately increases Quilp's vitality wherever he can and that such an increase usually accompanies an outburst of offensive behaviour on the dwarf's part. Thus, we find appropriate insertions in an account of monstrous conviviality:

> As he spoke, Daniel Quilp drew off and drank three small glass-fuls of the raw spirit, and then with a horrible grimace took a great many pulls at his pipe, and swallowing the smoke, discharged it in a heavy cloud from his nose. This feat accomplished he drew himself together in his former position, and laughed excessively.
> "Give us a toast!" cried Quilp rattling on the table IN A DEXTEROUS MANNER with his fist AND ELBOW ALTERNATELY, IN A KIND OF TUNE.

The vitality of Quilp's malice is strengthened in the following:

> The one eye was upon the old lady always, and if she so much as stealthily advanced a tea-spoon towards a neighbouring glass (which she often did), for the purpose of abstracting but one sup of its sweet contents, Quilp's hand would overset it in the very moment of her triumph, and Quilp's mocking voice implore her to regard her precious health. And IN ANY ONE OF THESE HIS MANY CARES, from first to last, Quilp never flagged nor faltered.

The rhetoric is so successful that Dickens can deliberately draw attention to Quilp's unreality:

> He soon cast his eyes upon a chair into which he skipped with uncommon agility, and perching himself on the back with his feet upon the seat, was thus enabled to look on and listen with greater comfort to himself, besides gratifying at the same time that taste for doing something fantastic and monkey-like, which on all

---

[1] First Edition of *MHC* (1840), vol. i, p. 105. The proofs have not survived.

occasions had strong possession of him. Here, then, he sat, one leg cocked carelessly over the other, his chin resting on the palm of his hand, his head turned a little on one side, and his ugly features twisted into a complacent grimace . . .

The child uttered a suppressed shriek on beholding this agreeable figure; in their first surprise both she and the old man, not knowing what to say, AND HALF DOUBTING ITS REALITY, looked shrinkingly at it.

Possibly the most physically repulsive character in Dickens's novels is Uriah Heep. Here, Dickens's loathing of the hypocrite is expressed in its most virulent form. Yet the novelist also insists more than once that David is attracted as well as repelled by Heep. An insertion in the corrected proofs, for example, deliberately draws attention to this strange attraction:

There I saw him, lying on his back, with his legs extending to I don't know where, gurglings taking place in his throat, stoppages in his nose, and his mouth open like a post-office. He was so much worse in reality than in my distempered fancy, that afterwards I WAS ATTRACTED TO HIM IN VERY REPULSION, AND could not help wandering in and out every half hour or so, and taking another look at him.[1]

David's ambivalent attitude towards Uriah might be explained by the argument that Uriah is a projection of David's own animal-like sexuality directed against Agnes. Although there is an admixture of sexual feeling of some sort in all David's other romantic attachments from Little Em'ly to Dora, it is significant that sexual feeling appears to be missing from his relationship with Agnes both before and after marriage. My point, however, is that David's ambivalence must be shared by the reader if it is to be convincing. As certain revisions in the manuscript indicate, the reader must experience both the physical revulsion against Heep and the appeal of his animal-like vitality.[2] Thus Dickens hit upon a

[1] Corrected proofs of *DC*, Chap. XXV, p. 271; cf. *DC*, pp. 383–4.
[2] Original MS. of *DC*, Vol. IB, Chap. XVI, pp. 6–7 ('rapturous' substituted for 'virtuous' in proof, while MS. reads 'pinched', proofs and all other versions read 'pointed' which may be a printer's error that went uncorrected [another treacherous character who cruelly misuses his power over others has pinched nostrils which dilate and contract, see *TTC*, Bk. II, Chap. VII, pp. 102–3]; cf. *DC*, pp. 234–6.

characteristic gesture of Heep which expresses his hypocrisy
and is both repulsive and vital:

> He had a way of writhing when he wanted to express enthusiasm,
> which was very ugly; and which diverted my attention from the
> compliment he had paid my relation, to the SNAKY twistings of
> his throat and body.
> "A sweet lady, Master Copperfield!" said Uriah Heep. "She has
> a great admiration for Miss Agnes, Master Copperfield, I believe?"
> I said, 'Yes," boldly; not that I knew anything about it,
> Heaven forgive me!
> "I hope you have, too, Master Copperfield," said Uriah. "But
> I am sure you must have."
> "Everybody must have," I returned.
> "Oh, thank you, Master Copperfield," said Uriah Heep, "for
> that remark! It is so true! Umble as I am, I know it is *so* true!
> Oh, thank you, Master Copperfield!"
> He writhed himself quite off his stool in the excitement of his
> feelings.

The epithet 'snaky', which is added in revision, strengthens
the vital, sexual, and treacherous associations suggested by
'writhing' and 'twisting'. A complex vision is presented.
Behind the simulation of a platonic regard for Agnes and the
protestations of 'umbleness lurks a vital repressed instinctive
life which reflects more than Uriah's primitive sexual appetite and ruthless ambition. Despite their idealization of girls
like Agnes and their profession of benevolence, Dickens and
his readers also shared the general lust of the age for wealth,
power, and primitive sexual experience.[1] With a profound

---

[1] By 1851, the industrial revolution had placed England in a position of
wealth and power hitherto unparalleled in human history. Perhaps it is not
surprising that the Victorians should have become increasingly intoxicated
with the dream of almost unlimited power (see Winwood Reade, *The Martyr-
dom of Man* [1872], pp. 512–14), or that Carlyle, Charles Kingsley, and even
Dickens should have sometimes warmly approved of physical violence in the
exercise of power (see below, p. 355). Partly also as a result of the industrial
revolution, prostitution and sexual depravity seem to have reached their
lowest depths ever. Henry Mayhew, 'Those That Will Not Work', *London
Labour and the London Poor*, vol. iv (1862), hardly does justice to the situation;
even Dostoyevsky was appalled on his visit to London in 1862 (see his account
quoted in David Magarshack's introduction to his translation of *A Gentle
Creature and Other Stories* (1950), pp. xi–xiv), and an exposure of the full
horror had to wait until W. T. Stead's 'The Maiden Tribute of Modern Babylon', *Pall Mall Gazette* (6–10 July 1885). Although Dickens scourged Victorian

irony, then, Uriah Heep touches the Victorian reader at the level of his own deep-seated hypocrisy. This hypocrisy demands that the 'dirty' animal nature with its 'nasty' secretions be made to appear as repulsive as possible:

But, seeing a light in the little round office, and immediately feeling myself attracted towards Uriah Heep, who had a sort of fascination for me, I went in there instead. I found Uriah reading a great fat book, with such demonstrative attention, that his lank fore-finger followed up every line as he read, and made CLAMMY tracks along the page (or so I fully believed) like a snail.

"You are working late to-night, Uriah," says I . . .

As I was getting on the stool opposite, to talk to him more conveniently, I observed that he had not such a thing as a smile about him, and that he could only widen his mouth and make two hard creases down his cheeks, one on each side, to stand for one.

"I am not doing office-work . . . I am improving my legal knowledge, Master Copperfield," said Uriah. "I am going through Tidd's Practice. Oh, what a writer Mr. Tidd is, Master Copperfield!"

My stool was such a tower of observation, that as I watched him reading on again, after this virtuous exclamation, and following up the lines with his fore-finger, I observed that his nostrils, which were thin and pinched, WITH SHARP DINTS IN THEM, had a singular and most uncomfortable way of expanding and contracting themselves—that they seemed to twinkle, instead of his eyes, which hardly ever twinkled at all.

"I suppose you are quite a great lawyer?" I said, after looking at him for some time.

"Me, Master Copperfield?" said Uriah. "Oh, no! I'm a very umble person." . . .

acquisitiveness from *OT* to *OMF*, he was himself a business man quite exceptional among writers and amassed a fortune of £93,000 (see *F*, vol. iii, p. 518), equivalent of about a million to-day. He exercised complete control over all his activities, from amateur theatricals to his own periodicals (see *W, passim*), and his mania for exerting an almost physical power over audiences at his public readings is notorious. He made at least one cynical remark about the sexual incontinence of his time (see Edgar Johnson, op. cit., vol. ii, p. 645) and some of his own interests in this respect can be gauged from ibid., vol. i, pp. 497–8, letters to Wilkie Collins (22 Apr. 1856, 22 May 1857), *C*, pp. 57, 81–2, as well as from the Ellen Ternan episode towards the end of his life. For a recent exposure of what was seething below the surface of Victorian respectability, see Steven Marcus, *The Other Victorians* (1966), though a more cautious view is taken in 'Underneath the Victorians', Brian Harrison's article on the book, and Mark Spilka's review of it, *Victorian Studies*, x (1967), 239–62, 293–5.

"Perhaps you'll be a partner in Mr. Wickfield's business, one of these days," I said, to make myself agreeable; "and it will be Wickfield and Heep, or Heep late Wickfield."

"Oh, no, Master Copperfield," returned Uriah, shaking his head, "I am much too umble for that."

Here again, David's notion of the slimy tracks exuded by Heep's lank forefinger, an idea emphasized in revision, suggests not merely a man who sweats offensively but also vital, sexual, and treacherous associations. Significantly, two of the few occasions in the novel on which David acts hypocritically occur in both this and the previous passage when he tries to make himself agreeable to Uriah. The result of all this on the novel is to lend the structural irony which relates to Heep's designs on Wickfield's daughter and business a depth of feeling that the melodramatic story would not otherwise communicate.

Complex though the vision of Uriah Heep is, it does not include the breezy affability which, as fully expressed in Pecksniff, is perhaps the most deadly mask the hypocrite can wear. Pecksniff's attractiveness is managed by a rhetoric of sympathy which is sustained from our first acquaintance with him during his knockabout encounter with the wind.[1] Though amoral in itself, Pecksniff's vitality serves an important moral purpose. If the question whether such wickedness as his should be represented as attractive is raised, the answer must be 'yes'. Unlike the moral philosopher, the artist may help us to experience our kinship with all that moves and breathes. Thus, Dickens may show us that Pecksniff's wickedness is a vital reality to which we feel instinctively drawn because it reflects the living, resilient evil within ourselves.[2]

This kind of revelation, however, is not only a matter of identity but of a certain critical distance. Dickens was aware

[1] Consider, for example, a resilience equal to all rebuffs, his animal spirits during the drunken spree at Todgers's, his lively attempt to woo Mary, his colossal unflinching cheek and inexhaustible resourcefulness in attributing his own vices to others when he denounces his three pupils in turn; see *MC*, Chaps. II, IX, LIV, IX, XXX, II, XII, XXXI, pp. 9–11, 139–40, 810–12 148–53, 480–5, 19—20, 209–10, 496–501.

[2] Cf. the motto Dickens intended for the story: 'Your homes the scene. Yourselves, the actors, here!', *F*. vol. ii, p. 59.

that Pecksniff's vital hypocrisy needed to be exposed ironically at every opportunity, as various revisions in the manuscript clearly show.[1] When Pecksniff, for example, during the coach journey to London, takes up a clever and cosy bourgeois standpoint on a moral question, Dickens carefully sets against it a gesture which is both lively and ironic:

"For" (he observed), "if every one were warm and well-fed, we should lose the satisfaction of admiring the fortitude with which certain conditions of men bear cold and hunger. And if we were no better off than anybody else, what would become of our sense of gratitude; which," said Mr. Pecksniff with tears in his eyes, AS HE SHOOK HIS FIST AT A BEGGAR WHO WANTED TO GET UP BEHIND, "is one of the holiest feelings of our common nature."

If the ironic contrast seems a little contrived here, how delicately Dickens could increase the power of his ironic vision of Pecksniff may be seen in certain revisions in the earliest portrait. Dickens originally began a page of his manuscript with [Pecksniff] 'was a moral man, and no mistake at a'[ll], broke off at this point, abandoned the page, turned over and began his new page, 'Mr. Pecksniff', which he erased, and continued, 'Perhaps there never was a more moral man than Mr. Pecksniff.' The subtle way in which 'Perhaps' together with 'never' hints at an ironic reading is a decided improvement. Again, Dickens began the following page with, 'Of his doings in the architectural way no other record existed than a framed plan which was suspended over the chimney piece in the back parlour and lettered', abandoned the page, turned over, and began the new page with a version which has a more powerful irony, 'Of his architectural doings, nothing was clearly known, except that he had never designed or built anything; but it was generally understood that his knowledge of the science was almost awful in its profundity.' Again, slight touches of subtle irony are added in the following paragraph: '⟨It was in ?the⟩ His genius lay in ensnaring parents and guardians, and pocketing premiums. A young gentleman's premium being paid, and the young gentleman come to Mr. Pecksniff's

[1] Original MS. of *MC*, Vol. IA, Chap. VIII, p. 37, Chap. II. pp. 17 and overleaf, 18 and overleaf; cf. *MC*, pp. 116, 12, 13.

house, Mr. Pecksniff ⟨took away⟩ BORROWED his case of mathematical instruments (if SILVER-MOUNTED OR OTHERWISE valuable)'.

Dickens usually presents a complex vision of characters, whether villains or otherwise, through the rhetoric of sympathy and irony. The character is deliberately conceived in terms of a complex effect, as we can see from the author's notes.[1] The material is then carefully selected and organized so as to create a well-balanced opposition of powerful effects which invites identification yet establishes critical distance. Thus, while we warm towards Pickwick, we are made critically aware of his narrow bourgeois view of the world. Mark Tapley is presented as a gay, engaging young man. Yet the irony of his psychic masochism, the drive to seek what is 'jolly' only in painful situations, questions his gaiety and the rationalization of his behaviour. Major Bagstock might have been a satirical figure only, without true substance, yet he conveys the impression of solidity. Irony draws attention to the sycophant behind the affectation of bluntness but the major is given so substantial and energetic a laugh that it almost chokes him. Irony exposes his conceit but the manner in which he goes about, puffing himself through puffing Dombey, expresses an undeniable vitality. There is an apt irony in Bagstock's deflation at his club after Dombey's fall but the major has a capacity for survival which warns us that such lively humbugs are not easily dismissed to limbo.[2] Dickens has to present Steerforth from a double viewpoint. His charm must convince the reader as it convinces David. So Steerforth is carefully made to please Peggotty, he is 'healthy weather' to the sick Barkis, delights the family in the houseboat, and even rouses Mrs. Gummidge from her general despondency. At the same time, however, there must be hints of the ironic truth, of that other very different personality behind the charm, the shallow selfish friend and the cynical seducer who makes use of others to gratify his momentary pleasure. So, that other side is given away in the story of the hammer attack on Rosa, through the hints of

[1] See above, pp. 173-4.
[2] *PP*, *passim*; *MC*, Chap. V, pp. 65-9; *D & S*, Chaps. XX, LVIII, pp. 271-3, 284, 814-15.

Miss Dartle and Miss Mowcher, by his own outbursts of cynicism and ruthlessness. Sympathy and irony are, in fact, so
closely interrelated in the basic concept of Steerforth's
character that they appear to fuse at many points. His
moments of remorse and his analysis of his own weakness
move our pity while they are also ironically foretelling a
crime that the unsuspecting David would not credit. Since a
structural irony is at work in the very sympathy which
Steerforth universally commands, his very charm is an ironic
fate which also involves an authentic tragic waste.[1]

Careful revision in the manuscripts frequently shows how
Dickens deliberately focuses his earliest impression of a
character through as powerful a complex effect as he can produce. Thus, Dick Swiveller is presented in the following manner:

At length there ⟨? slunk⟩ SAUNTERED up, on the opposite side
of the way—WITH A BAD PRETENCE OF PASSING BY
ACCIDENT—a figure conspicuous for its dirty smartness, which
after a great many frowns and jerks of the head, in resistance of
the invitation, ultimately crossed the road and was brought into
the shop . . . His attire was not, as he had himself hinted, remarkable for the nicest arrangement, but was in a state of disorder
which strongly induced the idea that he had gone to bed in it. It
consisted of a brown body-coat with a great many brass buttons
up the front and only one behind, a bright check neckerchief, A
⟨–?–⟩ PLAID WAISTCOAT, ⟨–?– dirty white⟩ SOILED WHITE
trousers, and a very limp hat, worn with the wrong side foremost,
to hide a hole in the brim. The breast of his coat was ornamented
with an outside pocket ⟨in which was thrust a very large⟩ FROM
WHICH PEEPED FORTH THE CLEANEST END OF A VERY
LARGE AND VERY ILL-FAVOURED handkerchief; ⟨and
though⟩ his DIRTY wristbands ⟨had were pulled ? down/? back⟩
WERE PULLED DOWN as far as possible and OSTENTAT-
IOUSLY folded back over his cuffs.[2]

Dick Swiveller's little stratagem is presented in such a way
that it is both ironic and vital. The insertion of 'with a bad

---

[1] *DC*, Chap. XXI, pp. 310, 315–17; my point is strengthened by also
taking into account the scene with Mrs. Gummidge deleted in proof for reasons
of space and reprinted in John Butt, '*David Copperfield*: From Manuscript to
Print', *Review of English Studies*, N.S., i (1950), 251, and in Sylvère Monod,
Dickens romancier, pp. 487–8. *DC*, Chaps. XX, XXII, XXI, XXVIII, XXII,
pp. 295, 292–3, 328 ff., 302–3, 317, 426, 321–3.
[2] Original MS. of *OCS*, Vol. IA, Chap. II, pp. 14, 16; cf. *OCS*, pp. 16–18.

pretence of passing by accident' draws attention to a double
irony in the situation. Swiveller believes he is deceiving
others, yet betrays his own deceit. At once, then, he is set at
a critical distance from the reader as something of a failure.
'Sauntered', a second thought which may well be an improvement, increases the liveliness of the manner in which Swiveller
attempts to put on a convincing act. The description of his
clothes is a good instance of how Dickens can convey both the
living reality of a man and the irony in his situation through
external detail. Swiveller's genteel defiance of his shabby
fate, which is to brighten many pages of the novel, earns a
certain admiration at once through the key phrase, 'dirty
smartness'. Yet this oxymoron already points to the irony in
his circumstances. The rest of the description is organized in
a distinct pattern. Each sprightly attempt at smartness
proclaims Swiveller's genteel pretensions which are at once
deflated by a sharp ironic revelation of the shabby reality.
Revisions in the manuscript intensify the attempted smartness ('plaid waistcoat', 'cleanest end', 'ostentatiously') and
the shabbiness ('soiled', 'very ill-favoured', 'dirty').

The earliest portrait of Micawber is handled in the same
deliberate manner:[1]

I went in, and found there a stoutish, middle-aged person, in a
brown surtout and black tights and shoes, with no more hair upon
his head (which was a large one, AND VERY SHINING) than
there is upon an egg, and with a very extensive face, which he
turned full upon me. His clothes were shabby, but he had an
imposing shirt-collar on. He carried a jaunty sort of a stick, with
a large PAIR OF rusty tasselS to it; and a quizzing-glass hung
outside his coat,—for ornament, as I afterwards found, as he very
seldom looked through it, and couldn't see anything when he did ...

"Under the impression," said Mr. Micawber, "that your pere-
grinations in this metropolis have not as yet been extensive, and
that you might have some difficulty in penetrating the arcana of the
MODERN BABYLON IN THE DIRECTION OF THE City Road—
in short," said Mr. Micawber, in another burst of confidence, "That
you might lose yourself—I shall be happy to call this evening, and
instal you in the knowledge of the nearest way." ...

So he put on his hat, and went out WITH HIS CANE UNDER

[1] Original MS. of *DC*, Vol. IA, Chap. XI, pp. 15–16 ('as' after 'ornament'
deleted in proof), 17; cf. *DC*, pp. 155–7, 159.

HIS ARM: very upright, and humming a tune when he was clear of the counting-house.

Micawber's dialogue is modelled on the same plan as the description of his appearance. The elaborate and elegant circumlocutions, like his jaunty manner and his attempt to cut an imposing figure through certain articles of dress, display considerable energy and proclaim pretensions to gentility. [That such is the case is confirmed a page or so later: 'He would . . . go out, HUMMING A TUNE with a greater air of gentility than ever.'] Yet, with an unconscious irony, Micawber undermines the impression he is trying to create through his elegant periphrases. He suddenly sinks into plain everyday English, offering a brief down-to-earth translation of his lofty expressions, which aptly comments on the contrast between his pretensions and his real situation. By elaborating one of Micawber's circumlocutions, Dickens deliberately increases the effect of bathos which follows.

Dickens readily arrives at a compassionate and detached vision of character through combining the idea of character *as the victim of catastrophe* with the idea of character *as the subject of deception*. Thus, the situation of a newly born workhouse orphan is made even more poignant by the contrast between his innocence and our knowledge of the fate which awaits him. Yet a vision which might have deteriorated into a crude sentimental preoccupation with the most helpless of all victims is set at some distance through the grim irony of the reflections we are invited to share with the author:

But now that he was enveloped in the old calico robes which had grown yellow in the same service, he was badged and ticketed, and fell into his place at once—a parish child—the orphan of a work-house—the humble, half-starved drudge—to be cuffed and buffeted through the world—despised by all, and pitied by none.

Oliver cried lustily. If he could have known that he was an orphan, left to the tender mercies of churchwardens and overseers, perhaps he would have cried the louder.[1]

---

[1] *OT*, Chap. I, p. 3. That this allegation of brutality was by no means an exaggeration is confirmed by the exposure of the scandal at the Hoo Union-Workhouse in *The Times* during Jan., 1841. See also David Roberts, 'How Cruel was the Victorian Poor Law?', and Ursula Henriques, 'Communication: How Cruel was the Victorian Poor Law?', *The Historical Journal*, vi (1963), 97–107, xi, 2 (1968), 365–71.

This type of vision is realized in a much more mature manner in *Great Expectations*. Unlike Oliver, Pip only begins life as the victim of circumstances. He quickly develops into the pathetic and ironic victim of his own self-deception. Irony ceases to be an external view of a puppet tugged by the strings of a mechanical fate, it becomes a scathing vision, surveying a world of doubtful values and penetrating the soul of a man with the shock of recognition.[1]

This compassionate and ironic vision of character as the victim of circumstance and self-deception is also to be seen, at one of its most mature stages of development, in Dickens's handling of William Dorrit's character. Revisions in the manuscript show the deliberate care with which Dickens focuses a powerful complex vision along these lines when the Marshalsea prisoner first appears in the story:

He was, at that time, ⟨a⟩ A VERY AMIABLE AND VERY helpless middle-aged ⟨?man⟩ GENTLEMAN, who was going out again directly. Necessarily, he was going out again directly, because the Marshalsea lock never turned upon a debtor who was not. HE brought in a portmanteau with him, which ⟨it was not⟩ HE DOUBTED ITS BEING worth while to unpack; he was so perfectly clear—like all the rest of them, the turnkey on the lock said—⟨about⟩ THAT HE WAS going out again directly.

He was a shy, retiring ⟨womanly NERVOUS⟩ man; well-looking, though in an effeminate style; with A MILD VOICE, CURLING HAIR, AND ⟨–?–⟩ irresolute hands—rings upon the fingers in those days—which nervously wandered to his trembling lip a hundred times, in the first half-hour of his acquaintance with the jail. ⟨After some days –?–⟩ His ⟨wife⟩ principal anxiety was about his wife.

A similar power and complexity is deliberately sustained in the vision of the development in Dorrit's character which follows later in the chapter:

The shabby ⟨old g⟩ OLD DEBTOR with the SOFT MANNER AND THE white hair, was the Father of the Marshalsea.

And he grew to be proud of the title. If any imposter had arisen to claim it, he would have shed tears in resentment of the attempt

---

[1] I leave aside the question of certain ambiguities in Pip's development which may offer a deeper irony; see K. J. Fielding, 'The Critical Autonomy of *Great Expectations*', *A Review of English Literature*, ii (1961), 83–6.

to deprive him of his rights. ⟨There was a⟩ A disposition BEGAN TO BE PERCEIVED in him, to exaggerate the number of years he had been there; it was generally understood that you must deduct a few from his account; he was vain, the fleeting generations of debtors said.[1]

Here, there is already a certain pathos and irony in the spectacle of the shabby old gentleman with white hair who is vain enough to exaggerate the time he has spent in the Marshalsea. Dickens, however, increases our tender concern by reminding us of Dorrit's wretched situation ('old debtor') and by referring to his weak character ('soft manner'). At the same time, by substituting 'A disposition BEGAN TO BE PERCEIVED in him' for 'There was a disposition in him', Dickens emphasizes the ironic distance which furthers a detached and critical view of the character.

[1] Original MS. of *LD*, Vol. IA, Bk. I, Chap. V, pp. 9, 14; cf. *LD*, pp. 58, 65.

VIII

MODES OF VISION

1. *Fragmentation of Vision*

'The presence of different modes in a narrative is something we must accept in his [Dickens's] novels, as in poetic drama', writes Kathleen Tillotson when she distinguishes and examines the modes of fairy-tale romance and melodrama in *Dombey and Son*. Philip Collins also draws attention to these modes and the critical problem which they pose: 'His [Dickens's] novels, too, present a remarkable mixture, of hilarious comedy, uninhibited pathos, moral earnestness, and melodramatic violence, to which few critics have done justice; they have tended to focus their attention on only one or two of these elements and to give their admiration to them alone.'[1] A critic might go even further than Collins and distinguish comic and satirical, melodramatic and tragic, sentimental and genuinely pathetic modes of vision in Dickens's fiction. The presence of these modes suggests a certain fragmentation of vision. How successful Dickens is in bringing the various modes together into a complex unity of vision will be discussed in the next chapter. First, the nature of each mode of vision must be examined separately.

2. *Sentimentality and Genuine Pathos*

Clearly, sentimentality may be an attribute of many kinds of emotional effect. In practice, the term is often applied to unsuccessful idealization or pathos, two effects which have earned a particular notoriety in Dickens's hands. It is usually

---

[1] Kathleen Tillotson, *Novels of the Eighteen-Forties*, pp. 175, 174–81; the same term is used by Northrop Frye, 'Theory of Modes', *Anatomy of Criticism* (Princeton, 1957), pp. 33–52. Philip Collins, *Dickens and Crime*, p. 25.

argued that sentimentality results from emotion in excess of a situation:

> The sentimental in art is betrayed by an emotional expression in excess of what the object of love or pity would normally arouse; or by the exaggeration of the benevolent character through bestowing upon it an incredibly warm heart that irradiates the soul with extraordinary kindness and pity. Both forms of sentimentality merge in the tears—tears of joy and tears of "sweet sorrow"—which flow through the Victorian novel whenever a loving heart catches a glimpse of either goodness or suffering.

It is difficult to see how genuine pity and pathos can be excessive in situations of extreme grief, such as death-bed scenes, and I. A. Richards has pointed out that the quantitative explanation covers only one kind of sentimentality.[1] Falseness rather than excess is, I believe, the real key to understanding all forms of sentimentality. Certainly there is a disproportion between the emotion and the situation. Nevertheless, the idea of excess may be misleading. The definition in *OED*, 'indulgence in superficial emotion', is on safer ground, particularly if we stress 'superficial'. A false emotion results in a weak effect. It would be much closer to the truth to argue that in sentimentality the emotion is unequal to the situation rather than in excess of it.

A situation may be so inadequately realized that it fails to arouse a genuine emotion. A frequent cause of sentimentality in Dickens's early work is a failure to find an 'objective correlative' for the emotion he wishes to convey. A good example is the attempt at an idyllic description of Oliver's sojourn in the country.[2] The happiness the boy is supposed to be experiencing is presented in vague abstract terms:

> Who can describe the pleasure and delight, the peace of mind and soft tranquility, the sickly boy felt in the balmy air, and among the green hills and rich woods, of an inland village! . . . It was a happy time. The days were peaceful and serene; the nights brought with them neither fear nor care; no languishing in a wretched prison, or associating with wretched men; nothing but pleasant and happy thoughts.

[1] Walter E. Houghton, *The Victorian Frame of Mind* (New Haven, 1963), p. 276; I. A. Richards, *Practical Criticism* (1949), pp. 258–61.

[2] *OT*, Chap. XXXII, pp. 237–9.

Frequently, we are not shown the occasion for Oliver's bliss but told about it instead. We tend to get a summary or, worse still, a digression into the generalizations of an essay:

> Who can tell how scenes of peace and quietude sink into the minds of pain-worn dwellers in close and noisy places, and carry their own freshness, deep into their jaded hearts! . . . The memories which peaceful country scenes call up, are not of this world, nor of its thoughts and hopes. Their gentle influence may teach us how to weave fresh garlands for the graves of those we loved: may purify our thoughts.

Where Dickens does use concrete images, they are the clichés of pastoral convention which arouse only weak feelings:

> The rose and honeysuckle clung to the cottage walls; the ivy crept round the trunks of the trees; and the garden-flowers perfumed the air with delicious odours . . . There was the little church, in the mornings, with the green leaves fluttering at the windows: the birds singing without: and the sweet-smelling air stealing in at the low porch, and filling the homely building with its fragrance.

From time to time, an unsuccessful idealization weakens the effect of the passage still further:

> Hard by, was a little churchyard; not crowded with tall unsightly gravestones, but full of humble mounds, covered with fresh turf and moss: beneath which, the old people of the village lay at rest . . . Every morning he went to a white-headed old gentleman, who lived near the little church: who taught him to read better, and to write: and who spoke so kindly, and took such pains, that Oliver could never try enough to please him . . . The poor people were so neat and clean, and knelt so reverently in prayer, that it seemed a pleasure, not a tedious duty, their assembling there together; and though the singing might be rude, it was real, and sounded more musical (to Oliver's ears at least) than any he had ever heard in church before.

It is instructive to compare this account of a child's blissful sojourn in the country with the description of the young boy's delightful holiday at Yarmouth in *David Copperfield*. That Dickens learned to overcome the basic weaknesses of the passage in *Oliver Twist* with a conscious rhetoric can be seen in the manuscript of the later novel:

It was beautifully clean inside, and as tidy as possible. There was a table, and a DUTCH CLOCK, AND A chest of drawers, and on the chest of drawers there was a tea-tray with a painting on it of a lady with a parasol, taking a walk with a military-looking child who was trundling a hoop. The tray was kept from tumbling down, by a bible; and the tray and the bible, if it had tumbled down, would have smashed a quantity of cups and saucers and a teapot that were grouped around it. Round the room there were some COMMON coloured pictures, framed and glazed, of Scripture subjects; such as I have never seen since in the hands of pedlars, without seeing the whole interior of Peggotty's brother's house again, at one view. Abraham IN RED going to sacrifice Isaac in blue, and Daniel in yellow cast into a den of green lions, were the most prominent of these. Over the little mantel-shelf, was a picture of the Sarah Jane lugger, built at Sunderland, with a real little wooden stern stuck on to it; a work of art, combining composition with carpentry, which I considered to be one of the most enviable possessions that the world could afford . . .

All this, I saw in the first glance after I crossed the threshold—child-like, according to my theory—and then Peggotty OPENED A LITTLE DOOR AND showed me my bedroom. It was the completest and most desirable bedroom ever seen—in the stern of the vessel; with a little window, where the rudder used to go through; a LITTLE looking-glass, just the right height for me, NAILED AGAINST THE WALL, AND framed with oyster shells; a little bed, which there was just room enough to get into; and a nosegay of seaweed in a blue mug on the table. The walls were WHITEWASHED as white as milk, and the patchwork counterpane made my eyes quite ache WITH ITS BRIGHTNESS. One thing I particularly noticed IN THIS DELIGHTFUL HOUSE, was the smell of fish; which was so searching, that when I took out my pocket-handkerchief to wipe my nose, I found it smelt exactly as if it had wrapped up a lobster.[1]

In this passage, the specific concrete detail provides an 'objective correlative' for the emotion Dickens wants to convey. The boy's delight in the charming interior of the house-boat is genuine and strong. Each item added in revision seems an improvement and increases the power of the effect. On the other hand, in the account of Oliver's sojourn in the country, the cumulative result is an increasingly weakened

[1] Original MS. of *DC*, Vol. IA, Chap. III, p. 25, corrected proofs of *DC*, Chap. III, p. 26; cf. *DC*, pp. 30–1.

effect. There are some indications in the manuscript of
Oliver Twist and elsewhere that Dickens also tried to improve
the effect of this account. Yet the direction of his revision,
here, is away from the specific and concrete towards abstract,
vague, and general ideas. Thus, 'quick decline' is substituted
for 'pain', 'tombs' for 'graves', and insertions increase the
general woolliness: 'which calls up solemn thoughts OF
DISTANT TIMES TO COME, and bends down pride AND
WORLDLINESS BENEATH ⟨before⟩ it'. The gushing
emotion of 'while tears of tranquil joy stole down his face' in
the manuscript and *Bentley's Miscellany* is only avoided in
the first edition by substituting 'in a perfect rapture', and
later in the manuscript, 'warm feelings' replaces 'gratitude
and affection'.[1] There is a further reason why the vision of
Oliver's bliss is false and that of David's delight is authentic.
Whereas the specific and concrete are particularly appropriate
to a child's viewpoint, the vague, the abstract, and the
general remind us we are only getting the adult's solemn
view of the child's vision. The reader cannot sympathize with
Oliver's bliss when even the boy's pastimes read like an
extract from one of those earnest nineteenth-century moral
tracts for children on how a good boy should behave:

In the morning, Oliver would be a-foot by six o'clock, roaming
the fields, and plundering the hedges far and wide, for nosegays of
wild flowers . . . for the embellishment of the breakfast-table.
There was fresh groundsel, too, for Miss Maylie's birds, with which
Oliver, who had been studying the subject under the able tuition
of the village clerk, would decorate the cages, in the most approved taste. When the birds were made all spruce and smart for
the day, there was usually some little commission of charity to
execute in the village.

In David's case, however, the strong nostalgic feeling for
childhood, which is in every reader, compels us to share
sympathetically in the boy's experience because it is genuinely
evoked, while a subtle reminder of the adult's point of view,
'such as I have never seen since in the hands of pedlars,
without seeing the whole interior of Peggotty's brother's

---

[1] Original MS. of *OT*, Vol. IB, Bk. II, Chap. IX, pp. 42, 43, 46, Chap. X,
p. 2; cf. *OT*, Chaps. XXXII, XXXIII, pp. 237, 238, 240.

house again, at one view', preserves us from the complete
identification with childhood that would mark the unsophisticated vision.

The powerful mood of nostalgia which pervades the early
part of *David Copperfield* is worth examining. In its authentic
bitter-sweetness, this nostalgia has some of the same essential
elements as pathos. Nostalgia, in fact, may well be a disguised form of self-pity. Mingled with the pleasure of happy
memories are grief at our eternal separation from the mother
and home of our infancy and tender regard for the helpless
lost child which, deep down within us, we remain. The sweet
and terrible vision of separation which nostalgia usually
conceals is brilliantly revealed in a striking incident from
David Copperfield, surely one of the finest instances of genuine
pathos in our literature:

I kissed her, and my baby brother, and was very sorry then;
but not sorry to go, for the gulf between us was there, and the
parting was there, every day. And it is not so much the embrace
she gave me, that lives in my mind, though it was as fervent as
could be, as what followed the embrace.

I was in the carrier's cart when I heard her calling to me. I
looked out, and she stood at the garden-gate alone, holding her
baby up ⟨as if⟩ IN HER ARMS for me to see. It was cold still
weather; and not a hair of her head, or a fold of her dress, was
stirred, as she looked intently at me, holding up her child.

So I lost her. So I saw her afterwards, in my sleep at school—a
solemn presence near my bed—looking at me with the same
intent face—holding up her baby in her arms.

The specific reference to the mother's arms, which handle
(and protect) the baby, shows how a deliberate rhetoric is
used to intensify the feeling and increases the power of the
vision in these concluding paragraphs of a chapter. A kind of
gloss on the feeling and vision here is offered in the next
chapter in which David returns to school and his mother dies
and which concludes:

I remembered her, from that instant, only as the young mother
of my earliest impressions, who had been used to wind her bright
curls round and round her finger, and to dance with me at twilight
in the parlour . . .

The mother who lay in the grave, was the mother of my infancy; the little creature in her arms, was myself, as I had once been, hushed for ever on her bosom.[1]

The nostalgia and the pathos in the early chapters of *David Copperfield* are a triumph because Dickens does adequate justice to the complexity of the experience he is presenting. He grants us the tender joys but does not spare us the sharp pain and bitter grief of childhood. Whenever pathos fails in his work, it is because he tries to avoid or soften the element of pain. The result, in such cases, is not pathos at all but a bogus emotion. This can be seen in a sentence from the description of Oliver's sojourn in the country:

Oliver often wandered here; and, thinking of the wretched grave in which his mother lay, would sometimes sit him down and sob unseen; but, when he raised his eyes to the deep sky overhead, he would cease to think of her as lying in the ground, and would weep for her, sadly, but without pain.[2]

Nostalgia, as Walter Houghton has shown, was one of the prevailing moods of Victorian England. This mood may well help to explain the appeal of *David Copperfield* to Dickens's contemporaries. But it is interesting to see how Dickens presents his vision of childhood, in this novel, with authentic feeling and yet avoids the simple and naïve escapism into which some of his most illustrious contemporaries rushed in moments of panic. Consider, for example, the following passage from a novel which was published the same year that the serialization of *David Copperfield* began:

God has given us each our own Paradise, our own old childhood, over which the old glories linger—to which our own hearts cling, as all we have ever known of Heaven upon earth. And there, as all earth's weary wayfarers turn back their toil-jaded eyes, so do the poor speculators, one of whom is this writer . . . turn back in thought, at least, to that old time of peace—that village church—that child-faith—which, once lost, is never gained again—strange mystery—is never gained again—with sad and weary longing!

[1] Original MS. of *DC*, Vol. IA, Chap, VIII, p. 22½ ('away' after 'go' added in proof, proofs read 'a silent presence'); cf. *DC*, p. 121. Ibid., Chap. IX, p. 133.
[2] *OT*, Chap. XXXII, p. 238.

Or consider this stanza from an early poem of Tennyson's:

> Thrice happy state again to be
> The trustful infant on the knee!
> Who lets his waxen fingers play
> About his mother's neck, and knows
> Nothing beyond his mother's eyes.
> They comfort him by night and day;
> They light his little life alway;
> He hath no thought of coming woes;
> He hath no care of life or death.

Froude and Tennyson present a sentimental vision of child-hood here, not because they indulge in tender and pleasurable emotion but because they ignore the elements of pain and grief which Dickens makes a part of his nostalgic vision in *David Copperfield*.[1]

The unsuccessful death-bed scene in Dickens's novels does not fail because such details as it presents are unreal. A Victorian country parson's diary, for example, records a death-bed scene identical in many ways with several such scenes in Dickens's fiction:

I never saw death look so beautiful. There was no bandage round the chin. The pretty innocent child face looked as peaceful and natural as if the child were asleep and the dark curls lay upon the little pillow. I could hardly believe he was dead. Leaving the face still uncovered the poor mother knelt with me by the little bedside while I prayed for them all. She was deeply touched and most humbly grateful. Before I left the room I stooped and kissed the child's forehead, and the mother did the same. It was as cold and as hard as marble . . . Margaret Davies told me that before Little Davies died he saw a number of people and some pretty children dancing in a beautiful garden and heard some sweet music. Then someone seems to have called him for he answered, 'What do you want with me?' He also saw beautiful birds.

---

[1] W. E. Houghton, op. cit., pp. 79–81, 85–6, 344–5. *DC* was universally liked; see George H. Ford, *Dickens and His Readers*, pp. 126–8, *Dickensiana*, pp. 104–9, 261–3, and cf. Dickens's letters to M. De Cerjat (29 Dec. 1849), to Revd. James White (13 July 1850), *HD*, pp. 208, 216. J. A. Froude, *The Nemesis of Faith* [1849] (1904), p. 116, quoted by Houghton, op. cit., p. 344. Froude's novel was in Dickens's library; see *Catalogue of the Library of Charles Dickens*, p. 49. Alfred Lord Tennyson, 'Supposed Confessions of a Secondrate sensitive Mind not in unity with itself', ll. 57–65; first published in *Poems, Chiefly Lyrical* (1830).

The authenticity of such a scene, drawn from real life, is confirmed by other documentary evidence. Such pictures of death are, therefore, untrue only in what they suppress. A conventional attitude towards the death of a loved one dwelt upon certain indisputable facts but ignored others and repressed or subdued certain emotional reactions to death. The elements which tended to be suppressed or toned down were suffering, grief, and horror. The Victorians stood on the edge of a great abyss of religious doubt. Whenever they looked death in the face, therefore, they demanded consolation above all.[1] And, for a nation with a phenomenal population explosion, mushrooming towns, and overcrowded slums, death must have seemed to remind the Victorians of its presence most frequently in its most disturbing forms, those of infant mortality and the slaughter of youth.

Dickens was prostrate with grief at the death of his young sister-in-law, on whom Little Nell was modelled. A phrase from the epitaph on Mary Hogarth's grave, which Dickens composed, 'Young, Beautiful, and Good', is echoed by the tolling of the bell at Nell's funeral, and in writing *The Old Curiosity Shop* Dickens was concerned with this traumatic experience: 'The many friends it [the tale] won me, and the hearts it turned to me when they were full of private sorrow, invest it with an interest in my mind which is not a public one, and the rightful place of which appears to be "a more removed ground". ' Certainly the intention of Little Nell's death was consolation, as Dickens made clear on completing the scene, 'I resolved to try and do something which might be read by people about whom Death had been, with a softened feeling, and with consolation', and in his instructions to his illustrator, 'I want it to express the most beautiful repose and tranquility, and to have something of a happy look, if death can.'[2] This seeking for consolation is, however, what ruins

---

[1] *Kilvert's Diary*, ed. William Plomer (1944), 24 Dec. 1878, pp. 340–1. Cf., for example, Hare's account of his mother's death, Augustus Hare, *The Years with Mother* (1952), 3 Mar. 1868), p. 264: 'With the morning light my dearest Mother has seemed to become more rapt in holy thoughts and visions, her eyes more intently fixed on the unseen world. At last, with a look of rapture she has exclaimed, "Oh, angels, I see angels!" and since then pain seemed to have left her.' See also Houghton, op. cit., p. 277.

[2] He was so overcome that no serial parts of *PP* and *OT* appeared during June 1837. See Edgar Johnson, *Charles Dickens*, vol. i, p. 197, for the epitaph

Nell's death as an exercise in pathos. Far from indulgence of
emotion, the manuscript shows a conscious effort at restraint:

> For ⟨Nell⟩ SHE was dead. There, upon the ⟨little lowly⟩ LITTLE
> bed, she lay at rest. The solemn stillness was no marvel now. ⟨The
> presence of that sleeping white form the very air within the room
> seemed hushed.⟩
> She was dead ⟨and the strong heart⟩. No sleep so beautiful and
> calm, so free from trace of pain, so fair to look upon. She seemed
> a creature fresh from the hand of God, and waiting for the breath
> of life; not one who had lived and suffered death . . .
> Where were the traces of her early cares, her sufferings and
> fatigues? All gone. That was the ⟨only⟩ true death before their
> weeping eyes. Sorrow ⟨and strife⟩ was dead indeed in her, but
> peace and perfect happiness were born; imaged in her tranquil
> beauty and profound repose. ⟨God's love was manifest on earth.⟩
> . . . So shall we know the angels in their majesty, after death.

The consolation theme which unifies the passage is stressed
when the schoolmaster pronounces the concluding moral: 'It
is not on earth that Heaven's justice ends. Think what earth
is, compared with the World to which her young spirit has
winged its early flight; and say, if one deliberate wish expressed in solemn terms above this bed could call her back to
life, which of us would utter it!'[1] This conclusion touches on
the problem of earthly suffering which has been evaded in
the description of Nell's death. The trouble with the scene is
not that emotion is in excess of the situation but that the
emotional effect is feeble. It is said that Dickens had Cordelia
in mind;[2] certainly a strong genuine pathos was required to

and cf. *OCS*, Chap. LXII, p. 542. The identification between Mary and Nell
is made absolutely clear in Dickens's letter to Forster (7 Jan. 1841), *F*, vol. i,
p. 187: 'Dear Mary died yesterday when I think of this sad story.' Preface to
the First Cheap Edition of *OCS* (1848). To John Forster (17 Jan. 1841), *F*,
vol. i, p. 187; to George Cattermole (22 Dec. 1840), *HD*, p. 37. The dominant
intention to provide consolation is confirmed by the 'tail piece . . . giving some
notion of the etherealized spirit of the child' which concludes the novel; see the
letter to Cattermole (14 Jan. 1841), *HD*, p. 39.

[1] Original MS. of *OCS*, Victoria and Albert Museum, Forster Collection,
47. A. 8 (Vol. IIB), Chap. LXXI, pp. 7–8 (First Edition of *MHC* omits 'That
was . . . eyes'; if this was deleted in proof, as seems likely, it is further evidence
of Dickens's conscious attempt at restraint). Sylvère Monod, *Dickens romancier*, p. 167, comments on the restraint shown by revision in the first paragraph. Cf. *OCS*, pp. 538–9.

[2] George H. Ford. op. cit., pp. 69–70.

move the reader. But such a pathos and an uncompromising insistence on consolation are incompatible. Dickens's vision fails because he ignores the limitations of his rhetoric. The rhetoric of pathos subscribes to certain conditions imposed by a genuine emotional reaction. Pity is a complex emotion. The absence of pain will result in something bogus, a sickly superfluity of the sweet and tender element which now, of course, appears to be over-indulged while the vision is correspondingly impoverished.

Nell's death should be carefully compared with what Dickens came to make of the death-bed scene. Thus, although he repeats the same basic error of rhetoric in his account of Little Paul and Jo's deaths, the effect is much less sickly and he complicates his effect and vision with irony—the child who pays no attention to his doting father, the naïvety of Paul and Jo. On the other hand, Mrs. Dombey's death is deeply moving.[1] The two essential elements of pathos are present. Pain is 'sympathetically induced' through little Florence Dombey's distress. A tender regard is conveyed through the embrace of dying mother and small daughter. Restraint is successful in this scene because there is a strong emotional effect which may gain from a certain degree of understatement:

The lady lay upon her bed as he had left her, clasping her little daughter to her breast. The child clung close about her, with the same intensity as before, and never raised her head, or moved her soft cheek from her mother's face, or looked on those who stood around, or spoke, or moved, or shed a tear.

Apart from the mother's smile, there is no note of consolation to soften the pain of her end; on the contrary, death is 'the dark and unknown sea' upon which the mother drifts away. There is irony as well as pathos in the mother and daughter's embrace, which involves a reversal of roles, for the child, seeking comfort for her grief in the maternal arms, becomes 'that slight spar' to which the mother is 'clinging fast' as she drifts away upon the ocean of death. There is irony, too, in Mrs. Chick's callous belief that Mrs. Dombey will recover if only she shows a little of the Dombey grit. Yet when she

[1] *D & S*, Chap. I, pp. 9-10.

urges the dying woman to rouse herself, this callousness also increases our pity for Mrs. Dombey. Irony and pathos, therefore, are closely interrelated here. In addition, the reader's concern is made still more acute. The terror and suspense of dying are not evaded but realized through the ticking of the watches which not only draws attention to the passing of time and life but also symbolizes the fearful beating of the pulse and heart:

There was no sound in answer but the loud ticking of Mr. Dombey's watch and Doctor Parker Pep's watch, which seemed in the silence to be running a race . . .
The race in the ensuing pause was fierce and furious. The watches seemed to jostle, and to trip each other up.

The vision here is not simple or naïve. Compared with the account of Nell's end, it explores death as a fairly complex experience. The vision has moral implications, in that it sets a compassionate vision of love against an ironic view of the callous arrogance of the Dombey will. Furthermore, the vision does not shrink from the possibility that love's final agony may not escape, and may even provoke, the world's callous reaction. Nor does it avoid the tragi-ironic conclusion that death is a mystery which may seem to mock love's final gestures. Mrs. Dombey's death invites a deep involvement certainly, but also establishes a critical detachment that encourages subtle and searching inquiry.

Gridley's death in *Bleak House* is also a considerable achievement.[1] Here, Dickens does not spare us the painful state to which Chancery has reduced Gridley. The manuscript shows how the author intensifies this element in his effect:

Upon a plain canvas-covered sofa lay the man from Shropshire—dressed much as we had seen him last, but so changed, that I ⟨saw⟩ RECOGNIZED no likeness in ⟨him⟩ HIS COLOURLESS FACE AT FIRST to what I recollected.

An appeal to the reader's tender concern completes an effect of genuine pathos:

His voice had faded, with the old expression of his face, with his strength, with his anger, with his resistance to the wrongs that

[1] Original MS. of *BH*, Vol. IB, Chap. XXIV, pp. 22-3, corrected proofs of *BH*, Chap. XXIV, p. 248; cf. *BH*, pp. 350-1. Ibid., pp. 351-2.

had AT LAST subdued him. The faintest shadows of an object full of form and colour, is such a picture of it, as he was of the man from Shropshire WHOM we had spoken with before.

The irony in Gridley's situation is also intensified:

He had been STILL writing in his hiding-place, and STILL dwelling on his ⟨wrongs⟩ GRIEVANCES, hour after hour. A table and some shelves were covered with manuscript papers, and with worn pens, and a medley of such tokens.

So is his heroic defiance:

But, you know I made a fight for it, you know I stood up WITH MY SINGLE HAND against them all, you know I told them the truth to the last, and told them what they were, and what they had done to me; so I don't mind your seeing me, this wreck.
"You have been courageous with them, many AND MANY a time," returned my Guardian.

His wrongs have only 'AT LAST subdued him'. Through a rhetoric of sympathy and irony, Dickens deliberately focuses a complex vision of Gridley as the heroic and tragic dupe of Chancery whom we admire yet pity and also observe at a critical distance:

"I thought, boastfully, that they never could break my heart, Mr. Jarndyce. I was resolved that they should not. I did believe that I could, and would, charge them with being the mockery they were, until I died of some bodily disorder. But I am worn out. How long I have been wearing out, I don't know; I seemed to break down in an hour. I hope they may never come to hear of it. I hope everybody, here, will lead them to believe that I died defying them, consistently and perseveringly, as I did through so many years."

3. *Melodrama, Sensation, and Suspense*

The belief that Dickens provided each instalment of his serials with a sensational ending and distorted the natural development of his narrative in the process is still being circulated. It is very largely a myth.[1] Though Dickens sometimes

[1] Q. D. Leavis, *Fiction and the Reading Public* (1932), pp. 152 9. Two reprints (1965, 1968) repeat the error, though K. J. Fielding drew attention to it in

concludes a serial part with the simple kind of suspense
ending, like Charles Darnay's re-arrest, many of his serial
'curtains', like the discovery that Lady Dedlock, Tulkinghorn,
or the Marquis St. Evrémonde, is dead, terminate a particular
state of uncertainty and show the theatre's influence rather
than that of the serial. Very often, the most dramatic incident
in a number, like the finding of Steerforth's body, William
Dorrit's collapse, or Merdle's suicide, occurs at the beginning
or in the middle of a serial part.[1]

A study of Dickens as a conscious artist should note the
responsibility he exercised in handling the serial form.
Whenever he acknowledged the restrictions imposed by the
serial form on his work or discussed its difficulties with other
authors, he almost invariably had in mind not the question of
suspense but the importance of getting incident into each
number and the problem of overall unity which this posed.[2]
He thought in terms of an effective 'curtain' at the end of the
chapter rather than the serial part. Many of his notes prominently indicate the 'curtain' of a chapter and he may well
intend this to create suspense: '*Mr. Tulkinghorn and Lady
Dedlock. Each watching the other.* open that interest and leave
them so' (Chap. XII). On the other hand, Dickens may
deliberately avoid a strong suspense 'curtain' at the end of a
number. He originally intended to end No. XV of *Dombey
and Son* with the shocking climax of what is now Chapter
XLVII: Dombey discovers that Edith has eloped with
Carker and savagely strikes his daughter who runs from the
house. Unwilling to leave his readers in so painful a state of
suspense, however, he transposed Chapters XLVII and

'The Critical Autonomy of *Great Expectations*', *A Review of English Literature*,
ii (1961), 75; see also Kathleen Tillotson, *Novels of the Eighteen-Forties*, pp.
27–45. For a list of the serial divisions, see K. J. Fielding, 'The Monthly
Serialization of Dickens's Novels', 'The Weekly Serialization of Dickens's
Novels', *The Dickensian*, liv (1958), 4–11, 134–41, and T. Hatton and A. H.
Cleaver, *Bibliography of the Periodical Works of Charles Dickens* (1933). See
also Archibald C. Coolidge, Jr., *Charles Dickens as Serial Novelist* (Iowa, 1967).
    [1] *TTC*, Bk. III, Chap. VII, pp. 277–8; *BH*, Chaps, LIX, XLVIII, pp.
811–12, 664–5; *TTC*, Bk. II, Chap. IX, pp. 121–2; *DC*, Chap. LV, p. 795;
LD, Bk. II, Chaps. XIX, XXV, pp. 647–50, 705–6.
    [2] See Dickens's preface to the First Edition of *PP* (1837) and his letters to
Mrs. Brookfield (20 Feb. 1866), Miss King (9, 24 Feb. 1855), the Hon. Mrs.
Watson (1 Nov. 1854), John Forster (25 Aug. 1859, Miss Emily Jolly (17 July
1855), *HD*, pp. 599, 357, 360, 345, 485. 374.

XLVIII: 'The Thunderbold chapter originally intended for the last of the No. and the middle chapter meant to have led up—but the Thunderbold chapter being written first, place altered, to leave a pleasanter impression on the reader' (memoranda for No. XV).[1] Again, the sensational ending of one particular serial part was not originally planned. Throughout most of No. IV of *Our Mutual Friend*, suspense has been carefully worked up as Mr. Inspector waits all night at the riverside to arrest Gaffer Hexam. The number ends with the tantalizing discovery that Hexam's boat has been found empty and adrift. This may appear a clear case of deliberate sensationalism. Yet the author's plans reveal that he had intended the material in the first chapter of No. V to be included in the final chapter of No. IV. The title of this first chapter (XIV) in No. V, 'The Bird of Prey Brought Down', had originally been the title of the final chapter (XIII) in No. IV which can be seen on the plan to have been changed to 'Tracking the Bird of Prey'. The outline notes for Chapter XIII contain the instruction: 'Kill Gaffer retributively. "Many a slip" for Mr. Riderhood'. On completing No. IV, Dickens discovered that he had overwritten it by six pages for he adds to the memoranda for No. IV, 'The No. overwritten and chapter divided into two, and carried on into No. V', and to the memoranda for No. V, '6 pages of the No. brought forward. 20 to write'. Reasons of space have therefore dictated the 'curtain' of No. IV which thus indicates a responsible artist's refusal to cramp the natural development of his story within the divisions of the serial form.[2] Again, the interpolation of the present Chapter II of *Bleak House* after the first number had been written offered Dickens an opportunity to conclude the number with a sensational 'curtain'. The present number ends on a comparatively mild note with the pathetic spectacle of the neglected Jellyby children whom Esther Summerson has begun to take in hand; the interpolated chapter ends on a strong note of suspense with Lady Dedlock's mysterious fainting. There are no reasons, other than certain subtle artistic ones to be discussed later, why

[1] Original MS. of *BH*, Vol. IA; original MS. of *D & S*, Vol. IA.
[2] *OMF*, Bk. I, Chap. XIII, p. 169; see the transcript in Ernest Boll, 'The Plotting of *Our Mutual Friend*', *Modern Philology*, xlii (1944), 105–6.

Dickens should not have ended with the interpolated chapter. Had he been a purely sensational writer he could hardly have resisted the temptation. Yet there is no indication of hesitation, in either the revised plan or the manuscript, as to where the interpolated chapter shall go.[1]

When suspense of the sensational type occurs in Dickens's fiction, it rarely exists as a simple effect. It is usually complicated by sympathy or irony, or both, and often by terror or horror. Sympathy is essential to the proper working of suspense. Unless we are involved with the characters, our interest in what happens to them will remain faint and suspense will seem a contrived, heartless piece of machinery. This is the trouble with the scene in which Lady Dedlock learns that Tulkinghorn's threat to reveal her shameful past to her husband is to remain poised over her head. The scene is presented through dialogue of this calibre:

"I am to drag my present life on, holding its pains at your pleasure, day by day? . . . It is necessary, you think, that I should be tied to the stake? . . . I am to remain on this gaudy platform, on which my miserable deception has been so long acted, and it is to fall beneath me when you give the signal?"

It is understandable that Lady Dedlock should retain some sort of a mask before Tulkinghorn, but fatal that her reaction to the situation should be presented through clichés. We get an indication of her true feelings only at the end of the chapter in a brief dumb show which fails to impress us. Since we do not experience her anxiety in the only way we can—through 'the sympathetic induction of emotion'—the suspense in her situation remains outside us and seems a mechanical trick of the plot. When a similar situation is presented through a character's genuine feelings, the suspense works naturally. Thus, Esther Summerson's anxiety lest she betray her mother's guilty secret involves the reader in a concern for both women:

At no time did I dare to utter her name. I felt as if I did not even dare to hear it. If the conversation anywhere, when I was present, took that direction, as it sometimes naturally did, I tried

_____

[1] For a full discussion on this interpolated chapter, see below, pp. 335-7.

not to hear—I mentally counted, repeated something that I knew, or went out of the room.[1]

A character's sensations will ensure a complex, satisfying form of suspense, provided they record a predicament which stimulates an emotional reaction in the reader. Dickens handles suspense of this type with great skill at the close of the tenth serial part (and first book) of *Oliver Twist*:

In the short time he had to collect his senses, the boy had firmly resolved that, whether he died in the attempt or not, he would make one effort to dart up stairs from the hall, and alarm the family. Filled with this idea, he advanced at once, but stealthily.

"Come back!" suddenly cried Sikes aloud. "Back! back!"

Scared by the sudden breaking of the dead stillness of the place, and by a loud cry which followed it, Oliver let his lantern fall, and knew not whether to advance or fly.

The cry was repeated—a light appeared—a vision of two terrified half-dressed men at the top of the stairs swam before his eyes—a flash—a loud noise—a smoke—a crash somewhere, but where he knew not,—and he staggered back . . .

"Clasp your arm tighter," said Sikes, as he drew him through the window. "Give me a shawl here. They've hit him. Quick! How the boy bleeds!"

Then came the loud ringing of a bell, mingled with the noise of fire-arms, and the shouts of men, and the sensation of being carried over uneven ground at a rapid pace. And then, the noises grew confused in the distance; and a cold deadly feeling crept over the boy's heart; and he saw or heard no more.[2]

The assumption of Oliver's viewpoint is crucial here. The loss of consciousness facilitates a natural shift of viewpoint in the next chapter so that suspense is maintained not only over the month between the tenth and eleventh parts but for the next five chapters (two monthly numbers). But viewpoint is crucial in another way. It is carefully used to create sympathy for Oliver. First, there is moral approval at his secret resolve to warn the family. Then there is sympathy for him in his fear and confusion ('knew not whether to advance or fly', 'a vision . . . swam before his eyes'). Finally, there is pity for him in his wounded half-conscious plight ('a crash some-

---

[1] *BH*, Chap. XLI, p. 580, Chap. XLIII, p. 591 (cf. Chap. XXXVII, p. 518).
[2] *OT*, Chap. XXII, pp. 163–4.

where, but where he knew not', 'staggered back', 'the sensation of being carried over uneven ground at a rapid pace', 'noises grew confused in the distance', 'a cold deadly feeling crept over the boy's heart', 'he saw or heard no more'). Sikes's cry, 'How the boy bleeds!' adroitly interprets what Oliver feels here, while his sensations throughout are handled convincingly yet with restraint.

Suspense may be complicated by irony in an equally effective manner. Thus, when Nancy tries to get away from Sikes to keep the appointment on the bridge, suspense and dramatic irony work closely together. Structural irony is, in itself, a form of suspense, since it hints at more than it states. By lifting a corner of the veil, it draws attention to the mystery beyond and whets the reader's curiosity. Yet structural irony appeals to more than simple curiosity; it excites an awareness that a pattern of fate is developing. The emphasis shifts from 'What will happen next?' to 'What has destiny in store?' Structural irony is engineered in *Bleak House*, for example, by several devices which also create and maintain suspense: the pointing hand of the Roman, say, or the Ghost's walk 'machinery', or the cold sunlight which falls upon Lady Dedlock's portrait in the shape of the bend sinister, heraldic sign of bastardy. A particularly skilful example of ironic foreshadowing as a complex type of suspense can be seen in the 'curtain' which falls on Sikes's flight:

He resolved to drown him, and walked on, looking about for a pond: picking up a heavy stone and tying it to his handkerchief as he went.

The animal . . . skulked a little farther in the rear than usual, and cowered as he came more slowly along. When his master halted at the brink of a pool, and looked round to call him, he stopped outright.

"Do you hear me call? Come here!" cried Sikes.

The animal came up from the very force of habit; but as Sikes stooped to attach the handkerchief to his throat, he uttered a low growl and started back.

"Come back!" said the robber.

The dog wagged his tail, but moved not. Sikes made a running noose and called him again.

The dog advanced, retreated, paused an instant, turned, and scoured away at his hardest speed.

The man whistled again and again, and sat down and waited in the expectation that he would return. But no dog appeared, and at length he resumed his journey.

Sikes's fear the dog will betray him does not fully account for the effect here and, though the incident suggests the murderer's final isolation, it has a further ironic significance. The dog dies with its master, springing for his shoulders as he hangs from the chimney stack. It is a projection of Sikes, almost his familiar. In attempting to destroy it, Sikes is unwittingly enacting his own pursuit and foreshadowing the very means by which he will die. The phrase, 'made a running noose', is repeated in the later scene with a further ironic touch, 'made a strong running noose'. On a second reading, the suspense is enriched with an extra grim quality as Sikes attempts to lure the dog to its death and the dog tries to evade him.[1]

The power and complexity of vision which Dickens focuses through a fairly intricate rhetoric can be seen to advantage, if we compare his comparatively sophisticated handling of the Newgate Novel with Harrison Ainsworth's treatment. It seems reasonable to compare Sikes's flight after Nancy's murder with Jack Sheppard's escape after his mother's violent death. Although Jack has caused his mother's death, guilt plays no part in Chapter XXIV, 'The Pursuit', and in Chapter XXV, 'How Jack Sheppard Got Rid of His Irons', there is only one very brief outburst, at the conclusion of which Ainsworth comments: 'This strong feeling of remorse having found a natural vent, in some degree subsided, and he addressed himself to his present situation.' Remorse appears in earnest only in Chapter XXVI, 'How Jack Sheppard Attended His Mother's Funeral', when Jack has got rid of his irons and is comparatively safe for the moment. Though Jack is arrested at the funeral towards the end of the chapter, there is very little suspense here. In Chapter XXIV, the suspense is restricted to the external and the physical. Whenever his pursuers close in on him, at the very last moment, by the sheerest good fortune—a convenient covered

[1] *OT*, Chap. XLIV, pp. 338–41; *BH*, Chap. XII, p. 153; *OT*, Chap. XLVIII, pp. 370–1, Chap. L, pp. 391, 390. (There is a further irony in the fact that it is Sikes's frightening the dog away and its continued loyalty which give away his last refuge, Chap. XLIX, p. 379.)

drain, a beggar mistaken for the thief, a sudden shower of rain—Jack escapes. The narrative is not without a momentary excitement but it is without depth. We get no insight into Jack's sensations or feelings. There is no co-ordination of sympathy and suspense. Only in Chapter XXV, when Jack has temporarily evaded his pursuers, do sympathy and suspense begin, for a few paragraphs, to function together:

He was now almost driven to despair. Wet as he was, he felt if he lay down in the grass, he should perish with cold; while, if he sought a night's lodging in any asylum, his dress, stained with blood and dirt, would infallibly cause him to be secured and delivered into the hands of justice. And then the fetters, which were still upon his legs—how was he to get rid of them?[1]

Sikes's case is handled very differently. Like Jack, he is responsible for the violent death of a loved one but, unlike Jack, he feels himself throughout to be pursued not only by the law but by horror and guilt. Finally, his footsteps are dogged by what appear to be manifestations of a super- natural retribution. By a careful exploitation of Sikes's viewpoint, by a constant record of his emotional reactions, the reader is involved sympathetically in his fate. The incident of the fire may eventually stress Sikes's isolation but, by drawing him (however momentarily) into communion with his fellow men, it also forges a link between Sikes and the reader through a common humanity. The mechanisms of guilt, too, are a deep-seated inheritance which the normal reader can share with the worst criminal. Sikes's guilty flight is also pervaded by a subtle irony for, in attempting to escape, he is repeatedly driven by an inner compulsion back to Lon- don, the scene of his crime.[2] His feelings and actions, from the accusation which he finds everywhere to his attempt to do away with his dog, point towards the fate which finally over- takes him and, indeed, assist its progress. It is important to establish horror as well as guilt as part of Sikes's experience

---

[1] *Bentley's Miscellany*, vii (1840), 95, 94; the opening chapters of *Jack Sheppard* began to appear in *Bentley's Miscellany*, v (1839), while *OT* was being concluded and Ainsworth's novel owes much to the immediate vogue created by it.

[2] For the mechanism involved, see Theodor Reik, *The Unknown Murderer*, tr. Dr. Katherine Jones (1936).

for a combination of the two will finally destroy him. Dickens's handling of Nancy's spectre might well be compared with an incident in Reynolds's *Mysteries of the Court of London*[1] in which we find sensationalism of the worst kind. A woman has murdered a man who has tried to make violent love to her. Compelled to spend the night with the corpse, she believes she is ravished by it:

She felt the first marble-cold touch of the hand of the corpse! . . . as the touch of the dead traced its way by very slow degrees over her own plump flesh, she could feel the animal heat in herself gradually retiring beneath the appalling contact which she was thus doomed to experience. Was it not—oh! was it not hell upon earth?—and had not her punishment already begun in this world with a foretaste of the horrors of Satan's Kingdom? . . . as if this foretaste of posthumous punishment were to be crowned with all the horrors conceivable by mortal imagination,—the corpse slowly, but surely and resolutely, glued its lips to the mouth of the milliner and sent with its awful caress an ice-chill throughout her whole frame.

The irony of the woman's punishment is certainly apt, here, but the overwhelming impression is one of disgust. Reynolds's attempt to exploit both sexual sensation and charnel horror fails because a sympathetic involvement with the victim is impossible for any reader other than a confirmed necrophilist. In Dickens's vision of the haunted Sikes, however, the murderer is not simply flesh and nerves but a human being. Divine retribution is not reduced to the level of the beast but remains superior to man in its dignity and terror:

At times he turned, with desperate determination, resolved to beat this phantom off, though it should look him dead; but the hair rose on his head, and his blood stood still, for it had turned with him and was behind him then. He had kept it before him that morning, but it was behind now—always. He leaned his back against a bank, and felt that it stood above him, visibly out against the cold night-sky. He threw himself upon the road—on his back upon the road. At his head it stood, silent, erect, and still—a living grave-stone, with its epitaph in blood.

[1] G. W. M. Reynolds, *The Mysteries of the Court of London* (1849–56), vol. ii, chap. cxxxv, pp. 43–6; *OT*, Chap, XLVIII, p. 368.

When the attempt at terror or horror fails in Dickens's fiction, it does so (as in the spurious kind of pathos) through weakness of effect rather than through over-indulgence in emotion. In his account of Ralph Nickleby's suicide,[1] for example, Dickens begins quite well. Ralph's vision of death as he contemplates the miserable squalid graveyard provides a fine realistic setting for the mean and sordid affair which suicide usually is. The moment of merriment, in which Ralph hysterically joins, adds a convincing human touch. The rest of the account, which seems an anticlimax, does not indicate restraint but a dearth of true feeling. Dickens no sooner turns the spotlight on Ralph's exit than he ceases to be a human being and becomes a theatrical villain. The vacuum of feeling has to be filled somehow and Dickens falls back on the stereotyped gestures of contemporary melodrama and an attempt at Jacobean bombast which reads like a parody. The attempt at tragic soliloquy, however, is serious and ambitious. It seeks to explore Ralph's inner life, to reveal (as in Macbeth's case after his wife's death) the soul which finds but a reflection of its own spiritual emptiness in the external world. Unfortunately, inflated tragic dialogue is totally out of key with the meanness of Ralph's end. Obvious anachronisms, like the body thrown on the dunghill, seem ridiculous in the realistic setting. In his concluding paragraphs, Dickens uses a technique he later employs in a masterly fashion to describe the end of Tulkinghorn and the Marquis St. Evrémonde. Suspense as to what has happened to the victim is built up and the discovery of the body presented as a shock. The scene in *Nickleby*, however, has no real terror or horror. Preliminary staginess of the worst kind has helped to ruin the build-up. That Ralph has hanged himself is made too obvious and the shock of discovery correspondingly lessened. The mystification of the people who investigate the situation remains an intellectual puzzle; it does not create atmosphere. The final paragraphs, which should provide the climax of an effect, fail because, in spite of a contrived

---

[1] *NN*, Chap. LXII, pp. 802–7. The realism of the graveyard setting is confirmed by G. E. Walker, *Gleanings from Graveyards* (1839), *Burial Ground Incendiarism, or the minute anatomy of grave-digging in London* (1846). Dickens possessed 'Walker's Lectures on the Condition of Metropolitan Grave Yards, *four series*'; see *Catalogue of the Library of Charles Dickens*, p. 89.

attempt to suggest an awe-inspiring fate, the episode is devoid of terror or horror:

They pressed forward to see; but one among them thrusting the others aside with a loud exclamation, drew a clasp knife from his pocket and dashing into the room cut down the body.

He had torn a rope from one of the old trunks, and hanged himself on an iron hook immediately below the trap door in the ceiling—in the very place to which the eyes of his son, a lonely desolate little creature, had so often been directed in childish terror, fourteen years before.

In his study of Dickens as a sensation novelist, W. C. Phillips does not discern any development in Dickens's treatment of terror or horror, and he particularly singles out Merdle's suicide as an instance of what he claims 'is least admirable in his [Dickens's] art' and is 'not the excrescence of immaturity, but a constant quality of Dickensian fiction'. Yet if we compare Merdle's suicide with Ralph Nickleby's we are bound to concede a power and verisimilitude in the incident from *Little Dorrit* absent in the episode from the earlier novel. A careful examination reveals that Dickens is successful in the case of Merdle's suicide because he presents a strong convincing impression of horror. Indeed, the manuscript and proofs show that he deliberately makes the effect as powerful as possible:[1]

There was a bath in that corner, from which the water had been hastily drained off. Lying in it, as in a ⟨sort of⟩ GRAVE OR sarcophagus, with a hurried drapery of sheet and blanket thrown across it, was the body of a heavily-made man, ⟨of⟩ WITH AN OBTUSE HEAD AND coarse, <u>MEAN</u>, common features. A skylight had been opened, to release the steam with which the room had been filled; but, it hung, condensed into water-drops, HEAVILY upon the walls, and HEAVILY upon the face and figure in the bath. The room was still hot, and the marble of the bath still warm; but, the FACE AND figure were clammy to the touch. The

---

[1] W. C. Phillips, *Dickens, Reade, and Collins*, pp. 14, 17, 193. Original MS. of *LD*, Vol. IIB, Bk. II, Chap. XXV, p. 19 (after 'sit' proofs read 'down' which is not in MS.), Chap. XXIV, p. 16, corrected proofs of *LD*, Bk. II, Chap. XXV, pp. 534, 530; cf. *LD*, pp. 705–6, 701. See also William McDougall, *An Introduction to Social Psychology*, pp. 116–17: 'Fear and disgust are very apt to be combined . . . It is the emotion we call loathing, and, in its most intense form, horror.'

WHITE MARBLE AT THE bottom of the bath was veined with a dreadful red. On the ledge at the side were an empty laudanum-bottle and a TORTOISE-SHELL HANDLED penknife—soiled, but not with ink.

"Separation of jugular vein—death rapid—been dead at least half an hour." This echo of the physician's words ran through the passages and little rooms, and through the house, while he was yet straightening himself from having bent down to reach to the bottom of the bath, and WHILE HE was yet dabbling his hands in water; REDLY veining it ⟨like⟩ AS the marble WAS VEINED, before it ⟨turned to⟩ MINGLED INTO one tint . . . Physician was glad to walk out into the ⟨free⟩ night air—was even glad, in spite of his great experience, to sit upon a door-step for a little while: ⟨being⟩ FEELING sick and faint.

The revisions stress the mean ugly appearance of the dead man while the effect of squalid horror is intensified. The heavy condensation of steam into water-drops on the corpse adds a sinister touch to the squalor, in view of what is to come; it suggests those other drops with which Merdle's life has oozed away and later, sure enough, we are told that blood and water mingle together. A striking contrast is achieved by the insertion of 'white marble' which truly throws up the colour of the blood into a 'dreadful' prominence. This idea is intensified in the next paragraph when all, as in Macbeth's dreadful vision, is turned to one red. Dickens can afford to increase the effect of horror, here, for a good aesthetic reason. The element of disgust in this effect is under control in all kinds of subtle ways. We are never shown the wound, for example. The oozing of blood is suggested indirectly as we have seen. The severed jugular vein is referred to once, in the cold medical language of the physician as he gives his diagnosis. Nevertheless, the idea of the bleeding vein is thrust repeatedly at the reader in another form. It is not white flesh but the white marble of the bath that is veined with red. Dickens can, in fact, multiply the notion of the bleeding vein because it is now safely displaced on to inanimate objects. In all these ways, then, the element of disgust is distanced. Dickens, therefore, goes on to indicate that the scene really was disgusting through the physician's reaction when he got out into the street. Yet there is still a further kind of distancing at work in this description. In one of his revisions, Dickens specifies that the penknife, with which Merdle has cut his throat, is 'tortoise-shell handled'. This detail, together with the ironic understatement that the knife is 'soiled, but not with ink', is intended to refer the reader back to the close of the previous chapter. There, Merdle had called on the Sparklers to borrow a penknife and was offered one with a mother-of-pearl handle:

"Thank you," said Mr. Merdle; "but if you have got ⟨a darker one⟩ ONE WITH A DARKER HANDLE, I THINK I should prefer ⟨a darker one⟩ ONE WITH A DARKER HANDLE."

"Tortoise-shell?"

"Thank you," said Mr. Merdle; "yes. I THINK I should prefer tortoise-shell." . . .

"I will forgive you, if you ink it."

"I ⟨won't⟩ 'LL UNDERTAKE NOT TO ink it," said Mr. Merdle.

The irony of Merdle's remark is deliberately echoed in the description of the suicide and its significance made plain. The effect of carrying the reader back to the earlier incident is to free him from the oppressive horror of the moment and to set Merdle's suicide in a wider context of time and fate. In handling Merdle's suicide, Dickens uses restraint only in the sense of 'distancing'. In fact, the need to 'distance' indicates a strong effect.

The distinction between feebleness and power, then, marks the difference between crude theatrical melodrama in Dickens's work and a melodrama which appears to be that of life itself. Any complete vision of life must do justice to its melodramatic moments. A vision which makes any pretence to verisimilitude cannot shun the horrible meanness and squalor which accompany at least one form of violent death.

4. *Tragedy*

Though Dickens's vision reflects authentic tragic experience, it is rarely the pure vision of high tragedy. What we usually find is tragi-comedy, or a melodramatic type of tragedy, or tragedy of the pathetic kind. The nature of the tragic forms in Dickens's fiction can be better understood if we take into account his rhetoric as well as his vision.

The complex vision of tragedy is focused, as Aristotle has rather vaguely indicated, by a complex effect. Aristotle, however, stresses the catharsis of the emotions involved rather than any interaction between the two elements in the effect. But I. A. Richards, in surveying Aristotle's theory of tragedy, draws attention to the balance between pity and terror. Yet both Aristotle and Richards (although the latter recognizes there may be 'other allied groups of equally discordant impulses' involved) ignore irony as an element in the complex group of reactions which make up the tragic effect. A. W. von Schlegel has gone so far as to find irony incompatible with the authentic tragic experience, 'No doubt, wherever the proper tragic enters, every thing like irony immediately ceases.'[1] It is, however, the very incompatibility between the various elements which enables a balance in the complex effect to occur. If the complex effect of tragedy then does, in my view, include a tension between pity, terror, and irony, it will be seen to exhaust and reconcile all the basic attitudes towards a tragic situation, other than indifference. The vision of tragedy, that is, binds us to the agony of the world, preventing our flight from our own anxiety, by sympathetic involvement in the fate of tragic victims. While through 'aesthetic distancing', of which irony is the most important form, we are further removed from both our own anxiety and our own involvement to a critical and objective vantage point.

There are two factors in Dickens's narrative art which tend to inhibit the full development of a tragic vision. These factors derive not so much from the polarization of good and evil in Dickens's fiction as from the effects and vision that Dickens considers appropriate to weakness on the one hand and to an energetic evil on the other. There is a considerable development in Dickens's concept of weakness which is plain enough if the case of Little Nell is compared with that of Amy

---

[1] Aristotle, *Poetics*, vi. 2, tr. Thomas Twining [1812], *Everyman Library* (1941), p. 14; I. A. Richards, *Principles of Literary Criticism*, pp. 245–6; A. W. von Schlegel, 'Shakespeare', Lecture XXIII, *Lectures on Dramatic Art and Literature*, tr. John Black, revised by A. J. W. Morrison (1861), p. 370.

Dorrit or Richard Carstone. Both Richard and Nell are menaced by an evil fate but, in Nell's case, the weakness is entirely in her situation and the wickedness that menaces her remains an external one. In the passage which was added to Chapter I in the first cheap edition of *The Old Curiosity Shop*,[1] Dickens makes it clear that Nell's story is to be taken as 'a kind of allegory' of innocence menaced by evil. The figures, that is, are emblematic rather than human. The figure of helpless innocence in Dickens's fiction becomes more human. This is what makes Amy Dorrit more acceptable than Nell. Amy's happiness is threatened not by an allegorical evil but by her father's selfishness and Arthur Clennam's blindness. Richard Carstone, however, becomes the prey of an external evil through a weakness of character which this same evil has fostered.[2] Weakness of any kind, as we might expect in Bagehot's 'sentimental radical' and the age of benevolence,[3] evokes a compassionate vision. Maturity in Dickens demands that this vision should also be a critical one. And, for the naïvely pathetic and frequently sentimental picture of Nell, we eventually get the mature, sympathetic, and ironic portrait of Richard. Although the shift is from an external to an internal view of weakness, Dickens seldom allows an inner experience of terror to enter fully into his vision of weakness. The weak may be threatened by evil but the evil is hardly ever shown as part of their subjective experience. Yet the real terror of evil is not its interference in the events of our lives, not what it may do to our bodies, but to our souls. It is the contagious quality of evil which is so terrible. The terror of such a contagion seldom spreads, or threatens to spread, to the weak character in Dickens's novels. Oliver prays that Sikes will not make him steal; here, wickedness is only a physical action which, compelled from without, leaves innocence untouched. Although Miss Flite describes the

---

[1] The interpolated passage begins, 'I sat down in my easy chair', and concludes, 'resolved to go to bed and court forgetfulness'. See the First Cheap Edition of *OCS* (1848), pp. 8–9, and its preface. Neither the original MS. of *OCS*, Vol. IA, Chap. I, p. 18, nor the First Edition of *MHC*, vol. i (1840), pp. 46–7, contains the passage.

[2] *BH*, Chaps. XIII, XXIII, XXXV, pp. 167, 322, 493.

[3] Walter Bagehot, 'Charles Dickens', *National Review*, vii (1858), 458–86; the relevant passage is quoted in Humphry House, *The Dickens World*, p. 170. See also House's chapter on 'Benevolence', ibid., pp. 36–54.

terrible fascination of the evil to which Richard succumbs, even in his case we are never shown the terror of this experience at work in Richard himself.[1] Terror as a subjective experience or as an atmosphere which surrounds a character tends to be restricted to Dickens's villains. Such a terror is either the hell which they endure on earth or a warning to others which accompanies their fate. One notable exception is the dreams and hallucinations which sometimes afflict the apparently innocent. Thus, Dickens's main social thesis in *Bleak House* is the responsibility of the upper and middle classes for the condition of England yet he excludes Esther Summerson from any censure on this score. The contagious evil corrupting society is well expressed by the diseases which are bred in the slums but spread throughout all classes. Dickens assures us that such diseases punish the highest in the land yet it is Esther who catches smallpox from Jo. It is only in the delirium resulting from smallpox that Esther experiences the terror of an identity with evil, the horror of damnation, which is concealed in the following symbolical terms:

Dare I hint at that worse time when, strung together somewhere in great black space, there was a flaming necklace, or ring, or starry circle of some kind, of which *I* was one of the beads! And when my only prayer was to be taken off from the rest, and when it was such inexplicable agony and misery to be a part of the dreadful thing?[2]

Dickens overtly protects the innocent reputation of the weak in his world but a deep, perhaps unconscious, irony sometimes insists on their share in the common guilt. Irony, too, plays a role in the punishment of Dickens's villains and he skilfully engineers some sympathy for them; though we seldom pity them in the deepest sense and grimly approve of their punishment. As Aristotle has warned us, 'the fall of a very bad man from prosperous to adverse fortune . . . may be pleasing from its moral tendency' but 'it will' not 'produce . . . pity . . . For our pity is excited by misfortunes undeservedly suffered'.[3]

---

[1] *OT*, Chap. XXII, p. 162; *BH*, Chap. XXXV, pp. 498–9. Pip is all the more an authentic tragic figures because he does experience the terror of contagion.

[2] *BH*, Chap. XXXV, p. 489; see also above, pp. 152–3.

[3] Aristotle, *Poetics*, xiii. 4, p. 25.

The result of these two inhibiting tendencies in Dickens's narrative art is that the elements which might have been united into a full tragic vision frequently remain in a fragmented state. What we often find is either compassion without terror or terror without compassion, though irony is a fairly constant factor.

Carton's death or the shipwreck at Yarmouth is perhaps Dickens's nearest approach to a tragic scene in the Aristotelian sense. In the scene at the scaffold, the opportunities for terror are almost unlimited, yet Dickens chooses to muffle this effect in favour of pathos and admiration for Carton's heroic self-sacrifice:

> He has not relinquished her patient hand in getting out, but still holds it as he promised. He gently places her with her back to the crashing engine that constantly whirrs up and falls, and she looks into his face and thanks him.

Moreover, there is an emphasis throughout on consolation. This is true of the comfort which Carton gives to the little seamstress, the religious sentiments, and Carton's prophetic thought. Dickens invites a comparison with the tragic passion of Christ's crucifixion: 'Nor should I have been able to raise my thoughts to Him who was put to death, that we might have hope and comfort here to-day. I think you were sent to me by Heaven.'[1] But Christ's tragic passion does not spare us the terror and horror of physical agony, the crown of thorns, the nails in the hands and feet, the spear in the side. What Dickens leaves out can be seen in this true account of a victim at the foot of the guillotine:

> All the way to the place of execution, Madame Bergeret consoled and encouraged her companions, and she assented to their petition that she should suffer last, that she would see them

---

[1] *TTC*, Bk. III, Chap. XV, pp. 355–8. If we compare Dickens's treatment of the scene with what was probably his source, Madame Roland's death as described by Thomas Carlyle, *The French Revolution* [1837], People's Edition (1872), vol. iii, bk. v, chap. ii, p. 179, we can observe how eagerly and extensively Dickens has exploited the very brief hints for pathos and consolation in Madame Roland's comforting of the dejected Lamarche. *The Catalogue of the Library of Charles Dickens*, p. 98, records that Dickens possessed a copy of Madame Roland, *Ses Mémoires; avec une Notice sur sa Vie, des Notes et des Éclaircissements historiques par Berville et Barriére*, 2 vols. (Paris, 1820).

through the dread portal before her. Therefore, when her turn at length came, the ground around the scaffold was one sea of blood, for a hundred and nineteen persons had perished that day. Thus, on descending the steps of the cart, Madame Bergeret slipped and stumbled.[1]

That final realistic touch which describes Madame Bergeret's slipping in the blood brings before our eyes the guillotine's full terror and horror in a way that the statistics (which Dickens also uses) and even the reference to 'sea of blood' do not. Dickens weakens his tragic impression because he fails to balance terror adequately against pathos.

He cannot be accused of doing this in the great shipwreck scene at Yarmouth.[2] The manuscript shows that he intensifies the effect of terror wherever he can. Revisions stress the storm's terrible superhuman strength:

As we struggled on, nearer and nearer to the sea, from which this mighty wind was blowing dead on shore, its force became MORE AND MORE terrific. Long before we saw the sea, its spray was on our lips, and showered salt rain upon us. The water was out, over miles and miles of the flat country adjacent to Yarmouth; and every sheet and puddle lashed its banks, and had its stress of little breakers setting HEAVILY towards us. When we came within sight of the sea, the waves on the horizon, caught at intervals above the rolling abyss, were like glimpses of another shore with towers and buildings. When at last we got into the town, the people came out, all aslant, AND WITH STREAMING HAIR, to their doors, MAKING A WONDER OF ⟨to⟩ the mail that had come through such a night.

I put up at the old inn, and went down to look at the sea; staggering along the street, ⟨afraid of falling⟩ WHICH WAS STREWN WITH SAND AND SEA-WEED AND WITH FLYING BLOTCHES OF SEA-FOAM; AFRAID OF FALLING slates and tiles; and holding by people I met, at angry corners.

After describing the anxiety of everyone concerned, he

---

[1] Cited by Augustus Hare, op. cit., pp. 256–7.

[2] Original MS. of *DC*, Vol. IIB, Chap. LV, pp. 13–14 and overleaf ('I saw' was altered to 'I seemed to see' and 'everywhere' after 'nature' deleted in proof), 16–18 ('plainly' added, 'for' before 'the sea' and 'four' deleted, and 'two' substituted for 'three' in proof), 18–18½; cf. *DC*, pp. 787, 788, 792–4, 794–5.

deliberately makes it clear that all nature's terrible forces have been unleashed:

The tremendous sea itself, when I could find sufficient pause to look at it, in the agitation of the blinding wind, the flying stones and sand, and the awful noise, confounded me. As the high watery walls came rolling in, and, at their highest, tumbled into surf, they looked as if the least would engulf the town. As the receding wave swept back with a hoarse roar, it seemed to scoop out deep caves in the beach, as if its purpose were to undermine the earth. When some white-headed billows thundered on, and dashed themselves to pieces before they reached the land, every fragment of the late whole seemed possessed by the full might of its wrath, rushing to be gathered to the composition of another monster. Undulating hills were changed to valleys, undulating valleys (with a solitary storm-bird sometimes skimming through them) were lifted up to hills; masses of water shivered and shook the beach with a booming sound; every shape tumultuously rolled on, as soon as made, to change its shape and place, and beat another shape and place away; the ideal shore on the horizon, with its towers and buildings, rose and fell; the clouds flew fast and thick; I SAW A RENDING AND UPHEAVING OF ALL NATURE EVERYWHERE.

In describing the shipwreck, he increases the effect of terror by deliberately centring it on a particular and immediate danger and he consciously introduces a new effect, that of pity:

One mast was broken short off, six or eight feet from the deck, and lay over the side, entangled in a maze of sail and rigging; and all that ruin, as the ship rolled and beat—which she did without a moment's pause, and with a violence quite inconceivable—beat the side as if it would stave it in. Some efforts were even then being made, to cut this portion of the wreck away; for, as the ship, which was broadside on, turned towards us in her rolling, I descried her people at work with axes, especially one active figure with long curling hair, conspicuous among the rest. But, a GREAT cry, which was audible even above the wind and water, rose from the shore at this moment; for the sea, sweeping over the rolling wreck, made a clean breach, and carried men, spars, casks, planks, bulwarks, HEAPS OF SUCH TOYS, into the boiling surge.

The second mast was yet standing, with the rags of a rent sail, AND A WILD CONFUSION OF BROKEN CORDAGE flapping to and fro. The ship had struck once, the same boatman hoarsely said in my ear, and then lifted in and struck again. I understood

him to add that she was parting amidships, and I could readily
suppose so, for the rolling and beating were too tremendous for
any human work to suffer long. As he spoke, there was another
great cry ⟨from the beach fo⟩ OF PITY FROM THE BEACH;
FOR four men arose with the wreck out of the deep, clinging to the
rigging of the remaining mast; uppermost, the active figure with
the curling hair.

There was a bell on board; and as the ship rolled and dashed,
like a desperate creature driven mad, now showing us the whole
sweep of her deck, as she ⟨–?–⟩ turned on her beam-ends towards
the shore, now nothing but her keel, as she sprang wildly over and
turned towards the sea, the bell rang; and its sound, the knell of
those unhappy men, was borne towards us on the wind. Again we
lost her, and again she rose. Two men were gone. The agony on
shore increased. Men groaned, and clasped their hands; women
shrieked, and turned away their faces. Some ran wildly up and
down along the beach, crying for help where no help could be. I
found myself one of these, frantically imploring a knot of sailors
whom I knew, not to let those three lost creatures perish before
our eyes . . .

The wreck, even to my unpractised eye, was breaking up. I
saw that she was parting in the middle, and that the life of the
solitary man upon the mast hung by a thread. Still, he clung to it.
He had a singular red cap on,—not like a sailor's cap, but of a
finer colour; and as the few yielding planks between him and
destruction rolled and ⟨rolled⟩ BULGED, and his anticipative
death-knell rung, he was seen by all of us to wave it. I saw him
do it now, and thought I was going distracted, when his action
brought an old remembrance to my mind of a once dear friend.

How consciously Dickens is working for the effect of pity here
can be seen when he qualifies his reference to the second
great cry from the crowd on the beach by the phrase 'of pity'.
Other revisions show that he deliberately increases the effect
of terror. The tempest reduces men, casks, spars, and other
wreckage to mere 'heaps of such toys' in its dreadful play. In
addition to a tattered sail, 'a wild confusion of broken cordage'
is flapping about. The few planks between the last man and
destruction not only 'rolled' but also 'bulged' ominously.
Pity and terror are also nicely and deliberately balanced at
the conclusion of the chapter:

A fisherman, who had known me when Emily and I were
children, and ever since, whispered my name at the door.

"Sir", said he, with tears starting to his weather-beaten face, WHICH, WITH HIS TREMBLING LIPS, WAS ASHY PALE, "will you come over yonder?"

The old remembrance that had been recalled to me, was in his look. I asked him, TERROR-STRICKEN, leaning on the arm he held out to support me:

"Has a body come ashore?"

He said, "Yes."

"Do I know it?" I asked then.

He answered nothing.

But, he led me to the shore. And on that part of it where she and I had looked for shells, two children—on that part of it where some lighter fragments of the old boat, blown down last night, had been scattered by the wind—among the ruins of the home he had ⟨made desolate⟩ WRONGED—I saw him lying with his head upon his arm, as I had often seen him lie at school.

There is a further effect in this conclusion. It has been argued that the washing up of Steerforth's body among the ruins of the home he has wronged is an instance of Dickens's use of coincidence at its worst.[1] Yet, in my view, this is not coincidence at all, for behind the appearance of chance is the reality of design. The apt irony of this retribution implies fate —a divine providence at work. The incident has, in fact, been carefully prepared through structural irony. The manner of Steerforth's punishment is most apt; in committing his offence, he has misused the sea and his interest in boats and sailing and he is punished through the sea in a shipwreck. Again, we are told that he is spending his time cruising, after his desertion of Em'ly.[2] The precise shape which Steerforth's death will assume has also been carefully foreshadowed twice.[3] During that first fatal meeting between Steerforth and Em'ly we learn that: 'Steerforth told a story of a DISMAL shipwreck (which arose out of his talk with Mr. Peggotty), as if he saw it all before him—and little Em'ly's eyes were fastened on him all the time, as if she saw it too.' The insertion of 'dismal' in the manuscript shows with what conscious irony Dickens was preparing Steerforth's fate. There is a

[1] For example, George Gissing, *Charles Dickens*, p. 62.

[2] See above, p. 248; *DC*, Chap. XLVI, p. 672.

[3] Original MS, of *DC*, Vol. IB, Chap. XXI, p. 26; cf. *DC*, p. 316. Ibid., Chap. XLVI, pp. 673-4.

second ominous hint during David's final interview with Mrs. Steerforth and Rosa Dartle before the catastrophe:

As I moved away from them along the terrace, I could not help observing how steadily they both sat gazing on the prospect, and how it thickened and closed around them. . . . a mist was rising like a sea, which mingling with the darkness, made it seem as if the gathering waters would encompass them. I have reason to remember this, and think of it with awe; for before I looked upon those two again, a stormy sea had risen to their feet.

Unless we grasp and accept the element of divine intervention in Steerforth's fate, much significant detail in the shipwreck scene and the real terror of the storm is lost upon us. In his description of the 'tremendous sea' Dickens carefully stresses that it represents a cosmic force let loose ('a rending and upheaving of all nature everywhere'). The stormy sea and inundation are potent archetypal symbols of the catastrophe engineered by cosmic powers. In dream and myth, the overwhelming ocean or flood frequently represents divine retribution or the reaction of the offended forces of Nature.[1] Significantly, Dickens insists that the waves 'looked as if the least would engulf the town' and adds about each receding wave that it seemed 'as if its purpose were to undermine the earth'. That Dickens thought of Steerforth's fate as brought about by a cosmic will is confirmed by a sentence which occurs at the beginning of the following chapter in the manuscript and one set of corrected proofs but was deleted in a second set and is omitted in the first edition. The men carrying Steerforth's body, covered with a flag, hesitate to lay him in the same room as Ham:

They felt as if it were not right to lay him down in the same quiet room. ⟨While I tried to consider what it would be best to do, the wind plucked at the flag, as if it were eager to get underneath and see its work.⟩[2]

In discussing Dickens's tragic vision, perhaps we need to use something like the distinction which Northrop Frye makes

[1] Genesis, 6:5–7, 17. The tribulations which Odysseus endured at the hands of an angry ocean resulted from his offending the sea-god, Poseidon, *Odyssey*, bk. i. Cf. C. G. Jung, *Psychological Types*, pp. 326–8.

[2] Original MS. of *DC*, Vol. IIB, Chap. LVI, p. 19, corrected proofs of *DC*, Chap. LVI, p. 565; cf. *DC*, p. 796.

between 'high' and 'low mimetic tragedy'. Dickens's tragedy usually stands somewhere between high tragedy and the journalistic use of the term. The subjects of his tragedy are such as we might find described at length in the newspapers of his own time: a shipwreck, a fatal accident, a murder, a trial on a capital charge.[1] Certainly, Dickens often presents tragedy as public spectacle. Nevertheless, his tragic vision has some of the characteristics of high tragedy. At times he uses the spectator's reaction to a situation as a means of conveying tragic emotion, thus involving the reader in an almost dramatic experience that lends the effect some of the theatre's intensity. This device, a parallel to the use of the chorus in classical tragedy, can be seen in its most effective form during the shipwreck scene in *David Copperfield*. Dickens also succeeds, here, in conveying a tragic impression of waste. When Steerforth is cast up on the hearth whose gods he has offended,[2] his posture in death recalls the hero of David's schooldays.

5. *Comedy*

The range of Dickens's comedy is extremely wide. It includes farce, burlesque, parody, the mock-heroic, bathos, satire, the comedy of humours, the comedy of manners, and 'high' comedy. Of course, these comic forms sometimes overlap. This apart, the reason why such a profuse mixture does not usually result in a fragmentation of Dickens's comic vision can be found, I believe, in the complex unity of effect and direction which all his comic forms tend to preserve. Dickens's comedy is very frequently ironic and critical; it is almost invariably full of life and often sympathetic in other ways.

Even farce is by no means always used for its own sake.

[1] Northrop Frye, op. cit., pp. 37–40; Frye insists that no value-judgement is implied in his distinction. Accounts of such episodes tended to be much fuller in the Victorian press than in today's newspapers and they often aimed at a tragic impression; the boasted objectivity of our journalism may well be a case of having 'supp'd full with horrors'.

[2] Like the Romans, whom they resembled in so many other ways, the Victorians experienced a feeling of sanctity about the home; the other side to this particular picture should not blind us to the authenticity of this feeling. See also Houghton, op. cit., pp. 341–8.

True, instances of pure farce do occur, particularly in the earlier fiction. Winkle, for example, is locked out of his lodgings in his night attire and mistakenly supposed by an irate husband to be eloping with his wife. During a scuffle, Fagin hurls a pot of beer at Charley Bates but its contents drench Bill Sikes. Moments of pure farce survive as late as *Our Mutual Friend*, yet they remain moments. When the Lammles depart for their honeymoon, a servant is struck on the head by a heavy flying shoe. On the other hand, much of Dickens's earliest farce does have some sense of direction. The farcical adventures of the Pickwickians during the field day, for instance, are part of the mock-heroic vein which runs through the book. The farcical episodes of Winkle's horsemanship and his skating at Dingley Dell ironically deflate his sporting pretensions. The criticism, here, is mild enough but the sense of direction becomes much more pronounced in the later novels. The farcical events during Flora Finching's wedding and honeymoon deflate her romantic pretensions with a keen irony. As Dickens's art develops, farce frequently becomes an instrument of satire. Thus, General Fladdock's inglorious entrance is but one incident in the American satire of *Martin Chuzzlewit*, a satire which aims at exposing the ironic contrast between transatlantic delusions of grandeur and the truth about the United States (as Dickens sees it). The satirical use of farce in the later novels may be more subtle. Dinner at Mrs. Jellyby's degenerates into a farce since this is precisely what Mrs. Jellyby's neglect has reduced her household to. Against the confusion of domestic slapstick, Dickens ironically sets Mrs. Jellyby's serene unconcern for her own home and her fanatical preoccupation with 'two hundred healthy families cultivating coffee and educating the natives' in Africa:

All through dinner; which was long, in consequence of such accidents as the dish of potatoes being mislaid in the coal scuttle, and the handle of the corkscrew coming off, and striking the young woman in the chin; Mrs. Jellyby preserved the evenness of her disposition. She told us a great deal that was interesting about Borrioboola-Gha and the natives; and received so many letters that Richard, who sat by her, saw four envelopes in the gravy at once.

Again, the superior pose which Young Barnacle affects through the wearing of an eye-glass comes to grief, ironically enough, through the monocle's behaviour:

He had a superior eye-glass dangling round his neck, but un-unfortunately had such flat orbits to his eyes, and such limp little eyelids, that it wouldn't stick in when he put it up, but kept tumbling out against his waistcoat buttons with a click that discomposed him very much . . . He was under a pressing and continual necessity of looking at that gentleman, which occasioned his eye-glass to get into his soup, into his wine-glass, into Mrs. Meagles' plate, to hang down his back like a bell-rope, and be several times disgracefully restored to his bosom by one of the dingy men. Weakened in mind by his frequent losses of this instrument, and its determination not to stick in his eye, and more and more enfeebled in intellect every time he looked at the mysterious Clennam, he applied spoons to his eye, forks, and other foreign matters connected with the furniture of the dinner-table.

It is particularly appropriate to make Young Barnacle a farcical figure. He and his class are reducing the nation's political and administrative life to Circumlocution, to a fruitless slapstick in which the logical chain of cause and effect that should ensure the dispatch of the nation's business has been broken.[1]

Parody and burlesque also offered Dickens opportunities for both irony and direction. The aping of others, in word or deed, may result in a discrepancy between what is mimicked and the mimicry that can be used as an instrument of comedy or a weapon of satire. Certainly Dickens was conscious of burlesque as a comic form and of its ironic possibilities:

. . . a man in a broad-skirted green coat, with corduroy knee smalls and grey cotton stockings, was performing the most popular steps of a hornpipe, with a slang and burlesque caricature of grace and lightness, which, combined with the very appropriate character of his costume, was inexpressibly absurd.

[1] *PP*, Chap. XXXVI, pp. 514–16; *OT*, Chap. XIII, p. 85; *OMF*, Bk. I, Chap. X, p. 122; *PP*, Chaps. IV, V, XXX, pp. 46–50, 60–2, 411–12; *LD*, Bk. I, Chap. XXIV, p. 285; *MC*, Chap. XVII, pp. 288–9; *BH*, Chap. IV, p. 40; *LD*, Bk. I, Chaps. X, XVII, pp. 108, 208.

Sometimes, the burlesque has little direction. Thus, an Inspector of Police may be seen in a whimsical moment as an abbot. At other times, the underprivileged may enrich the social comedy by directing their burlesque against the privileged. On being scolded by his mistress, a boy servant mimics penitent actions. When two of the commercial gentlemen at Todgers's take down the Pecksniff girls to supper, their disappointed colleagues follow them in pairs, one gentleman of each couple miming the part of a lady. On the other hand, burlesque may be frankly satirical as when the servants at the soirée in Bath are shown as aping their masters' manners in a way which Sam Weller finds ridiculous. The way in which children burlesque their elders provides a rich source of irony. Thus, Bartholomew Smallweed represents the absurd pretensions of the adolescent who in trying to be adult only reminds us all the more clearly that he is an adolescent. The burlesque may be given a social orientation. Thus, the Artful Dodger, Fagin's other boys, and Charley Neckett draw attention to the social conditions which forced children to become adults before their time. Burlesque may even bring the critically ironic vision of a novel to one of its sharpest points of focus as when Trabb's boy mimics the snobbish Pip to his face on his return to his home town. Occasionally, burlesque attains the stature of 'high' comedy. Such is the case with Guppy's performance as Esther's would-be lover. During his first proposal to Esther, Dickens anatomizes the lawyer's clerk, making us aware of the ironic contradiction between his ardent romantic posture and preoccupation with sordid, material interests. The squalid reality is only completely exposed, however, when Esther reveals her disfigurement. The extensive passages added to this scene in proof show how deliberately the irony in Guppy's lively embarrassment is exploited to the full. The first interpolation (' "A kind of a giddy sensation . . . into the corner behind him" ') draws attention to Guppy's extreme state of shock and thus exposes all the more forcefully the completely physical nature of his regard for Esther. A second passage which was added (' "I am bound to confess . . . the present proceedings" ') shows Guppy performing a complete *volte-face* in his attitude towards Esther, eagerly approving of her

request that he stop trying to serve her by making inquiries
into her history. In an even longer interpolation (' "I beg
your pardon, miss . . . Much obliged" '), the extreme shod-
diness of Guppy's attitude, with its materialistic and legal
approach to a human relationship, is brought home when he
gets Esther to repeat in front of a witness that there has never
been a promise of marriage. The final interpolation ('but
when we last looked back, Mr. Guppy was still oscillating in
the same troubled state of mind') adds an effective 'curtain'
to the scene. It recalls Guppy's former romantic posture (now
a source of embarrassment) and sets it beside his present
concern with avoiding any action for breach of promise. Our
awareness that there is no foundation for Guppy's anxiety
lends the burlesque a further irony.[1]

Sometimes, Dickens's use of parody has little point to it.
His brief skit on the pastoral style in *Dombey and Son* is an
example. Occasionally, the irony in his parody is managed
somewhat crudely. A servant, for instance, affects genteel
speech at the soirée in Bath but betrays himself by putting
his 'h's' in the wrong places. Parody, however, may well be an
instrument of the highest comedy. Thus, a parody of the
unrequited lover's agonized sentiments forms part of Guppy's
romantic posture. The ghastly parody to which Chadband
reduces Biblical language is examined critically through an
ironic contrast between the lofty poetic phrases and the low
occasions on which they are squandered. The device of
parallelism enables Dickens to deflate Chadband's preten-
tiousness with frequent anticlimax. A shrewd deletion in the
manuscript shows Dickens consciously ensuring bathos: 'you
are to us a pearl, you are to us a diamond, you are to us a
gem, you are to us a jewel ⟨of price⟩'.[2]

Dickens uses bathos very often, frequently in association
with the mock-heroic. True, he can use mock-heroic ideas
without critical purpose, as when he refers to 'Wilfer Castle'.

[1] *PP*, Chap. XLI, p. 580; *OMF*, Bk. I, Chap. III, p. 24; *MC*, Chaps. XI,
IX, pp. 172, 145; *PP*, Chap. XXXVII, pp. 520–7; *BH*, Chap. XX, pp. 274–5;
OT, Chap. VIII, pp. 53, 56–7; *BH*, Chap. XV, pp. 209–10; *GE*, Chap. XXX,
p. 232; *BH*, Chap. IX, pp. 122–6. Corrected proofs of *BH*, Chap. XXXVIII,
pp. 382–4; cf. *BH*, pp. 542–6.
[2] *D & S*, Chap. LX, p. 852; *PP*, Chap. XXXVII, p. 523; *BH*, Chap. IX,
p. 125. Original MS. of *BH*, Vol. IB, Chap. XIX, p. 30; cf. *BH*, p. 269.

On the other hand, the mock-heroic idea may be given critical direction through being coupled with bathos:

Mrs. Pott, who would have looked very like Apollo if she hadn't had a gown on: conducted by Mr. Winkle, who in his light-red coat, could not possibly have been mistaken for anything but a sportsman, if he had not borne an equal resemblance to a general postman.[1]

Bathos is particularly effective in dealing with the pretentious and the pompous. Dickens makes critical comedy out of the inquest in *Bleak House* by ironically contrasting the masquerade of judicial forms with the trivial and squalid details of a parochial setting. The revisions in the manuscript show an almost Augustan care for 'the art of sinking':

At the appointed hour arrives the Coroner, for whom the Jury-men are waiting, ⟨in the first floor apartment⟩ AND WHO IS RECEIVED WITH A SALUTE OF SKITTLES FROM THE GOOD DRY SKITTLE-GROUND ATTACHED TO THE SOL'S ARMS. The Coroner frequents more public-houses than any man alive. The smell of sawdust, beer, tobacco-smoke, and spirits, is inseparable in his vocation from death in its most awful shapes this being another aspect of the wisdom to which we are indebted for our Chancery and many other blessings. He is conducted by the beadle and the landlord to the Harmonic Meeting Room, where he puts his hat on the piano, and takes a Windsor-chair at the head of a long table, formed of several short tables put together, and ⟨covered with glutinous rings in involutions⟩ ORNAMENTED WITH GLUTINOUS RINGS IN ENDLESS INVOLUTIONS, made by pots and glasses. As many of the Jury as can crowd together at the table sit there. The rest get among the spittoons and pipes, or lean against the piano. Over the Coroner's head is A SMALL IRON GARLAND, the pendant handle of a bell, which rather gives the Majesty of the Court the appearance of going to be hanged presently . . . Mr. Tulkinghorn is received with distinction, and seated near the Coroner; between that high judicial officer, A BAGATELLE-BOARD, and the coal-box.[2]

Dickens's satire uses irony as its general method of attack and, as he matures, it gains in power and becomes more

[1] *OMF*, Bk. III, Chap. XVI, p. 610; *PP*, Chap. XV, p. 200.
[2] Original MS. of *BH*, Vol. IA, Chap. XI, pp. 6–7 ('this . . . blessings' deleted in proof); cf. *BH*, pp. 145–7.

ambitious in direction. At first, as in *Pickwick*, he aims at
scattered targets, like the postures adopted by lawyers and
judges, nonconformist ministers, and newspaper editors and
the satire remains peripheral. Later, the satire comes to
occupy a much more central position in a novel's grand
design and is organized into an effective unity. The power
which the satire of *Bleak House* gains through its unity and
central position is particularly impressive. The charade of
justice, the reactionary delusions of members of the ruling
class like Lord Boodle and Sir Leicester Dedlock, the divine
right of Coodle and Doodle to govern England, the irrelevant
philanthropy of do-gooders like Mrs. Jellyby and Mrs. Pardiggle, the general air of unreality in which the upper and
middle classes live are all shown to contribute to 'the condition of England' and are castigated with a vigorous satirical
irony. How this irony works can be seen in a neat summary of
the national disgrace which Chancery has become:

To see everything going on so smoothly, and to think of the
roughness of the suitors' lives and deaths; to see all that full
dress and ceremony, and to think of the waste, and want, and
beggared misery it represented; to consider that, while the sickness of hope deferred was raging in so many hearts, this polite
show went calmly on from day to day, and year to year, in such
good order and composure; to behold the Lord Chancellor, and the
whole array of practitioners under him, looking at one another and
at the spectators, as if nobody had ever heard that all over England the name in which they were assembled was a bitter jest: was
held in universal horror, contempt, and indignation: was known
for something so flagrant and bad, that little short of a miracle
could bring any good out of it to any one: this was so curious and
self-contradictory to me, who had no experience of it, that it was
at first incredible, and I could not comprehend it. I sat where
Richard put me, and tried to listen, and looked about me; but
there seemed to be no reality in the whole scene, except poor
little Miss Flite, the madwoman, standing on a bench, and nodding
at it.[1]

It is often not easy to distinguish satire, the comedy of
manners, the comedy of humours, and 'high' comedy in Dickens's

[1] *BH*, Chaps. XII, XL, IV, VIII, XII, pp. 160-1, 164, 562, 36-45, 99-110,
161-2; Chap. XXIV, pp. 344-5.

fiction, so successfully does he blend two or more of these
forms into a rich amalgam. Irony and a critical sense of
direction, usually present in all these forms, help to make
this union a particularly close one. On the other hand,
satire may oust the higher forms of comedy altogether, as in
the American scenes of *Martin Chuzzlewit*, or satirical elements and the general comedy may not be fully integrated in
a harmonious whole. Satire in Dickens's fiction appears more
satisfying when it is successfully mixed with true comedy;
when it occurs alone or is too dominant, the critical note is
apt to appear strident and the irony cold and calculating.
Comedy proper contributes an element of sympathy. Even
such masterpieces of satirical art as Mrs. Jellyby and Mrs.
Pardiggle are not so satisfying as Guppy (who does, of course,
have his satirical aspect as the petty lawyer's clerk trying to
make his influence felt in high society and seeking to marry
above himself). In Mrs. Jellyby and Mrs. Pardiggle's effect on
us, we can detect a faint suspicion of irritation which has not
been assimilated aesthetically. Guppy, however, never ceases
to delight us. But, then, Dickens had known in his youth what
it was to be a lawyer's clerk, to hope and strive for a better
future, and to dream of marrying above himself only to be
rejected. It is not surprising that he is able to communicate
to the reader his own deep-seated sympathy with Guppy.
Thus, even though Guppy may appear vulgar when he says
he cannot face the food in front of him during his first proposal to Esther, he only expresses what we all feel, and sympathize with, on such occasions.[1]

Winkle, Snodgrass, and Tupman provide a very simple
version of the comedy of humours. The type of simple characterization involved here presents the mask or *persona* in its
most rudimentary form. In such a comedy, irony results when
a disaster shatters the *persona*, thus revealing that this was
the complete personality. For example, Tupman fails as a
lover and collapses as a character. Bumble ceases to be really
Bumble after his defeat by his wife and his public humiliation.
On the other hand, Winkle can be repeatedly shown up as an
inadequate sportsman only because there are several kinds of
sport which he can take up and the comic catastrophes, here,

[1] *BH.*, Chap. IX, p. 125.

are not as disastrous as those which involve love or social status. In less simple forms of the comedy of humours, the *persona* may become complex as it does in characters like Pecksniff or Micawber. In such cases, irony results from the contradiction between the mask and the inner life. Exposure, here, does not involve a collapse of the character.

One of the most consistent factors in Dickens's comedy is a structure with the ironic pattern also found in his tragedy and melodrama. Though not inherently comic therefore, this pattern helps to articulate the moral vision in Dickens's comedy and explains some of its ironic power. The manuscripts show how deliberately Dickens exploited this pattern of structural irony in some of his very successful comic scenes.

The episode in which Bumble is trounced and then publicly humiliated by his wife[1] is based upon two archetypal comic situations. The man with great matrimonial expectations discovers that marriage is a dingy trap. He tries to make a stand against the wife but is soundly trounced. A rich source of music-hall humour, these situations also occur in infinite variety in the comic postcard. Yet the power and sense of direction of Dickens's scene does not derive so much from the basic situations as from the ironic pattern imposed on these situations and the social and moral vision focused through structure and its effect. Bumble's defeat is not simply a domestic set-back. A significant emendation in the manuscript stresses that it is Bumble's dignity which is at stake. A dignity, however, which rests upon fancy dress, a personality which seeks its only meaning in outward forms, is not only highly vulnerable but also masks a great void and risks a total collapse:

There are some promotions in life, which, independent of the more substantial rewards they offer, acquire peculiar value and ⟨importance⟩ DIGNITY from the coats and waistcoats connected

[1] Original MS. of *OT*, Victoria and Albert Museum, Forster Collection, 47. A. 3 (Vol. IIA), Bk. II, Chap. XIV, pp. 28 (from *Bentley's Miscellany* onwards the text omits 'Promote . . . multitude' and from the 1846 edition onwards the text reads 'beadle of his hat and lace'), 30–1 (the passage was replaced by ' "Mrs. Bumble, ma'am!" said Mr. Bumble, with sentimental sternness'), 36 (the passage occurs between 'full possession of the field' and 'Mr. Bumble was fairly taken by surprise'); cf. *OT*, Chap. XXXVII, pp. 267–70.

with them. A field-marshal has his uniform; a bishop his silk apron; a counsellor his silk gown; a beadle his cocked hat. Strip the bishop of his apron, or the beadle of his cocked hat and gold lace; what are they? Men. Mere men. Promote them, raise them to higher and different offices in the state; and divested of their black silk aprons and cocked hats they shall still lack their old dignity and be somewhat shorn of their influence with the multitude. Dignity, and even holiness too, sometimes, are more questions of coat and waistcoat than some people imagine.

Bumble is given a general significance, here. He becomes a comic cipher for the England which bases its authority on fancy dress, an England which in this respect is briefly glimpsed as Bumbledom writ large. By being promoted master of the workhouse, Bumble has sought an increase in his authority and already, ironically enough, he feels his dignity seriously weakened. Yet Bumble's fall is complicated by a further factor. The beadle had hardly married for love but he had expected a peaceful domestic life, as a passage in the manuscript, which was not printed, makes particularly clear:

"Is that"—said Mr. Bumble with sentimental sternness "is that the voice as called me a irresistible duck in the small one-pair? Is that the creetur that was all meekness, mildness, and sensibility?"

"It is indeed, worse luck"—replied his helpmate; "not much of sensibility though, or I should have had more sense than to make the sacrifice I did."

"The sacrifice Mrs. Bumble?"—said the gentleman with great asperity.

"You may well repeat the word" rejoined the lady "It ought to be never out of my mouth gracious knows."

"I am not aware that it ever is Ma'am"—retorted Mr. Bumble. "It's always coming out of your mouth Ma'am, but is always there. Mrs. Bumble, Ma'am."

The present scene is, therefore, linked again to Bumble's past. Bumble has acquired a termagant for wife and, ironically enough, he had believed he was getting a perfect lamb. Again, the invective of the disgruntled couple consists of commonplaces of comic marital recrimination which yet have a subtle well-directed irony here. Repeatedly in the novel

Dickens makes it clear that Bumbledom is the creation of an acquisitive society. The marriage of Mrs. Corney and the beadle represents the final degradation of such a society. The institution which should express the consummation and stability of human love is reduced to a squalid financial manœuvre:

"The Board allow you coals, don't they, Mrs. Corney?" affectionately inquired the beadle, pressing her hand.
"And candles," replied Mrs. Corney, slightly returning the pressure.
"Coals, candles, and house-rent free," said Mr. Bumble. "Oh, Mrs. Corney, what a angel you are!"
⟨"Don't!" remonstrated Mrs. Corney.
"Don't!" cried the Beadle "I must; I can't help it. Love Mrs. Corney can't be⟩
The lady was not proof against this burst of feeling.[1]

The ironic vision and its critical sense of direction are made clearer by the deletion in the manuscript, since the references to Bumble's overpowering passion and the perks he will gain are more sharply juxtaposed. When the cash nexus has become substituted for human relationships, all values will tend to be restricted to the financial meaning of the term. Yet human values will not be denied in the long run:

"I sold myself," said Mr. Bumble, pursuing the same train of reflection, "for six teaspoons, a pair of sugar-tongs, and a milk-pot; with a small quantity of second-hand furniture, and twenty pound in money. I went very reasonable. Cheap, dirt cheap!"
"Cheap!" cried a shrill voice in Mr. Bumble's ear: 'You would have been dear at any price; and dear enough I paid for you, Lord above knows that!"

'Sold' and 'paid', 'cheap' and 'dear' are loaded with a double meaning, for, although Mr. Bumble had calculated in financial terms, the final cost is counted in human terms. Again, Mrs. Bumble knows nothing of love yet the word she repeatedly uses, 'sacrifice', belongs to the language of love.

No doubt a man's physical subjection by his wife is a huge

[1] Original MS. of *OT*, Vol. IA, Bk. II, Chap. V, pp. 38–9; cf. *OT*, Chap. XXVII, p. 199.

joke which involves the inversion of normal roles. Yet Bumble's case is not simply knockabout humour since the comedy has effective shape and direction. Bumble's castigation is precipitated by trying to assert what he believes to be his superior masculine authority and he does enjoy a moment of apparent triumph and hubristic swagger as Mrs. Bumble dissolves into tears:

> Mr. Bumble took his hat from a peg, and putting it on, rather rakishly, on one side, as a man might, who felt he had asserted his superiority in a becoming manner, thrust his hands into his pockets, and sauntered towards the door, with much ease and waggishness depicted in his whole appearance.

That Bumble's defeat is not merely physical but has ironic and moral significance is made clear in another passage of the manuscript which was not printed:

> "I couldn't have believed it" said Mr. Bumble as he crawled down the passage arranging his disordered dress "She didn't seem one of that sort at all. If the paupers knew of this, I should be a parochial bye-word."

This passage may have been meant to link Bumble's private and public humiliations and to stress that both episodes are part of the same ironic fate. The passage was almost certainly cut because the idea in the final sentence is immediately realized. Irony attains its sharpest edge in Bumble's decisive humiliation in front of the paupers he has terrorized so long. Bumble's offences are essentially public ones. His vulnerability lies in public exposure. The *lex talionis* demands with an apt irony that abuse of parochial authority should be redressed by parochial humiliation.

The henpecked Jack-in-office is a particularly suitable culprit for public exposure. So is the hypocrite whose secret misdeeds have inflicted extensive social harm. Casby is not simply a blood-sucking landlord. He represents that unholy alliance between outward respectability and ruthless acquisitiveness which disfigured Victorian affluence and helped to keep the richest society the world had ever known chained to a hell of misery and squalor. Dickens correctly sees Casby's *persona* as the people's deadliest enemy. The poor are not

simply being cruelly exploited; they are being duped by
their exploiters about who is really responsible, a much more
complex situation. The weapon Dickens launches against
Casby is not indignation alone but a scathing irony. Only the
exposure of the patriarchal pose can begin to break the
exploiter's power. Truth must be the spearhead of the assault
on social evil. Dickens attacks something more fundamental
than the system of rack-rent or its landlords. He attacks the
deception which allows such evil to spawn and flourish in a
dark corner of society. This explains the precise form of
Casby's public exposure:

He appeared to be meditating some Patriarchal way out of his
⟨difficult⟩ DELICATE position, when Mr. Pancks, once more
suddenly applying the trigger to his hat, shot it off again with his
former dexterity. On the preceding occasion, one or two of the
Bleeding Heart Yarders had obsequiously picked it up and handed
it to its owner; but, Mr. Pancks had now so far impressed his
audience, that the Patriarch had to TURN AND stoop for it
himself.

Quick as lightning, Mr. Pancks, who, for some moments, had
had his right hand in his coat pocket, whipped out a pair of
shears, swooped upon the Patriarch behind, and snipped off ⟨his⟩
SHORT THE sacred locks ⟨all round⟩ that ⟨fell⟩ FLOWED
upon his shoulders. In a paroxysm of animosity and rapidity,
Mr. Pancks then caught the BROAD-BRIMMED hat out of the
ASTOUNDED Patriarch's hand, cut it down into a mere stewpan,
and fixed it on the Patriarch's head.

Before the frightful results of this desperate action, Mr. Pancks
himself recoiled in consternation. A ⟨–?–⟩ BARE-POLLED,
GOGGLE-EYED, big-headed, ⟨?blundering⟩ LUMBERING personage stood staring at him, not in the least impressive, not in the
least venerable, who seemed to have started out of the earth to ask
what was become of Casby . . . Mr. Pancks deemed it prudent to
use all possible dispatch in making off, though he was pursued by
nothing but the sound of laughter in Bleeding Heart Yard.[1]

As Dickens deliberately stresses by his revisions, Casby is
shorn of the venerable *persona* which constitutes his hypocritical relationship with society. His deceptive appearance

[1] Original MS, of *LD*, Vol. IIB, Bk. II, Chap. XXXII, pp. 26–7; cf. *LD*,
pp. 802–3.

is the means by which he has been able to offend against society. The *lex talionis* with its apt irony demands that his deceptive appearance be destroyed before the tenants he has deceived. The ironic justice in the manner of Casby's exposure directs our critical and moral attention to the grave social danger of a *persona* taken at its face value.

IX

THE NATURE OF VISION

1. *Complexity and Unity*

Two major characteristics of Dickens's vision help to blend its different modes in a complex unity.[1] One of these characteristics, the introverted quality of his vision, will be discussed in the next section. The other is a complex theme which dominates his vision and finds effective expression through the rhetoric of sympathy and irony.

This theme is a view of life as an ironic tragi-comedy of deception; often there is also a melodramatic element in this complex view. True, Dickens is less successful in blending the different elements of this vision in the earlier novels. In *Pickwick*, for example, deception is frequently explored as a comic—only occasionally as a tragic—idea, though the emergence of a tragi-comic vision largely accounts for the success of the episodes in the Fleet Prison. On the whole, Dickens shows increasing skill in combining the various elements of his vision as he matures. Thus, the compassionate and critical views of life embodied separately in Mr. Pickwick and Sam Weller are brought more closely together in *David Copperfield* and life, with its comedy and tragedy, pathos, and melodrama, is seen as a continuum of experience by being filtered through a single consciousness. The compassionate and ironic visions combine through the narrator's viewpoint as he looks back on his earlier naïvety and self-deception with feeling but also with the distance and hindsight which time provides. In *Great Expectations*, this complex kind of viewpoint is combined with a tightly organized plot which hinges on tragi-comic self-deception. The result is an extremely effective

---

[1] Complexity implies unity. *OED* defines the noun 'complex', as a 'complex or complicated whole', and the adjective as 'comprehending various parts united or connected together; ... composite, compound' and 'consisting of parts ... involved in various degrees of subordination'.

structural irony and pathos as the twists of fate find Pip
sadly and searchingly wanting. And around Pip are grouped
several characters with expectations, comic and tragic delusions, which also come to nothing.

On the other hand, the opening chapter of *Bleak House*, in
which Dickens uses omniscient viewpoint, shows how intimately he learned to combine the various modes of vision in a
view that has unity and yet does justice to different aspects
of an experience. Revisions in the manuscript stress his
deliberate use of the rhetoric of sympathy and irony to focus
a vision of Chancery with power and complexity:

On such an afternoon, if ever, the Lord High Chancellor ought
to be sitting here—as here he is—WITH A FOGGY GLORY
ROUND HIS HEAD, SOFTLY fenced in with crimson cloth and
curtains, addressed by a large advocate with great whiskers, a
little voice, and an interminable brief, and outwardly directing
his contemplation to the lantern in the roof, where he can see
nothing but fog. On such an afternoon, some score of members of
the High Court of Chancery bar ought to be—as here they are—
mistily engaged in one of the ten thousand stages of an endless
cause, tripping one another up on slippery precedents, groping
knee-deep in technicalities, running their goat-hair and horse-hair
warded heads against walls of words, and making a pretence of
equity with serious faces, as players might. On such an afternoon,
the various solicitors in the cause, some two or three of whom have
inherited it from their fathers, who made a fortune by it, ought to
be—as are they not?—ranged in a line, in a long matted well (but
you might look in vain for Truth at the bottom of it), between the
registrar's red table and the silk gowns, with bills, cross-bills,
answers, rejoinders, injunctions, affidavits, issues, references to
masters, masters' reports, mountains of nonsense, piled before
them. Well may the court be dim, with wasting candles here and
there; well may the fog hang heavily in it, as if it would never get
out; well may the stained glass windows lose their colour, and
admit no light of day into the place; well may the uninitiated
from the streets, who peep in through the glass panes in the door,
be deterred from entrance by its owlish aspect, and by the drawl
languidly echoing to the roof from the padded dais where the Lord
High Chancellor looks into the lantern that has no light in it, and
where the attendant wigs are all stuck in a fog-bank! This is the
Court of Chancery; which has its decaying houses and its blighted
lands in every shire; which has its worn-out lunatic in **every**

madhouse, AND ITS DEAD IN EVERY CHURCHYARD; which has its ruined suitor, ⟨begging and borrowing⟩ WITH HIS SLIPSHOD HEELS AND THREADBARE DRESS, BOR-ROWING AND BEGGING through the round of every man's acquaintance; which gives to monied might the means abundantly of wearying out the right; which so exhausts finances, patience, courage, hope; so overthrows the brain and breaks the heart; that there is not an honourable man among its practitioners who would not give—who does not often give—the warning, "Suffer any wrong that can be done you, rather than come here!"

Who happen to be in the Lord Chancellor's court this murky afternoon besides the Lord Chancellor, the counsel in the cause, two or three counsel who are never in any cause, and the well of solicitors before mentioned? There is the registrar below the Judge, in wig and gown; and there are two or three maces, or petty-bags, or privy-purses, or whatever they may be, in legal court suits. These are all yawning; FOR NO CRUMB OF AMUSE-MENT EVER FALLS FROM Jarndyce and Jarndyce (the cause in hand), which was squeezed dry years upon years ago. The short-hand writers, the reporters of the court, and the reporters of the newspapers, invariably decamp with the rest of the regu-lars when Jarndyce and Jarndyce comes on. Their places are a blank. Standing on a seat at the side of the hall, the better to peer into the curtained ⟨part⟩ SANCTUARY, is a little mad OLD woman IN A SQUEEZED BONNET, who is always in court, FROM ITS SITTING TO ITS RISING, and always expecting some ⟨indefinable⟩ INCOMPREHENSIBLE judgement to be given in her favour. Some say she really is, or was, a party to a suit; but no one ⟨knows⟩ KNOWS FOR CERTAIN, BECAUSE NO ONE CARES. She carries something in a reticule which she calls her documents; but they are principally consisting of paper matches and dry lavender. A SALLOW prisoner has come up, in custody, for the half-dozenth time, to make a personal application "to purge himself of his contempt"; which, being a solitary sur-viving executor who has fallen into a state of conglomeration about accounts of which he had ever any knowledge, he is not at all likely ever to do. In the meantime his prospects in life are ended. Another RUINED suitor, who periodically appears from Shropshire, and breaks out into efforts to address the Chancellor at the close of the day's business, and who can by no means be made to understand that the Chancellor is legally ignorant of his existence after making it desolate for a quarter of a century, plants himself in a good place and keeps an eye on the Judge,

ready to call out "My Lord!" IN A VOICE OF SONOROUS
COMPLAINT, on the instant of his rising. A few lawyers' clerks
and others who know this suitor by sight, linger, on the chance of
his furnishing some fun, and enlivening the dismal weather a
little.

Jarndyce and Jarndyce drones on. This scarecrow of a cause
has, in course of time, become so complicated, that no man
alive knows what it means. The parties to it understand it least;
but it has been observed that no two Chancery lawyers can talk
about it for five minutes, without coming to a total disagreement
as to all the premises. Innumerable children have been born into
the cause; innumerable young people have married into it;
innumerable old people have died out of it. Scores of persons have
deliriously found themselves made parties in Jarndyce and
Jarndyce, without knowing how or why; whole families have
inherited legendary hatreds with the suit. The little plaintiff or
defendant, who was promised a new rocking-horse when Jarndyce
and Jarndyce should be settled, has grown up, possessed himself
of a real horse, and ridden away into the other world. Fair wards
of court have ⟨become⟩ FADED INTO mothers and grandmothers; A LONG PROCESSION of Chancellors has come in
and gone out; the legion of bills in the suit have been transformed into mere bills of mortality; there are not three Jarndyces
left upon the earth perhaps, since old Tom Jarndyce ⟨cut his
throat⟩ in despair BLEW HIS BRAINS OUT AT A COFFEE-
HOUSE IN CHANCERY-LANE; but Jarndyce and Jarndyce
still drags its dreary length before the Court, perennially hopeless.

Jarndyce and Jarndyce has passed into a joke. That is the only
good that has ever come of it. It has been death to many, but it is
a joke in the profession.[1]

Dickens makes clear that the Court of Chancery is a mere
charade of justice. The irony in the deliberate deception
which is being practised is brought out in the description of
the lawyers. They are 'players' in costume, 'making a pretence
of equity with serious faces'. Their very wigs, which seek to
impress the court with the majesty of justice, are only a
ridiculous head-gear manufactured from the hair of goats and
horses. Their parade of legal argument is a solemn mockery.

[1] Original MS. of *BH*, Vol. IA, Chap. I, pp. 2–4 ('costly' inserted before
'nonsense' in proof, proofs read 'carries some small litter in', 'documents;
principally', 'accounts of which it is not pretended that he', 'scarecrow of a suit',
'and trotted away into the other world'); cf. *BH*. pp. 2–4.

This court of law is no more concerned with truth than with justice. The judge is preoccupied with maintaining a legal fiction rather than with acknowledging some awareness of a man he has helped to ruin. In the paragraph which follows this passage, we are even told that the court encourages 'trickery', 'evasion', and 'false pretences of all sorts'. 'Groping' and 'floundering' are an obvious consequence of deception. The fog symbolizes deception and self-deception as well as confusion. The presiding genius of deception and confusion is the Lord Chancellor, who wears 'a foggy glory round his head'; the word, 'glory', and the idea of a halo, normally associated with a very different context, are loaded with irony and it is interesting to note that the image was a happy second thought which shows Dickens using irony and symbolism together consciously.

The tragi-comic concept of Chancery is made clear enough in the final paragraph; elsewhere Dickens deliberately increases both the tragic and comic elements in his vision. In bringing Chancery's victims before our eyes, he deliberately emphasizes their wretched plight and shows us Chancery's effect on them, thus enlisting our pity for their tragically pathetic fates. To Chancery's toll of worn-out lunatics, he consciously adds the 'dead in every churchyard' and those reduced to 'slipshod heels and threadbare dress, borrowing and begging'. He goes further and shows us individual victims, the 'RUINED suitor from Shropshire', and 'a SALLOW prisoner' who has unwittingly committed contempt of court through a legal technicality. On the other hand, the victims are comic as well as tragically pathetic figures. Some spectators linger in the court in the hope of getting a laugh out of the man from Shropshire's behaviour. The insertion of the phrase, 'in a voice of sonorous complaint', makes Gridley's protest all the more ridiculous, for the dignity of his deep vibrant voice is to be outraged when the judge successfully evades him yet again. There is something cruelly absurd, too, about the predicament of the prisoner caught up in the Kafka-like idiocy of legal machinery. The comic situation also has a keen irony. Some of the victims are not only trapped in a web of deception but actively cling to it, trusting that the very court which has ruined them will somehow bring about their

salvation in the end. The tragic and comic visions coalesce
particularly well in the spectacle of Miss Flite. The poor little
deluded woman, who has grown 'old' and 'mad' in the course
of her obsession with Chancery and who never ceases to
haunt the court 'from its sitting to its rising', is viewed with
a conscious pathos and irony. Dickens brings out the irony all
the more sharply by describing the judgement Miss Flite
expects in her favour as 'incomprehensible' instead of 'in-
definable'. He provides an extra touch of comedy and pathos
by referring to the 'squeezed bonnet' and once more stresses
the irony and pathos in her situation by adding that, far from
her case being settled, no one either knows or cares what it is.

A strong element of farce is mixed with the general comedy
and satire. The lawyers' knockabout clowning with words and
arguments is matched by the suitors' buffoonery; Miss Flite's
'documents', for example, consist of matches and lavender,
the prisoner is in the habit of popping up, as absurdly as a
jack-in-the-box, to try to purge his contempt, Gridley waits
for his cue to pounce on the judge with his useless cry of
protest. The farce reaches its climax at the end of the chapter
when the judge forestalls Gridley by a dexterous disappearing
act. Of course, this farce has direction. It implies that the
whole proceedings are little better than a slapstick performance and thus helps to reinforce the impression of Chancery
as a charade of deception.

An element of sensation is also merged in the over-all vision,
for the account of Chancery's victims culminates in a scandalous suicide. Terror is increased through the addition of
circumstantial detail, which lends immediacy, when Dickens
substitutes 'blew his brains out at a coffee-house in Chancery
Lane' for 'cut his throat'. All the same, there is also a suggestion of farce in Tom Jarndyce's final desperate act.
Indeed, this is the tragedy of real life in which farce and
melodrama play a part and hysterical laughter relieves our
darkest distress and anxiety. Here, a kind of terror is also
associated with a grim ironic comedy. Dickens lays deliberate
stress on time as an agent of Chancery, thus lending his
vision of the cavalcade of whole generations a sense both of
relentlessness and of distance. Fair wards of court have not
'become' but 'faded into' mothers and grandmothers while

'a long procession' of Chancellors has passed on. Earlier, Dickens had pointed out that, by this time, 'no crumb of amusement ever falls' from the proceedings of Jarndyce and Jarndyce in court. It is a different matter when the case is viewed in a wider perspective. Dickens now follows up his tragi-comic panorama of the people involved in the interminable suit by insisting that it is simultaneously both 'death to many' and 'a joke'.

The way in which different modes are blended in a rich and complex over-all vision, here, points towards the achievement of Dickens's pupil, Dostoyevsky. Nevertheless, Dickens is not always so successful in combining different modes. One mode, like the dyer's hand, may turn all to its own complexion. As Kathleen Tillotson points out, Dickens allows the complex figure of Edith Dombey, which requires a naturalistic mode, to be drawn into the melodramatic sphere of Carker; she is thus 'not a tragic heroine, but a tragedy queen'. On the other hand, novels like *Bleak House* and *Little Dorrit* are marvels of complexity and power. Moreover, a study of significant revisions in the manuscript of, say, *Bleak House*, together with the author's notes for this novel, now published in their entirety, shows how deliberately Dickens worked for this power and complexity at almost every phase of planning and execution.[1] By examining the author's blueprint alongside his narrative practice, we catch glimpses of Dickens at the very moment when he is deliberately translating a complex vision, by means of a rhetoric itself complex, into the substance of a work of art.

Deception is a particularly fruitful theme for the novelist who wishes to give unity to his vision and, at the same time, wants to exploit the complexity and power which a combination of the various modes of vision and their associated

---

[1] See, for example, Marmaladov's drunken confession, or the scandalous appearance of Marmaladov's widow and children outside the General's residence after the funeral, Fyodor Dostoyevsky, *Crime and Punishment* (1866), pt. i, chap. ii, pt. v, chap. v; see also George H. Ford, *Dickens and His Readers*, pp. 193–6, for an account of Dickens's influence on Dostoyevsky. Kathleen Tillotson, *Novels of the Eighteen-Forties*, pp. 177–80. H. P. Sucksmith, 'Dickens at Work on *Bleak House*: A Critical Examination of His Memoranda and Number Plans', *Renaissance and Modern Studies*, ix (1965), 47–85; for my argument that the notes are mainly a plan for the novel rather than a résumé, see 48–52.

effects offer him. Deception provides rich material for irony; but it does more than this. Deception may lead to tragedy and to comedy and so it is also liable to involve terror, pathos, and the other types of sympathy.

The tragi-comedy may be both public and private. A truly comprehensive vision will include both. Thus, in *Bleak House*, a single though not a simple scrutiny explores a world of comic delusion among the ruling class, in their social, political, judicial, and philanthropic aspects, whose result is the contemporary 'condition of England', a national tragedy signified by the ugly painful farce of Chancery, by the squalid Brickmaker's family, the illiterate Jo, and the pestilent slum of Tom-all-Alone's. A note registers with satirical irony one delusive starting-point of this national tragi-comedy: 'No Govt. without Coodle or Doodle. Only two men in the country' (Chap. XL). On the other hand, Dickens shows how deception leads to tragedy and comedy in a more personal, less public sphere. Thus, we find the tragic irony of Richard's delusion, which is cured only at the point of final failure and death, and the comic irony of Guppy's self-deception, so very plain in the notes for his final offer to Esther: 'handsome proposal' (memoranda for Nos. XIX and XX); 'Mr. Guppy's magnanimity' (Chap. LXIV).

The complex vision must find a rhetoric which will communicate it to the reader. This rhetoric is suggested by two notes, which indicate the pathos of Richard's tragedy and the structural irony at work in his fate: 'The two Wards, the subjects of the unhappy story of Jarndyce and Jarndyce' (Chap. IV); 'The shadow of Miss Flite on Richard' (Chap. XXIV). It is those two words, 'unhappy' and 'shadow', which are so revealing and indicate the link between vision, structure, and a rhetoric of sympathy and irony.

Indeed, Dickens's notes reveal two instances in which both vision and rhetoric compelled him to modify original plans for the construction of *Bleak House*. Both concern the Dedlocks. Dickens's problem with the Dedlocks was that they had to fulfil a double function. The satirical vision required that, as typical members of the ruling class, they be anatomized with a cold irony, as they are in the early part of the novel. Yet the comprehensive vision, which sees the more private world of the Dedlocks in terms of a tragic irony and pathos, also required that, as individuals, they must be pitied as well as punished. While the novel was moving towards their catastrophe, then, a careful readjustment of sympathy towards the Dedlocks had to occur, if on the human level the reader was to be involved in their fate. The complexity of vision here is being built up throughout the course of their story.

The notes and manuscript show how conscious Dickens was of this process.[1] The readjustment of sympathy towards Sir Leicester Dedlock, for instance, is held over in the memoranda for No. XVI, 'Sir Leicester? Very little. *reserve for next time. Hold him in*', and begins in earnest in the following number. The outline for Chapter LIV carefully records a 'curtain' which, by emphasizing the husband's magnanimity as well as his distress, is calculated to earn our approval and awaken our pity: 'Sir Leicester swoons—compassionate and sorrowful. not angry.' This effect is deliberately strengthened by revisions in the manuscript. The human relationship between Sir Leicester and his wife is stressed. The verbal formula 'It is she', possibly a second thought, is repeated in a kind of counterpoint with the pronoun, 'he', thus subtly reflecting the concern for Lady Dedlock uppermost in her husband's mind. Yet the careful substitution in proof of 'almost to the exclusion of himself' for 'not himself' indicates the complexity of Sir Leicester's reaction to the shock, setting him up not as an unconvincing ideal of husbandly virtue but as an authentic human being whose genuine concern for another person is mixed with a little for himself in a moment of real crisis:

IT IS ⟨The woman⟩ SHE, in ⟨–?–⟩ ASSOCIATION with whom, saving that she has been ⟨a main part⟩ FOR YEARS ⟨THE⟩ A MAIN ⟨ROOT⟩ FIBRE OF THE ROOT of his dignity and pride, he has never had a selfish thought. It is she whom he has loved, admired, honoured, and set up for the world to respect. It is she,

---

[1] Original MS. of *BH*, Vol. IIB, Chap. LIV, p. 14 ('the' before 'main' altered to 'a' in proof), Chap. LVI, p. 26, Chap. LVIII, p. 14 ('through' altered to 'throughout' in proof, proofs read 'sleet and snow'), Vol. IA, Chap. II, p. A (proofs also read 'the fire', First Edition reads 'a fire'), corrected proofs of *BH*, Chap. LIV, p. 527; cf. *BH*, pp. 744, 761–2, 788, 9.

who, at the core of all the CONSTRAINED formalities and
conventionalities of his life, has been a stock of LIVING tenderness and love, susceptible as nothing else is of being struck with
the agony he feels. He sees her, ⟨not⟩ ALMOST TO THE EX-
CLUSION OF himself; and cannot bear to look upon her cast
DOWN from the high place she has graced so well.

Similarly, in the notes for Chapter LVI, the brief outline of
urgency and distress alone evokes our sympathy: 'Sir Leicester ill. To him, Mr. Bucket. "Save her"—Hurry in pursuit'.
Yet revisions in the manuscript reinforce the effect of tragic
pathos, which is mixed with suspense, and also draw attention to the irony in Sir Leicester's physical collapse that
suggests a spiritual fall too:

He fell down, this morning, a handsome stately gentleman;
somewhat infirm, but of a fine presence, and with a well-filled
face. He lies upon his bed, an aged man with sunken cheeks, the
decrepit shadow of himself. His voice was rich and mellow; and he
had so long been thoroughly persuaded of the weight and import
TO MANKIND of any word he said, that his words really had
come to sound as if there were something in them. But now he
can only whisper; and what he whispers sounds like what it is—
mere jumble and jargon . . .
He points again, IN GREAT AGITATION, at the two words.
They all try to quiet him, but he points again with increased
agitation. On their looking at one another, not knowing what to
say, he takes the slate once more, and writes, "My Lady. For
God's sake, where?" And makes aN ⟨terrible⟩ IMPLORING moan.

The proud reactionary voice with which Sir Leicester imagined
he made pronouncements of world-wide importance is exposed as a meaningless babble, and yet we feel for him in the
helplessness and distress of his personal tragedy.

The memoranda for No. XVIII show that Dickens considered narrating Lady Dedlock's pursuit entirely from
Esther's viewpoint: 'All Esther's Narrative? No.' His decision
not to do so is qualified by the reminder that suspense must
be maintained through the whole number: 'Pursuit interest
sustained throughout'. Clearly, a shift of viewpoint to a
different scene and characters, at the moment when Bucket
decides to return to London with his discovery hinted at but

still kept secret, 'Mr. Bucket⟨'s excitement⟩ "I have got it by the Lord!" ' (Chap. LVII), will keep the suspense at a high level of intensity. Yet Dickens reminds himself in his first entry for Chapter LVIII: '*Carry on suspense*'. The suspense can, in fact, only be carried on in this chapter through, and as it affects, Sir Leicester and may be exploited to create further sympathy for him, a complex effect of sympathy and suspense already beginning in the outline for Chapter LVI. This complex type of suspense should perhaps be contrasted with the more simple type, aiming at pure sensation, in the notes for Chapter LIX: 'Guster causes delay—"Bring her round somehow in the Lord's name!" '. Significantly, the viewpoint throughout Chapter LVIII repeatedly shifts to that of Sir Leicester, recording his anxiety at first hand, and revisions in one of these passages in the manuscript intensify the suspense and sympathy:

Sir Leicester lying in his bed can speak a little, though ⟨very indistinctly⟩ WITH DIFFICULTY AND INDISTINCTIVE-NESS. He is enjoined to silence and to rest, and they have given him some opiate to lull his pain; for his old enemy is very hard with him. He is never asleep, though sometimes he seems to fall into a dull waking doze. He caused his bedstead to be moved out nearer to the window, when he heard it was such inclement weather; and his head to be so adjusted, that he could see the ⟨falling⟩ DRIVING snow and sleet. He watches it as it falls, ⟨by the hour together⟩ THROUGH THE WHOLE WINTRY DAY.

Upon the least noise in the house, which is kept hushed, his hand is at the pencil. The old housekeeper, sitting by him, knows what he would write, and whispers "No, he has not come back yet, Sir Leicester. It was late last night when he went. He has been but a little time gone yet."

He withdraws his hand, and falls to looking at the sleet and snow again, until they seem, BY BEING LONG LOOKED AT, to fall so thick and fast, that he is obliged to close his eyes for a minute on the giddy whirl of white flakes and icy blots.

HE BEGAN TO LOOK AT THEM AS SOON AS IT WAS LIGHT. The day is not yet far spent, when he conceives it to be necessary that her rooms should be prepared for her. It is very cold and wet. Let there be good fires.

Lady Dedlock's case is somewhat different. In the manu-script, the pages of Chapter II are numbered A, B, C, D, E, whereas Chapter I ends on page 6 and Chapter III begins on page 7.

A comparison of the plans for Nos. I and II with the manuscript reveals that, in both manuscript and plans, the present numbering of Chapters III and IV has been altered from II and III; but the numbering of Chapter V has not been tampered with in either plan or manuscript. The present Chapter II, therefore, was interpolated *after* the first number was written, but *before* the second number or its plan were composed.

Why was this done? Certainly Dickens decided he must show as soon as possible that the Dedlocks were a major group of characters along with the Chancery and Bleak House groups. But more important, Dickens's ironic vision, his feeling for organic unity, his skill in construction combined to insist that the worlds of Chancery and the Dedlocks be linked as aspects of a single satirical view. The link is reinforced by the opening sentence of Chapter II and by the title, 'In Fashion', which was altered from 'In the Fashionable World' to make it a careful parallel to 'In Chancery'.

The satirical view of Lady Dedlock is developed at length in Chapter II, but what of that later vision whose tragic irony requires that she be seen as a sympathetic figure? In addition, Dickens does not completely assimilate certain melodramatic elements in Lady Dedlock's story into a genuine tragic experience. Yet he tries. Wisely, for instance, he keeps Lady Dedlock off-stage during the pursuit. Wisely, he appreciates that, since her story will be largely told in the form of sudden revelations, a sudden readjustment of sympathy for her at such times will seem contrived and reinforce the jerky artificial quality of the melodrama. Thus, a germ of sympathy must be planted earlier which will blossom naturally.

Clearly, Lady Dedlock's destiny is on the move from that entry in the notes which provides the climax and 'curtain' of Chapter II: '*Lady Dedlock. Law Writer.* work up from this moment.' But her fate is prepared even earlier. In the third paragraph of the chapter, almost immediately after referring to the Ghost's Walk, Dickens writes:

My Lady Dedlock ⟨was bored to death by the keeper's lodge in the ?early twilight⟩ (WHO IS CHILDLESS), looking out in the early twilight from her boudoir at a keeper's lodge, and seeing the light of the fire upon the latticed panes, and smoke rising from the chimney, and a child, ⟨?stealing⟩ CHASED BY A WOMAN, running out into the rain to meet the shining figure of a wrapped-up man coming through the gate, has been put quite out of temper.

In one flash, Dickens shifts from the omniscient viewpoint to Lady Dedlock's and we sympathize with her childless predicament. Yet the matter is more complex. Lady Dedlock is not childless, though she herself thinks so—a point which gains by the careful juxtaposition of this opening and the mystery of Esther's birth with which the next chapter begins. This was clearly in Dickens's mind, to judge by his solitary entry for Chapter III in his notes: 'Esther Summerson. Lady Dedlock's child'. In the single qualifying clause, 'who is childless', we have not only the embryo of Lady Dedlock's tragic fate but the rhetoric through which the vision of her destiny will be focused. For while the statement is ironical, masking a shameful truth which bears the seed of tragedy, the feeling aroused by the statement, in conjunction with what follows, is sympathy for Lady Dedlock. Both the vision and the rhetoric, here, are calculated: in the manuscript, this vital clause, 'who is childless', was inserted as a second thought. The insertion of 'chased by a woman' also draws our sympathetic attention to Lady Dedlock's predicament.

Does Dickens offer us a prospect of any enduring reality beyond delusion? True, in many novels, he fails to relate his view of love and goodness adequately to his vision of deception. Yet, in this respect, *Little Dorrit*, repeatedly described as his darkest novel, is also his most profoundly optimistic. The significance of the prison image is obviously the key to a full understanding of *Little Dorrit*. Society, as Dickens's notes confirm, 'Society like the Marshalsea' (II, Chap. VII), is a prison. So is the world.[1] Yet what does the prison symbol ultimately mean? To Trilling it represents the negation of the will, which paralyses the creative spirit.[2] This is certainly

---

[1] Original MS. of *LD*, Vol. IIA; a transcript of the complete memoranda and number plans together with my argument that these notes were mainly a plan and not a résumé will appear in my forthcoming critical edition of *Little Dorrit* to be published by Houghton Mifflin in their Riverside series of university critical editions. *LD*, Bk. II, Chap. XXX, p. 763.

[2] Lionel Trilling, introduction to *LD* (1953), pp. vi–ix. The introduction is reprinted in *The Dickens Critics*, pp. 279–93.

one of its meanings but what Trilling's argument overlooks is that the negation of the will is also the starting-point for spiritual progress towards enlightenment, a process in which Arthur Clennam is engaged.

Almost all the novel's major characters are incarcerated in a jail of deceit or self-deception. This idea helps to unify the novel and Dickens explores its tragic, melodramatic, and comic possibilities with irony and sympathy. Mrs. Clennam is shut up in the delusion of her narrow self-righteousness but a crippling guilt restricts her to her room. As Dickens indicates in a note: 'PARALLEL IMPRISONMENTS—his mother's and the Father of the Marshalsea's' (I, Chap. VIII). Merdle's guilt for his criminal deception shackles him with his complaint and the gesture in which he seems to take himself into custody. William Dorrit's entire life is a prison of delusion. Fate gives him the wealth to realize his pretensions to gentility. Yet when fate exposes him to society as a former jailbird he reassumes the genteel posture of the Father of the Marshalsea. Life is, as it were, a delusion within an hallucination. Strip one veil of deception away and another veil hangs behind it.

Arthur Clennam is also imprisoned in a delusion, namely his stubborn belief that love is no longer for him. Significantly, it is in prison that the scales fall from his eyes, an enlightenment stressed symbolically by his deliverance from the Marshalsea. This conclusion to the second book brings out all the irony in William Dorrit's release from the Marshalsea which concluded the first book. Intended as parallel scenes, they stress that William Dorrit was not released from that other prison of delusion and indicate the full meaning of Arthur's deliverance. Significant also is the sense of alienation from society which Arthur and Amy experience and through which they move towards their union. When all the veils of delusion have been stripped away, love alone remains, the only ultimate, enduring human reality. Arthur and Amy's love must not be interpreted narrowly as primarily a sexual union. Amy Dorrit is shown as the epitome of womanly love in its widest aspects. Here, we are in the presence not so much of 'Beatrice', as Trilling suggests, still less of the 'Paraclete in female form', as of the *hieros gamos* or mystic marriage, an

archetype of redemption which occurs both within and outside Christianity.[1] For once, the Victorian reticence about
sexuality works for Dickens rather than against him. So does
the Victorian emphasis on Amy's maternal qualities, since
both are typical of the genuine archetype. True, Arthur's
financial ruin rises out of an uncharacteristic act and his
reluctance to marry Amy while she has wealth seems to us a
curious Victorian notion about what is manly. Yet Dickens's
deeply introverted feeling incorporates both of these as the
stages of a ritual in a more profound vision. The sacred union
of Amy and Arthur cannot take place while there are ties to
the world. The final delusions of wealth and station, even as
regards the decent soul, must be swept aside. Dickens consciously determined on a calm conclusion to the novel. In
the notes, he writes: '*Very quiet conclusion*' (II, Chap. XXXIV).
Yet this is not simply a case of bringing the reader quietly out
of the stress of the story and leaving him at peace. By an
insertion in the corrected proofs, Dickens deliberately juxtaposes the sacred couple's serenity and the world's turmoil:

They went QUIETLY down into the roaring streets, inseparable
and blessed; and as they passed along in sunshine and in shade,
the noisy and the eager, and the arrogant and the froward and
the vain, fretted, and chafed, and made their usual uproar.

This conclusion is the nearest we get in Dickens's novels to
T. S. Eliot's 'still point of the turning world'.[2]

2. *Introversion*

During the last two decades, scholars have noted discrepan-
cies between the objective world of Victorian England and
Dickens's picture of it. Thus, Humphry House claims that
Dickens mixes different periods in his novels, confuses the
regimes in workhouses under the old and new poor laws,
exaggerates the inadequacy of workhouse dietaries, and
evades certain ugly truths about crime and sanitation.

[1] Trilling, op. cit., p. xvi; cf. C. G. Jung, *Psychology and Religion*, pp. 438–
58, *Psychology and Alchemy*, tr. R. F. C. Hull (1953), p. 36.
[2] Corrected proofs of *LD*, Bk. II, Chap. XXXIV, p. 626; cf. *LD*, p. 826.
T. S. Eliot, *Four Quartets*, 'Burnt Norton', ii.

Philip Collins argues that Dickens is not fair to the ragged
schools in *Our Mutual Friend* or the Middlesex magistrates in
David Copperfield, and that his first-hand knowledge of the
prostitute is never allowed to appear in his fiction. K. J.
Fielding points out that Dickens renders less than justice to
the Department of Practical Art in *Hard Times*. William O.
Aydelotte even suggests that we should not look to Dickens
and other social novelists, like Disraeli, Mrs. Gaskell, and
Charles Kingsley, for a historically valid portrait of social and
economic conditions in the England of Marx and Mills. Such
fiction 'reflects principally not the times but the author'.
Sheila M. Smith approaches the problem by distinguishing
between a kind of fiction, like Reade's, which for all its strict
adherence to the facts remains propaganda and a fiction, like
Dickens's, which may get some of the facts wrong yet,
through imagination, presents the essential truth of a situation.[1] The special quality of the imaginative truth Dickens
offers us may be defined, I believe, with great precision.

Dickens's vision is very largely an introverted one. This
explains why the following attitude towards historical truth
meets with his approval:

As he was not one of those rough spirits who would strip fair
Truth of every little shadowy vestment in which time and teem-
ing fancies love to array her—and some of which become her
pleasantly enough, serving, like the waters of her well, to add
new graces to the charms they half conceal and half suggest, and
to awaken interest and pursuit rather than languor and indifference—as, unlike this stern and obdurate class, he loved to see the
goddess crowned with those garlands of wild flowers which

[1] Humphry House, *The Dickens World*, pp. 21–2, 28–33, 93–6, 94, 215,
220 (the mixture of periods has been commented on by Kathleen Tillotson,
Novels of the Eighteen-Forties, pp. 110 ff., but for a later debate on conditions
under the Old and New Poor Laws, which is more detailed and more accurately
researched than House's account, see David Roberts, 'How Cruel was the
Victorian Poor Law?' and Ursula Henriques, 'Communication: How Cruel
was the Victorian Poor Law?', *The Historical Journal*, vi (1963), 97–107, xi,
2 (1968), 365–71); Philip Collins, *Dickens and Education*, p. 92, *Dickens and
Crime*, pp. 160–3, 113–15; K. J. Fielding, 'Charles Dickens and the Department
of Practical Art', *Modern Language Review*, xlviii (1953), 270–7; William O.
Aydelotte, 'The England of Marx and Mill as Reflected in Fiction', *Journal
of Economic History*, Supplement VIII (1948), 42–58; Sheila M. Smith, 'Truth
and Propaganda in the Victorian Social Problem Novel', *Renaissance and
Modern Studies*, viii (1964), 75–91.

tradition wreathes for her gentle wearing, and which are often freshest in their homeliest shapes,—he trod with a light step and bore with a light hand upon the dust of centuries, unwilling to demolish any of the airy shrines that had been raised above it, if any good feeling or affection of the human heart were hiding thereabouts.[1]

Obviously, such an attitude has its weaknesses, yet it cannot properly be understood as lying or evasion. There is a clear connection with Dickens's views on fact and fancy and with the idealistic tendencies in his fiction. The core of the attitude here is that the imagination can create a vision of an eternal quality, such as the goodness of human affection, which has more value than the accuracy of historical facts. It is very easy to depreciate such an attitude, particularly from the extraverted standpoint. Since the terms 'introversion' and 'extraversion', 'introverted' and 'extraverted', are widely employed so loosely as to overrate or underrate the positive and negative aspects of these two basic attitudes to life, the terms are used here strictly according to C. G. Jung's definition in his classic work on the subject:

Extraversion means an outward-turning of the libido [i.e. psychic energy]. With this concept I denote a manifest relatedness of subject to object in the sense of a positive movement of subjective interest towards the object. Everyone in the state of extraversion thinks, feels, and acts in relation to the object, and moreover in a direct and clearly observable fashion, so that no doubt can exist about his positive dependence upon the object ... Introversion means a turning inwards of the libido, whereby a negative relation of subject to object is expressed. Interest does not move towards the object, but recedes towards the subject. Everyone whose attitude is introverted thinks, feels, and acts in a way that clearly demonstrates that the subject is the chief factor of motivation while the object at most receives only a secondary value.

Whereas the extraverted attitude seeks its truth in external facts, the introverted attitude tries to find it in the eternal

---

[1] *OCS*, Chap. LIV, p. 400. Certainly, during 1843–55 Dickens was very actively and directly concerned with contemporary affairs from which he turned away in his later work. Thus, he became more introverted. See K. J. Fielding, 'Dickens and the Past: The Novelist of Memory', *Experience in the Novel*, ed. Roy Harvey Pearce (New York and London, 1968), pp. 120–1.

validity of the primordial images. The introverted attitude ventures into the world of external facts only to select what will confirm its subjective values and beliefs.[1]

Certainly, on the face of it, it would be difficult to find a more extraverted age than that of the Victorians. In the task of transforming their environment men's energies were turned outwards as never before. The industrial revolution gathered momentum throughout the early years of the nineteenth century and by the Great Exhibition of 1851 Britain was clearly the workshop of the world. In the later Victorian period, expansion was also expressed by conscious imperialism. The age is characterized by an almost feverish activity and a preoccupation with endeavour and accomplishment on the grand, sometimes the grandiose, scale. In twenty-five years (1825–50), for example, England and Scotland was covered with substantially our present network of railways and most of this development occurred in a single decade (1840–50). Treasure was poured forth. As regards sheer output, the writers too are children of their time. Everywhere, we find giants of industry and feats of production.

If literature ever seeks to correct the one-sidedness of an age or at least reflects what the age denies, it is not surprising that much typically Victorian literature presents an introverted vision. It can be seen, for instance, in Carlyle's *Sartor Resartus* (1833–4), Tennyson's *The Lady of Shalott* (1833), Matthew Arnold's *The Forsaken Merman* (1849) and *The Scholar Gipsy* (1853), D. G. Rossetti's *The Blessed Damozel* (1850), Browning's *Childe Roland to the Dark Tower Came* (1855), William Morris's *The Blue Closet* (1858), Bulwer-Lytton's *Zanoni* (1842) and *A Strange Story* (1863), Emily Brontë's *Wuthering Heights* (1847), Sheridan Le Fanu's *Uncle Silas* (1864) and *In a Glass Darkly* (1872), Lewis Carroll's *Alice's Adventures in Wonderland* (1865) and *Through the Looking-Glass* (1872). Introversion may assume an active or a passive form.[2] The Victorian preoccupation with the Middle Ages may involve a genuine quest for values to confront the contemporary world, as in Carlyle's *Past and Present*

---

[1] C. G. Jung, *Psychological Types*, pp. 542, 567, 434-5, 480-2.
[2] Ibid., p. 567.

(1843), or it may become pure escapism. A passive form of
introversion can be seen in the day-dream quality of much
Victorian poetry and in William Morris's later prose romances.

Dickens's introverted vision is of the active kind. Unlike
so many of his contemporaries, he sets his face against the
Middle Ages:

> "Don't you doat upon the Middle Ages, Mr. Carker? . . . So full of
> faith! So vigorous and forcible! So picturesque! So perfectly re-
> moved from commonplace! Oh dear! If they would only leave us a
> little more of the poetry of existence in these terrible days!" . . .
> "Those darling byegone times, Mr. Carker," said Cleopatra,
> "with their delicious fortresses, and their dear old dungeons, and
> their delightful places of torture, and their romantic vengeances,
> and their picturesque assaults and sieges, and everything that
> makes life truly charming! How dreadfully we have degenerated!"[1]

He may reject the Middle Ages with an unsubtle irony here,
but his rejection springs from a profound attitude. Generally,
Dickens tries to face his own age, to realize his introverted
vision in the context of his own time. He usually wrests his
symbols from the present, not the past, and so can view his
own age directly in the light of introverted values. He writes
of 'the romantic side of familiar things'. He finds his wasteland in the Black Country of *The Old Curiosity Shop*. He
criticizes Coketown harshly in *Hard Times* and yet by also
seeing the lighted mill by night as a 'fairy palace' suggests
the factory has more to it than dirt, monotony, and oppression.
That Dickens respected the inventor and what the machine
could perform can be gathered from his picture of Doyce.
Dickens discovers poetry in the contemporary city and takes
the very image of a congested urban mass as a symbol of the
flux of life:

> The roar soon grew more loud, the passengers more numerous,
> the shops more busy, until she was carried onward in a stream of
> life setting that way, and flowing, indifferently, past marts and
> mansions, prisons, churches, market-places, wealth, poverty,
> good, and evil, like the broad river side by side with it, awakened
> from its dreams of rushes, willows, and green moss, and rolling on,
> turbid and troubled, among the works and cares of men, to the
> deep sea.

[1] *D & S*, Chap. XXVII, pp. 384, 387.

Again, Dickens shows that a railway journey is an emblem of the course of Death.[1] He expresses the anger of the gods not only through elemental forces like the sea and weather but also through natural forces which man has locked up in his attempt to tame his environment, through the fal lof a house, or a drowning in a river lock, or a death caused by a steam locomotive:

A trembling of the gound, and quick vibration in his ears; a distant shriek; a DULL light advancing, quickly changed to two red eyes, and a fierce fire, dropping glowing coals; an irresistible bearing on of a great roaring and dilating mass; a high wind, and a rattle—another come and gone, and he holding to a gate, as if to save himself!

He waited for another, and for another. He walked back to his former point, and back again to that, and still, through the WEARISOME vision of his journey, looked for these approaching ⟨?again⟩ MONSTERS. He loitered about the station, waiting until one should stay to call there; and when one did, and was detached for water, he stood parallel with it, watching its heavy wheels and its brazen front, and thinking what a cruel power and might they had. Ugh! To see ⟨them slowly⟩ THE GREAT WHEELS SLOWLY turning and to think of being run down and crushed! . . .

He . . . felt the earth tremble—knew in a moment that the rush was come—uttered a shriek—looked round—saw the red eyes, bleared and dim, in the daylight, close upon him—was BEATEN DOWN, CAUGHT UP, AND whirled away upon a jagged mill, that spun him round and round, and struck him limb from limb, and ⟨cast his mutilated⟩ LICKED HIS STREAM OF LIFE UP WITH ITS FIERY HEAT, AND CAST HIS MUTILATED fragments in the air.

Dickens reveals that the dragon and other fabulous monsters are still abroad though now we call them machines. He exposes a devil in a lawyer like Vholes, a lawyer's clerk like Heep, a dilettante politician like Harthouse, or a shabby genteel psychopath like Rigaud. He shows us an underprivileged schoolmaster like Headstone subject to demoniacal possession.[2]

---

[1] Preface to the First Edition of *BH* (1853); *OCS*, Chap. XLV, pp. 335–6; *HT*, Bk. I, Chaps. X, XI, XII, pp. 64, 69, 80; *D & S*, Chap. XLVIII, p. 668, Chap. XX, pp. 280–2.

[2] *LD*, Bk. II, Chaps. XXX, XXXI, pp. 785–6, 793–4; *OMF*, Bk. IV,

Jung and others have described a particular introverted way of viewing the world which seems to me strikingly similar to Dickens's vision in many respects:

They . . . are often preoccupied with images from the collective unconscious. Even precise observations of reality does not stop the subjective factor from working—such people cannot see buses or trams without thinking of fiery dragons, trees have faces, and inanimate objects spring to life; they think they see people who are not really there, and have curious experiences with 'ghosts' . . . If . . . he remains faithful to his irrationality . . . the objective world will appear a mere make-belief and a comedy.[1]

In Dickens's hands, the rhetoric of sympathy and irony is well able to communicate this introverted vision of a spiritual universe pervading the material world. This vision is all the more impressive in that Dickens does not try to deny or weaken our immediate perception of the tangible world but renders it with a remarkable verisimilitude. The rhetoric of sympathy enables Dickens to explore and present the common bond between all things and to involve the reader in this process of viewing the world as a vital experience, to make him feel his identity with all creation. Not only is animism characteristic of the introverted vision but so also is the awareness of a force which permeates all things, a primitive identity.[2] Yet to *be* all things not only means to sympathize

Chaps. I, XV, pp. 635–6, 801–2. Original MS. of *D & S*, Victoria and Albert Museum, Forster Collection, 47. A. 22 (Vol. IIB), Chap. LV, pp. 7 ('they' after 'power and might' altered to 'it' in proof), 8; cf. *D & S*, pp. 776–7, 779. *BH*, Chaps. XXXVII, LX, pp. 535, 820; *DC*, Chap. XXV, p. 381; *LD*, Bk. II, Chap. VI, pp. 493–4; *OMF*, Bk. III, Chap. XI, p. 555. 'Genteel demon' is the single phrase with which Dickens characterizes Harthouse in his notes for Chap. XIX, bound in with the original MS. of *HT*, and Harthouse is referred to as 'agreeable demon', *HT*, Bk. II, Chap. III, p. 133. Although Dickens decided in the corrected proofs of *HT*, Chap. XXX, 42, to soften Harthouse's own description of his attempted seduction of Louisa by altering 'a smoothness so entirely diabolical' to 'a smoothness so perfectly irresistible' and this was the form which appeared in *HW*, ix (22 July 1854), 529, he emended this in the First Edition (1854), p. 275, to 'perfectly diabolical'; cf. *HT*, Bk. III, Chap. II, p. 232.

[1] Frieda Fordham, *An Introduction to Jung's Psychology* (1953), pp. 42–43; C. G. Jung's *Psychological Types*, p. 504.

[2] Ibid., pp. 479–80; Arthur O. Lovejoy, 'The Fundamental Concept of the Primitive Philosophy', *The Monist*, xvi (1906), 357–82; C. G. Jung, *The Structure and Dynamics of the Psyche*, tr. R. F. C. Hull (1960), pp. 63–6.

with them in the sense of 'the sympathetic induction of emotion' or the *participation mystique*,[1] it also offers the basis for the higher forms of sympathy. It is the foundation of mature love and compassion. The power which permeates all things is, in the final analysis, the loving joy which allows to all things their essential being. It is this delight in all creation which Garis would deny Dickens.[2] Yet this delight reflects Dickens's (and the reader's) identity with life and energy of every kind, even pain and even evil. On the other hand, the ironic factor in Dickens's complex rhetoric helps to focus his introverted vision in two ways. First, structural irony recognizes the existence of a spiritual order at work in the universe and makes its presence felt. Secondly, by exploring the nature of appearance, by constantly tearing away veils of delusion, irony enables Dickens to shake our confidence in the value of many things in the material world. Since introversion withdraws value from objects, it can afford a critical view of the external world from a detached standpoint. The introverted vision is particularly useful, therefore, in examining extraverted forms and relationships. It has a deadly knack of exposing the superficiality of social institutions and social attitudes. This helps to explain the scathing manner in which Dickens's fiction hardly ever ceases to denounce society, Parliament, bureaucracy, courts of law, the legal, financial, and political worlds, workhouses, schools, and so on. In this respect, Dickens's vision is not necessarily reactionary. A complex rhetoric, which seeks a common identity between things and yet can simultaneously expose their spiritual bankruptcy, may afford a searching view of social life that has great positive value. Thus, Dickens frequently sums up an unhealthy state of society through an effective image, the fancy dress masquerade. He perceives an identity between the falseness of an empty society and its addiction to gaudy costumes and frivolous ceremonial. This is not a fanciful resemblance, it is a genuine 'correspondence'. It can be no accident that one state of affairs reflects the other. It indicates a grave spiritual truth. Only the introverted vision could

---

[1] See Lucien Lévy-Bruhl, *How Natives Think*, tr. Lilian A. Clare (1926), *passim*, for a full explanation of this term.

[2] *The Dickens Theatre*, p. 16.

have revealed the ironic fate of France's *ancien régime* in so depreciative and yet so profound a manner as this:

Dress was the one unfailing talisman and charm used for keeping all things in their places. Everybody was dressed for a Fancy Ball that was never to leave off. From the Palace of the Tuileries, through Monseigneur and the whole Court, through the chambers, the Tribunals of Justice, and all society (except the scarecrows), the Fancy Ball descended to the common Executioner: who, in pursuance of the charm, was required to officiate "frizzled, powdered, in a gold-laced coat, pumps, and white silk stockings." At the gallows and the wheel—the axe was a rarity— Monsieur Paris, as it was the episcopal mode among his brother Professors of the provinces, Monsieur Orleans, and the rest, to call him, presided in this dainty dress. And who among the company at Monseigneur's reception in that seventeen hundred and eightieth year of our Lord, could possibly doubt, that a system rooted in a frizzled hangman, powdered, gold-laced, pumped, and white-silk stockinged, would see the very stars out!

The vision is not limited to its immediate historical context but has universal validity. It implies a warning to Victorian England, believed to stand on the brink of revolution throughout much of Dickens's lifetime and frequently criticized by him for being preoccupied with fancy dress and ceremonial.[1] Again, in the dust-heap symbol of *Our Mutual Friend*, Dickens intuitively finds an identity between the amassing of wealth and excrement, a genuine correspondence (as we know today) since the acquisition of gold is partly motivated by an anal complex. Yet through this symbol Dickens is also able to depreciate the acquisitive society with such a devastating irony because it exposes a gap between what is desirable and disgusting which corresponds to, and derives from, an ambivalent, infantile attitude towards excretion.

Introversion, together with a rhetoric which affords both detachment and an awareness of the mystical unity of things, enables Dickens to view his world from what can only be described as a cosmic standpoint. Such a standpoint entails all the complexity of a metaphysical vision which comprehends both benevolent and malevolent forces at work in the

---

[1] *TTC*, Bk. II, Chap. VII, pp. 101–2; see, for example, his article, 'Court Ceremonies', *The Examiner* (15 Dec. 1849), reprinted in *MP*, pp. 161–4.

universe. It is a tribute to the active character of Dickens's introversion that it can discover part of the complex pattern of a spiritual order in a contemporary scientific idea. Referring to the 'zymotic' theory of contagion, which became fashionable during the great cholera epidemic of 1848–9, Dickens goes on to explore the functioning of a moral and metaphysical design:[1]

Those who study the physical sciences, and bring them to bear upon the health of Man, tell us that if the noxious particles that rise from vitiated air were palpable to the sight, we should see them lowering in a dense black cloud above such haunts, and rolling slowly on to corrupt the better portions of a town. But if the moral pestilence that rises with them, and in the eternal laws of outraged Nature, is inseparable from them, could be made discernible too, how terrible the revelation! Then should we see depravity, impiety, drunkenness, theft, murder, and a long train of nameless sins against the natural affections and repulsions of mankind, overhanging the devoted spots, and creeping on, to blight the innocent and spread contagion among the pure. Then should we see how the same poisoned fountains that flow into our hospitals and lazar-houses, inundate the jails, and make the convict-ships swim deep, and roll across the seas, and over-run vast continents with crime. Then should we stand appalled to know, that where we generate disease to strike our children down and entail itself on unborn generations, there also we breed, by the same certain process, infancy that knows no innocence, youth without modesty or shame, maturity that is mature in nothing but in suffering and guilt, blasted old age that is a scandal on the form we bear.

That this is not simply a social comment which uses an analogy but a view of the world from a cosmic standpoint is confirmed by the apocalyptic passage which follows:

Oh for a good spirit who would take the house-tops off, with a more potent and benignant hand than the lame demon in the tale, and show a Christian people what dark shapes issue from amidst their homes, to swell the retinue of the Destroying Angel as he moves forth among them! For only one night's view of the pale

---

[1] See Dr. E. V. Mainswaring's explanation of the 'zymotic' theory in *The Lancet*, cited in John W. Dodds, *The Age of Paradox*, p. 339: 'The disease is probably caused by persons inhaling a noxious gas.' *D & S*, Chap. XLVII, pp. 647–8.

phantoms rising from the scenes of our too-long neglect; and from the thick and sullen air where Vice and Fever propagate together, raining the tremendous social retributions which are ever pouring down, and ever coming thicker!

Dickens's spiritual vision is no abstraction nor, apart from occasional lapses like the heavenly music or angelic presences in the hour of death, is it just a convention. Dickens was well read in occult literature. His library contained such works as A. Calmet's *Phantom World: or the Philosophy of Spirits, Apparitions, etc.* (1850), Abbé de Mountfaucon de Villar's *The Count de Gabalis: Being a Diverting History of the Rosicrucian Doctrine of Spirits* (1714), Catherine Crowe's *Night Side of Nature: or Ghost Seers* (1848), W. C. Dendy's *Philosophy of Mystery* [*on Ghosts, Poetic Phantasy, Mysterious Forms and Signs, Mysterious Sounds, Fairy Mythology, Demonology, Dreams, Somnambulism, etc.*] (1841), J. Ennemoser's *History of Magic*, tr. W. Howitt, *with appendix of remarkable Apparitions, Dreams, Second Sight, Somnambulism, Predictions, Divinations, Table-turning, Spirit Rapping* by Mary Howitt (1854), and Jung–Stilling's *Theory of Pneumatology* (1834).[1] Yet his vision of the occult reflects more than reading. It conveys the genuine *numinous* quality of supernatural experience and thus indicates true introversion. This is why Dickens is usually so successful in making us feel the presence of the spiritual world.[2] We find that 'shadowy company' which 'attended Florence up and down the echoing house, and sat with her in the dismantled rooms' and Mrs. Boffin's encounter with the faces equally convincing:

"I was sorting those things on the chest, and not thinking of the old man or the children, but singing to myself, when all in a moment I felt there was a face growing out of the dark . . . So I thought of the new house and Miss Bella Wilfer, and was thinking at a great rate with that sheet there in my hand, when, all of a sudden, the faces seemed to be hidden in among the folds of it, and I let it drop . . . but the moment I came near the bed, the air got thick with them . . . and I even felt they were in the dark behind the side-door, and on the little staircase, floating away into the yard."

[1] *Catalogue of the Library of Charles Dickens*, pp. 17, 24, 25, 27, 42, 66.
[2] *D & S*, Chap. XXIII, p. 321; *OMF*, Bk. I, Chap. XV, p. 190, Bk. II, Chap. II, pp. 238–40, Bk. I, Chap. I, p. 5.

We do not question Jenny Wren's experience of the unearthly children who comfort her in her pain or of the strange flowers which she believes she smells:

"I smell roses till I think I see the rose-leaves lying in heaps, bushels, on the floor, I smell fallen leaves till I put down my hand—so—and expect to make them rustle. I smell the white and pink May in the hedges, and all sorts of flowers that I never was among."

Dickens's introverted vision successfully conveys the presence not only of benevolent but also of malevolent forces, like the corpse that menaces Gaffer Hexam with a weird life:

What he had in tow, lunged itself at him sometimes in an awful manner when the boat was checked, and sometimes seemed to try to wrench itself away, though for the most part it followed submissively. A neophyte might have fancied that the ripples passing over it were dreadfully like faint changes of expression on a sightless face; but Gaffer was no neophyte and had no fancies.

The introverted view discerns strange signs in familiar things. The omen here warns Gaffer of the precise manner of his coming death. But Gaffer is uninitiated.

The apparently contradictory nature of the forces which the introverted vision reveals at work in the Dickens universe raises an interesting metaphysical problem. A genuine complexity, as distinct from a confused mixture, implies unity. Certainly, Dickens argues through the unified structure of his later novels for some single order at work in his universe. For example, in a passage in his *Life of Dickens*,[1] which deserves to be read very carefully, Forster rightly praises the skilful construction of *Bleak House*. Approvingly, he explains how an organic unity is built up in which all 'tends to the catastrophe'; that behind the appearance of chance lies the reality of design. Though Forster does not use either the words 'irony' or 'fate', he implies both. He notes the ignorance of 'the chief persons in the tale' and the inexorability of the processes 'drawing them on insensibly, but very certainly, to the issues that await them'. The plot, therefore, is not a clever mechanism with the author pulling the strings: it demonstrates a 'machinery', in the old sense, at work, an

[1] *F*, vol. iii, pp. 20–3.

ironic providence or fate, pursuing, exposing, punishing, rewarding. That this is Dickens's idea of fate is confirmed by the discussion of Jonas's character in the preface to the first cheap edition of *Martin Chuzzlewit* (1849):

But, so born and so bred; admired for that which made him hateful, and justified from his cradle in cunning, treachery, and avarice, I claim him as the legitimate issue of the father upon whom those vices are seen to recoil. And I submit that their recoil upon that old man, in his unhonoured age, is not a mere piece of poetical justice, but is the extreme exposition of a plain truth . . . nothing is more common in real life than a want of profitable reflection on the causes of many vices and crimes that awaken the general horror. What is substantially true of families in this respect, is true of a whole commonwealth. As we sow, we reap.

That final image of nemesis as a natural law is echoed in *David Copperfield*, *Hard Times*, and Dickens's other novels.

Yet this idea may appear to be no more than that character is fate, and that we punish ourselves by a discipline of natural consequences, an idea expressed by other mid-Victorian writers, Charles Kingsley for instance:

Men can and do resist God's will, and break the law, which is appointed for them, and so punish themselves, by getting into disharmony with their own constitution and that of the universe; just as a wheel in a piece of machinery punishes itself when it gets out of gear.[1]

Certainly, Richard Carstone's fate in *Bleak House* seems to be very largely of this type. Dickens carefully indicates in his notes that Richard's decline springs from certain traits of character: 'New traits in Richard *Yes*—slightly' (memoranda for No. III) and 'Richard? YES. Carry through, his character —developing itself' (memoranda for No. VI). A note stresses

---

[1] Cited in Guy Kendall, *Charles Kingsley and His Ideas* (1947), p. 131. Cf. the description of Mrs. Bedonebyasyoudid's nature in *The Water Babies* [1863] (1893), pp. 196–7: 'I cannot help punishing people when they do wrong. I like it no more than they do; I am often very, very sorry for them, poor things; but I cannot help it. If I tried not to do it, I should do it all the same. For I work by machinery, just like an engine; and am full of wheels and springs inside; and am wound up very carefully, so that I cannot help going.'

moral disapproval of one of Richard's outstanding traits: 'Bayham Badger? YES. *To introduce Richard's unreliability*' (memoranda for No. VI). The notes go on to sketch Richard's moral deterioration: 'Richard. "O! It's all right enough. Let us talk about something else" ' (Chap. XVII); 'RICHARD. Downward Progress. Jarndyce & Jarndyce. The army' (Chap. XXIII); 'Richard's progress—distrust of Mr. Jarndyce naturally engendered by the suit' (Chap. XXXVII); Richard's decline—*carry on*' (Chap. XXXIX). Moreover, in his portrayal of Richard's end, Dickens shows a Christian view apparently similar to Kingsley's. Richard accepts responsibility for his own decline, he is penitent, he seeks and finds forgiveness and reconciliation. But Christian thinking is the core of Kingsley's view, whereas a vague though sincere Christian feeling colours Dickens's more complex, if less intellectual, view.

Thus, Dickens seems to come close to determinism when he insists, in Chapters XIII, XVII, and XXIII of *Bleak House*, on the fatal influence of the atmosphere of 'Jarndyce and Jarndyce' in which Richard has been reared. Again, outside forces seem to be sweeping Richard off as he is driven away by his solicitor at the end of Chapter XXXVII, an extremely sinister picture which symbolizes what is happening to Richard at Vholes's hands. That Dickens was conscious of what he was doing here can be seen in his notes. He ends his outline for Chapter XXXVII: 'driving away to Jarndyce & Jarndyce. *Close with that.*' Kingsley denied the reality of evil, but Dickens makes us feel its very presence. He refers to Richard's solicitor as "*Vholes*, the evil genius" (Chap. LX)— something quite satanic.

In the introduction to his *Westminster Sermons*, Kingsley tried to find a Christian providence at work in nature, even to reconcile the God of love with the dark destructive side of evolution; but Dickens often presents fate as an altogether sinister force. No one could describe the working out of Lady Dedlock's destiny as Christian, or even moral in any rational sense. Judged even by the narrowest and most harsh of Victorian attitudes towards fornication, her punishment is out of all proportion to that offence. Yet Dickens indicates the real 'crime' in the scrap of Lady Dedlock's monologue

recorded in the notes: ' "My enemy alive and dead" ' (Chap.
LV). She has wished Tulkinghorn dead, she explains further
in the text; she actually feels guilt for his murder, and his
vengeance pursues her from beyond the grave. Here is that
terrible 'omnipotence of thought' of which Freud writes in
Totem and Taboo and Theodor Reik in *The Unknown Murderer* and which, together with the law of talion, provides the
basis of primitive justice. Neither could anyone justify Ada's
fate according to either a Christian or a rational ethic. She
suffers because she is unfortunate enough to love Richard.
This is the problem of evil in one of its most acute forms;
a problem which only the tragic vision can bear to look upon
and transcend. As we can see from a note, Dickens does not
intend that the ugly problem which Ada's fate poses should
be shirked: 'Still the same shadow on my darling' (Chap. L).
The word 'shadow' is used very often in the notes when
Dickens is indicating the sinister element in fate at work.

Behind the veil of Dickens's moral sense and his vague
Christian feelings, dark primitive gods appear to demand
their sacrifices, exert their ancient taboos and execute their
terrible justice. Even Ada is warned by Miss Flite in something like the old classical manner, her engagement to Richard
is finally opposed by Mr. Jarndyce on the grounds of Richard's
character, and although she accepts Mr. Jarndyce's advice
for a time she eventually rushes into a secret marriage. The
supernatural, 'Foreshadowing Legend of the country house'
(memoranda for No. II), may work itself out in natural events,
the illegitimate daughter, Esther, may feel she embodies the
curse on the Dedlocks, but Esther's terror of the old house
and its legend, which Dickens describes so effectively in
Chapter XXXVI, is unmistakably *numinous* and, as we have
seen, the dread of an unseen presence here is deliberately
intensified.[1] In this category of fate as a sinister, supernatural
agency, there is the cruel fascination of which Miss Flite
speaks; an almost magical power emanating from the mace
and seal in the Court of Chancery; a fatal attraction which
will draw Richard too:

"There's a cruel attraction in the place. You *can't* leave it. And

[1] *BH*, Chap. XXXVI, pp. 514–15; see above, pp. 105–8.

you *must* expect . . . my dear, I have been there many years, and I have noticed. It's the Mace and Seal upon the table."

What could they do, did she think? I mildly asked her.

"Draw," returned Miss Flite. "Draw people on, my dear. Draw peace out of them. Sense out of them. Good looks out of them. Good qualities out of them. I have felt them even drawing my rest away in the night. Cold and glittering devils!"[1]

This concept of fate can be seen brooding and shaping in so many of Dickens's notes for *Bleak House* and is clearly to be realized through a rhetoric of structural irony: 'The shadow of Miss Flite on Richard' (Chap. XXIV); the destiny building up for Tulkinghorn, 'Begin grim shadow on him' (Chap. XLI) and the dumb omens which might have warned him, 'If it said now, Don't go home! *High and mighty street*' (Chap. XLVIII); '*shadowing forth of Lady Dedlock at the churchyard*' (Chap. XVI).

A genuine introversion, as distinct from introspection, will not lead to the kind of subtle preoccupation with man's complex moral conflicts found so frequently in George Eliot's or Henry James's fiction, but to the metaphysical, even mystical, vision of good and evil revealed in its more advanced forms in the work of Blake or Nietzsche. A criticism, like Garis's,[2] which sets a subtle and complex view of man's moral conflicts as the highest to which art can aspire will not do justice to Dickens's vision. Its complexity, in general, lies elsewhere. True, Dickens seems to be trying to present a vision of some single order at work in the universe. Yet this single order appears to be divided by an inner contradiction. The complexity of Dickens's vision, here, lies in an almost Manichaean view that the universe is governed by the dual spirit of benevolence and malevolence, and that divine providence is both love and a dark chastising force. It may be foolish to suppose that Dickens was theologically aware of the Manichaean problem which his metaphysical vision of the universe raises. Dickens would probably have been horrified at the suggestion that his fiction was advocating a heresy. His Christian beliefs, though vague, were certainly sincere. Yet the very vagueness of Dickens's doctrinal thinking gave

[1] *BH*, Chap. XXXV, p. 498.
[2] Robert Garis, op. cit., pp. 48, 117.

sufficient scope for his work to reflect a spiritual problem of modern man. Some idea of this problem can be gained by considering the curious contradiction in western man between Christian and pagan values. I do not refer, here, simply to the failure of many Christians to live up to their religion but to the widespread flourishing of pagan alongside Christian attitudes in the same people. Dickens fully approved when rebellious natives in Jamaica were summarily flogged and hanged and when mutinous sepoys in India were blown to bits at the mouths of cannon. That it comes as a shock to learn this only shows how far we are from recognizing the problem. Some commentators have argued that western man was never completely christianized. Others have thought that Christianity was too idealistic a religion to subdue the old Adam. It certainly seems as if the old gods and their cruel values have lived on, deep within modern man's soul. We can see this in other Victorians besides Dickens. Carlyle, for example, and even a decent thoughtful Christian like Charles Kingsley enthusiastically approved of the most horrifying violence in the interests of what they believed to be justice and good order.[1]

When Dickens examines the problem of suffering and of God's nature in a specifically Christian context, the result is significantly unimpressive. Stephen Blackpool, who represents the case of man crucified by the contemporary world, puts the tragic irony of the situation well:

"How 'tis . . . that what is best in us folk, seems to turn us most

[1] See Dickens's letter to M. De Cerjat (13 Nov. 1865), *HD*, pp. 590–1; K. J. Fielding, '*Edwin Drood* and Governor Eyre', *The Listener* (25 Dec. 1952), 1083–4; George H. Ford, 'The Governor Eyre Case in England', *University of Toronto Quarterly*, xvii (1948), 227–8; Dickens's letter to Miss Coutts (4 Oct. 1857), *Coutts*, p. 350; 'The Perils of Certain English Prisoners', *CS*, p. 179. Philip Collins, *Dickens and Crime*, p. 346, points out that, although Dickens generally objected to his periodicals containing articles about executions, he printed an account of the blowing to pieces of leaders of the Indian Mutiny, *HW*, xvii (27 Mar. 1858), 348–50. H. Godwin Baynes, *Germany Possessed* (1941), *passim*; Sigmund Freud, *Civilization and Its Discontents*, tr. J. Riviere (1930), *passim*; C. G. Jung, *Psychology and Alchemy*, pp. 11–12, *Psychology and Religion*, p. 28; Thomas Carlyle, 'Dr. Francia' [1843], 'The Nigger Question' [1849], *Miscellaneous Essays*, People's Edition (1872), vol. vii, pp. 1–54 (esp. 37–49, 53), 79–110; *Charles Kingsley: His Letters and Memories of His Life*, ed. his wife (1880), vol. i, pp. 340–2. Cf. Walter E. Houghton, *The Victorian Frame of Mind*, pp. 210–13, 216–17.

to trouble an' misfort'n an' mistake, I dunno. But 'tis so. I know 'tis, as I know the heavens is over me ahint the smoke. We're patient too, an' wants in general to do right. An' I canna think the fawt is aw wi' us.

In his notes, Dickens plans a Christian answer: 'STEPHEN AND RACHAEL Bear and forbear The star that leads the way' (Chap. XXXIV). A careful revision in the manuscript stresses that Stephen is able to attain a Christian view of forbearance returned for suffering, which transcends his earlier concept of providence, through the star of divine guidance with its strong New Testament associations:

"It ha' shined upon me," he said reverently, "in my pain and trouble down below. It ha' shined into my mind. I ha' LOOK'N AT IT AN thowt o' thee, Rachael, till the muddle in my mind have cleared awa, above a bit, I hope."[1]

The muddle turns out to have been only in Stephen's mind, a paranoid delusion of a persecuting fate. It is dispelled by a compassionate Christian love which is also enlightenment. The irony was a double one. Stephen was deceived in thinking that providence was cruelly ironic. Unfortunately, the solution, which is expressed with the conventional, sometimes the sentimental, Christian feeling of Dickens's time, fails to convince us. It is much less impressive than that other vision of malevolent energy at work in the universe which is usually fresh and compelling in Dickens's fiction and points to a deeper conviction.

Though it has obvious links with his own vague Christian beliefs and the tearful benevolence of the age, Dickens's compassionate vision is effective only when it reflects his own natural and profoundly compassionate feelings. When he avoids conventional Christian postures and sentimentality, Dickens's rhetoric is admirably suited to the task of presenting a dualistic vision of the universe. His rhetoric of sympathy may stir within us that sense of compassionate involvement with mankind which, as in Balzac's *The Atheist's Mass*, surpasses the language of creeds. While his rhetoric of irony

[1] *HT*, Bk. II, Chap. V, pp. 148–9. Original MS. of *HT*, Chap. XXXIV, p. 30; cf. *HT*, Bk. III, Chap. VI, pp. 272–3.

may offer us an almost pagan detachment, may even give play to those old gods whom we can sometimes hear laughing cruelly within ourselves at the fates of humankind. At its best, Dickens's vision is comprehensive and complex enough to take in our equal and contradictory passions for justice and for mercy.

APPENDIX

A COMPLETE TRANSCRIPT OF THE ALTERNATIVE TITLES IN THE ORIGINAL MANUSCRIPT OF *HARD TIMES*

(Friday January 20th 1854)

Mr. Gradgrind
Mrs. Gradgrind

Stubborn Things
Fact
Thomas Gradgrind's facts
 John
⟨George⟩ Gradgrind's facts
Hard-headed Gradgrind
The Grindstone
Hard heads and soft hearts
The Time Grinder
Mr. Gradgrind's grindstone
⟨The Family Grindstone⟩
⟨Hard Times⟩
 general
The ⟨universal⟩ grindstone
Hard Times
Heads and Tales
Two and Two are Four
Prove it
Black and White

According to Cocker
Prove it!
Stubborn things
⟨Facts are stubborn things⟩
 Facts

⟨John⟩
⟨Thomas⟩
The ⟨Thomas⟩
 ⟨Thomas⟩

Mr. Gradgrind's ⟨grindstone⟩

⟨Mr. Gradgrind's⟩ grindstone

⟨These real times days⟩
 ⟨There's no⟩
⟨No such thing Sir⟩
⟨Extremes meet⟩
⟨Unknown quantities⟩
Simple arithmetic
A ⟨mere⟩ matter of calculation
A mere question of figures

Hard Times
Two and Two are Four
⟨Calculation⟩
⟨According to Cocker⟩
⟨Damaging Facts⟩
Something tangible
Our hard-headed friend
Rust and dust.

BIBLIOGRAPHY

A. MANUSCRIPTS AND CORRECTED PROOFS

All MSS. and corrected proofs of the novels listed below are in the Forster Collection at the Victoria and Albert Museum with the exception of the MS. of *Great Expectations* which is in the Townshend Collection at the Wisbech and Fenland Museum.

DICKENS, CHARLES. Original MS. of *Bleak House*. 47. A. 27 (Vol. IA), 47. A. 28 (Vol. IB), 47. A. 29 (Vol. IIA), 47. A. 30 (Vol. IIB). The author's notes are bound in at the beginning of the serial part to which they correspond.

—— Corrected proofs of *Bleak House*. 48. B. 15.

—— Original MS. of *David Copperfield*. 47. A. 17 (Vol. IA), 47. A. 18 (Vol. IB), 47. A. 19 (Vol. IIA), 47. A. 20 (Vol. IIB). The author's notes, with the exception of those for No. I, are bound in at the beginning of the serial part to which they correspond. The author's notes for No. I are in 48. E. 1.

—— Corrected proofs of *David Copperfield*. 48. B. 14.

—— Original MS. of *Dombey and Son*. 47. A. 13 (Vol. IA), 47. A. 14 (Vol. IB), 47. A. 15 (Vol. IIA), 47. A. 16 (Vol. IIB). The author's notes are bound in at the beginning of Vol. IA.

—— Corrected proofs of *Dombey and Son*. 48. B. 16.

—— Original MS. of *Great Expectations*. No press or shelf mark or catalogue number. Some memoranda of the author's are bound in at the end of the single volume.

—— Corrected proofs of *Great Expectations*. 48. E. 24. A portion of the proofs only.

—— Original MS. of *Hard Times*. 47. A. 31. The author's notes are bound in at the beginning of the single volume.

—— Corrected proofs of *Hard Times*. 48. E. 27, 48. E. 28. The proofs are bound in with two separate volumes.

—— Original MS. of *Little Dorrit*. 47. A. 32 (Vol. IA), 47. A. 33 (Vol. IB), 47. A. 34 (Vol. IIA), 47. A. 35 (Vol. IIB). The author's notes for Nos. II–X and XI–XX are bound in at the beginning of Vols. IA and IIA respectively. The notes for No. I are in 48. E. 1.

—— Corrected proofs of *Little Dorrit*. 48. B. 17. There are also some proofs and a MS. slip in 48. E. 24.

—— Original MS. of *Martin Chuzzlewit*. 47. A. 21 (Vol. IA), 47. A. 22 (Vol. IB), 47. A. 23 (Vol. IIA), 47. A. 24 (Vol. IIB). The author's very brief notes for Nos. IV and VI are bound in at the beginning of those numbers.

—— Corrected proofs of *Martin Chuzzlewit*. 48. E. 24. A portion of the proofs only.

—— Original MS. of *The Old Curiosity Shop*. 47. A. 5 (Vol. IA), 47. A. 6 (Vol. IB), 47. A. 7 (Vol. IIA), 47. A. 8 (Vol. IIB).

—— Corrected proofs of *The Old Curiosity Shop*. 48. E. 27. A portion of the proofs only.

—— Original MS. of *Oliver Twist*. 47. A. 1 (Vol. IA), 47. A. 2 (Vol. IB), 47. A. 3 (Vol. IIA), 47. A. 4 (Vol. IIB). The MS. is incomplete. This version of the novel is divided into three books; the numbering of chapters after the end of the first book (Chap. XXI), therefore, differs from that in all printed versions except the serial version in *Bentley's Miscellany*.

—— Original MS. of *A Tale of Two Cities*. 47. A. 36 (Vol. A), 47. A. 37 (Vol. B).

I have consulted but not used the MSS. of *Barnaby Rudge* and *Edwin Drood* which are also in the Forster Collection. The only MSS. of novels I have not consulted are those of *Our Mutual Friend*, which is in the Pierpont Morgan Library, New York [though I have referred to the complete transcript of Dickens's notes in Ernest Boll, 'The Plotting of *Our Mutual Friend*', *Modern Philology*, xlii (1944), 96–122], and of *Pickwick Papers* and *Nicholas Nickleby* which survive only in scattered fragments; the location of these fragments is given in Ada B. Nisbet, 'Charles Dickens', *Victorian Fiction: A Guide to Research*, ed. Lionel Stevenson (Cambridge, Mass., 1964), pp. 46–7.

B. PRINTED BOOKS

I have listed only works by (or edited by) Dickens, and the place of publication is London unless otherwise stated. Full details of other works consulted are given in the notes.

DICKENS, CHARLES. *The Posthumous Papers of the Pickwick Club*. First Edition. 1837.

—— *Oliver Twist; or, the parish boy's progress*. First Edition. 3 vols. 1838.

—— *The Life and Adventures of Nicholas Nickleby*. First Edition. 1839.

—— *Master Humphrey's Clock*. First Edition. 3 Vols. 1840–1. Contains *The Old Curiosity Shop* and *Barnaby Rudge*.

—— *The Life and Adventures of Martin Chuzzlewit*. First Edition. 1844.

—— *Dealings with the Firm of Dombey and Son, Wholesale, Retail, and for Exportation*. First Edition. 1848.

—— *The Personal History, Adventures, Experiences, and Observations of David Copperfield the Younger of Blunderstone Rookery*. First Edition. 1850.

DICKENS, CHARLES. *Bleak House*. First Edition. 1853.

—— *Hard Times: For these times*. First Edition. 1854.

—— *Little Dorrit*. First Edition. 1857.

—— *A Tale of Two Cities*. First Edition. 1859.

—— *Great Expectations*. First Edition. 3 vols. 1861.

—— *Our Mutual Friend*. First Edition. 2 vols. 1865.

—— *The Mystery of Edwin Drood*. First Edition. 1870.

—— *Works*. The First Cheap Edition. 17 vols. 1847–68.

—— *Works*. The Charles Dickens Edition. 21 vols. 1867–75.

—— *Works*. The New Oxford Illustrated Dickens. 21 vols. 1947–58.

—— *Miscellaneous Papers*. Ed. B. W. Matz. 1908.

—— *Letters of Charles Dickens to Wilkie Collins 1851–1870*. Ed. Lawrence Hutton. 1892.

—— *The Letters of Charles Dickens 1833–1870*. Ed. his Sister-in-law and his Eldest Daughter [Georgina Hogarth and Mamie Mary Dickens]. 1903.

—— *Charles Dickens as Editor: Being Letters Written by Him to William Henry Wills His Sub-Editor*. Ed. R. C. Lehmann. 1912.

—— *The Letters of Charles Dickens*. Ed. Walter Dexter. Nonesuch Press. 3 vols. 1938.

—— *Letters from Charles Dickens to Angela Burdett-Coutts 1841–1865*. Ed. Edgar Johnson. 1953.

—— *The Letters of Charles Dickens*. Ed. Madeline House and Graham Storey. Pilgrim Edition. Vol. 1. 1965.

—— *The Speeches of Charles Dickens*. Ed. K. J. Fielding. Oxford, 1960.

DICKENS, CHARLES (ed.). *Household Words*, i–xix (1850–9).

—— *All the Year Round*, i–xxiii (1859–70).

INDEX

Abrams, M. H., 33
Adam, 197
Adler, Alfred, 187
Aeschylus, 227
'Affective fallacy', 28
Ainsworth, William Harrison, 295-6
Alexander the Great, 51
Alison, Archibald, 159
Allingham, William, 177
Allot, Miriam, 44-5
Almack's, 154
Alterton, Margaret and Craig, Hardin, 71, 73-4, 110
America, 74
American Notes, 100
Apollo, 316
Aristotle, 5, 44, 132, 133, 151, 152, 157, 227, 244, 302, 304, 305
Arnold, Matthew, 122, 342
Ashley, Robert, 25
Axton, William F., 226
Aydelotte, William O., 340
Aylmer, Felix, 85

Bagehot, Walter, 168, 303
Bain, Alexander, 159, 167, 171
Baker, Ernest A., 16
Ballou, R. O., 206
Balzac, Honoré de, 356
Barnaby Rudge
    Characters: Gashford, 259; Gordon, Lord John, 262; Haredale, Reuben, 73-4; Rudge, Mr., 73; Tappertit, Simon, 260; Varden, Dolly, 251-2; Varden, Gabriel, 251
    Text and Writing of: Editions, First, 360; MS., 360; Popish Riots, 73-4
Barnard's Inn, 102-3
Bath, 237, 314, 315
Baynes, H. Godwin, 355
Beadnell, Maria (later Mrs. Winter), 188, 190-1, 192, 194, 195
Bear, Great (Charles's Wain), 219
Beardsley, M. C., *see* Wimsatt, W. K., Jrn., and Beardsley, M. C.
Behn, Mrs. Aphra, 43

Bell, Sir Charles, 172
Benjamin, Edwin B., 227
Bentham, Jeremy, 167, 168
Benthamism, 92
Bentley, Eric, 226
Berg Collection, New York Public Library, 211
Bergeret, Madame, 305-6
Berners Street, 179
Bible, 209, 280, 310, 315
Black, John, 302
Black Prince, 102
Blackwood's Edinburgh Magazine, 113, Tale of Terror in, 77-9, 81-2
Blake, William, 354
Bleak House
    Characters: Augusta ('Guster'), 335; Badger, Bayham, 352; Boodle, Lord, 317; Boythorn, Lawrence, 92-3, 103-4, 105, 121, 132, 258; Brickmaker's family, 332; Bucket, Inspector, 90-2, 230, 257, 334-5; Carstone, Richard, 66-7, 93, 107, 123-4, 156, 174-6, 206-10, 230, 234, 243, 244, 248, 260, 303-4, 312, 317, 332, 351-2, 353, 354; Chadband, Mr., 44, 58, 63, 259, 315; Clare, Ada, 93, 156, 174, 175, 206-10, 332, 353; Coodle and Doodle, 317, 332; Coroner, 316; Dedlock, Lady Honoria, 91-2, 96, 105-9, 137, 143, 234, 243, 259, 290, 291, 292, 294, 332-7, 352-3, 354; Dedlock, Sir Leicester, 104-8, 137, 143-4, 240, 317, 332-5; Dedlocks, 353, 107-8, treatment of, 332-7; Flite, Miss, 175-6, 208-10, 244, 303-4, 317, 327, 330, 332, 353-4; Gridley ('Man from Shropshire'), 240, 288-9, 327-8, 329, 330; Guppy, William, 66, 120, 155, 234, 243, 314-15, 318, 332; Hawdon, Captain ('Law-Writer', 'Nemo'), 336; Hortense, 259; 'Jarndyce and Jarndyce', 66, 230, 243, 244, 248, 327, 328, 331, 332, 352; Jarndyce, John, 93, 208, 244, 257, 289, 352, 353; Jarndyce, Tom, 328;

Prayer Book, doxology, 164
'Preliminary Word, A', *Household Words*, 219, 220
Prest, T. P., 8, 108–9
'Proposals for Amusing Posterity', *Household Words*, 46
Pugh, Edwin, *Dickens Originals, The*, 177

Quintillian, 5
Quirk, Randolph, 69

Radcliffe, Mrs. Ann, 43, 78
Rationalism, 168
Reade, Charles, 340
Reade, Winwood, 267
Regnier, Mons., Dickens's letter to, 23
Reik, Theodor, 296, 353
Reinhardt, Kurt F., 206
Reynolds, G. W. M., 8, 23, 27, 261–2, 297
Ricardo, David, 92
Richards, I. A., 15, 278, 302
Richardson, Samuel, 205
Ricks, Christopher, 112
Roberts, David, 274, 340
Roland, Madame, 305
Romans, 311
Romanticism, 168
Rosenberg, Marvin, 226
Rossetti, D. G., 342
Rotch, Benjamin, 259
'Royal Book of Nursery Rhymes, The', 220
'Ruffian, The', *All the Year Round*, 17
Russians, 83, 84
Rymer, J. M., 8, 108–9, 240–1

Sade, Marquis de, 205
Sadleir, John, 213
Saint Giles's, 154
Sala, G. A. H., 17
Schlegel, A. W. von, 302
Sedgewick, G. G., 140, 141, 142, 145, 147, 151
Seven Dials, 220
Shakespeare, William, 62, 78, 138, 158, 209, 226, 286, 298, 300, 311
Shipley, Joseph T., 2
Siegfried, 251
Simpson, Evelyn M., 226

Sisyphus, 67
Sketches by Boz, 79; 'Black Veil, The', 74, influenced by Warren's 'Early Struggles', 'Grave Doings', 'The Thunderstruck—The Boxer', 79; 'Criminal Courts', ('The Old Bailey', *Morning Chronicle*), source provided by Thomson's 'Le Revenant', 79; 'Pawnbroker's Shop, The ',70; 'Visit to Newgate, A', final episode influenced by Thomson's 'Le Revenant', 79
Smallpox, 153
Smith, Adam, 116, 223
Smith, Sheila M., viii, 69, 340
Smollett, Tobias, 54, 228
Socrates, 145
Sophocles, 151, 227
Spaniards, 83
Speeches of Charles Dickens, The, ed. K. J. Fielding, xiii, 47, 153, 154, 361
Spencer, Herbert, 171, 172
Spilka, Mark, 262
Spontaneous Combustion, 36
Stang, Richard, 10, 14, 250
Stead, W. T., 267
Stephen, Sir James Fitzjames, 1–3, 11, 28
Stephen, Leslie, 119
Sterne, Lawrence, 227, 228
Stevenson, Lionel, 360
Stoehr, Taylor, 9
Stoker, Bram, 36
Stonehouse, J. H. (ed.), *Catalogue of the Library of Charles Dickens*, 26, 87, 170, 172, 226, 228, 284, 298, 305, 349
Stout, G. F., 88, 89–90, 99, 110
Sucksmith, H. P., 9, 28, 79, 331, 337
Surtees, R. S., 228

Taine, H. A., 9
Tale of Two Cities, A
    Characters:Carton,Sidney,238, 305; Darnay, Charles (Evrémonde), 238, 239, 290; Defarge, Madame Thérèse, 237–8, 239, 262; Evrémonde family, 238; Manette, Lucie, 239; Pross, Miss, 238; St. Evrémonde, Marquis, 63, 252, 262, 266, 290, 298, 347; seamstress, little, 305; Vengeance, the, 238